HTML 3

ELECTRONIC PUBLISHING ON THE WORLD WIDE WEB

HTML 3

ELECTRONIC PUBLISHING ON THE WORLD WIDE WEB

Dave Raggett
Jenny Lam
Ian Alexander

Addison-Wesley

Harlow, England • Reading, Massachusetts • Menlo Park, California • New York
Don Mills, Ontario • Amsterdam • Bonn • Sydney • Singapore • Tokyo • Madrid
San Juan • Milan • Mexico City • Seoul • Taipei

Addison Wesley Longman Limited
Edinburgh Gate
Harlow
Essex
CM20 2JE
England

Cover designed by odB Design & Communication, Reading
and printed by The Riverside Printing Co. (Reading) Ltd.
Typeset by CRB Associates, Norwich.
Text design by Sally Grover.
Cartoons by Fred Volans.

Printed and bound in the United States of America.

First printed 1996.

ISBN 0-201-87693-0

British Library Cataloguing in Publication Data
A catalogue record for this book is available from the British Library.

Library of Congress Cataloging in Publication Data applied for.

PREFACE

This book is for anyone and everyone who wants to put information on the World Wide Web. Here you will find an organized and detailed description of the Web publishing language, HTML, written for both the complete novice (What is the difference between the Web and the Internet? What is a browser? What is HTML?) and for the advanced user. Whether you or your organization are new to the idea of publishing on the Web, or whether you are an experienced Webmaster looking for the perfect HTML companion book to supplement your reading, *HTML 3: Electronic Publishing on the World Wide Web* will be immensely useful to you. The book contains teach-yourself material, reference material and a wealth of examples drawn from the arts, literature, science, mathematics and classics to make the HTML language truly accessible to everyone.

New HTML features included

The book covers many new HTML features which are likely to find their way into a new HTML 3 standard. These include style sheets for HTML documents which will be supported by Microsoft this year, a new standard HTML tag for multimedia applications, and features for more sophisticated forms and tables. You will even find a chapter on marking up maths, chemistry and other scientific material for publishing on the Internet. This, a whole new area of HTML, is likely to implemented in the near future.

Which versions of HTML does this book cover?

Those already familiar with HTML will be aware that the language does not have a closely defined set of features. To start with there is more than one 'version' of HTML and, to complicate matters further, different browsers have developed their own special HTML features or 'extensions'. To make it clear to which 'version' of the language a given feature belongs, and also whether that feature is an extension peculiar to one or other browser, we have used a system of icons.

This icon means a feature belonging to HTML 2 – a formal specification of HTML which was written up by Dan Connolly as an RFC for the Internet Engineering Task Force in 1995.

Netscape, Microsoft and others have added a number of HTML extensions. These are marked with this icon.

In March 1995 Dave Raggett published the preliminary specification for HTML 3 as the *HTML 3.0 Internet Draft* which was made openly available on the Web for discussion and comment.

This icon indicates a feature which was proposed in the HTML 3.0 Internet Draft by Dave Raggett.

This icon indicates a proposed HTML 3.0 feature now implemented by one or other browser vendor.

Since publishing his HTML 3.0 draft, Dave Raggett has been assimilating comments and suggestions on the proposal and has revised many aspects of his specification accordingly. These revisions, along with some entirely new features, are likely to find their way into an official HTML 3 standard to be agreed by major browser vendors during 1996.

New features which are *likely* to incorporated into an eventual HTML 3 standard are indicated with this icon.

The authors point out that HTML is very much a moving target and, although they have done their very best to keep up to date, things are changing all the time. The latest on HTML is available on the Web itself and references to the relevant pages are given in the text.

About the authors

Having worked in conjunction with Tim Berners-Lee, Mark Andreessen, Dan Connolly and others involved in shaping the Web from the start, Dave Raggett is one of the lead architects of HTML. Dave defined HTML+ and also HTML 3.0 and set up and co-chaired the Internet Engineering Task Force HTTP working group, responsible for the international standards associated with the Web protocol. Dave is currently Visiting Scientist at the World Wide Web consortium where he continues to pursue a major role in HTML development. He works closely with member organizations and recognized experts in the field, refining and testing the Hypertext Mark-up Language. Recently, Dave has worked with the consortium to bring together companies including IBM, Microsoft, Netscape Communications Corporation, Novell, Spyglass and SoftQuad for joint work on HTML development activities. The aim is to establish international standards for HTML features such as multimedia objects, style sheets, forms, scripts, tables and high quality printing, as well as improved access for the visually impaired. Many of these features are explained in this book and are likely to be included in a formal definition of the HTML 3 standard to be finalized during the course of 1996.

Jenny Lam and Ian Alexander are technical writers who aim to explain and present technology to a wide audience. Ian is also a software engineer who teaches requirements engineering, builds prototypes and runs a Web site.

An insider's perspective

This book offers more than a simple description of HTML as an online publishing language. There is a history of the Web and an explanation of the technology behind it. We plot the development of HTML and look at the rationale behind its various features with a critical eye. Much of this discussion is aimed at the non-technical reader and is as much as possible free from jargon and hype. The authors also offer valuable insights into the Web community – the technical people involved in HTML development: how they work, their culture, their aspirations and so on.

VRML – the virtual reality modelling language

Dave Raggett is also known for coining the term 'VRML' the virtual reality modelling language – a language to be used to generate three-dimensional interactive graphical virtual 'worlds'. Virtual reality in the context of the Web is an up-and-coming topic and is also discussed in the book at an introductory level.

The Web and society

The authors believe that the merits of any new technology should be considered in the context of society as a whole. With this in mind a section of the book is devoted to the effects of the Web on how people might work, interact and do commerce in the future. We include an account of one of the

An explanation of the characters in the cartoons in this book.

ADRIAN ANORAK

Adrian is always in his head, he lives in the virtual world of the Internet, which consists of a world-wide web of interlinked nodes, represented here by a lily pond.

PRUNELLA

Prunella is Adrian's aunt. She treats Adrian as the small boy she embarrassingly once knew, and probably still thinks he is.

LILY POND

Virtual pond in Prunella's garden, representing the waters of Cyberspace. The water-lily leaves are nodes on the web.

FRED FROG

Fred lives in the pond, hopping from leaf to leaf. He is of course a virtual frog, unlike Adrian who only imagines he is virtual (well, maybe . . .) Fred is naturally derisive (Brrrekk!)

first cyber-cafés. You may guess from some of our cartoons and examples that we imagine that the Web may become part of life, but not vice versa!

Overall structure

The book starts off by explaining basic concepts of the Web at 'layman level' and giving background information about how and why HTML was conceived and the roles played by key companies and people in its development and evolution. There is also a chapter written for the novice on the process of designing a simple Web site which is illustrated with real examples from the Web and an amusing imaginary *Theatre on the Web*. This simple but informative example shows a seating plan, playwrights and so on, all marked up in HTML. The beginner learns about HTML Life Cycle, structuring a Web site, navigational aids, and the importance of requirements and testing.

Early chapters are complemented by tighter and more definitive sections explaining the concepts and terminology of HTML, giving a firm grounding for understanding later chapters in the book.

We cover:

- **Character mark-up** including subscripts, superscripts, font size, text colour and so on.
- **Paragraph mark-up** including how to attach a style to a paragraph to give it a particular colour or font and text flow around graphics.
- **Lists**: bulleted lists, numbered lists, lists within lists, roman lists.
- **Hypertext links** including how to jump to a particular place in a document rather than simply to the beginning, use of relative URLs, how to make a graphic 'clickable', client and server-side image maps and so on.
- **Tables** including design principles, merging tables cells, automatic alignment, fancy borders, and more.
- **Fill-out forms** including design principles and practices, syntax of latest forms widgets.
- **Maths equations**, chemistry, special bracketing, matrices.
- **Style sheets** including how to reference an external style sheet; how to apply local styles applicable to say, a single paragraph; and the various stylistic properties that can be associated with the various HTML elements.
- **Multimedia on the Web**: how to insert images, video clips, Java applets and other applications into your document. This chapter includes discussion about the new `OBJECT` element which is likely to be the standard way to insert images and other media into HTML documents in the near future.
- **Graphics** on the Web including a discussion of graphics formats and which are applicable under which circumstances: GIF, JPEG and PNG.
- **Appendices** consisting of convenient reference material, an entertaining and informative glossary, a handy set of symbol definitions, and an aide-mémoire with examples of common tags.

Our thanks to...

Our thanks first to Fred Volans for livening up the book with her wonderful cartoons.

We would also like to thank Kevin Hughs (EIT), Bert Bos, Håkon Lie (World Wide Web consortium), Kirkpatrick Sale and Martin Lam for their contributions to the text, and Alan Mordue, Clare Axel-Berg, Julian Diller and Mike Billson for reading the manuscript.

We are particularly grateful to Tom Stone and Karen Mosman (Addison-Wesley) for their valued efforts in diplomacy and negotiation, and to the indefatigable Sheila Chatten and Nicky Jaeger (also Addison-Wesley).

This book would not have been possible had it not been for Grandma and Grandpa Lam for distracting children and associated guinea-pigs and rabbits at critical moments, a service which cannot be underestimated in its value.

We would like to thank HarperCollins Publishers for permission to use the quote on p. 89, and to acknowledge the following organizations and individuals whose Web sites appear in the text and in the colour plates:

Text MovieNet (image on p. 3); Berkeley Museum of Paleontology (images in Chapter 5 *and* colour section); HotWired (images in Chapter 5: Copyright © 1995 HotWired Ventures LLC. All rights reserved. Icons designed by Max Kisman); Mystic Fire (images in Chapter 5: © Jon-Marc Seimon, Mystic Fire Video, 1995); the Estate of the late Alan Watts (image on p. 101: Copyright © Alan Watts); American Stock Exchange (image in Chapter 10: used with permission of Paul Nobile, Director of Advertising for the American Stock Exchange, Inc.); the Louvre site (image in Chapter 11); Chris's World (images in Chapter 11 *and* colour section); David Siegel (images in Chapter 11 *and* colour section); Cameo Graphics (images in Chapter 11 *and* colour section); Library of Congress (image in Chapter 12).

Colour section The Times (image used with permission of the Times Newspaper Group, San José CA); University of Illinois; Elizabeth Fischer; Patches and Bailey; YAHOO!, Inc. (text and artwork copyright © 1996 by YAHOO!, Inc. All rights reserved. YAHOO! and the YAHOO! logo are trademarks of YAHOO!, Inc.); IndiaWorld; Audubon Society; James Farron, Alex Feldman and Boise State University (Gilbert and Sullivan Archive images); the Online Bonsai Collection; Randy D. Ralph; Banff National Park (bird-watching images); New England Aquarium; George Phillips (periodic table image); The Japan Information Center of Science and Technology (image: JICST Copyright); Hewlett-Packard; Schoolhouse Videos and CDs (image used with permission of Jeff and Penny Gift, Schoolhouse Videos and CDs); WeatherLinks.

We would also like to acknowledge that artwork for the cover illustration was taken from the original interface design by Diverse Interactive, London (http://www.diverse.co.uk).

Dave Raggett, Jenny Lam, Ian Alexander
Boston and London, April 1996

CONTENTS

1 WHAT IS THE WEB?

In this chapter:

- Components of the Web explained for the lay person
- How is the Web different from the Internet?
- Bulletin boards and the Web
- The role and importance of HTML and HTTP as open standards
- The World Wide Web consortium

1.1 Introduction

From your home in the small English town of Chipping Sodbury, you decide to find out what's on tonight in Bath, the famous city only 15 miles away. A company publishes 'What's On in Bath' online and you have read that this is available on http://www.bath.info.uk/ as a series of Web 'pages' on the Internet. You decide to take a look. You switch your computer on and start it up in the usual way. Just as you might click on an icon to start up your desktop publishing package, so you click on the icon to load your World Wide Web browser. This is a piece of software which allows you to display certain kinds of information obtained across the Internet.

Your modem, which connects your computer to the telephone line in the street via an ordinary household telephone socket, makes a series of electronic beeps as it dials up the nearest Internet point of presence and puts you onto the 'Net. Via the interface provided by your Web browser, you can now enter the Internet address – otherwise known as the URL – of the file containing the front page of What's On in Bath. As with all other information on the Web, this would start with 'http://', for example:

http://www.bath.avon.uk/

HTTP is the name of the Web's own transmission **protocol**. Web pages are sent over the Internet to your computer courtesy of HTTP. Do not make the rather common mistake of confusing the Web with the Internet itself: the Internet simply provides a medium for the Web to run on, just as a telephone line provides the medium for telephone conversations. What the Web does is to provide the technology for publishing, sending and obtaining information over the expanse of the Internet. How the Internet actually works may be a matter of interest, but the ordinary Web user does not need to know about it in any detail.

What is a protocol?

A protocol consists of salutations which are exchanged between computers: 'good morning', 'be with you in a tick', 'file coming down the line now' and so on. Each service on the Internet has its own protocol – its own personal way of sending files around the system. The protocol for the Web is HTTP. File Transfer Protocol (FTP) is another common protocol that you may have heard of.

After a few seconds, the front page for What's On in Bath arrives at your computer. This (fictitious) home page would have perhaps a photo showing the famous Roman Baths on the first page, together with a short paragraph introducing the town and a menu of icons to call up specific information on Bath's museums, parks, bus-tours and so on. These icons provide hypertext links for you to click – on-screen 'buttons' enabling you to home in on the information you want. Hypertext links are in many ways the most important feature of the Web. In the case of our imaginary Web pages, clicking on hypertext buttons mostly displays data held on computers somewhere in Bath itself. Sometimes, however, a hypertext link may fetch a file from somewhere quite different on the Internet. If you click on the title of a play taking place in Bath, information about the performing company may be fetched across the Internet from a computer thousands of miles away in the US. From that point onwards, you might be able to call up pages telling you about other plays by the same company. With the Web, you can depart on your own private 'tour' of information on a chosen subject whenever the inclination takes you. This is by virtue of the hypertext links which span the globe.

You can also pay for services and goods over the Web. You could, for example, decide to order some tickets for a play by filling in a form displayed on a 'page' of the online magazine – you might buy a £20.00 seat for *As You Like It* at the Bath Playhouse and pay securely by credit card. The example screen below is taken from a different application – movie information on the Web. You can see now what a Web page looks like. The Web page is the first in a series which allows you to see which films are on at a cinema in Houston. You can click on any of the buttons to see more specific information including reviews and times of showings. The page is shown on a Macintosh computer. The browser displaying the Web page is the Netscape browser. This is one of about 30 Web browsers available for use.

Accessing the Web from work

If you are using a computer in your office which is connected up directly to the Internet via a LAN (local area network) then you do not need a modem link to access the Web. This is in many ways preferable because downloading information from the Internet will be that much quicker.

You can see buttons on the screen to click on: these are the hypertext links. There are two types: underlined words and pictures. These buttons serve to fetch up new information across the Internet. Also you can

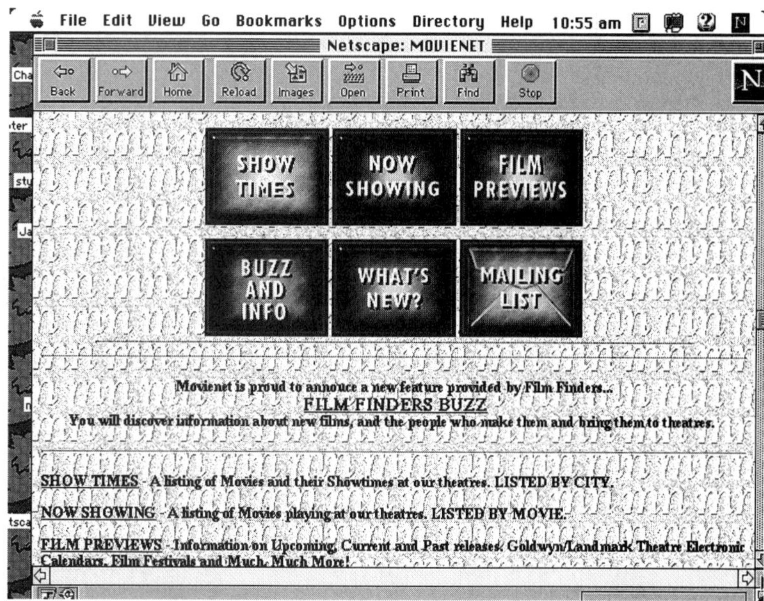

see the title of the page, in this case 'MovieNet', and a URL at the bottom of the screen telling you where the information came from, in this case http://www.movienet.com/movienet/moviep.html.

Looking at this screen and other pages from the Web you can see that the Web provides:

- A means for publishing online information. The Web enables you to lay out the text and graphics of the 'pages' on the screen, and insert titles, photos, captions and so on.
- A means for retrieving online information via hypertext links, at the click of a button. You can also use Web search programs to find the information you want.
- An interface for looking at information retrieved. This is done by virtue of a Web browser.
- Forms for conducting commercial transactions across the Internet.
- Web pages may also include other applications, for example spreadsheets, video clips, sound clips and so on. This idea is relatively new and is explained towards the end of Chapter 2 which looks at how the Web will change in the future.

The Web is therefore simultaneously a means of online publishing, a way of accessing, storing and retrieving information, and a means of sending, acquiring and querying data across the Internet. Most importantly, the Web allows the use of hypertext links that can take you to any computer on the Internet. All these functions work by using the hardware – the wires, the cables, the computers, the satellite links – that is used to send information from computer to computer using the Internet protocols.

What is a URL? This is a much simplified explanation for the novice

Given the fact that there are vast numbers of Web servers, how can HTTP possibly locate just the file you want from somewhere on the Internet? The answer is through the use of the URL, the *Universal Resource Locator*. This is rather like the telephone number of a computer on the Internet, together with information appended to specify the exact file to be sent to your machine.

Taking the URL for our fictitious Web pages in Bath, UK, we can see quite clearly the general pattern that URLs adopt. Look at

```
http://www.bath.avon.uk
```

more closely.

- `http` is the name of the Web protocol used to access the data across the Internet.

- `www.bath.avon.uk` is the Internet name – or the *domain* name – of the computer on which the information is stored. The 'www' indicates that this is a World Wide Web server. 'uk' is the country code for the United Kingdom.

To be more specific about the file you want from the server in question, you add to the URL a *path* and a file name. For example:

```
http://www.bath.avon.uk/time_tables/buses.html
```

which would point to a file called buses.html in a directory called time_tables. We can imagine that `buses.html` contains bus time-tables for the city of Bath which can conveniently be called up on your screen.

URLs can specify files to be accessed using protocols other than http. A URL beginning with `ftp://` points to a file to be fetched using FTP – the File Transfer Protocol. Meanwhile `mailto://` links to an application which allows you to send an email message to a pre-defined address, and `news://` points to a USENET newsgroup and uses the Network Transfer Protocol transfer data.

There are various conventions when it comes URLs. Take the letters '.com' for instance. These mean 'company' as in:

```
http://www.movienet.com
```

which you may recognize as the URL for the Web screen shown earlier. Non-profit making organizations may use '.org' and educational establishments use '.edu'.

Similarly there are codes for countries. A URL may end in '.us' for the United States, '.fr' for France, '.au' for Australia and so on. Some of the conventions for URLs are listed in Appendices E and F.

How are email addresses different from URLs?

Email addresses follow a different format: `name@name.name.domain`. For example: `tiptoes@hawks.uni.edu`.

The string of letters *following* the `@` identifies the machine to which the mail will be sent, while the name of the person to deliver the mail to is given directly *before* the `@` sign. There may be more than one person logging into the machine to read their mail. This is why the name of the person becomes important in an email address.

1.2 Why has the Web become so popular?

Before the Web, the Internet was largely the domain of computer nerds and others who delighted in the abstract and concise. Interfaces to early Internet applications required almost mathematical precision to operate, and programs like FTP and Telnet were purely command-line based. Later, when file retrieval services such as WAIS and Gopher became popular on the Internet, these had the advantage of being menu-driven, but they were still rather cumbersome.

While the Internet was still using interfaces suitable for the more technically inclined, software for the home and office market had long ago departed from command-driven applications. The idea of a graphical interface using windows, which originated from work at Xerox Parc in the 1970s, was popularized in the early 1980s, primarily through the Apple Macintosh. The PC then followed suit with the introduction of Windows in the mid-1980s. At the same time, windowing systems were introduced to the UNIX workstation market, which is now dominated by the X11 interface. It has, however, taken until the mid-1990s to introduce a simple and reliable user interface for accessing information over the Internet. The Web's popularity has doubtless been in part because it offers a simple point-and-click interface, which immediately makes it more accessible to a much wider range of users. Another important factor must have been email, which, as it has gained popularity, has made the idea of sending information across networked computers that much more acceptable.

A long-distance jump
<A HREF="http://www.norge.org/docs/norse.html">

What is the Internet?

The Internet is a vast network of interconnected computers. Just as AT&T, France Telecom, British Telecom, and other country-wide and regional telephone networks are now all joined up to make a global telephone system, so it is with the Internet: each of the many thousand computer networks which make up the Internet are joined together on a global scale, so that any Internet computer can locate and talk to any other.

How can your computer know how to find someone else's computer on the other side of the world? Just as each telephone in the world has its own unique telephone number, so each computer connected to the Internet has its own computer number. This is known as its IP address. However, because IP addresses consist of long series of numbers which are cumbersome to remember and type in, you rarely come across them in everyday Internet use, and most people prefer to use the parallel system of naming computers. This is the system of Internet host names, sometimes called Internet addresses or even domain names. While a computer on the Internet may have an IP address like 17.254.0.63, it may have a more manageable Internet host or *domain* name like www.drizzle.org. Servers consult a globally distributed directory to map each host name onto the corresponding IP address.

Once you are connected to the Internet, you can theoretically 'dial' anywhere you want. This gives you tremendous freedom. The cost of Internet access remains the same regardless of whether you talk to a computer in Australia, England, the US or the next town. This is because you pay only for the time spent on the line to your nearest Internet point of presence. And as when you make a phone call to another country, you are hardly aware that your voice is travelling along foreign telephone lines, so it is (theoretically) with the Internet. Although data sent from a computer linked to a network at an office in Paris may travel across various constituent networks on its route to Los Angeles, as a user you don't have to worry about the path it takes. The only evidence you will have that the information requested comes from a long way off is when a part of the Internet system is in heavy use and you have to wait to 'get through'.

1.3 Other services on the Internet

The Web is just one of many services on the Internet; that said, it is the easiest to use and the one that appeals most to the ordinary user who is not technically minded. It is certainly now the most popular. Other information services include Gopher, WAIS and Veronica and FTP. Many Web browsers have facilities for summoning up information held by Gopher or FTP servers (a server is a computer which holds the files for distribution – see Section 1.2) *as well as* from Web servers. A reference to a file on a Gopher or FTP server can be inserted into an HTML document as a hypertext link containing a URL. The user clicks on the reference, and the file is fetched accordingly without further ado from anywhere in the world.

The French system Minitel – used in ways similar to the Web

It is interesting to note that the French have been using a public system of information access for a number of years which has in many ways occupied the same niche as the Web although it is not nearly so sophisticated nor as versatile. Called Minitel, the system consists of hardware in the form of a computer, keyboard and modem originally given away free to subscribers to France Telecom, the national French telephone company. Very easy to use, and extremely popular – most homes have one – Minitel has existed as a household 'pet' for over 10 years. Using your Minitel you dial up the Minitel online service and then proceed through a number of menus and pages to book yourself on a train, read the latest recipe for *Mousse chocolat à l'anglaise*, inspect your bank balance, book hotel rooms and so on. Le Minitel is so much an accepted part of French life that you often hear on French radio programmes something like: 'pour les renseignements, tapez le numéro 392 sur votre Minitel' (enter 392 on your Minitel for more information). Minitel is financed by the suppliers of information, not the user. In other words, a company or individual wanting to put information on a Minitel page pays France Telecom for the privilege. Customers pay only the cost of a local phone call to access information on the system. The popularity of Minitel was certainly due in part to the *messageries roses* ('little pink messages') which were sent by users who realized with enthusiasm that Minitel provided an uncensored medium.

Current applications of Minitel are a long way from the reason for Minitel's introduction in 1978. Orginally Minitel was to offer a more economical way of giving access to telephone directories. However, the system was much more popular than expected. Today, 12 000 online services are available to French users who, at home, may want to check the state of their bank accounts, play electronic games, look at the times of films at their local cinema, meet anonymously *à compute*, read a newspaper, learn the results of a sports event or do their shopping, air their opinions during an interactive TV programme – even obtain legal advice. Somewhat to the dismay of the government, the system has also been enthusiastically utilized by Trade Unions to coordinate industrial action, and by students to organize demonstrations.

1.4 Basic components of the Web

The basic components of the Web are shown in the following illustration. They are:

- Web servers are computers which hold the information for distribution over the Internet. In the example application in the diagram, a Web server would hold the text and graphics of the online magazine What's On in Bath, and another might hold information on seats available for a particular concert. The magazine would be formatted using the Web's own publishing language HTML. Data on seats available and prices to pay would be held in a database with links to forms published using HTML.

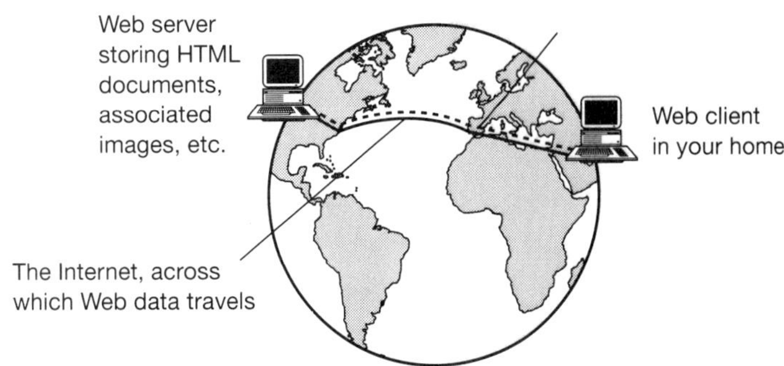

Simplified view of components of the Web.

- Servers can be PCs, Macs or UNIX workstations: it's the server software which makes them special, rather than the computer itself. That said, servers need to be fairly up-market machines. Servers do need to be left on all the time, so that people can access the information on them whenever they want. Another important point about servers: they are relatively difficult to set up. If you are a non-technical person who wants to publish on the Web, the best thing to do is to rent some space on someone else's server.
- Web clients are the PCs, Macs and other computers connected to the Internet that can retrieve information from Web servers. A Web client is the computer on your desk. PCs, Macs, UNIX workstations and even simple terminals can run client software. Different client software is marketed (or given away free) for different platforms. Thus Mosaic has a Mac implementation and a PC implementation.
- The protocol HTTP is used to transmit files between servers and clients. When you click on a hypertext link, or when you fill out a form on a Web document, the results of your action need to be sent across the Internet as quickly as possible and then understood by a server at the other end. Instructions such as 'send me this file', 'get me that image' are carried by the Web communications protocol HTTP, the Hypertext Transfer Protocol. HTTP is the 'messenger' which fetches files to and from servers, and delivers results to your computer every time you click with a request. HTTP has its counterparts in other Internet services: FTP (file transfer protocol) and Gopher are protocols which obtain different sorts of information from across the Internet.
- Browsers and viewers are software needed by a Web client for displaying text, images, video clips and so on. This is supplied under the umbrella name 'browser', of which Mosaic and Netscape are probably the best-known examples. Browser software gives you the ability to scan through information retrieved from Web servers rather

as you would browse through a book. It also give you facilities for saving and printing out information obtained on the Web.

Client and server are common terms used throughout the computer industry. A client makes requests; the server satisfies those requests. Thus a client on the Web might make a request to a server for a file, a picture or even music to be sent to it. In practice, people tend to use 'client' and 'server' to mean either the physical machine itself or simply the software necessary to assume these respective roles. The Web is a prime example of what is known as a client–server architecture: instead of having one big machine to which terminals, PCs and other smaller machines log on, a client–server arrangement has a mixture of machines which make requests to each other for files.

1.5 A universally understood publishing language: HTML

To publish information for global distribution on the World Wide Web, you need a universally understood publishing language, a kind of mother tongue which all computers on the Web can potentially understand. You also need a commonly understood communications protocol for sending published information 'down the wire' from computer to computer. This should enable users to download information to their machine at the click of a button, and also to send information back (your address, a credit card number, a query to a database and so on) with little effort.

The publishing language used by the Web is called HTML – HyperText Mark-up Language. Using HTML you can specify which parts of your text are headings, ordinary paragraphs, bulleted lists, in bold or italics, and so on. You can use HTML to insert tables into documents, to write equations, to import images and to format fill-out forms for querying databases at a distance. (Some of these features are peculiar to HTML 3 and are not supported by earlier versions of HTML. See Chapter 3.) The language is very flexible and not difficult to use, although, as with all tasks associated with computing, patience is a necessary virtue for authoring hypertext. Part of the Web's appeal is that almost anyone with a reasonable PC, Mac or UNIX computer can publish information without being unduly technical. Judging by the variety of publishers on the Web today, HTML is within the grasp of many. A simple example of HTML can be seen at the beginning of Chapter 3.

Searching for information on the Web

How do you find the information you want on a Web containing millions of documents? The answer is through special programs constructed for the purpose. Known by names such as WebCrawler, Yahoo and Lycos, these search programs are freely accessible over the Web itself and extremely easy to use. All you have to do is to enter the appropriate URL to call up the interface to the search program you want and then enter keywords for the program to look for. At the click of a button off goes the search program through a kind of enormous yellow pages of the Web. This is constantly being updated by 'robot' software which looks at new material placed on the Web and indexes it according to content. You can access a number of these programs via `nearnet.gnn.com`.

A key point that has brought about the success of the Web is that it is multi-platform. What this means is that it doesn't matter what kind of computer you are using; you can still view information published on other, normally incompatible, machines. Thus a PC user can access information published on a Mac; a Mac can access information published by a PC; even UNIX users will find that they are compatible with everyone. The trick is that HTML can be assimilated by each computer in its own way. What happens when an HTML document gets to its destination is up to the computer on the receiving end. It can display paragraphs in Helvetica 20 point if it pleases, and headings in Times 14 point bold, if that is the font available. While the document is transmitted from computer to computer in a standard format, individual *browsers* may display it quite differently, depending on the capabilities of the hardware and software in the computer on the receiving end.

HTML and its relationship to SGML

Early work on representing documents focused on the rendering instructions needed to print the documents out. Work by IBM on GML, the Generalized Mark-up Language, focused on an alternative approach whereby standard document structures such as headers, paragraphs, lists and so on were marked up by tags inserted into the document text. The emphasis on document structure rather than rendering instructions made it dramatically easier to move documents from one system to another, whether for display on simple terminals, line printers or sophisticated typesetting machinery.

This work led to the Standard Generalized Mark-up Language which is an international standard ISO 8879:1986. SGML allows you to define a grammar for marked-up documents defining the ways in which tags can be inserted into documents. For instance, list items only make sense in the context of a list and table cells only make sense in the context of a table. SGML's formal way for describing the grammar is called the Document Type Definition.

Global hypertext makes worse the problems in moving documents from one system to another, for example we have Macs, PCs, a variety of UNIX boxes, simple terminals and even speech I/O for visually impaired people. SGML proved ideally suited for this application. Tim Berners-Lee chose SGML to define the HTML document format for the World Wide Web. HTML is formally an application of SGML. The set of HTML tags and the ways that they can be inserted into documents are formally defined by the HTML Document Type Definition (DTD).

DTDs are rather intimidating to the uninitiated. This book tries to act as a guiding hand to explain the HTML mark-up language and how to apply it to create documents for publishing over the Web. HTML is not a static document format but is evolving rapidly from its simple beginnings as conceived by Tim Berners-Lee.

1.6 HTML and HTTP as open standards

HTML and HTTP continue to be developed as open standards. What this means is that they are non-proprietary specifications and free for anyone to use. Quite different from commercial software packages developed by a particular company, they are part of the standard Internet suite of software specifications which have been developed cross-company and cross-nation under the auspices of the Internet Architecture Board. As such, they are fully compatible with existing Internet communication protocols such as TCP/IP as well as other Internet standards; they can also be used by anyone without payment.

Virtual conversations of the past

You can actually look at the email exchanges between Marc Andreessen, Tim Berners-Lee, Dan Connolly, Dave Raggett and other Web enthusiasts which took place in the early stage of Web development. The information is archived and available via the IETF (Internet Engineering Task Force) pages on the Web.

It is strange to think that when these conversations took place in late 1992 and 1993, no one realized that the Web would be so widely used in years to come. None would have guessed that Marc Andreessen was to become a millionaire as a result of Web technology.

1.6.1 Anyone can have a go at designing HTML and HTTP

The development of both HTML and HTTP has been open to public interest and scrutiny in a way which software developed by companies never is. HTML and HTTP have been developed semi-formally by a small number of very dedicated individuals in a variety of research establishments, small companies and university departments from all over the world. No single company or organization can be attributed the Web standards – there is no single place for which one can confidently state 'this is where they wrote HTML and this is where they will brew the next version of the Web protocol'. Instead there has been a loose network of developers who have worked informally together, cross-company and cross-nation, communicating their ideas and critiquing each others' designs by email. It is quite extraordinary how the apparent anarchy of Web development by email has materialized into something tangible at the end of it.

Anyone can potentially contribute to the development of Internet standards and HTML and HTTP are no exceptions. To register your interest and receive information on Internet standards and developments, you join the appropriate *working groups* by going on their mailing lists.[1] A working group consists of a loosely self-organized group of people making technical and other contributions to the engineering and evolution of the Internet and its technologies. Working groups meet at Internet Engineering Task Force meetings which occur about three times a year. Not unlike a science fiction convention in spirit, IETF meetings are held over a period of about four days in large corporate-style hotels, generally in the US but also in Europe. Beards and pony-tails used to abound; less so recently. It is up to your own company or university to pay travel costs and accommodation.

An IETF working group has no formal voting and the basic principle is rough consensus and *running code*. This is a different approach from that

[1] Look on the IETF home page for pointers to working groups.

adopted in a more commercial environment. Disputes are resolved by discussion and demonstrations of software developed – there is nothing like doing an experiment and getting results to prove your point.

What is the Internet Engineering Task Force?

The Internet Engineering Task Force is the standards and development body of the Internet. The IETF is a large open international community of network designers, operators, vendors and researchers concerned with the evolution of the Internet architecture and the smooth operation of the Internet. It is open to any interested individual. The technical work of the IETF is done in its working groups, which are organized by topic into several areas, for example security, network routing, and applications. HTML and HTTP are in the applications area of the IETF.

The internal management of the IETF is handled by the area directors. Together with the Chair of the IETF, they form the *Internet Engineering Steering Group* (IESG). The operational management of the Internet standards process is handled by the IESG under the auspices of the *Internet Society*. The *Internet Architecture Board* (IAB) is a body of the Internet Society responsible for overall architectural considerations in the Internet. It also serves to adjudicate **disputes in the standards process**.

There are two types of Internet documents: *Internet-Drafts* and *Request for Comments* (RFCs).

- Internet-Drafts have absolutely no formal status and can be changed or deleted at any time. They put down proposals for standards.
- RFCs are the official document series of the IAB and define standards, and are archived permanently (that is, they are never deleted, and once an RFC is published, it will never change); however, it is important to note that not all RFCs are standards.

RFCs and Internet drafts are accessible over the Web. Begin at http://www.ietf.cnri.reston.va.us.

How should you dress for an IETF meeting?

The Tao of the Internet – A guide for New Attendees of the Internet Engineering Task Force by Gary Scott Malkin, Xylogics, Inc., October 1994, discusses what you should wear at an IETF working group meeting: 'Since attendees must wear their name tags, they must also wear shirts or blouses. Pants or skirts are also highly recommended.' You are discouraged from wearing suits because it is embarrassing to find that everyone else is wearing shorts and sandals (in hot weather!). But apparently: 'There are those in the IETF who refuse to wear anything other than suits. Fortunately, they are well known (for other reasons) so they are forgiven this particular idiosyncrasy.'

1.6.2 Public utility, not private

Those involved in the development of Web standards enjoy the idea that the Internet belongs to the people of the world. The Web enthusiast wants the protocols and other Web standards to be available to anyone who wants to use them. This feeling is demonstrated in the song, the *Net Flag*, which can be found 'somewhere on the Internet'. The first verse runs as follows:

> The people's web is deepest red,
> And oft it's killed our routers dead.
> But ere the bugs grew ten days old,
> The patches fixed the broken code.
>
> Chorus:
>
> So raise the open standard high
> Within its codes we'll live or die
> Though cowards flinch and Bill Gates sneers
> We'll keep the net flag flying here.

1.6.3 The World Wide Web consortium

The World Wide Web consortium has been recently formed to fulfil the potential of the Web through the development of open standards. This is the first time that Web enthusiasts who previously worked by email have joyously come together to form a band. The consortium consists of a number of people who have made substantial contributions to the Web. To date (late 1995) the band includes:

- Tim Berners-Lee on lead vocals. He heads up the team. From the United Kingdom.
- Dave Raggett on HTML 3 and the Arena Browser. From the United Kingdom.
- Dan Connolly (editor of HTML 2.0 Internet Draft). From the US.
- Henrik Frystyk on HTTP 1.0 and the W3C Reference Library. From Denmark.
- Håkon Lie on style sheets and Arena (actually working in France at INRIA, see below). From Norway.
- Jim Gettys on HTTPng – he is also one of the principal authors of X-windows. From the US.
- Phil Hallam-Baker on Web security issues. From the United Kingdom.
- Bert Bos on style sheets and layout. From the Netherlands.
- Rohit Khare on security protocols. From the US.

- Jim Miller on how the content of Web pages may be given some kind of rating. From the US.
- Karin Moulder as Web Master. From the US.

Most of the people involved are located in the Laboratory of Computer Science at the Massachusetts Institute of Technology in Boston although a team is also being established at INRIA in France. Sponsored by member organizations in industry, the consortium undertakes work in specific areas related to its charter and is currently looking at document formats, protocols, security over the Web and payments. The work is done by a small design team and then assessed by review boards set up by consortium member companies. When some consensus has been achieved 'in house' the consortium may then work with standards bodies such as the IETF to further promote the acceptance of specifications. The review boards elected by the members may in turn co-opt external people to improve the quality and usefulness of their opinions. Reference code created by the consortium is subject to a wide-range licence which allows it to be used for any purpose, commercial or otherwise. The consortium also seeks improvements to the Web by organizing workshops and conferences. You can look at the consortium's Web pages on http://www.w3.org.

Members of the World Wide Web consortium at the MIT site. From left to right are Henrick Frystyk Neilsen, Anselm Baird-Smith, Jay Sekora, Rohit Khare, Dan Connolly, Jim Gettys, Tim Berners-Lee, Susan Hardy, Jim Miller, Dave Raggett, Tom Greene, Arthur Secret, Karen MacArthur.

1.6.4 Keeping to standards

One problem in developing standards via the IETF is that the process takes a long time. Now that the Web has become rather trendy, every programmer and his dog wants to get involved. The mailing list associated with the HTTP and HTML working groups has become unmanageably long and the sheer amount of email flying about is so great that many developers spend almost all of their time reading and answering email, leaving little time for actually coding or designing the standards themselves.

The World Wide Web consortium is now working jointly with Microsoft, Netscape, Spyglass Mosaic, Sun Microsystems and others to define a new HTML standard.

It comes as no surprise then to find that the more adventurous companies have come up with the goods in a hurry themselves rather than waiting around. Netscape Communications Inc. are a case in point – seeing a demand for a Web browser, they produced one and this now has 75% of the browser market. They have also extended the HTML langauge by adding their own tags to it. Waiting for the IETF to ratify new tags proposed in new standards is asking too much of an organization making a living by selling Web technology. That said, Netscape have not departed from HTML standards arbitarily and have implemented most of HTML 2.0 and many ideas from HTML 3.

The purists believe that *ad hoc* extensions to HTML are likely to cause trouble in the long run, particularly as many of the new tags are associated with font and colour which should be the province of style sheets. It is now important to roll over to a properly defined standard and to phase out certain proprietary features of HTML which have been introduced. If this is not done, so many variants of HTML will be in use that problems of incompatibility will invariably arise with browsers displaying and handling documents in ways unintended by authors. Lack of international standards may lead to the domination of one company over communications on the Internet, in much the same way that Microsoft dominated the market for the PC.

1.7 How does the Web fit in with dial-up 'bulletin boards'?

Many people are familiar with the dial-up bulletin board. CompuServe, America Online, Delphi and Prodigy provide such a service by issuing information online covering everything from weather and sports, travel, TV, business and financial data, to specialized news and discussion groups. Increasingly such services also give access to the Internet but, if Internet access is really what you want, there is no need to go through such an intermediary.

Before you use a bulletin board service, you must become a subscriber. When you do so you get a package through the post which includes software, manuals and so on. Once you have installed the software on your hard disk, you 'dial up' the service simply by clicking on the appropriate icon on the screen. Your computer automatically sets up your modem, then connects to a central computer owned by the bulletin board company over the telephone line, checks your password and access rights to information held, and finally displays the menus, icons and so on which allow you to look at information on chosen subjects. You can download games to your computer, look at the text of magazines available online, and even 'talk' to other subscribers to the service via special interest forums: the bulletin board is a bit like a cross between a radio station and a newspaper. There is generally a monthly subscription on top of the initial joining fee with extra payments for using certain specialist information which falls outside of the central core of standard data and services available to all subscribers.

The large bulletin board companies do not use the Internet although they can give you access to it. The bulletin boards to date do not by and large use the Internet communications protocol TCP/IP. Instead, bulletin board companies rely on 'private' proprietary protocols, with custom-built interfaces to match.

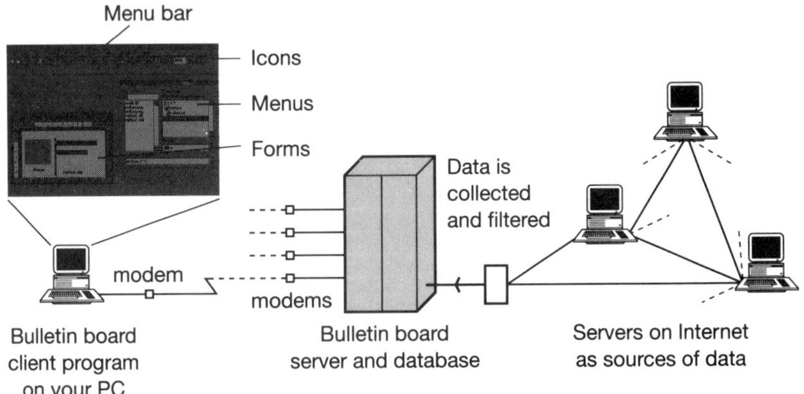

How a bulletin board service works. The information is stored on the host machine(s). These may be mainframes or groups of powerful UNIX boxes. Proprietary protocols make the connection between the host and your machine at home or at work. The client software displays the system of menus on your machine and provides the interface to the service.

Although the bulletin board offers a popular service, it has one big disadvantage. It offers a closed environment: the information it provides is published via one company, the bulletin board company itself. Although the data may come from a variety of sources, it is not the case that anyone can publish information on the system (although there is a certain amount of free-for-all in the 'chat' groups which give an opportunity for users to exchange notes and advice on particular topics). Those who have heard of the wide expanses of the Internet find this aspect of the bulletin board disappointing. Like a person who finds their radio can only tune into one station, when there are thousands broadcasting, bulletin board users feel itchy to find out what is going on elsewhere – they want the freedom to roam.

In future the companies which at the moment provide more conventional dial-up bulletin board services are likely to become 'middle men', offering value-added services on the Web which help users access quality information, rather than get lost in the chaos. Just as publishers vet what ends up in specialist (paper) journals and magazines, so there will no doubt be companies on the Internet who ensure that their customers see a good selection of online papers and articles.

2
FROM CERN TO CYBERSPACE

In this chapter:

- How the Web began – discussion of events and circumstances which led to its present popularity
- Recent innovations to the Web such as plug-in modules and Java
- Virtual reality applications: the Web of the future?
- Visions of how the Web will benefit society, with critique

2.1 Introduction

The first chapter described the technology of the Web for the relatively non-technical reader, and explained how Web standards are developed. If you want to know more about the curious evolution of the Web from its first conception to the popularity it now enjoys, this is the chapter you should read. Apart from a chronological history of events (Table 2.1), we discuss the changes in Web technology which have taken place over the past few years, and look at the future of the Web as virtual reality takes off.

Any new technology bears thinking about not just in terms of what it can do but also in terms of how (and if) it can be used to the benefit of the world in general. Accordingly we have summed up and discussed some of the visions and excitement of Web enthusiasts and critics.

Table 2.1 Chronological history of the Web: summary of events in its development.

Date	*Event*
August 1990	Tim Berners-Lee and Robert Cailliau submit a Web proposal at CERN where they work in the computer science department.
October 1990	Prototype Web browser runs on a NeXT computer at CERN. This is the machine which Tim Berners-Lee first used to develop his ideas on the Web.
January 1991	The first Web servers outside of CERN are set up.
August 1991	The World Wide Web is discussed in the user group alt.hypertext on the Internet.
September 1991	The www-talk mailing list is started.
December 1991	Tim Berners-Lee gives a 'poster' demonstration of his Web browser at the conference Hypertext '91.
January 1992	The possibilities of introducing graphics into the Web are discussed.
July 1992	Pei Wei releases his Viola browser.
January 1993	50 Web servers exist worldwide.
February 1993	Marc Andreessen of NCSA first proposes the `IMG` element which would allow graphics to be used on the Web so that it would no longer be a text-only system.
March 1993	Lou Montulli releases Lynx 2.0a which is a text-based browser for terminals and computers running under DOS without Windows.
April 1993	NCSA Mosaic for X 1.0 is released. This browser is for use on UNIX workstations only and is responsible for much interest in the Web.
August 1993	Mac Mosaic and WinMosaic are released from NCSA. The Web is thus available to a much wider 'audience'.
October 1993	Over 500 Web servers exist worldwide. Rob McCool proposes the Common Gateway Protocol (CGI).

Table 2.1 (*cont.*)

Date	*Event*
September 1993	Web traffic has grown by 1000 per cent in 6 months.
November 1993	Mosaic for X is released which supports simple on-screen fill-out forms.
May 1994	International Web conference in Geneva, May 1994. 380 people attend.
May 1994	At the International Web conference, Dave Raggett presents ideas to support 'distributed virtual reality' and establishes the name VRML. Mark Peche, one of the main enthusiasts in this area, demonstrates a simple 3-D modelling tool in which you click on geometrical shapes to move from one point of view to another.
June 1994	Over 1500 Web servers exist worldwide.
July 1994	MIT and CERN announce the World Wide Web consortium.
October 1994	Second international WWW conference in Chicago with 1300 participants.
December 1994	Third Internet World Conference in Washington with 11 000 participants.
December 1994	Netscape Communications Corporation releases version 1.0 of its browser. This is the first major browser and soon overtakes Mosaic as the browser most commonly in use.
February 1995	After a period of uncertainty in the world of Web politics, CERN in Switzerland, where the Web was first conceived, passes responsibilities to INRIA in France.
March 1995	Dave Raggett releases the Internet draft for HTML 3 with provision for more sophisticated forms, tables, maths and a number of other new features.
April 1995	Fourth Internet World Conference in San Jose, California. 200 exhibits and more than 60 sessions.
April 1995	Third International WWW conference in Darmstadt. Many large computer companies send delegates, marking the graduation of the Web into the world of big business.
May 1995	The official version 1.0 of the Virtual Reality Modelling Language is released.
September 1995	Style sheets become an issue to allow Web authors finer control over font, colour and other aspects of layout. Netscape continues to add proprietary extensions to HTML in an attempt to keep the customer satisfied meanwhile.
November 1995	W3C work-group on style sheets to report on the work so far and kick style sheets into motion.

Table 2.1 (*cont.*)

Date	*Event*
December 1995	Netscape release version 2.0 with a built-in HTML editor plus support for 'plug ins', frames for newspaper-style layout, Java and scripting.
Late 1995	W3C are re-implementing Arena as a WYSIWYG editor with support for HTML 3 and style sheets. To be released in 1996.
Late 1995	A number of companies are releasing WYSIWYG editors for HTML. HoTMetaL has however been available for some time.
Late 1995	A standard method of embedding information in HTML documents is under consideration. Microsoft, Netscape, Spyglass Mosaic and Sun Microsystems are likely to agree on the `OBJECT` tag for this purpose.

2.2 How the Web began

The World Wide Web began life in the place where you would least expect it – at CERN, the European Laboratory for Particle Physics in Geneva, Switzerland. CERN is a meeting place for physicists from all over the world, highly abstract and conceptual thinkers who engage in the contemplation of complex atomic phenomena occurring on a minuscule scale both in time and in space – a surprising place indeed for the beginnings of a technology which would, eventually, deliver everything from tourist information, online shopping and advertisements, to financial data, weather forecasts and pornography to your personal computer.

Tim Berners-Lee is the inventor of the Web. In 1989 Tim was working in a computing services section of CERN when he came up with the concept, although at the time he had no idea that it would be implemented on such an enormous scale. Particle physics research often involves collaborations between institutes from all over the world. Tim had the idea of enabling researchers from remote sites right across the world to organize and pool information together. But far from simply making available a large number of research documents as files which could be downloaded to individual computers, he suggested that you could actually link the text in the files themselves. In other words, there could be cross-references from one research paper to another. This would mean that while reading one research paper, you could quickly display part of another paper which held directly relevant text or diagrams. Documentation of a scientific and mathematical nature would thus be represented as a 'web' of information held in electronic form on computers across the world. This Tim thought could be done by using some form of hypertext, some way of linking documents together by using buttons on the screen which you simply clicked on to jump from one paper to another. Before coming to CERN, Tim had already worked on document production and text processing and had developed his first hypertext system, 'Enquire', in 1980 for his own personal use.

2.2.1 Hypercard

Although already established as a concept by academics as early as the 1940s, it was the advent of the personal computer that brought hypertext out of the cupboard. In the late 1980s, Bill Atkinson, an exceptionally gifted programmer working for Apple, came up with an application called *Hypercard* for the Mac. Hypercard enabled you to construct a series of on-screen 'filing cards' containing textual and graphical information. Users could navigate through these by pressing on-screen buttons, taking themselves on a tour of the information in the process. An art gallery in London used Hypercard to present information about their paintings. Readers could guide themselves through the 'museum' by simply pointing and clicking with the mouse.

Hypercard set the scene for more applications based on the filing card idea. Toolbook for the PC was used in the early 1990s for constructing hypertext training courses with 'pages' with buttons to go forwards and backwards or jump to a new topic. Behind the scenes, buttons would initiate little programs called *scripts*. These would control which page was presented next or even run a small piece of animation on the screen. Guide was a similar application for UNIX and the PC.

Hypercard and its imitators caught the popular imagination. However, there was one limitation of these packages still to be sorted out: hypertext jumps could only be made to files on the same computer. Jumps to computers on the other side of the world were still out of the question. Nobody had implemented a system which involved hypertext links on a global scale.

2.2.2 The introduction of the domain name system

By the beginning of the 1990s, the Internet had grown to the point where it became a viable substrate for global hypertext.

A key advance was the introduction of the domain name system for computers on the Internet. The domain name system is the naming system most familiar to everyday users for computers on the Internet today. A domain name comprises a series of letters separated by dots, for example: `www.kttie.com` or `www.seft.edu`. These names are the easy-to-use alternative to the much less manageable and cumbersome IP address numbers. IP addresses are used internally by the Internet and today are normally hidden from view, but this was not always so. It was only when a program called DNS (Distributed Name Service), which maps domain names onto IP addresses, came into use that IP addresses became 'hidden' in this way. DNS was an absolute breakthrough in making the Internet accessible to those who were not computer nerds. Email addresses became simpler as a result of its introduction: previous to DNS email addresses had all sorts of hideous codes such as exclamation marks, per cent signs and other extraneous information which specified the route to the other machine.

2.2.3 Choosing the right approach

Global links seemed feasible but it was a matter of finding the correct approach to implementing them. Using an existing hypertext package might seem an attractive proposition but this was impractical for a number of reasons. For a start, any hypertext tool to be used worldwide would have to take into account that there were many types of computer linked to the Internet – PCs, Macs, UNIX machines and simple terminals. Also, there were many desktop publishing methods – WordPerfect, Word, LaTex, Troff, SGML and so on – for producing information. Commercial hypertext packages were computer-specific and couldn't easily take text from other sources, and besides they were far too complicated and involved tedious compiling of text into internal formats to create the final hypertext system.

What was needed was something very simple, at least to start with. Tim Berners-Lee demonstrated a basic but attractive way of publishing text by developing some software himself, and also a protocol for retrieving other documents' text via hypertext links. The text format was named HTML and his hypertext implementation was demonstrated on a NeXT workstation, which provided many of the tools he needed to develop his first prototype. By keeping things very simple Tim encouraged others to build upon his ideas and design further software for displaying HTML and for setting up their own HTML documents ready for access.

Tim's implementation also drew upon ideas from SGML and could be implemented on any machine.

2.2.4 Large companies are unconvinced of the importance of the Internet

In early 1992 Dave Raggett at HP Labs in Bristol had also become interested in hypertext, and sent out a message across the Internet (via the 'news group' alt.hypertext) to announce that, now that the Internet was sufficiently robust, and now that hypertext had come into vogue, the time had come for a system of hypertext-linked documents across the world which used the Internet as its medium. He suggested a 'skunk-works' project – a project which isn't sanctified by senior management but can be done as a part-time activity by those who believe in its necessity and importance. Such a project would evolve a platform-independent interpreted system looking similar to

Microsoft Help but with hypertext links which spanned the Internet. Dave originally suggested that such a system could be based on a subset of LaTex, a way of marking up text used by academics in scientific fields.

Back came messages from Universities saying that such a system was just what they needed to access information on different types of computer cross-campus, and also, back came messages that Tim Berners-Lee *et al.* already had a working prototype of such a system at CERN. There seemed no point in duplicating work, so Dave turned his attention to what Tim was doing.

Many other individuals were in Dave's position in that they too had seen a need for a global hypertext system. However, at the level of senior management, large companies were quite unconvinced that the Internet would be a success and the need for a global hypertext system simply passed them by. To many large commercial organizations it was unclear that there was any money to be made from the Web, and there was a misconception that the Internet was mostly for academics. In some companies senior management were assured that the telephone companies would be providing the technology for global communications of this sort, anyway. The result was that individuals working in research laboratories in the commercial sector were unable to devote much time to Web development. This was a bitter disappointment to some researchers who would gratefully have committed almost every waking moment to the cause of shaping what they imagined was THE communication system of the future.

As the WWW project grew to take in people from further afield, a small band of enthusiasts communicated their ideas via the WWW-talk mailing list. During early 1993, for example, these included Tim Berners-Lee, Dave Raggett, Marc Andreessen, Dan Connolly and Jay Webber.

2.3 The Web takes off

Even if senior management were not particularly interested in the Web, others were. In 1993 Marc Andreessen and Eric Bina at NCSA, the National Center for Supercomputing Applications in Illinois, got funding from DARPA[1] and produced the Mosaic browser. Rob McCool, also at NCSA, wrote the Web server software. Before you knew it UNIX users were downloading the software. In software R & D (research and development) it was not uncommon to find a small crowd of 'techies' around a computer beaming with excitement. 'Is it a new computer game?', you would ask. 'No, come and see. *This* is Mosaic – it's *amazing*'.

[1] DARPA was the Defense Advanced Research Projects Agency (USA), formerly ARPA whose ARPAnet was the direct precursor of the Internet.

The Mosaic browser was ported to a number of UNIX platforms and then to the Mac and PC. Mosaic was immensely popular. Although there were Mac and PC versions of the Mosaic browser, when Netscape released their browser the number of people using the Web from their computers at home increased dramatically. Netscape did its best to make sure that even those relying on a low bandwidth connection (i.e. modem) from home were able to use the Web effectively.

2.3.1 Everyone goes crazy about the Web

During 1994 the popularity of the Web was apparent from the number of attendees at conferences. The first International WWW conference sponsored by CERN was held in Geneva in May 1994 and had 300 or so attendees. Soon after, in June of the same year, a conference on the Internet was held in Prague, with the Web featuring very strongly. There were well over a thousand people attending from over a hundred countries. The Third International conference in Washington in December 1994 had 11 000 participants. No longer just full of 'techies', conferences developed a large business-class following, too.

These conferences coincided with the start of what was to develop into a kind of mania for the Web, an unmitigated enthusiasm which was not predicted even amongst those directly involved in Web research and development. By mid-1995 an enormous amount of very diverse information could be obtained over the Web from equally diverse sources.

Surprising and curious things had already begun to happen during early 1994. Normally quiet and retiring programmers suddenly realized that there was nothing to stop them talking to the world without the hassle of face-to-face conversation. The Web suited them ideally. A vast number of home pages blossomed and all at once you could find out what music a complete stranger liked, muse over amateur poetry published by someone a thousand miles away, or read someone's CV over the Web. People put their Persian cats on the Web and displayed their holiday snaps on the Web; it was rumoured that you could even hear pet dogs bark over the Web. So numerous and effusive were the home pages which appeared during 1994 that one couldn't help wondering if some deep-seated need was unintentionally met by the Web technology. It was as though thousands of people had discovered the amateur radio enthusiast in them.

The development of HTML

The original HTML was limited in that you could not include tables, forms, graphics or 'nested' lists in documents. Mark-up was therefore comparatively simple.

Dave Raggett was involved in the design work for extending HTML to meet the needs of professional publishing on the Web since 1992. This work led to an Internet Draft for HTML+ in mid-1993 and this work played an important role in encouraging NCSA to add support for fill-out forms for Mosaic. At the first World Wide Web conference organized by CERN in May 1994, it was agreed that the work on HTML+ should be carried forward to lead to the development of the HTML 3 standard. Dave, together with CERN, had developed a proof-of-concept browser for this work, called Arena. It demonstrated text flow around a figure with captions, resizable tables, image backgrounds, maths and other features.

The preliminary specification for HTML 3 was published as an Internet Draft in March 1995. Since then work on HTML 3 has focused on pieces of the specification, leading to revised proposals first for tables and then for other areas of the specification.

How does HTML 2 fit into the scheme of things? Prior to the first World Wide Web conference in 1994, many browser writers were 'inventing' their own HTML as suited them in a rather *ad hoc* manner. HTML 2 was an attempt to define HTML based on current practices at that time and to formalize the evolving features of the language in writing. It was written up as an Internet RFC by Dan Connolly.

Following the programmers and their Web pages came student groups and organizations who started to use the Web as a new medium, much as students in the 1960s embarked on using offset litho technology as a new medium for printing underground student publications. Behind the students with their experimental graphics and layouts came small adventurous companies, followed by larger sedate organizations advertising their services on the Web. Newspapers started to use the Web; academics published on it. In the music business, many bands put information on the Web and by the middle of 1995 even everyday information such as the times of movies showing started to appear.

To date much of the information available over the Web is one-way, in the sense that, by and large, you browse through it and read it or maybe send simple information back via fill-out forms. Future applications of the Web will stretch far beyond the current applications with 'collaborative' use of the Web where several people use the medium to 'talk' and 'meet' in cyberspace. These future uses of the Web are further discussed towards the end of this chapter.

On the conferencing circuit

The Internet 94 conference was held in the Palàc Kultury – the Palace of Culture – in Prague. About a mile from the old town, the Palàc Kultury occupies a key position on top of a wooded hill. A modern concrete building with a commanding position over Prague, its architecture speaks of its foundations in communist Czechoslovakia. Nobody then could even have dreamed that the Palàc Kultury would ever host a massive conference about global communications. In the communist era Czechs were not even allowed to watch Western television.

The more technical delegates could be easily spotted, somewhat disorientated, in the streets even before the conference began. The many fine beer guts betrayed a common interest amongst Internet visionaries from all over the world, an interest which the conference organizers had happily anticipated.

On their arrival at the Palàc Kultury delegates found the conference registration area hard to find, for the building seemed so incredibly vast. The only clue that they were in the right place was cardboard signs for the *Terminal Room.* Instinctively delegates hurried to this home from home and, to everyone's dismay, suddenly there it was! Behind an enormous glass frontage was a giant room in which were seated about a hundred young men appearing on first glance to be playing a kind of computer bingo. Each had a computer screen in front of him (there were no women) and a keyboard at which he typed in bursts and fits. Others were waiting in silent anticipation, possibly for a program to run, for a distant computer to answer back, who could say. To whom or to what were these people talking? Why were they there? What was going on? For those not accustomed to Internet conferences, it was hard to tell. 'I'll meet you back here in two hours', a technical delegate said to his wife as he stepped forward to join the silent communicators.

Registration for the conference was a complicated process but at the end there were rewards. Delegates were given two cut-glass tumblers of questionable taste and could collect a pair of Internet socks in green with embroidered earths in blue from a nearby stand. After registering they then filtered slowly towards a bar which occupied a corner of a large hall with a panoramic view over Prague. Beer was a 'trivial price' and before long everyone had settled in. A great time was had by all in this area during the following days. For the techies, the combination of Web fandom and beer,

Internet conferences always feature a 'terminal room' towards which technical delegates seem magically attracted...

of Internet and coffee, was simply unbeatable. Everyone was in their element, enthusing over protocols, arguing over mark-up languages, dreaming about servers and cyberspace, and of course, meeting friends who, for the most part, had been previously 'virtual' on the Internet.

The less technical delegates – that is, the managerial and business sections – were not so taken with chatting and software gossiping as were the techies and dutifully attended as many lectures as possible, taking it all very seriously. While the bar staff appeared bemused by the whole affair, waitresses serving buffet lunches, ducking though the fog of effusive Internet jargon, seemed unable to understand how so little attention was being paid to the Czechoslovakian cuisine. Attendees' wives, for whom the electronic world of the Internet sounded far inferior to the one outside, wanted to go and see Prague itself with its Art Nouveau buildings, wooded hillsides, old streets, museums and wonderful bridges and palaces. One group of Internetters, who were at last persuaded to go into town during the evening to look at the sights, walked across the Nuseleský Most bridge and then along the wide boulevard of Sokolskà. With enthusiastic gestures, a wife pointed out the ornate facades of cherubs, leaves and blossoms carved on the 19th century stone buildings they passed. 'Yes', said one of the conference attendees, 'you can see how the patterns repeat. If you constructed a bit map of each section of the pattern, it wouldn't take that much memory to construct a virtual image of the street.'

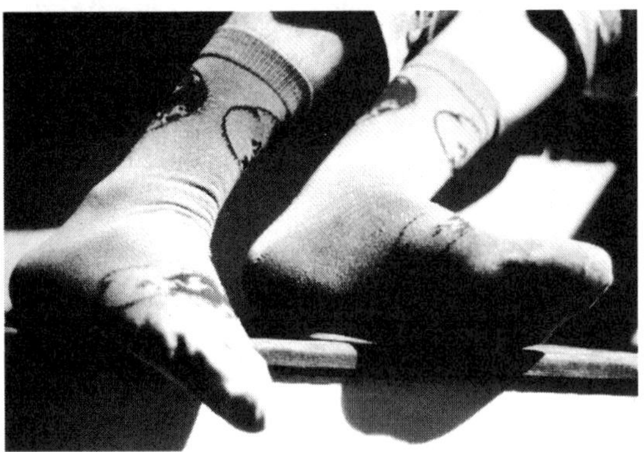

One of the authors models a pair of Internet socks. The words 'Prague June 1994' are carefully embroidered on the instep. These were given out by the RARE stand at the conference.

2.3.2 The role of Mosaic and Netscape in promoting the Web

The Web really took off with the development of Mosaic at the National Center for Supercomputing Applications at the University of Illinois. Mosaic extended the features specified by Tim Berners-Lee, for example by adding images, nested lists and fill-out forms. In late 1993, Jim Clark, founder of SGI, recruited key people from NCSA to set up the Netscape Communications Corporation which was immensely successful.

Netscape has gone on to add support for text flow around images, the ability to control relative font sizes, background images, support for tables and, more recently, a newspaper-style layout with frames and an ability to extend HTML with plug-in software modules. The primary people driving the evolution of HTML are in fact in the company Netscape itself. Netscape has implemented a number of HTML 2.0 and HTML 3 elements and added its own innovations.

2.3.3 Standards work continues nonetheless

Standards work has continued in the wake of this furious pace of innovation in the private sector. This is pursued through the IETF with the foundation of the HTML working group. This group has until recently focused on defining a standard for HTML based on current practice in mid-1994.

2.3.4 Development of HTTP as the Web protocol

The initial protocol for the Web was very, very simple. The clients sent a request: 'GET this filename' and the other end sent back the file and closed the connection. And that was it. No content type to tell you what kind of file was being sent. No status code. Just the file. The client therefore had to guess what it had been given and this developed into a fine art. First the browser would look at the file extension to see if there was a clue there, like .GIF or .HTML, and then it would look at the beginning of the file in case the first few bytes gave the game away – all rather precarious.

Then along came MIME, a kind of multimedia extension to email. This was soon adapted to HTTP so that now, when you got back the file, you actually got a status code and a content type. The content type would tell you the file was text-html, video-mpeg, image-gif and so on, giving the browser a chance to call up the correct viewers to display the file as need be. The burden of finding out what kind of file it was now moved to servers. On UNIX and DOS, servers still play this game of 'guess the file format', whereas on the Mac this is stored as part of the file itself.

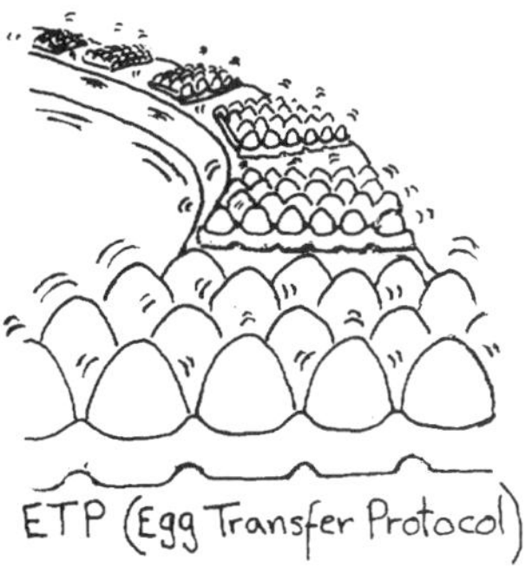

The HTTP we use today was the product of a collaboration between CERN and a group in NSCA. Innovations since that time have been security features such as Netscape's secure socket layer, and more recently the ability to keep the connection to the server open for multiple requests. We can look forward to a radical new protocol, HTTPng, which is designed to support much more efficient connections to servers and the interleaving of multiple messages over a single connection. HTTPng should herald a new host of applications as the Web goes object-oriented.

The HTTP consortium aims to roll out HTTPng along with style sheets and future improvements to HTML and the standardization of HTML 3.

2.3.5 The WWW consortium

The World Wide Web consortium was created in late 1994 and the team staffed up during the summer of 1995. The consortium is focusing on a number of areas: HTML 3, security and payments, content rating, and the next generation of the HTTP protocol. The consortium offers a more streamlined process for achieving consensus as well as carrying out longer-term research needed for the next generation of the Web. The consortium works closely with the IETF to ensure its specifications are subject to the best possible public review.

In the short term, however, the hothouse of commercial innovation is emphasizing short-term issues in enhancing HTML. The standards groups are working to ensure that HTML first of all provides a formal specification for core HTML standards as a basis for testing interoperability and to try to pull HTML back on track for a viable long-term role. In part the short-term problems are caused by the deficiencies of the current Web protocol. For example, if Microsoft wants to add a new feature to HTML there is no easy way to prevent these extensions being seen by other browsers. This forces extensions to be written in such a way as to minimize their impact on the installed base of browsers with the result that HTML is being pulled in different directions, losing its elegance and suffering from featuritis.

2.3.6 Style sheets take over many of the stylistic aspects of a document

Recognizing the need for authors to have control over the look-and-feel of Web documents, however, the concepts of style sheets began to be evolved during late 1994 with concrete proposals emerging from the Web community during 1995. Browsers will be able to download style sheets from central locations and overlay documents with settings included in the style sheet description. Style sheets get a chapter to themselves in this book (Chapter 14) and you should read this if you want to understand more about how they work.

2.4 More variety on the Web

The Web is expanding not only in terms of how much information is on it, but also in terms of the variety of information it holds. The figure below illustrates this general trend. On the left-hand side you can see the Web as it started, predominantly a medium for publishing information in textual form, and then with photos, diagrams and so on. Towards the right-hand side of our diagram we show the latest features at the time of writing: the introduction of plug-in modules, the Java programming language to enable all manner of small applications to be sent down the wire and used within Web applications, and so on.

More variety on the Web. From being a simple text-based system, the Web now supports a variety of media.

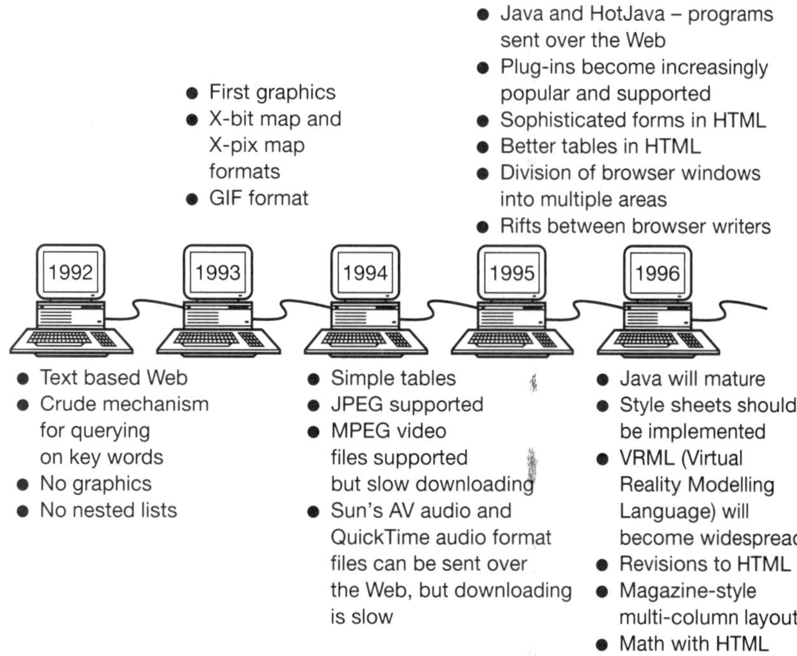

• First graphics
• X-bit map and X-pix map formats
• GIF format
• Java and HotJava – programs sent over the Web
• Plug-ins become increasingly popular and supported
• Sophisticated forms in HTML
• Better tables in HTML
• Division of browser windows into multiple areas
• Rifts between browser writers
1992
1993
1994
1995
1996
• Text based Web
• Crude mechanism for querying on key words
• No graphics
• No nested lists
• Simple tables
• JPEG supported
• MPEG video files supported but slow downloading
• Sun's AV audio and QuickTime audio format files can be sent over the Web, but downloading is slow
• Java will mature
• Style sheets should be implemented
• VRML (Virtual Reality Modelling Language) will become widespread
• Revisions to HTML
• Magazine-style multi-column layout
• Math with HTML

Many of the new features of HTML are associated with this departure away from the simple document and towards a Web which combines text, graphics, video, audio, applications like spreadsheets, front ends to databases, virtual reality applications and all sorts of other 'objects'. Even as we write, companies are inventing new HTML elements to cope with the new diversity of information, for example the new `INSERT` element (see Chapter 16).

2.4.1 What is Java?

At the time of writing a popular buzzword is Java. Java is a programming language which allows programmers to write small applications to be sent over the Web and executed on the client on the receiving end. It's an object-oriented language related to C++. What's so special about it is that programs can be sent to any machine with the right browser to understand them, and furthermore the code will run safely without any risk of adversely affecting the client.

From the user's point of view Web documents suddenly become much cleverer. It's as though your browser automatically creates features, such as the ability to run a spreadsheet or play a piece of animation, in front of your eyes, without you having to load any extra software. The code required to do such tricks is compiled into a special binary format and executed by a Java interpreter in your machine. Java applications are called 'applets' ('small applications' – it would be another thing entirely to send full-blown application software over the Web!) and are small pieces of code which rely on libraries of Java 'classes' in the browser. These libraries mean that the browser has a certain amount of processing knowledge *in situ*: the browser knows how to create a window, respond to events, paint things within a window, draw text within a window and so on. The applets arriving across the Web capitalize on this knowledge and utilize the library routines to do something useful, like display a simple spreadsheet or a piece of animated graphics to the user.

What happens if the applet calls upon a class which is not available at the client end? In such cases the class has to be fetched over the Internet, a process which may indeed be rather slow. It is best to limit the number of these 'additional' classes for this reason.

2.4.2 HotJava

HotJava is a browser which can handle Web documents and these little guest Java programs which can be downloaded to clients. It is available currently as an alpha release for a limited number of platforms, including certain Sun workstations, Windows NT 3.5 and Windows 95. In due course HotJava will be available for other platforms too.

2.4.3 Media types and their importance on the Web

Java programs are by no means the only things coming down the wire now: you can access a variety of other types of file too. A browser can sense what type a file is and therefore know what to do with it by using the **Internet media type**. The Internet media type is a code sent with the file. The browser uses this code to work out what software is needed to interpret and display the data. Without it a browser would not know what sort of animal the file was. Some examples: the Internet media type for an HTML document is text/HTML and for a JPEG image, image/JPEG.

Once the media type has been recognized, and the correct software called up to deal with the file, the information in the file can be displayed *embedded* in the document, that is, displayed in an area of the document as though it were simply part of it. Another way of looking at this is that information can be 'plugged in' to a document – indeed the phrase 'plug-in' is commonly used to describe the downloading of embedded files which are not in HTML and which require software at the browser end to come to the rescue and display them.

Netscape's version 2.0 of its browser allows, for example, a PDF file to appear down the wire. The browser sees that this has an Internet media type Application/PDF. It then calls up the Adobe Acrobat reader to display the PDF file. Once the media type is known, the browser loads the correct application software and interprets the file.

2.5 Virtual reality

2.5.1 Introduction

This section is about a new kind of application which may appear on the Web in the next year or so, and which has a magical attraction for a number of software developers. This is the area of networked virtual reality (VR) – the creation of three-dimensional imaginary and simulated worlds on a computer screen which are fully interactive from the point of view of users.

You will no doubt have seen computer or video games which have some kind of three-dimensional element. Now imagine that you yourself are portrayed in some quite realistic iconic form inside an environment rather like a computer game. There are buildings, rooms, tables, chairs, books, TVs and all sorts of other modern devices for you to interact with. By moving the mouse and clicking, you move yourself around to meet other animated figures of your colleagues and friends, move towards them, away from

The joys of virtual gardening at the click of a mouse button.

them, talk to them, even pass objects to them. Many of the 'props' in this curious on-screen stage are clickable: drawers open, books reveal their contents, a TV goes on and can change channels, and a video can be played. Other objects are more surreal in their behaviour: a door opens into another world; a red 3-D arrow passes by, signalling its importance by flashing at you and following you around. You click on it and an important mail message appears for you to read. Navigation might involve clicking on signposts and going down corridors to new 'places'. The three-dimensional world is at once a place to be, and at once an interface to a whole world of information in cyberspace.

This is some of the essence of virtual reality. Although to many the idea of virtual reality is somewhat far-fetched and indigestible, those involved in the creation of virtual reality software and techniques find the idea quite compelling. They emphatically believe that it is the way that the Internet, or its equivalent, must go.

2.5.2 But what is cyberspace?

Cyberspace is, according to Kevin Hughs[2] in his book *From Web to Cyberspace*, 'an interconnected computer-mediated environment in which all prior media are represented'. This kind of statement mere mortals find difficult to understand and further elucidation was sought. Others have suggested that cyberspace is the 'universe of Network accessible resources', but this also seems impenetrable. Dave Raggett on the subject:

> This is the idea that you have a network of computers which provide access to the set of all network accessible resources.

What are these 'resources'? They are the phone calls, recorded messages, films, photographs, drawings, books, computer games, three-dimensional representations of rooms, stores, landscapes and offices being used over the Internet. At the moment cyberspace is limited in some ways, but enthusiasts of virtual reality applications expect things to change radically within the next few years. It won't be long, they explain, before we'll be seeing applications which render very realistically the interiors of buildings and which allow you to interact with people in them.

2.5.3 Virtual reality and science fiction

If you think that this sounds like science fiction, bear in mind that many of the ideas in virtual reality have indeed been inspired by science fiction novels. A book called *Snow Crash* by Neil Stephenson, published in 1988, was certainly

[2] Kevin Hughs is a computer scientist working in the area of virtual reality. He is the author of *From Web to Cyberspace*, published by himself in 1995. Do read this book if you are interested in the ideas of virtual reality. Contact him for a free copy on http://www.eit.com.

one of the motivating forces behind many of the leading lights in virtual reality research. Others were inspired by computer games such as Doom – not by their violent content, but by their graphics. Dave Raggett said:

> Doom and Wolfenstein 3-D were amongst the first games to show 3-D textured virtual reality running on a PC. I liked the way you could look through rooms and corridors, and the way you could look outside to the other world. Also it had these marvellous sprites, 2-D animation which looked like 3-D.

Doom demonstrated that VR was an idea whose time had now arrived and that it was now feasible on a fast PC. In a restricted context 3-D environments were now possible, but fully general 3-D modelling software was much more expensive: it was by restricting and simplifying the view on the 'world' that good effects could be achieved.

The other thing that Dave came across was a package called SuperScape which ran on a fast PC and allowed you to build 3-D scenes using powerful object-oriented tools and a palette for textures of objects, and so on. It showed that you could indeed build simple 3-D graphical editors to construct 3-D virtual spaces such as your cubicle at work. Clearly, not only was VR practical on everyday equipment, but there were simple VR editors waiting to be used. With this in mind Dave ran a workshop at the Geneva conference on the Web on the subject of VR and went on to describe the full vision at the Internet Society conference in June 1995, where he established the name VRML – *Virtual Reality Modelling Language*. Mark Peche then demonstrated a simple 3-D modelling tool in which you clicked on geometrical shapes to move from one point of view to another.

Dave, however, wanted to take more advantage of the high performance, low cost 3-D graphics software recently available, such as RenderWare from Criterion. The algorithms for drawing 3-D graphics had improved tremendously so that it was now possible to do scenes with large numbers of textured polygons with reasonable frame rates (see the later section on techniques). On slower machines you would need to reduce the window size in which the graphics were displayed, but it was still possible to achieve impressive results on even modest hardware.

2.5.4 What will the virtual world be like?

In *Snow Crash,* the author foresees a telecommunications world monopoly providing the infrastructures for the 'metaverse', a kind of simulated world. The metaverse starts with a street running round the equator and little by little people buy parcels of land along the street to put up properties – a shared model for those who can afford to buy into it. The metaverse operates according to strict rules which provide the continuity needed for stable development, and in the book it is a place where people work, play and so on.

As a result of *Snow Crash* many of the discussions in the VR mailing list were about creating a metaverse out of a Web of VRML pages. The *Snow Crash* enthusiasts saw the Web as suffering from the distraction of hypertext links: they wanted to place the VRML models on some common underlying framework, like a 'street', rather than simply have a number of almost 'separate' models woven together by hypertext links. With hypertext links, there is obviously no such thing as a definite space as such. In a way, Dave Raggett explains, there are two camps of people: those who want a kind of metaverse and agree on some world coordinate system so that we can start rebuilding America in cyberspace, and those who think we can progress with hypertext towards some useful goal. Dave:

> Right now, hyperspace links, or let's say cyberspace links if you like, can be dealt with by simple computers. Simple computers couldn't handle large complex models. Using hypertext links you approach one part of the model at once – you only view one bit at a time which is OK to do even on today's machines. To implement a whole street requires much better computers than anything we have today.

Virtual reality applications will include 3-D images of people together with objects – books, files, TVs, telephones, and so on, just as in the real world:

> You'll be able to click on a file or book in a bookcase to read its contents, click on a TV to start a video. Objects will have expected 'behaviours': a book will fall to the 'ground'; a TV will change channels. The idea is to make cyberspace as natural as possible an environment. Hypertext links to other environments might be through doors – you click on the door, it opens and there you are in a different world!, a bit like the cupboard in C.S. Lewis's *The Lion, the Witch and the Wardrobe.*

Virtual reality scenarios

To give you a better idea of what virtual reality might be like, here are some 'scenarios' from Kevin Hughs' book. They give more of the flavour of possible virtual reality applications to come. You should read Kevin's book if this has made you curious to know more.

Scenario 1: Tour and lessons on the Web

A number of students gather at Virtual Academy's home page, where they await their professor, Dr Hoffman, who is a noted historian and Websurfer. He shows up and asks the students to follow him to an art site in France, where he will begin talking about impressionism and showing many examples.

The students follow him to a page with a number of pictures of artwork. He drags two into the conversation and talks about the particular colours that the artists used. He goes to a page that has a picture of a colour wheel and talks about why the particular colours that were chosen work so well; they are complementary colours. He asks students to go off and find some good examples of artwork with similar colour schemes; he gives them a list of about half a dozen links to sites at which they can start searching. After about ten minutes they re-group and each one drags their offering onto the page....

Scenario 2: Entertainment at home over the Internet

MediaDude magazine, one of the hippest pre-teen digital publications, is hosting a show tonight, one that features a presentation by computer expert Phil Fargo and a concert by the DEC rock group Severe Tire Damage, and Max really wants to go. He gets to MediaDude's server and selects an image of their auditorium. The show is $5. Max enters his Dad's Visa and gets into the page. Fargo is discussing the finer points about modem cards and he's putting up a number of slides as he continues. Max drags and copies the slides in a directory on his hard disk – he's not stupid. He sees a mistake on the slides and would like to put a note on the page correcting the error, but he doesn't have permission to do it and it's not such a big deal anyway. Since he was some minutes late, Max asks the server for the first five minutes of the talk and briefly reviews them.

After the lecture, there's a question and answer period, and after that the Severe Tire Damage logo appears on the page. They're about to play! Max connects their CU-SeeMe reflector and the audio is a little choppy; he doesn't care about the video since he's going over 14.4 from home and the band is putting up live colour shots on the page every two minutes or so....

Science on the Internet

Uses of VR in the context of the Internet are many. For example, scientific papers can consist of interactive exhibits of experiments: a scientific journal may be a world in which data can be played back and experiments rerun with different parameters. Scientific journals could thus be highly interactive.

Health: Cycling through virtual streets

There are a number of exercise machines that use virtual landscapes to encourage progress; while climbing stairs or pedalling a bike, one can ride through a town – or take a tour of a favourite city. It is certainly possible to create engaging biofeedback systems (real cycling is of course far preferable!).

Much telepresence work and simulation work is being done in the medical field. Its traditional use of high technology to do visual imaging has encouraged the development of high-speed collaborative systems. But beyond all of the various work being done for surgeons and medical staff, there are many applications for the patient as well. Users can connect to a hospital's advice service and manipulate a 3-D body to show exactly where the pain is; they can use sliding scales to indicate the kind of pain they are feeling. People can make use of medical expert systems or take courses in basic health, learn new exercises or access their medical charts.

Cyberspatial etiquette

Kevin Hughs includes these points about how you and the world around you should 'behave' in cyberspace. They are interesting not least because they give something of the curious flavour of possible future cyberspace. Kevin emphasizes that: 'these are guidelines and not rules – but if cyberspace architects follow them, we can create common spaces that are more livable and usable.'

- Create but don't confuse.
- When in doubt, keep things real.
- By default, your avatar should be opaque to all.
- It is not polite to pass through someone.
- If you do pass through someone, your appearance should become transparent or changed in some way to denote this action.
- The appearance of objects should not be changed when they are passed through unless they have been programmed to do so.
- It is best to be yourself; otherwise, assume a neutral shape and gender.
- It is impolite to teleport into and out of places unannounced.
- For short distances it is best to walk.
- You can only exist in one place at a time.
- Users should be made known in some way to all others in the vicinity.
- Users may decide who to see and display according to any criteria.
- Identical objects cannot be in more than one place at once. Aliases, agents and symbolic objects must be visually distinct.
- It is best to keep structures within a consistent range of height and dimension.
- For places meant to be visualized by others, it is best to stick with Cartesian space.
- For structures meant to be travelled by others, it is best to stay away from overlapping, extradimensional constructions.
- Objects should appear the same as far as possible to their viewers.

- Users cannot sense into domains into which they are not allowed. Only owners of objects can change their outward appearance, unless such objects are in the public domain.
- Users should be close to each other in order to converse, unless a virtual communications medium is used.

2.5.5 Techniques of virtual reality

This book is not the place to look if you are after a technical description of the issues involved in creating VR worlds. However, we do offer a very brief discussion of the principles of VR software for the non-technical reader.

Images may be composed of polygons

In virtual reality software, scenes are generally represented in terms of polygons. Even a person's face can be represented as a number of polygons and you may be familiar with the idea of a wire frame model which consists of a framework of simple polygons which form the contours of a three-dimensional object. The wire frame model can be stretched and compressed to simulate the movement of the object in question.

When a room is displayed on a screen, it generally consists of a number of polygons which are then treated in various clever ways to give the illusion of space and three dimensions. Remember that virtual reality is in many ways a cheat! Computer processing power is not to be wasted, so when a room or other view is displayed, polygons not in the field of view are culled and the rendering engine only loads in polygons which are visible to the user. Polygons are sorted with respect to depth so that they may be given different treatment according to whether they are near or far away from the viewer.

Managing the level of detail

Polygons are painted from the deepest to the closest using changing tones as appropriate. The illusion of depth may be given by other cues such as detail of textural rendering. Objects may have a lot of detail close up but far away there is no need to waste a lot of computing time on them for they only show up as a few pixels. If there are a lot of objects in the scene then they may not be able to have as much detail as if relatively few objects were present. This is an optimization problem: the computer has to figure out the best level of detail that is worth having for a given object in the context of the scene in general.

Close-up objects may have texture painted on their side like wood, marble or paper. Far away, however, this would be too computationally expensive and textures may be dropped. The number of polygons for 3-D solids is also reduced the further away they are. Distant objects might even be just a two-dimensional shape – it is unlikely that the user would notice.

Polygons which overlie each other cannot be truly sorted with respect to depth and are rendered using a slower and more expensive technique called Z *buffering* to compute how they should be rendered with respect to the scene.

Surface properties and lighting

A polygon will normally have a material associated with it, telling you how shiny it is (if it is shiny it will reflect light within a narrow range of angles) or whether it is matt (in which case light is scattered in all directions). Materials also have colours which they assume in the absence of any special lighting. In other words, some polygons 'glow' a certain colour even though there is no 'light' to illuminate them.

In a VR application, there often isn't enough time to deal with clever lighting models in real time so you have to cheat when it comes to how materials appear under various lighting conditions. Areas like tables, walls and other surfaces are divided up into smaller polygons and then just some of those are coloured as though illuminated at compile time. In other words certain polygons are permanently rendered lighter, or brighter, whichever effect is most realistic. An effect more costly in terms of computing power is *radiosity* where scattered light from walls, ceilings and so on is calculated and used to make interior scenes more true to life.

Moving through scenes

Static images are one thing. In a VR environment you need to consider much more carefully how you are going to create the illusion of movement and play off the computing power needed to create this illusion against the power needed to create detailed graphics. Consider the number of frames you can show per second. Below 10 frames per second everything looks too jerky. Above 10 frames per second, the brain perceives the illusion of motion with smoothness. At 30 frames per second there is no noticeable flicker.

If you decide to go for 10 frames per second, you have only a tenth of a frame to compute the changes and display them. This is your budget and it's not very much. You have to update your view of the virtual world so that anything which moved (including yourself in the world and your resulting perception of it) is portrayed correctly. The low-level 3-D graphics routines have to re-compute which things are now visible and update the screen accordingly. If sound is involved, you also have to update the sound and keep it in synch with the images. In practice, the graphics routines cannot maintain these frame rates if the model gets complex. As a result, part of the time budget is spent loading and unloading parts of the virtual world. For example, as you come to a virtual door, the system has to load up what is behind the virtual door before you actually click to open it. So, in a network, this process of downloading pieces and building them can go on in the background as part of our budget. Outdoors we rely on a fog so that far away, buildings fade into a mist, bounding the number of objects we have to deal with. Inside, the boundaries are imposed by rooms.

The problem of very complex models

For VR models you might want to download the entire model of the particular virtual world and run it on your computer. The problem is that models may be extremely large. So, instead of downloading the whole model already constructed, instead of sending the geometry files for defining each individual polygon and also pix maps for defining each texture, you choose an entirely different route. What you do instead is to send down a *description* of what you want constructed. This is especially appropriate in distributed VR, as would be the case over the Web.

Suppose the server wants a house to appear on your screen. It sends an instruction down the wire saying 'I want a house drawn please' (the computer is ever so 'umble and polite). At the other end the client, seeing that a house is required, reads the instructions for drawing a house from its disk. It knows that 'house' is a specific class of object for which it has a number of instructions for rendering, and looks for these on its hard disk. Thus it draws the house, using a number of initialization parameters sent down the wire which specify also the sub-class of house – 1930s English suburban detached, Victorian Sheffield terrace, New England colonial, ranch-style, or whatever – and perhaps a floor plan. The computer thus uses descriptions of object classes held on disk to carry out the instruction given down the wire to draw the scene. Even classes of wall coverings such as brick, wood, pebble-dash, and so on could be held on the client computer ready to be used when need be. The time for downloading models is thus dramatically reduced.

Colour

The more colours you have in a scene, the more memory your computer needs. PCs do not have enough memory to cope with complex colouring in animation sequences and various tricks are therefore used to get around the limitations. One idea used a lot in computer games is to have only a few things lit up at a time: the rest are dark areas where the eye will forgive the lack of detail. With 8-bit indexed colours you can do special effects such as animation very cheaply (in terms of memory) and certain effects like flashing lights can be achieved by keeping the image data fixed and changing just the colours apportioned to them.

Meeting in shared virtual environments over the Web

How do you meet people in shared virtual environments over the Web? A Web server will be responsible for a particular region of the virtual space, for example a group of rooms or an area in an external space. As a user approaches and enters this region, your browser is registered with the server for that region. That server then keeps track of all the people in that region, so that as you move around in it, your machine sends update messages to tell the server what you are doing and where you are moving. The server in exchange sends you messages about the movements of all the other people in that region. If you move from one region to another, then the server 'moves' you to other servers in charge of those regions which you have now entered. In this way a virtual world of arbitrary portions can be assembled from an arbitrary number of servers.

As well as being able to see other people in the same virtual place you may want to be able to talk to them. When you speak to somebody, your voice is compressed. The compressed samples are then sent to a server for that region. The server then has to blend the speech information from all the people in that region so that people who are far away from you will sound fainter than people who are close to you.

This is very much a research topic right now: is it possible to blend multiple sound sources efficiently without uncompressing sound samples? Uncompressing them would introduce an additional delay.

2.6 Is the Web a good thing?

Some Web developers believe that they are 'quietly changing the world' and are almost evangelical about the Internet. The following points summarize some of their ideas about how this new technology will benefit the world. Following each point we present the extreme other side of the argument, that the Web may not necessarily be of such benefit after all. The comments – which are included in italics – are those of Kirkpatrick Sale who has written extensively about the social and environmental consequences of introducing new technologies. His book, *The Luddites and their War on the Industrial Revolution: Lessons for the computer age*, will be published by Addison-Wesley in Spring 1996.

Readers interested in the Web in the context of society will also find Section 2.7 worth reading. This consists of a more middle of the road appraisal of the technology written by Martin Lam who had an extensive career in the British civil service and more recently, in computer consultancy looking into the profitability and feasibility of new technologies.

- The Web will close up national boundaries and enable us to see right into other people's cultures. As we access information produced by other countries over the Internet, our perception of them will change. We will be able to see how other countries work by calling up all sorts of hitherto difficult-to-find information about them over the Web. For example, national school curricula will be on the Web. This means that educationalists in the US will be able to see how they do things in Ireland or contrast their ideas with those of the UK. Similarly, anti-pollution legislation in the US could be compared with its equivalent in India or Japan. This electronic proximity will have global knock-on effects. It will become easier for the ordinary person to participate in the democratic process and harder for politicians to shield voters from obtaining information.

One must always ask, first, what is the problem that this particular tool or machine or technology is designed to solve? Then, is it necessary or important or desirable, considering all the costs, now and in the future, to ourselves and to our ecosystems? Who will benefit, who will suffer?

Sale points out that knowledge is power, but that its use demands wisdom, rooted in experience.

Yes, it is possible to get a lot of data about other countries and cultures, but who wants it and why? To whom will it give information, and will any get wisdom thereby? We can already know a great deal about other countries and people if we need to, but I can't see that this kind of knowledge, which has increased mightily in recent decades, has done anything to solve or even to address the world's problems. Generally the more we know, the more we are likely to interfere. Would it not make more sense to start to learn about our own country, better yet our town and region, our own specific ecosystem and all its species; and once we can safely say that we really know home, and have solved all the problems right here, then we might offer some few the luxury to delve into other lands.

- The Web is a powerful tool for organizing information to our benefit. By cross-referencing information on the Web with hypertext links that scan the globe, the world's knowledge will be structured more efficiently and could be more effectively used to everyone's benefit. For instance, a mere click of the mouse button will give statistics on Sandwich Terns issued by an English nature reserve. Another click and you can summon up the evidence that, by overfishing waters around Iceland, the numbers of breeding Sandwich Terns in England have decreased.

  The easier it is to access information from diverse sources, the more sensible and informed will be decisions about issues such as conservation.

Again, the idea that what we need most is the world's knowledge is a false and silly one. Human societies already have an immense supply of this information, increasing exponentially in the past century, and it has done nothing to make any of the world's deepest problems more tractable – indeed hunger, poverty, economic disparity, ignorance and environmental decay are only increasing. We already have 100 000 scientific journals – even if we knew what was in them, do you suppose that we would have some addition to the knowledge theatre that would change these problems? Not likely. As to Sandwich Terns: that is exactly the problem; it is precisely the use of high-tech fishing fleets that has led to the overfishing, next to which 'summoning up evidence' is trivial. It is the totality of the high-tech assault that must be understood, against which any individual use of the computer to monitor it is negligible.

Sale voices an obvious twin concern: that we monitor but cannot act; and that technology cannot heal the wounds caused by technology.

- The Web will lead to virtual communities. The Web will enable close relationships to be formed with people in the same town or on the other side of the world ... friendships, working relationships, business relationships, relationships with those sharing a common interest, and so on. These will form the basis for virtual communities on a global scale. People will interact across the Internet using new media which enable you, for example, to project an image of yourself into a virtual meeting room, or appear on an imaginary beach! Conversations will be able to be recorded and filed for later editing or reviewing.

Here Sale points out a major weakness in the ill-thought-out claims made for the brave new technologies.

A joke. Relationships, perhaps, but not communities: flesh and blood, place-based, nature enclosed, different and contrary-minded people, pubs and shops and green-market. What we have to concentrate on is how to re-create communities, the very social institutions that industrialism has been trying to eliminate for centuries, not make artificial ones.

- The Web will mean you can shop without leaving your home. You will be able to order all sorts of things via the Internet, including specialist goods from shops worldwide. This will benefit not only those living in isolated areas or inner city locations where it is too dangerous to go out at night, but also those who are simply too busy to shop or who want to buy items which are available only by 'mail order'. People with unusual needs will find that they can easily see what a specialist shop in, say, Germany has, and order direct over the Web. You will be able to save time for better things by using the Web to plan your shopping trips in advance.

Sale likens the 'innocent' technology of the Web to its roots in materialist culture.

Of course you can shop: the whole point of this stuff is to increase consumption. In general, computers are yet another technology used to increase production (and destroy the world's systems and species in the process) and inevitably somebody has to buy the products at the end of it. This cycle of excessive production and consumption contributes to the most wasteful and polluting economy that the world has ever known.

- The Web will mean you get a wider choice of home entertainment. With the ability to download films, music, animated sequences, video and computer games over the Internet – you will be able to click on the item you want and pay over the Web – a wider range of entertainment will reach your home. People with a particular and rare taste in films will find specialist companies providing for their needs over the Internet. Meanwhile larger media conglomerates will provide material for mass consumption. Small specialist providers can co-exist with the large companies because their audience is drawn from all over the world.

  With the coming of techniques such as VRML (Virtual Reality Modelling Language) new media will appear, including three-dimensional virtual worlds to 'play in' from the comfort of your home.

Sale echoes Aldous Huxley's and George Orwell's views of the future, with 'prolefeed' for the supine masses.

What a dire prospect, the stuff of 'entertainment' and celebrity and sports and sitcoms, the poisons that eat at the very soul of society and turn it into a reflectionless mush. Great access to all kinds of soulless junk is not an advance in human achievement.

- The Web will reduce the need to travel. The need for stressful commuting to work will decrease as you will be able to work with your colleagues over the Web from home. As the Web develops you will be able to look at all manner of documents together over the Web, converse and 'appear' in virtual offices on the screen. Machinery will be monitored remotely over the Internet as the output of measuring devices. Access to databases via the Web will become commonplace and you will be able to apply for mortgages, jobs, and so on without leaving your computer screen.

Sale thinks gloomily about the ecology of future human societies.

Would that it would be reduced! It will not be: our technology is designed to make great numbers of people travel continually, hence the tourist revolution and the vast increase in road travel in the past 30 years. It is possible to do a lot of things in the high-tech home (but what a grisly home it will be) but, guaranteed, that will not reduce other kinds of travel, for business and pleasure (pleasure? jet travel?) and simple rootless anxiety. And would they stay at home to learn the ecosystems pulsing around them? No, to learn Nintendo and Doom.

- The Web will encourage individualism. It will benefit small companies. Many Web developers see the application as something like a public train service or the telephone, to be used by the everyday person as a tool in the modern world. Rather than seeing the potential for a 'big brother' act on the part of large companies and institutions, which is the fear of some, the Internet community hopes that the Web will foster the sense of individuality and anarchy which has characterized the Internet so far.

Here Sale shows what he thinks of 'modern' Western ideals: thinly-disguised power politics married to industrial self-interest.

Individualism, the antithesis of community, is what industrialism is all about. The rootless, confused individual must ratify his or her existence by accumulating material possessions and acquiring meaningless power, spend and control. Large companies love it; there's nothing here that threatens the power of immense corporations, no matter how many consuming individuals and small companies exist.

- You will be able to educate yourself from home. Rather than commute to college you will be able to take courses over the Web, appearing in virtual classrooms where you could click on the teacher to add a question to a list of student queries to be answered next class. Experiments in science could be simulated by downloading and running programs on your screen. Assignments could be sent back to the teacher electronically via the Web.

Finally, Sale distinguishes education (which requires effort, conscious thought) from mere data or information.

Courses, maybe, but not education. All this high-tech version of connecting might possibly do is inform, it can't educate. Education is difficult, and most enormous industrial institutions, like universities, can't always do it. It takes the real world, nature, and teacher at one end of the log, student at the other, to teach properly, and even then it's not always successful. This high-techery is merely rapid and high data processing, something that high-school teachers might love, but then schools have long ago given up the true task of educere *– the drawing out of people so that they could give themselves a context in nature.*

2.7 The Web – another perspective

This is an attempt, resulting from many conversations with the authors of this book, to put the World Wide Web into perspective. The target is, of course, moving, in technology, scope and time; thus this note distinguishes between what is feasible now, what is likely to be possible soon, and, again, those developments which are rather more speculative and depend on changes and improvements which are envisioned but not yet to hand. Because 'everything flows', it is impossible for an overview of this kind to be definitive. There is a philosophical dilemma: many bullish forecasts contain some such phrase as 'one simply cannot imagine what new services and applications the future will bring'. This should stop forecasters in their tracks – but of course they go on predicting regardless. Moreover, if writers merely relate the marvels in store and do not mention possible problems they are naif and credulous; if they do justice to the problems they can be accused of being negative. However, in the rich harvest of commentary this is an attempt to separate the wheat from the chaff.

2.7.1 Analogies – anything quite like it?

Before a new drug or medical technique can be used in earnest most countries insist on lengthy tests of effectiveness, danger, and even, in such cases as assisted conception and the laboratory use of foetuses, ethics. For better or worse no such filtering is customary for innovations in mechanical, electronic, communication or computing technology. Society has little to say on such matters: on the one hand there are relatively few cases of subsidy or encouragement, and on the other hand little or no record of any invention which has been suppressed in the public interest – not explosives, nor atomic fission. Neither can red flag treatment for trains be kept up for long. However, guns are subject to licensing; society imposes penalties for careless driving and for neglect of safety rules for machinery and explosives. States tax alcohol and tobacco. The printed word is subject to rules about what is proper, and what is obscene or libellous. Perhaps only poison gas and narcotic drugs are, in principle, banned – and, lately, fluorocarbons.

Apart from such exceptions the main rule is to let the public vote for new technology with its purse. Its response is largely unpredictable:

sometimes it is reticent, as with the electric car and, for a time, ISDN; some people still prefer analog displays on watches to digital. However, most users have warmed, one might say, to refrigerators, microwave cooking, the Walkman, colour television, mobile telephones, satellite TV and, of course, PCs. Some people claim to despise remote control for the TV – but then resent having to get up to change the channel.

Sometimes, as with digital exchanges and transmission, the public did not even know what was in store and did not try to evaluate it. It has grudgingly come to use some of the new facilities, but without necessarily ascribing them to digitalization. The same may happen with digital radio and television. On the other hand the analog Group III fax has flourished to a degree which rivals sliced bread; Teletex, as an advance on telex, got nowhere; neither did videotext prosper commercially. One survivor, the French Teletel/Minitel, is being linked to the Web.

Thus, in general, when innovations appear the field is wide open for debate about what is good and bad; as in the case of the Web, enthusiasts risk over-icing the cake and attract accusations of hyperbole. The Web practitioners do not make things easy for ordinary people to understand the Web: they are, for example, unclear about what is meant by many terms: for example, the words 'interactive', 'multimedia' and 'secure' are used loosely without real clarification. Now we also have 'content'.

The detractors comprise a few Luddites – genuinely afraid that technological advances will reduce employment – or potential Unabombers, against computing in general – or, more respectably, people who intuitively feel, and argue, that the resources expended on, for example, the Web could be used to the greater benefit of mankind at large. However there is no indication that such a switch of resources would take place if there were no Web. For better or worse the same is true of most items of investment by the richer nations: improved health care, better opportunities for leisure and access to entertainment, and advances in research and education. It would be quite arbitrary to base 'postmodernist' criticism of the Web on the grounds that it is one more piece of consumerism by which the better qualified members of society equip themselves to increase their lead over those less well endowed by country or opportunity.

2.7.2 The striking achievement – a super database

For the Internet as such, the facility of linking so many users so simply by email and via interest groups and mailing lists is spectacular. For the Web the salient bull point must be the advent of a hypertext-linked database which enables users of a PC at one end of the world to find information stored in a number of other places thousands of miles apart. The use of hypertext for text, images, audio and even video clips on the Web is surely a notable advance over conventional online searching.

Online information provision (text and graphics in black and white) has been a growing business for some time; it has come a long way since the first teletype-based systems. Specialized databases, including those listing and illustrating chemical compounds, have become ever more ingenious. In most fields bibliographic searches can be extended to full text. There is, moreover, evident and growing competition between online and regularly updated distribution of CD-ROMs, a large number of which can be held in 'juke boxes' and called up within seconds. The new generation of 9 gigabyte CD-ROMs will be even more formidable. This rivalry is to the advantage of the user.

'Traditional' online is, however, unsatisfactory in some respects; one trouble with it is that different enquiry languages are used for different hosts, and only professional librarians and searchers relish this diversity. However, the online market is by no means dead or dying; new entrants into this market will attempt to operate on a continental or global level, giving a choice of languages – for example English, French, German. But they are also turning to the Web as a vehicle.

2.7.3 Electronic mail and bulletin boards

Like online information, electronic mail and EDI – electronic distribution of (trading) information – have been available from commercial value added networks (VANs) for some years. However, subscribers to different email systems cannot easily communicate. Worldwide standards in such fields have taken years to develop against the background of competing, but incompatible, commercial systems.

By contrast the Internet and the Web are far more widespread and far more accessible. This is partly because of the adoption, by a remarkable feat of common sense and common purpose, of generalized communication protocols. But another reason is that the costs of some at least of the communication links have not been charged in full to the users. This is partly because so many of the users are in academia, or in companies where calls are not logged rigorously – though there are now firms which are conscious of the call on their employees' time and their telephone bills and are discouraging extracurricular Web access.

It has undoubtedly helped the growth of the Web that its early costs were low. Online hosts and VAN suppliers have to live on their earnings and charges have therefore to be economic, allowing for copyright where it applies. Users have to subscribe and pay for access. By the same token, because online activity is economically based it serves only the market which can pay, and thus offers only what the market requires – that is, no trivia.

The Web rejoinder to this is that only professional users can afford to access online services in their present form. The majority of Web users, on the other hand, are not professional searchers and include a number of people who have the use of a PC and enjoy participating in what the Web has to offer. Against this it is alleged that much of what is stored is trivial, some of it of interest mainly to the enthusiasts (or exhibitionists) who set it up, and that this bulk of material makes it more difficult for serious users to find what they really want. Ironically, the super-abundance of material on the Web has given rise to ingeneous new software for searching and indexing the needles in the haystack. The scope for browsing is spectacular, and surveys show that much browsing is done for its own sake – that is, where the user does not have a definite object in view but browses for the hell of it. This may not be a bad thing – just as people may learn a lot from books culled at random from the shelves of a library. Serendipity lives.

In this regard it is claimed as an advantage and, indeed, as a feat, that the material on the Web is put up autonomously and without scrutiny or censorship, and can be largely accessed freely and without payment. This is heralded as a bonus by those who argue that the best thing about the Web is that it is democratic; others, not so sure, speak of anarchy – a term sometimes regarded in the fraternity as complimentary rather than pejorative. Pornography poses a problem for society – whether delivered by post, video, TV, or over the Web; there is a suspicion that it will be harder to monitor on the Web/Net and more difficult to keep from viewers, for example children, to whom many people would like it barred. The 'content' chip has been devised to achieve just this.

It is uncertain how cost factors will operate in the longer run on the Web. Already 'domain names' attract a registration fee. Some of the links, including the cheap backbone, originally set up under Defence auspices, but now run by commercial carriers, are overloaded at certain hours at current prices (notably when North America is awake), so that congestion inhibits the flow of traffic and therefore reduces both the quality of service and the volume of usage. The provision of regional 'caches' of the most sought-after pages will be a palliative, but for this to change the telecommunications carriers along the line will have to be able to make a commercial turn on the use of the links and the high-speed switching of broadband circuits. Network management on this scale will not be easy, but here again smart software is predicted to do the job. The assumption has to be that the market in turn will be willing to pay for the improvements, for example by a change in the Internet convention whereby charges are on a flat rate – i.e. no account is taken of distance or bandwidth. Enthusiasts believe that this is old-fashioned thinking, and that in the future there will be a superfluity of bandwidth to be used in faster transfer of all kinds of data and for new services not yet invented. If so, even the ubiquitous fax will feel the competition.

2.7.4 Services already provided or immediately feasible

There is little doubt about the good things the Web can already offer. The idea that users can post a note of problems they have and invite solutions can be helpful, both within firms and more generally. Schools and colleges can make contact with similar establishments in other places or abroad. Government departments can and do give news of their activities, prospective calls for tender or for participation in research projects. Advertisements for goods and services are available on Web sites. The cliché 'digital retailing' is to be heard in the land. The first Web real estate agents have started up, no doubt hoping to offer virtual reality tours of houses in the near future.

It is already open to lobbyists to use the Web to express their views and press them on their target audience – assuming that they have identified those addresses from which their public operates. Software is being distributed over the Net; this saves time in getting updates to users. There is a limit to how long the files can be in present circumstances; transmission time could be costly. Questions of payment also arise; often, as with 'shareware', payment is requested from the satisfied user as a matter of honour, not obligation.

Travel information can be accessed: availability of lodgings, maps of how to find a hotel, can be got from the Web. Bookings can be made, exploiting the more sophisticated use of fill-out forms and new interactive interfaces over the Web. Investment portfolio management is on offer. Shareholders will be able to get figures from the company database and analyse them.

At least one noted picture archive library can be accessed over the Web. That is to say, pictures can be identified by content and then ordered and paid for; they will be available for downloading at full size and resolution by ISDN; they are not image-indexed. Twenty years of US patent abstracts are available on the Web.

Teleworking will undoubtedly be facilitated by the Web; location will become progressively less relevant for activities related to answering enquiries, carrying out surveys, translation over the Net and so on. There will be more outsourcing of such services by companies and government. What is not clear is how far people will be willing, even with the support of the Web, to forego real contact with others even in return for the best electronic connections.

One important plus is that the Web has made it far more difficult for autocratic regimes to control the flow of news. Iran and China are among the countries where it is reported that the authorities are worried that subscribers to the Web can both receive and send information which the regime would rather keep dark. However, China has set up internal Internet networks which are allowed links with the rest of the world.

2.7.5 The near future

What enhancements of the Web are in store for the near future and what services will they support? There is no doubt that as transmission over switched broadband speeds up – between the main nodes, the routers, the servers and the subscribers – retrieval will become faster, traffic jams less frequent, and more and bigger pictures and longer audio and video sequences will be incorporated in the 'files'. Cheap central storage, faster transmission – and downloading into plentiful cheap storage – will enable users to access long texts, films, video sequences, novels, and anything else, including music. They will be able, at a decreasing price, to download to re-writeable optical disks. Customized news and other information will be delivered from the Web to the machine at your desk.

Some predict that the Web will bring an end to copyright. Whether this is so will depend partly on the attitude of Web users to regulation, and also on the practical arrangements, for example electronic tags, which prove possible for access to be recorded and for billing to take place. It would be wrong to assume that the important and legitimate interests involved here cannot be managed, but there could be practical problems – apart from resistance from some of the community.

In general the concept of confidentiality of information on the Web involves a paradox. Since the current assumption is that the Web is there for everyone, and that the incredible availability of what is stored is the Web's chiefest glory, it is not clear how the circle will be squared – that is, how some at least of the information held will be restricted to authorized users and some of it charged for (access can be recorded) without at best a complicated and expensive billing system (as with roaming international mobile phones) and at worst an abandonment of the current (almost literally?) free-for-all ethic. Apart from the danger to confidentiality from hackers there is a general problem of intellectual property rights in the context of electronic distribution of text, video and music – indeed of entertainment generally. To use encryption may be a solution – but presents the well-known difficulties relating to the degree of security the State can tolerate. The so-called Pretty Good Privacy may serve as a compromise.

However, for the sensitive identity, authorization and authentication checks used in monetary transfers, several rival security arrangements are in the offing. Insecurity of payment systems will not be a bar to executing commercial transactions on the Web though suppliers are still left to seek credit information on would-be customers. At the same time, once access to a page can be unambiguously recorded the way is open for advertising targeted at individuals who have shown interest in a given product. This will not be universally welcome. Junk email is already a problem.

Speech on the Web

Digital mobile radio relies on the digitization and then the compression of speech. The same, or similar, compression algorithms can be used to enable speech over the Web, provided that the modem is a fast one or the bandwidth into the user's installation is sufficient and enables the packets to arrive fast enough. Software recently made available over the Net enables speech to be transmitted, but currently not in duplex; so far there is no direct equivalent to initiating a call in conventional telephony; however, a user with two telephone lines can combine a local call on one of them with an international conversation over the Net. This may pose questions of legality in some countries. Videoconferencing over the Net, using ISDN, could be the next step.

Publishing

Once difficulties of volume and speed are overcome there is no reason why users should not be able to download material from the Web either integrally or selectively. Education professionals putting courses together will be able to choose their texts, images, sound and video from all available sources, including museums and art galleries. Lectures and demonstrations by famous professors will be called up at will. Indeed there is a prediction that the university as an institution will be partly overtaken by what will be a cheaper way of accessing learning material. (However, as with teleworking, economics apart, there must be some doubt about how far learners will forego human contact in favour of the screen.)

Doctors will be brought up to date more quickly by online information (encrypted if required) via the Web. For better or worse, patients too can access medical information. Religious guidance can be sought and offered. Politics we already have.

One inviting – or frightening – prospect here is that scientific journals will be able to publish speedily, on the Web, papers which would otherwise have been held up for months by the procedures of refereeing. The optimistic view must be that this very process will be accelerated if referees can be sent the paper over the Web and if the references in the paper are hypertext-linked and can therefore be verified by the referee. The trouble is not technical but ethical. If some impatient authors beat the gun by putting their work on the Web before any referee has got near it this could be dangerous. It is hard to see how it could be prevented, without infringing that universality which, as observed, is one of the proud achievements of the Web. As a risky compromise one publisher offers, or threatens, to publish papers sent to him at the same time as they are sent to the referees.

Games on the Web can be seen as a subset of publishing, at any rate if they are accessed and downloaded to the user's machine. However, there are also games which can be played with other participants, either one-to-one or in a common space. Trials of such games for children in hospital are already current. More of this can be expected, particularly with virtual reality (see below). Sound radio broadcasts are already possible on the Web. In the important area of the delivery of entertainment there will be competition not only from the cable and satellite interests but also from the telephone companies commanding broadband domestic links or their equivalent.

Buying and selling on the Web

Companies are already using the Web to advertise and list the goods they sell. Some offer a semi-permanent listing, others take trouble to make their pages more attractive and change their contents more often. In this sense the Web is already an auxiliary to mail order. There is no reason to doubt that once the payment arrangements are secure transactions via the Web, particularly repeat or regular orders for staples, will increase – and if so will, incidentally, mean more delivery of goods to the home; but forecasts that the volume of this trade will threaten the existence of shopping malls and retailing as we know it are surely hard to swallow when most consumers still like to see and touch the things they are buying. However, pioneer retailers are offering local delivery, with a charge, of goods ordered electronically. Auctions could take place on the Web.

There is the difficulty of how to apply sales or valued added taxes, or price maintenance, or other such provisions, to transactions implemented over the Web. Certainly there is the risk that consumers would buy in the States of the USA where the sales tax is least. At the limit the criticism – reflecting the claims made that the Web will take over commerce – is that the Web would become one vast grey market. Certainly it could make nonsense of customs tariffs and differences in consumer taxation between countries. Perhaps the resolution of this is that where goods – other than those which can be distributed electronically – are ordered from another jurisdiction they still have at some stage to travel across frontiers. Thus, paradoxically, Customs authorities might have more, not less, work to do as a result of Web transactions.

Virtual reality

An important consideration here is the extent to which the use of virtual reality will make 'window' shopping and buying via the Web far more attractive than the listing on a page as described above. In principle virtual reality can enable a shopping mall to be presented on the screen, with the shopper enabled to go into a chosen shop and to move through it perusing the virtual shelves. The prices can be made available by pointing the cursor to the goods concerned.

However, as with some other possible Web scenarios, to transmit all this assumes more bandwidth than could be economically available at present. Alternatively, therefore, it is proposed that storage local to the user could, in the future, hold a generic code representing common objects (not just cubes and cones but including, presumably, stores, shelves, groceries, books, cabinets, and so on). On a signal triggered by the customer and responded to by the advertiser, the stored objects would appear on the user's screen. As mentioned earlier a language – Virtual Reality Modelling Language (VRML) – is being developed which will in time facilitate the programming, transmission and storage of three-dimensional objects. One advantage claimed for this technique is that transmission/downloading time would no longer be a constraint; thus more trouble and pixels could be devoted to the definition of the really relevant images.

The same argument is used in favour of virtual reality to provide the background to eventual 'videophone' conversations via the Web: the image of your room and that of your interlocutors would not need to be transmitted; the available pixels could be used to give better definition to your face and expressions (assuming that this is an advantage in all cases). Alternatively, and rather less plausibly, you could choose for yourself a shape in which you would appear and converse with other avatars in a scenario of your, or their, choosing.

Government

We have noted already the potential of electronic means to elicit opinions and advice, and to facilitate lobbying. Some forecast that true democracy will thereby either be deepened – or superseded. Assuming that more people took advantage of this facility than, for example, at present write to newspapers, it is surely hard to see how such a bulk and multiplicity of views could be managed. Regular or selective electronic voting on matters of public policy would be more practicable. This general question of how to deal with a potential information overload is a constraint on many possible applications. It is of interest in this connection that the Web Consortium has itself invited comments from interested parties on drafts circulated over the Web. Hundreds of replies have been received, many lengthy. It has been impossible to do justice to all of them.

There is an extreme point of view that in some way government in the sense in which we know it will be superseded by the Web: new 'communities' will arise, and they will be able to agree on procedures and actions which affect them. There will, therefore, be less – or no – need for the State as such. By the same token laws would not be necessary. The argument is that if all the people with guns, or vehicles, or dogs, or houses, and those others who are interested in whatever it is can agree, via their electronic community, on the rules applying to the field, then general legislation would no longer be needed. Sometimes this vision is called a virtual parliament. This prediction surely leaves out of account the ingenious ways in which Society has needed to evolve the means of reconciling conflicting interests. For practical purposes it is surely more useful to consider how to turn the Web to advantage in improving the pattern of government than to expect to supersede it.

Another question is whether financial transactions over the Web can be accommodated within the present international system. Concern on this account does not take into account that the largest transfers of funds are already made electronically and the resultant globalization of corporate finance and freedom of capital movement already pose problems of supervision and enforcement. In any case there must be an assumption that somewhere there will be a record of transactions so that if need be they can be subject to check or recall – for example in civil or criminal proceedings. This constraint would, as observed earlier, not be welcome to those who believe in the anarchistic merits of the Web. Alternatively, judicious use of the Web for prompt propagation of figures of capital movements and currency reserves, which some countries would like to delay or obfuscate, could make speculation, crises and crashes less likely.

2.7.6 The more distant future, and society

We have tried to deal above, circumspectly, with the proximate future; more distant prospects are less penetrable. The rise and rise of the PC, with ever more functionality, leads to the prediction that with even higher chip integration, thin screens and lighter power supplies (not yet invented) people will be able to carry pocket-calculator-size machines with which they can access information sources and draw on unlimited computing power, using digital radio links, supported by satellite if necessary, from anywhere in the world. At the other end of the scale it is argued, with equal logic, that if computing power, decentralized to nodes and servers, becomes plentiful and cheap, then the terminal carried or used by an individual can be as dumb as they used to make them. If so, it is argued in return, then there will be the problem of safeguarding the personal information and the programs stored outside the individual's control.

This section has tried to consider some of the explicit social and economic effects of the Web in the context of the activities it supports now and is likely to facilitate in the near future. However, one more general and implicit possibility, which attracts some reproach, is that these developments will help to make the rich richer and the poor poorer. The grounds are that those who will gain by being able to access more information more readily and use it to greater advantage will be those who have benefited from educational opportunities made possible by a substantial investment in human resources as well as in communication hardware which only rich countries can undertake. It is a commonplace that the number of jobs – even in industrial countries – requiring non-intellectual labour is in decline; thus it is feared that the ability of the favoured to use information will push the others even further down.

The practical answer to this must be that in every society more people will, thanks to the Web or its equivalent, have easier and cheaper access to more information and will be able to use it to improve their knowledge, skills and qualifications – and keep them up to date. As the productivity of the society is thereby enhanced, so some of the additional resources generated will be available to help those who are in danger of being left behind.

The same phenomenon could occur at the international level, but this is nothing new. The international division of labour does not have to be static. All countries want to upgrade their skills and to aspire to activities which give a better return both to capital and to labour. The hidden hand of international economics has already helped programming to move to those emerging countries where education is of a good standard and wages are still relatively low. Thus, paradoxically, it is possible to envisage circumstances in which the Web helps such countries to improve the average earning power of their citizens rather than reduce it.

3
OVERVIEW OF HTML

In this chapter:

- Basic concepts and terminology
- Syntactic rules for HTML
- Formal structure of an HTML 3 document

3.1 Introduction

You will have gathered from previous chapters that HTML is the Web's own publishing language. To see samples of HTML on your screen, switch to viewing the 'source' of any page on the Web (most browsers have an option SOURCE under the VIEW option for doing this) and you will see the HTML which gave rise to the page in question. The HTML consists of a number of codes or 'tags' which the author has used to mark up the various components of the document – its paragraphs, headings, tables and so on – and also to insert graphics and hypertext links. Common tags you might spot in the source of a Web page are <P> for 'paragraph', <H1> for 'heading 1' and <UL> for 'unordered list'.

It is only when the document is processed by a browser that such codes 'come alive' and trigger off the various browser formatting routines which give rise to a properly presented document. A browser knows that <P> marks the beginning of a new paragraph; it knows that <B> signals bold text, and will display emboldened words accordingly. HTML is not like an ordinary WYSIWYG editor where you have precise control over layout on the screen and printing to paper: different browsers will display your document in different ways. A text-only browser will, for example, display a document differently from one which displays graphics. The recent use of style sheets to indicate the font, colour and other details of layout do of course give more control – see Chapter 14.

Note: The reference card with this book includes a list of all the HTML tags. The list tells you which tags are implemented and to which version of HTML they belong. It is most important that you consult this list when you use this book; we have attempted to keep the list as up to date as possible.

3.2 A simple HTML document to show tags

The HTML below shows the very simple mark-up of Edward Lear's 'The Owl and the Pussy Cat'. It is followed by a browser rendering of how the poem might appear on the screen once displayed by a browser. We have put the HTML mark-up in bold simply for the sake of clarity.

```
<Title>THE OWL AND THE PUSSY CAT</TITLE>

<H1 ALIGN=center>The Owl and the Pussy Cat </H1>

<P ALIGN=center><IMG SRC="dancing.gif">

<P>The Owl and the Pussy Cat went to sea in a beautiful pea-green boat.

<P>They took some honey and plenty of money wrapped up in a five-pound
note. The Owl looked up to the stars above and sang to a small guitar:
<Q>Oh lovely Pussy, oh Pussy my love, what a beautiful pussy you are.
</Q>Said Puss to the Owl <Q>You elegant fowl, how <I>charmingly</I> sweetly
you sing! Oh let us be married; too long have we tarried, but what shall we
do for a ring?</Q>

<P>They sailed away for a year and a day to the land where the bong-tree
grows. And there in a wood, a Piggy-wig stood with a ring at the end of his
nose. <Q>Oh Pig are you willing to sell for one shilling, your ring?</Q>
Said the Piggy: <Q>I will.</Q> So they took it away and were married next
day by the turkey who lives on the hill.

<P>They dined on mince and slices of quince, which they ate with a runcible
spoon. And hand in hand on the edge of the strand they danced to the light
of the moon.
```

This simple document might be rendered by a browser like this:

The Owl and the Pussy Cat

The Owl and the Pussy Cat went to sea in a beautiful pea-green boat.

They took some honey and plenty of money wrapped up in a five-pound note. The Owl looked up to the stars above and sang to a small guitar: "Oh lovely Pussy, oh Pussy my love, what a beautiful pussy you are." Said Puss to the Owl: "You elegant fowl, how *charmingly* sweetly you sing! Oh let us be married; too long have we tarried, but what shall we do for a ring?"

They sailed away for a year and a day to the land where the bong-tree grows. And there in a wood, a Piggy-wig stood with a ring at the end of his nose. "Oh Pig are you willing to sell for one shilling, your ring?" Said the Piggy: "I will." So they took it away and were married next day by the turkey who lives on the hill.

They dined on mince and slices of quince, which they ate with a runcible spoon. And hand in hand on the edge of the strand they danced to the light of the moon.

Looking at the mark-up:

- `<TITLE>` and `</TITLE>` are tags to give the piece we are writing a title. This title will be displayed across the top of the window containing the poem when it appears on the screen. Every HTML document must have a title.
- `<H1>` and `</H1>` are tags to give a heading to the poem. This is different from the title, for it appears as a heading to the poem itself, rather than as the title for the window displaying the document. `ALIGN=center` has the effect of centring the heading.
- `<IMG>` embeds an image. This also has an attribute `SRC` (to describe the SouRCe of the image) and an attribute `ALIGN` with a value '`center`'.
- `<P>` is the tag for a paragraph; the `ALIGN` attribute allows you to position the text.
- `<I>` and `</I>` are to mark up text in italics.

- <Q> and </Q> are to mark up a quote. The browser automatically puts the quote marks in for you when it displays the text. Note that **Q** is not widely supported yet.

How HTML is different

HTML takes a different approach to document representation from other document formats. As a mark-up language, HTML concentrates on the structural parts of a document: its paragraphs, headings, lists, tables and other structual components. HTML is less concerned with stylistic issues such as type of font, margin settings and so on, leaving these to be chosen either by the browser or specified in a style sheet. HTML allows the author to indicate the function of the parts of a document rather than how they should be rendered on the screen or printed out on paper.

Writing HTML documents and trying them out

How do you actually write an HTML document in terms of trying it out and displaying the results on your browser? There are three options.

1 Using an HTML editor

The easiest option for the novice may be to use an HTML editor to create your document. Having said that, there is no point in using an editor if you don't know what you want to do with it. In the same way that, say, a sewing machine is of no use unless you know about sewing, so an HTML editor is no use unless you have some idea of the capabilities of HTML and the design of HTML documents. You also need a knowledge of HTML to 'fine tune' the results, to get the effects you want, and to produce more complex parts of documents such as forms and graphics.

Many editors are available. The best thing is to search under 'editors' and 'HTML' on the Web and see what is currently available; they change all the time..

2 Writing HTML from scratch

Another possibility is to write HTML from scratch. This gives you the greatest control. To try out a simple piece, open a file using your favourite text editor or DTP package, read or type in any material you want to mark up and then simply add the HTML tags as required (you might try 'The Owl and the Pussycat' as your first experiment). Now save the file as plain text ('text only' is the option many DTP packages give).

What file extension should you use? You should use .HTM if you are using a PC or, for a UNIX file, use .HTML. On the Mac you can give it any name that is practical (although it is still conventional to use .HTML none the less).

To test out the document, you call up your browser. Now do 'Open File' and select the file you want from the Open File dialogue box. Magically the HTML is digested by the browser and behold the result is a neatly displayed document on the screen.

3 Converting documents in Word, FrameMaker and other DTP packages to HTML

There are also various tools which allow you to take DTP documents directly and convert them into HTML. Simple documents with headings and paragraphs convert best; tables, forms and other more complicated parts of a document may be better marked up manually. Hypertext links need to be dealt with carefully, as do graphics.

3.3 Start tags and end tags

You will notice that tags often come in pairs. This is because they mark up the structural parts of a document and it is generally the case that a **start tag** marks the beginning of such a part, while an **end tag** is generally used to mark the end of it. The end tag differs from the start tag only in that it has a slash '/' included following the opening bracket. The symbols '<', '>' and '</' are called **delimiters** since they delimit mark-up.

Some tags, such as <P> for 'paragraph', need not have a complementary end tag although you may put one in if you want. The end tag can simply be left out as the browser infers its presence. Other elements *must not* have an end tag, for example IMG. The more common elements which do not need an end tag are listed in Table 3.1. The common elements which must not have an end tag are listed in Table 3.2.

Table 3.1 Some of the common HTML elements which do not need an end tag.

Element name
P (Paragraph)
LI (List item)
OPTION
DT, DD
HEAD
BODY
HTML

Table 3.2 Some of the common HTML 3 elements which *must* not have an end tag.

Element name
HR (Horizontal rule)
IMG (inline figure)
BR (break)
COL (in tables)
META (in HTML body)
LINK
BASE
ISINDEX

3.4 Elements as structural parts of a document

Each structural part of a document is an **element**. Paragraphs are elements, as are tables, forms, lists and images. Each element is marked up by inserting a start tag to indicate its beginning and an end tag to indicate its end. A browser will usually employ a different formatting routine to display the elements of each different kind.

3.4.1 Element names

An element has an **element name**. The element name for a paragraph element is P; that for a simple hypertext link element, A; the element name for a top-level heading is H1. Element names are not case sensitive, although in this book we adopt the convention of placing all element names in upper case. You can type them in lower case or even in a mixture of cases.

3.4.2 Rules about the order of elements in a document

HTML mark-up cannot occur arbitrarily and must conform to the HTML document grammar. This grammar describes the tags which can be used, and the legitimate order in which they can be inserted into a document. This idea is explained briefly in Chapter 1 which talks about the relationship between SGML, the Standard General Mark-up Language, and HTML.

3.4.3 The content model

The **content model** relates to which elements can be included within a given element in the document. For example, in marking up a table, the TH (table header cell) element has a content model which includes text, lists, maths, graphics and so on. What this means is that within any TH element, you can include text, lists, maths, graphics and many other elements. The content model tells you that all of these things are allowed in the cell of a table.

3.4.4 Permitted context

The **permitted context** meanwhile relates to the context in the document in which an element can be used. For example, TH elements (that is, table header cells) can only be used in the context of a table row, TD. This makes perfect sense for it would be surprising if you could place a table cell in, say, a title or a heading, or in an ordinary paragraph. The context for TH elements is never a paragraph, nor a heading or list; it is always a table row.

3.4.5 Block-level elements versus character-level elements

There are two groups of elements: **block-level elements** and **character-level** elements. A working definition of these two groups is as follows. A block-level element is one which, when inserted into a document, has the effect of automatically terminating the preceding paragraph and throwing a paragraph break. For example, when you insert a figure in a paragraph using the block-level element FIG, the paragraph preceding the FIG element is terminated prior to FIG beginning.

Tables, forms, equations and lists are just some of the items inserted into a document by using block-level elements. The CLEAR attribute controls the way each block flows around obstructions such as figures and tables. The basic idea is that you might want to ensure that a paragraph or list begins after the figure or table in question. You can use the CLEAR attribute on a block element to ensure it is rendered in the position intended. The use of CLEAR is explained in Chapter 4 which deals with HTML generic attributes.

Note: The FIG element is an HTML 3 proposed element; it has not been implemented by browsers at the time of writing. However, FIG or its equivalent is likely to be implemented in the near future.

Character-level elements behave differently from block-like elements. Character-level elements include text itself, character entities, various font-style and character-emphasis elements, and the MATH element (you can put a math equation in a line of text). They also include hypertext links and inline graphics with the IMG element. All of these things form part of the text flow within a paragraph.

Some block elements have further structures within them. For example, a definition list contains pairs of terms and their corresponding definitions; a table starts with a caption followed by a list of rows; a figure starts with a caption followed by a figure description, and then a credit. Throughout this book we will use the terms block-level element and character-level element to indicate where a given element can occur, or to describe what an element can contain. In other words, the ideas of block- and character-level elements will appear in the descriptions of content model and permitted context. Some common block-level and character-level elements are shown in Tables 3.3 and 3.4, respectively.

Table 3.3 Some common block-level elements.

P	Paragraph
TABLE	Table
FORM	Form
H1...H6	Headings
ADDRESS	Address
DIV	Division
PRE	Preformatted text
BLOCKQUOTE	Longer quotations in the text
NOTE	Note
BR	Line break
FN	Footnote (HTML 3 not yet implemented)
UL	Unordered list
DL	Definition list
CAPTION	Caption
OL	Ordered list
FIG	Figure (HTML 3 not yet implemented)
HR	Horizontal rule

Note: You can have a look at the reference card provided at the back of this book to see what the status is for each of these elements. Remember different elements are implemented on different browsers and some HTML 3 elements are merely proposed at the time of writing.

Table 3.4 Some common character-level elements.

ABBREV	Abbreviation in text
ACRONYM	Acronym in text
AU	Author, for example of a poem or book
CITE	Citation. Sections tagged as citations are typically rendered in italics
CODE	A sample of computer code as might be included in online computer manuals
DEL	Delete text (for legal documents). Shown with strike-through
DFN	Definition of term

Table 3.4 (*cont.*).

`EM`	Emphasis, which most browsers will render as italics
`INS`	Inserted text (for legal documents)
`KBD`	Text to be entered at the keyboard (for use in computer manuals)
`LANG`	Local change in language used in text. Enables browser to get hyphenation and other aspects of rendering text on the screen right for the language in question
`PERSON`	Name of person (for indexing purposes)
`Q`	Short quotation. Typically quotation marks are added by the browser using the correct punctuation for the language in which the text is displayed. HTML 3 – not yet widely implemented
`STRONG`	Strong emphasis
`VAR`	Variable (for use in on-screen computer manuals)
`TT`	Teletype font: a fixed pitch typewriter font
`U`	Underlined
`S (STRIKE)`	Strike through. The text should be displayed with a horizontal line through it, for showing changes in the text, or for use in legal documents
`BIG`	Text to be displayed using a bigger font if possible
`SMALL`	Text to be displayed in a smaller font if possible
`SUB`	Subscript
`B`	Bold
`I`	Italic
`BLINK`	Causes characters to 'flash' on the screen
`SUP`	Superscript
`A`	Anchor element (for hypertext)
`IMG`	Image (for inline images as opposed to block-level images inserted using `FIG`)

3.4.6 The character set used for a document

Is the document to be written in English, German, Swedish, Portuguese or other language which is based on Roman letters? Or is it to be written in Arabic, Russian or Hindi and therefore with a completely different character set? Whatever the case, the browser must know which character set is involved so that it can display the document properly.

The HTTP specification indicates that the default character coding is ISO Latin-1 which is an 8-bit character encoding and which includes a range of accented characters suitable for Western European languages. The standards for HTML and HTTP allow you to specify other character encoding, for example the Japanese SHIFT-JIS which includes support for kanji, hirokana, katakana and romaji. We expect the 16-bit Unicode character encoding to become increasingly important as it covers a very wide range of the world's characters.

3.4.7 Including symbols and accented characters in documents

When you write an HTML document, normally you concentrate on typing the text of the document and inserting the various tags and attributes. However, certain symbols and special characters cannot be entered directly at the keyboard (they simply aren't there or they would be confused with symbols used in mark-up) and so have to be inserted 'manually'. For example, suppose you want to include a character such as <, Å, © or £ in an HTML document. You can specify such characters by using the appropriate **character entities**. A character entity is a sequence of characters which codes a particular symbol. For example, `<` is the symbol '<', and `Ê` is an uppercase E with a circumflex accent. The browser sees the character entity and displays the symbol accordingly. For example: `<P>Vous voulez du café?` would be rendered: Vous voulez du café? The character entities that you can use in HTML 3 documents are given in Appendix B.

Note: As an alternative to using character entities you can use Latin-1 character codes or Unicode codes.

There is also a parallel system of numeric entities. These are strings of numbers, as opposed to characters, to represent symbols. Numeric entities always start with the '#' symbol. Examples are `*` to display an asterisk and `$` to display a dollar sign. We recommend that you don't use the numeric character entities with HTML.

3.4.8 Non-breaking space characters, hyphens and spaces

Certain characters are taken to have a special meaning within the context of an HTML document. Two characters in particular may be interpreted by the browser to have specific effects in text formatting. These are:

- The space character. This is interpreted as a word space in all contexts except `PRE` for preformatted text, where it is treated as a non-breaking space.

  The character entities ` ` and ` ` denote respectively an en space and an em space. An en space is equal to half the point size; an em space is equal to the full point size of the current font. For fixed-pitch fonts, the browser can treat the en space as being equivalent to a single space character, and the em space as being equivalent to two space characters. They are not widely used yet.

- Non-breaking space (` `). This is treated in the same way as the space character except that the browser should never break the line at this point. By placing ` ` you ensure that a word stays together and does not get split across two lines.

See also the NOBR element which is a Netscape extension, and also its associated element WBR, both documented in Chapter 6.

- Hyphen. This is shown on the screen as a hyphen symbol in all circumstances and browsers may insert a break in the line as though the hyphen was a normal word space. A hyphenated word may therefore be split after the hyphen and before the second part of the word.

Note: Character entities are case sensitive. Do not make the mistake of altering the case. For example, `Â` is Å but `â` is å. A list of character entities is given in Appendix B.

There are a number of special entities used in HTML 3 and these are `©` for a copyright symbol, `®` for Registration mark, `&tm;` for Trade Mark, `` for a soft hyphen, and `&cbsp;` for conditional breaking space. Netscape extensions to HTML 2.0 include `®` and `©`.

Note: All entity names should be followed by a semicolon ';' even though this in theory is not required. In practice the semicolon is needed by browsers which otherwise may not display the entity correctly.

3.4.9 Standard units for widths in HTML 3

Several attributes specify widths as a number followed by an optional suffix. The units for widths are specified by the suffix: pt denotes points, pi denotes picas, in denotes inches, cm denotes centimetres, mm denotes millimetres, em denotes em units (equal to the height of the default font) and px denotes screen pixels. The default units are screen pixels. The number is an integer number or a real value number such as '2.5'. Exponents such as in '1.2e2' are not allowed.

3.4.10 Two modes for authoring an HTML document

You can author a document in two modes: a weaker, lax mode designed for compatibility with existing documents, and a stricter mode with a cleaner, more rigorous model of document structure. In the weaker, lax mode, you do not have to include a block-level element always as specified. For example, you should, strictly speaking, follow an LI element with a paragraph of text. But under the laxer model you can simply insert some text: typically browsers, when they see ordinary text when they are expecting a block element, will insert an invisible P element automatically.

If you are writing an HTML editor or a filter from other formats we recommend that you generate HTML which conforms to the stricter model.

If you are writing a browser, it is essential that this can accept documents written with the laxer model.

3.5 Including attributes in tags: introduction

In many cases you will want to extend a tag by including an **attribute**. Attributes give you much finer control over document layout and allow you to include the references to other files in hypertext links, amongst other things. Attributes can be used to control alignment of paragraphs, titles, tables and graphics, also text flow, font, the border around a table and so on. This chapter explains how to insert attributes into an HTML document. The more common HTML 3 attributes such as `ID`, `CLASS`, `LANG`, `STYLE` and `MD` are discussed in Chapter 4; other attributes are discussed in conjunction with HTML elements where they are appropriate.

3.5.1 `ALIGN` attribute to align text

Our first example shows a 'heading 1' element tagged in such a way that it would be displayed right-aligned:

```
<H1 ALIGN=right>The Owl and the Pussy Cat</H1>
```

The element name is `H1` while the attribute is `ALIGN`. The value of `ALIGN` is `right`. This is the same heading, but aligned centrally:

```
<H1 ALIGN=center>The Owl and the Pussy Cat</H1>
```

3.5.2 `SRC` attribute to specify a graphic

This example shows the use of the attribute `SRC` which is used extensively to specify the source of a graphic:

```
<P>The Owl looked up to the stars above and sang to a small guitar.
<FIG SCR=owl.gif></FIG>
```

Notice that the critical tag `<FIG SRC=owl.gif>` follows exactly the same pattern as `<H1 ALIGN=right>`. The element name is `FIG`, the attribute is `SRC` and the value is `owl.gif`.

3.5.3 `HREF` attribute to reference a file by name in a hypertext link

In this example we use another very common HTML attribute, `HREF` (Hypertext REFerence). This is used to specify a reference to a file in the context of a hypertext link. The tag itself is the **anchor** tag which has the element name A. It is used to include a hypertext link in a document.

```
<P>They sailed away for a year and a day to the land where the bong-tree
grows and there in a wood a Piggy-wig stood with a ring at the end of his
Nose. <A HREF="http://dsr.boo.com/tree.gif"> Picture of the Bong-tree</A>
```

The last two lines of the mark-up are dissected as follows. The element name is A and this has an attribute HREF with a value which corresponds to a URL. The text that the user will see on the screen, underlined or highlighted in some other way to indicate a hypertext link, is **Picture of the Bong-tree**. Clicking this will activate the link.

The important point here is that the value for HREF includes the characters '//', also '/' and ':'. The inclusion of these characters, and indeed any other characters which are not one of the following: letters, digits, periods (full stops to UK readers) or hyphens, necessitates the use of quotes around the attribute value.

3.6 General rules for writing attributes in HTML

The general syntax for including attributes in HTML follows the same pattern each time:

```
<TAGNAME ATTRIBUTE=value>
```

or, a slight variant:

```
<TAGNAME ATTRIBUTE="value">
```

If the attribute value consists entirely of letters, digits, periods (full stops) or hyphens then that value does not need to be placed in quotes. If, however, it contains characters other than those mentioned, then placing the attribute in quotes is essential.

3.6.1 Implied attribute values

In HTML you use such tags as:

```
<UL COMPACT>
<UL PLAIN>
<TABLE BORDER>
```

and various other constructs which appear not to be in the usual attribute–value pair format. In the DTD (a tight definition of HTML which encapsulates the rules of the language) these are actually short for fuller forms such as <UL COMPACT=compact>. You are recommended not to use the full form as this may confuse browsers. The SGML mechanism behind this is too technical to be included in a discussion at this level.

Note: A reminder: URLs are case sensitive! Make sure that they are correctly entered when you include them in hypertext links.

3.6.2 More than one attribute in a tag

You may need to include more than one attribute–value pair in a tag. This is certainly allowed. Here is an example:

```
<IMG SRC=owl.gif ALT="The Owl playing his guitar">
```

The attribute `SRC` has a value corresponding to the image to display. So much is obvious. However, what happens if your browser cannot display graphics? Should this be the case, the attribute `ALT` gives an alternative textual description of the picture. This idea is particularly useful for visually impaired people who may have a computer that will read aloud a description of a picture, or print it in Braille, rather than display the picture.

Note: Some attribute values (for example `SCR`, `HREF`, `ALT`[1]) allow entities in them, for example `ALT="Vous voulez du café?"`.

3.7 Formal structure of an HTML document

Our example document at the start of this chapter was purposely simple. It could have been even simpler; in fact, the simplest legal HTML document consists of a `TITLE` element and nothing else. In this section we look at the formal structure of an HTML document and acquaint the reader with the associated concepts.

Formally, each document starts with an `HTML` element, which contains a `HEAD` element followed by a `BODY` element. The HTML code below shows the structure of a document as seen in these terms. The head of a document relates to information about the document as a whole and specifies general links from the document to others. The document head is like the header in a memo, for example: it tells you what the document is, who authored it, its expiry date, to what other documents it is related, and all sorts of other *meta-information*.

Meanwhile the body of the document contains elements that are text, images, hypertext links, tables, lists and so on: it is in fact the main part of the document itself.

[1] These are all defined as CDATA in the DTD. The case matters and they can include character entities or numeric character entities.

```
<HTML>
<HEAD>
...
<BODY>
...
</HTML>
```

In practice you can generally omit <HTML>, <HEAD> and <BODY> and their equivalent end tags. This is because the browser software will be able to recognize the head and body elements even when the tags are missing. The mystery is explained because the browser, on seeing elements which it knows are not allowed in the head, can deduce that the head has ended and the body begun. That said, you cannot mix elements thereafter in the wrong order. All the elements associated with the document head must be at the start of the document and you cannot suddenly insert an element associated with the document head in the document body.

Real-world HTML frequently breaks these rules, for text often appears before the document head. While browsers do their best to cope, it is important to ensure that you do not add to the problem. To test your documents you can go to certain test pages on the Internet. You click on the version of HTML you want to test and submit your document URL. Errors are sent back to you in one form or other.

David Ornstein maintains the BrowserCaps pages dedicated to gathering information about HTML support by Web browsers. He includes a useful list of pointers to documents describing vendor extensions to HTML. For more information see: `http://www.halsoft.com/places/index.html/`.

4
HTML 3 GENERIC ATTRIBUTES

In this chapter:

- Discussion of NAME and ID attributes to specify the destination of a hypertext link (Section 4.2)
- The CLASS attribute to give an element a style (Section 4.3)
- The STYLE attribute for local style overrides (Section 4.4)
- CLEAR to control text flow (Section 4.5)
- The message digest attribute, MD (Section 4.6)
- The LANG attribute (Section 4.7)
- The SCRIPT attribute for referencing an external script (program) (Section 4.8)

4.1 Introduction

HTML includes a number of **generic attributes**, attributes which are common to a number of elements. For example, the CLASS element can be used together with paragraph elements, with list elements, with the anchor elements and so on. This chapter tells you about common attributes by giving you diagrams to show their effect and by including examples in HTML to show you how they work. The attributes in question are: CLEAR, ID, NAME, LANG, CLASS, STYLE and MD.

4.2 The ID and NAME attributes to specify the target of a hypertext link

4.2.1 Introduction

The ID and NAME attributes are all about jumping to specific places in documents. When you activate an ordinary hypertext link what happens is that the new document is fetched and displayed to you *starting at the top*: you are presented with the first 'page' of the document. However, suppose you want the file presented at a particular point, say halfway through the document and on a particular paragraph. This is where the ID attribute comes in, and also its cousin, the NAME attribute. The ID attribute is, at the time of writing, proposed but very likely to be implemented by browsers in the near future. The NAME attribute is already implemented, for example by Netscape.

4.2.2 Simple example of the NAME attribute

Back when hypertext was in its early days of construction, the idea of jumping to specific places in files was already addressed. Tim Berners-Lee decided to use a NAME attribute for this purpose and it's still in use today. We will try to show you how NAME works.

Take the following example. The reader is looking through an on-screen document on Garden Birds. A hypertext link saying More on finches is shown ready to be clicked. The author has arranged for a file *fin.html* to appear on the screen when this is done, and furthermore for the browser to display it starting at a second-level heading *Finches, Sparrows and Buntings*.

Here is the code:

```
<A HREF="fin.html#Finches">More on finches</A>
<A NAME="Finches"><H2>Finches, Sparrows and Buntings</H2></A>
```

The first line is what you put in the source file. It is a fairly straightforward hypertext link referencing the file fin.html, but with the extra code #Finches to direct the browsers to the right location.

The second line is what you put in the destination file (the file to be displayed once the link is triggered). Once again an anchor element is necessary, this time with the NAME attribute included. This has the value finches.

When someone clicks on the link, the browser finds the file `fin.html` to display and matches the reference `Finches` in the source anchor element with the same value of the named anchor in the destination file. The user is rewarded with:

> **<u>Finches, Sparrows and Buntings</u>**
> These are a large group of seed-eating birds which are found worldwide. Some are quite tame and cheeky, particularly the House Sparrow and the Green Finch, both of which frequent gardens. The Chaffinch has been known to appear on tables in outdoor restaurants and finish off the crumbs. It is partial to jam scones and cream.

Note: Named anchors should be named with a text string starting with a character from the set a–z or A–Z and should never be exclusively numeric. A value for `NAME` like '12' is not allowed, although 'bird33' is. Values for `NAME` are also case sensitive. No spaces are allowed before the '#' character.

4.2.3 Why use an alternative to `NAME`?

`NAME` is rather cumbersome to use: the way you have to insert an anchor element in the destination file is rather laborious. HTML needs a simpler way to specify headings, paragraphs, list items and so on as candidate destinations for hypertext links.

It has been suggested that in HTML 3 you should instead be able to give practically any element an ID. Once you have done this, it's a matter of simply specifying that ID as part of a hypertext link and the browser will know where to jump to. You don't have to place an anchor element in the destination file.

4.2.4 ID jumping to files on other servers

Can you jump to an ID from a file on a different server? You can. The URL notation used in specifying the destination of hypertext links allows for names of documents, their filenames and the server name as well as the # symbol to denote an ID. This means you can potentially jump to a particular paragraph in a document held on quite a different server, or a heading of a scientific paper held a thousand miles across the Web.

Current browsers do not support the idea of jumping to an element based on its ID value. They only support jumping to the anchor element with `NAME=value`. The transition issue is that if you provide a document with an

HREF to an ID, then existing browsers will not be able to find the ID value and will simply show the document at its beginning rather than go to the intended location. This, along with the small co-programming effort to support the ID mechanism, has been deterring the browser vendors from implementing this feature. ID is likely, however, to be implemented in the future.

4.2.5 Simple example of the ID attribute

In this example the reader sees a strange word highlighted and realizes with thanks that this is defined in the online glossary. He or she clicks on it immediately to see the file containing the glossary itself displayed just at the right point. This trick is accomplished by first giving each paragraph in the glossary a unique ID, for example:

```
<P ID=rumple> A rumple is the fold of fur which many rabbits have under
their chins. Well-fed rabbits almost invariably have large rumples.
```

Then, in the text of the document:[1]

```
<P>The rabbit soon settled down on the cushion with Tickles the
guinea-pig snuggling against her large white fluffy
<A HREF="glossary.html#rumple">rumple</A>
```

Clicking on the word 'rumple' in the text of the document takes you straight to the glossary definition of that word.

You could equally access the glossary files on distant servers – it's just a matter of including a URL together with a reference to the ID:

```
<A HREF="http://www.bump.com/animals/rabbits/glossary.html#rumple">
```

ID is also useful for scripting and style sheets to attach properties to a specific HTML element.

4.2.6 More examples of ID

More examples of ID can be found in Chapter 9 on hypertext links. These include a further bird-watching example (you've guessed it: at least two of the authors are keen birders) in which you jump to different birds in an online 'book' by clicking on the names of species.

[1] This example is partly for the benefit of the authors' children who are quite convinced that books on computers are more boring than anything else ever written. (They may very well be right!)

4.3 Giving an element a style: the `CLASS` attribute

4.3.1 Introduction: `CLASS` in the context of style sheets

`CLASS` allows you to differentiate different roles of HTML tags. This makes it easier to apply different styles based on the role played by each tag. The styles themselves may be specified in *style sheets* or with the `STYLE` element. Style sheets contain information about how various elements should be rendered on the screen, whether they should be a particular colour, use a particular font, and so on. They only control the stylistic aspects of a document, leaving the structural aspects to HTML. Style sheets are described in Chapter 14 to which you should refer for more detail.

The point about style sheets is that they will make a lot of the stylistic information now included in HTML documents redundant. The original designers of HTML had no intention of putting so much about fonts, borders, colour and so on into the language in the first place. Stylistic tags such as `FONT` only exist because authors were anxious for extra features, and companies such as Netscape and Microsoft have felt compelled to provide them. Also, up until now, style sheets have not existed. This is all set to change.

If you think about it, the more stylistic tags there are, the more complicated the HTML language becomes, and the less standardized. With so many versions of HTML and so much extraneous information about precise rendering, there is also less chance of documents being displayed correctly by each and every browser.

Style sheets have several advantages:

(1) They leave the document itself 'clean': easy to modify and easy for browsers to process.

(2) A structured document can equally be displayed using one style sheet or another. Because the structure of the document is intact and simple for the browser to understand, the stylistic information can easily be overlaid.

(3) Style sheets can be held centrally and reused for a number of related documents. Companies usually have corporate templates; they will have corporate style sheets too.

(4) Document exchange is much easier if the precise rendering instructions are kept separate from the structure of the document.

Downloadable fonts

With style sheets should come *downloadable fonts*. When you call up a document, a style sheet may arrive accompanied by any unusual fonts which the document employs. This solves the perennial problem of not having Boston Gothic Light or Harrow Hot Helvetica on your machine: it won't matter – they'll be sent to you down the wire.

4.3.2 Including styles for sub-CLASSed elements

Style sheets can be written as separate entities and then downloaded with the HTML document (see Chapter 14). Alternatively, you use the STYLE element in the document head to list styles to be used. For example:

```
<TITLE>Rock Music</TITLE>
<HEAD>
<STYLE TYPE="text/css">
H1.punk: font-colour=pink                        styles for classes of
P.loud: font-colour=fluorescent                  elements are specified
P.huge:font-size=60pt                            here for P and H1
</STYLE>
</HEAD>
<BODY>
<H1 CLASS=punk>Rock Music in Bath July and August
<P CLASS=loud>Performance dates are given below.
Click on a date for more information on          the H1 and P elements
reservations. Click on a location for maps of    are given a class by
how to get there, information on refreshments    using CLASS here
available, public transport and parking
facilities.
<P CLASS=huge>This page last updated July 7th
<P>Compiled by Pumpkin Software in conjunction with Music Month
<P CLASS=loud>Tel. Kenton 01-2345 if your band would like to be listed
here.
```

You can see that each style begins with an element name followed by a period (full stop) and then a name. For example: H1.punk or P.loud.

4.3.3 The idea of sub-classing explained in more detail

In our example H1.punk refers to a class of heading called 'punk'; P.loud refers to a class of paragraph called 'loud'. The CLASS attribute has been used to distinguish 'punk' headings from normal headings and 'huge' paragraphs from normal paragraphs.

```
<H1 CLASS=punk> Rock Music in Bath July and August
<P CLASS=loud>Tel. Kenton 01-2345 if your band would like to be listed
here.
```

The correct terminology for the process of associating an element with a given class is *sub-classing*. Thus you talk of sub-classing an element using the

CLASS attribute. The CLASS attribute will potentially be available with a large number of elements.

You can sub-class elements to get a variety of effects. Tables can be rendered in different styles in the same document; headings can be in larger fonts than usual; parts of a document can be sectioned off in their own particular style in contrast to the rest of the document; you can manipulate the margin settings, borders, colour and even type of bullet used in lists by using style sheets. For the MATH element, the CLASS attribute can be used to describe the kind of math expression involved. This can be used to alter the way that formulae are rendered by the browser and to support exporting the expression to symbolic math software. You could, for example, write a class 'chem' for chemical formulae which would use an upright font for variables instead of the default italic font.

4.4 The STYLE attribute

The STYLE attribute is a generic attribute available on most elements. STYLE takes as its value a text string specifying rendering information specific to the element. The notation used to specify this is specified in the document head within the STYLE element. The choice is likely to be between CSS, the Cascading Style Sheet language described in Chapter 14, and DSSSL-Online from the SGML community.

In the following example the STYLE attribute has been used to specify the stylistic rendering of a paragraph element. The notation is CSS. The end tag for the STYLE element has been inserted here although it is not strictly required.

```
<TITLE>Test Document</TITLE>
<STYLE TYPE="text/css"></STYLE>
<P STYLE="color: red; font-style small-caps">This text should be in small
capitals and colored red!
```

Note: The style specified using the STYLE attribute locally overrides any style specified for that element by a more general style sheet being applied to that document. This idea is further explained in Chapter 14.

4.5 CLEAR to control text flow

You will probably be familiar with the idea of text flow in desktop publishing packages. Word, for example, has options to control text flow around frames with the possibility of either flowing text around an image in a frame so that it flows like so:

... his organic yet electrifying style captures that sense of internal bewilderment and excitement which so characterize his early works and is still vivid today in these unique pieces. The unique

combination of strength of colour matches with beauty of line to give a sense of the unexpected, of the intimate and of the musical. On show now at the Roxborough Gallery, we recommend that you visit 'Jam for Tea' before the exhibition finishes at the end of the month.

or of arranging the text so that it is pushed under:

... his organic yet electrifying style captures that sense of internal bewilderment and excitement which so characterize his early works and is still vivid today in these unique pieces. The unique

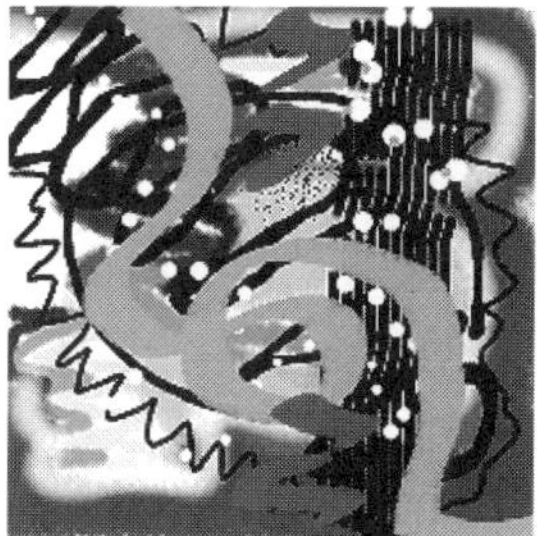

combination of strength of colour matches with beauty of line to give a sense of the unexpected, of the intimate and of the musical. On show now at the Roxborough Gallery, we recommend that you visit 'Jam for Tea' before the exhibition finishes at the end of the month.

HTML has an attribute called `CLEAR` which controls the flow of text around images and tables. In its current form as implemented by Netscape, `CLEAR` has already given the author some control over the positioning of text. In HTML 3 the `CLEAR` attribute went much further: not only did it allow you to say if you wanted text to flow around images and tables or not, it also enabled you to make the position of an element conditional on the width of the column next to the table or graphic in question. The HTML 3 version of CLEAR is unlikely to be implemented: style sheets will probably control most of this aspect of layout.

4.5.1 Netscape's simple implementation of CLEAR

Suppose you choose to place an image positioned to the right of the display window as shown below.

... his organic yet electrifying style captures that sense of internal bewilderment and excitement which so characterize his early works and is still vivid today in these unique pieces.

The unique combination of strength of colour matches with beauty of line to give a sense of the unexpected, of the intimate and of the musical. On show now at the Roxborough Gallery, we recommend that you visit 'Jam for Tea' before the exhibition finishes at the end of the month.

To get this kind of effect and to ensure that the next paragraph always begins below the image, you can, for example, with Netscape's current implementation of CLEAR, use the mark-up BR CLEAR=right:

```
<P><IMG SRC=painting.gif ALIGN=right>...his organic yet electrifying style
captures that sense of internal bewilderment and excitement which so
characterize his early works and is still vivid today in these unique
pieces.
<BR CLEAR=right>
<P>The unique combination of strength of colour matches with beauty of line
to give a sense of the unexpected, of the intimate and of the musical. On
show now at the Roxborough Gallery, we recommend that you visit 'Jam for
Tea' before the exhibition finishes at the end of the month.
```

The BR element acts to move the rendering position down until the margin is clear of the right-aligned obstructing image. If the image had been left-aligned you would have used BR CLEAR=left. If there were images on the left and the right margins then you would have used BR CLEAR=all.

The same method can be used to push headings under images so that headings are not left 'isolated' on the screen.

4.6 MD – the message digest attribute to check documents are unaltered since publication

4.6.1 Introduction

When a document points to another one it is sometimes critical to know that the reference document is the same as the author intended. This is the case, for example, with legal documents such as contracts which must not have been altered, and also with patents where it may be essential that diagrams referenced have not been tampered with.

The cryptographic community has developed techniques which effectively map a document to a number known as a message digest. Changing a single bit in the document changes the message digest in essentially a random way. The chances of finding two documents producing the same message digest are astronomically remote. The message digest starts with a prefix to identify the kind of message digest used, for instance MD5 is the prefix used for the well-known MD five algorithm and SHA is used for the US government's secure hash algorithm. MD5 generates a 128-bit number whereas SHA generates a 160-bit number. The number is represented as a string of hexadecimal digits with the most significant digit first and the least significant digit last. For the MD5 algorithm, this yields 32 hexadecimal digits. The MD attribute value is case insensitive.

4.6.2 Simple example

This is an example of a reference to an image from a patent:

```
<IMG SRC=invention.gif MD="md5:48a56912bd1258932b345c76533341d8">
```

When the browser is displaying a document and comes across a message digest for a link, it is expected to compute the message digest of the linked object and warn the user if there is a mismatch with the value on the link.

Note: In some cases authors may want to have several different versions of an object to take advantage of the capabilities of different browsers, whether they support video, Java, PNG or whether they are text-only browsers.

HTML 3 will include a VARIANT element which allows you to specify alternative bindings to objects. Basically it presents alternative bindings for the link so the browser can select which one is appropriate for its capabilities. A different message digest value will be required for each variant.

4.7 Localization of elements: the LANG attribute

The LANG attribute is used to control various aspects of hyphenation, kerning and typography which need to be changed according to the language of a document. This attribute determines the language that all (or a specific part) of your document is written in. For example you might write:

```
<P LANG="en.uk">
```

to show a paragraph of text which should be displayed using the conventions of UK English instead of US English. When the browser sees the LANG attribute, it may respond by doing a better job of hyphenation and also of kerning and ligatures. Quotation marks appropriate to the language may also be used when the browser realizes that it is displaying not, say, English, but Spanish. Dates can also be displayed to match the language in question: US dates are written month, followed by day; UK English dates are written day, followed by month. See Appendix G which gives information on writing HTML documents in different languages.

5
DESIGNING YOUR WEB PROJECT

This chapter, which makes no claim to being definitive, discusses the whole process of designing and writing HTML. It is intended for non-technical readers; most engineers should already be familiar with the main concepts. It covers:

- Specification (Section 5.2)
- Design with or without tools, including
  - design principles (Section 5.3.1)
  - whether texts should be chunky or creamy (Section 5.3.2)
  - how to structure hypertext into trees, nets, stars and lists (Section 5.3.3)
- Implementation with HTML tags (Section 5.4)
- Testing and debugging (Section 5.5)
- Rollout and maintenance (Section 5.6)

5.1 Introduction

Every journey begins with a single step, runs the proverb. When you look at some of the dazzling and complicated documents now on the Web, you may feel the task is impossible – or conversely that you must rush out and make your own at once. Both attitudes limit your ability to create. The truth is that you can make beautiful HTML documents, and that they can become complicated. You can succeed if you organize the task into sensible steps. These steps form a ladder, by analogy with real life, like this:

conception	specification
embryogenesis	design
childhood	development
exams	testing and debugging
adulthood	operational use (and further development)

The naive-looking comparison makes some important points, which your own experience will show to have at least some truth in them.

The most crucial moment in the whole life cycle is conception. A misconceived project with no definite specification is guaranteed to be a disaster. You absolutely must start at the beginning.

Even after starting well, things will go wrong unless you design and develop systematically. Children always learn to move and to communicate in a very particular order – the order which works. Some go fast, some slowly, but the order (babble, single words, short statements, longer sentences) is pretty much invariable.

Once developed, people everywhere go through testing and initiation stages. The mountain boy has to catch a cougar or a condor. The Apache has to sit out a sweat lodge. The westerner has to survive high school, university and driving tests. Your system isn't a system until it has proved that it works.

Only after all these stages can your HTML be considered mature, and even then it will go on developing and improving. You should aim to encourage continuing feedback from your readers to guide further development.

5.2 Specifying what you want

The vital first phase of any project consists of deciding what it is you want to build or procure. It may seem obvious, but you can't have what you want until you say what it is. Many systems of all sizes have failed simply because they were designed without clear requirements. When we talk about requirements, our friends say 'but that's just common sense'. So it is; but perhaps common sense is a rarer commodity than many people imagine.

Specification does not have to entail a lot of fuss: small HTML systems will be fine if specified as a one-page document (possibly pointing to sources of text and graphics).

Larger commercial systems may be best specified using a requirements or design tool, with the advantage that HTML can be generated automatically with the correct link and ID structures. You then have a much simplified job of tagging up, and testing can be systematized by comparing each piece of HTML with the requirement(s) which generated it.

5.3 Designing your HTML structure

Our friends who saw this chapter at once told us 'But no one designs their hypertext!'. Well, that is why so much of the Web is such a mess, and why it can be so frustrating when you want to find something. It is not a pleasure for readers to go round in circles, attempting to follow one dead link after another. It is not a delight to hunt up and down a tangled tree randomly arranged into branches with all the important stuff down one inconspicuous twig labelled 'Other Topics'.

You will not get your design right first time, so aim to throw one away.

Good hypertext is designed so that it matches the way its users approach it. You can only achieve such a structure by designing it according to its requirements. These may include, for example:

- structure of information to be presented
- intended readership
- information to be returned (in forms or email)
- marketing and public relations aspects (desired impression and image to be conveyed).

Corporate Web users generally want to impose their own style on their Web pages. They may employ graphic artists to design icons and logos, menu bars, and diagrams. Professional page designers may be involved in document layout. If the HTML is to be prepared by people with other backgrounds, the design department will typically produce a booklet of guidelines for authors, telling them not to use too many different typefaces, and laying down rules about diagram and image design. They are aware of the power of images in influencing people, and may specify colour schemes and use of the logo.

5.3.1 Design principles

Once you have a list of requirements, you can work out what sort of HTML system would meet the requirements. A good system is, by definition, one that satisfies its requirements exactly. Quality, in fact, is conformance to requirements. Your HTML has to be consistent, so that the same kind of thing is done the same way everywhere.

Since HTML naturally forms networks of documents, it is sensible to draw a diagram (or set of nested diagrams) illustrating how you want the network to behave. Do you need reverse links? Is there to be an index or table of contents? Now is the time to decide.

Small HTML systems can easily be designed by hand. It is helpful to have a supply of large plain drawing paper. A self-printing whiteboard (an expensive device, basically a rotating screen with a built-in photocopier) is a great luxury and convenience for the design of business systems: you discuss the design with your colleagues, sketch what you want on the board, and press the button for copies. Rich industrialists can achieve the same effect using a videoconferencing system, which allows them to share a drawing on their screens even if they are working at separate locations.

Large HTML systems may be designed using a computer-aided software engineering (CASE) tool. CASE tools let you put together a family of diagrams which can be checked automatically for internal consistency. This is nice if you have lots of hypertext pages with dozens of bi-directional links between them. The diagrams are best printed out in landscape format; you can then work directly from the printout to your HTML tags, ticking off each link anchor on the diagram as you insert it into the HTML.

This section describes the general principles of designing a properly linked hypertext (not necessarily represented in HTML). First, we look at the two main types of hypertext – in separate chunks, or in a large creamy flow of text. Secondly, we look at some ways of organizing numerous documents or chunks into manageable structures that your readers can understand, illustrating the approaches with examples from the Web.

You may be very familiar with linear documents like letters, or with hierarchical documents like textbooks, but quite unused to the design principles of networks like the Web's hypertexts. In fact, from a lofty visionary perspective, such as that of the inventor of hypertext, Ted Nelson, the whole of the World Wide Web is a single enormous hypertext! He kindly volunteered the following lines for this book:

> At last the world has populist, anarchic electronic publishing on networks.
>
> World Wide Web is like karaoke: anyone can do it, with no training, and that's great.
>
> Ted Nelson (Inventor of hypertext)

Nelson has for long made clear in his writings that the global, permanent, electronic medium he envisages should encompass all forms of knowledge, and be thoroughly indexed[1] and referenced with reusable components. The Web, simple-minded as it is, is certainly far from these goals of universal knowledge-sharing, so he is being polite when he praises it in the words quoted above. We agree with the sentiment 'anyone can do it', though perhaps we know enough to take issue with the phrase 'with no training'.

5.3.2 Different types of hypertext: Chunky versus creamy

The field of Hypertext has been enthusiastically visited, sorted, organized, disorganized and reorganized by academics and techies who love to expatiate on the subject, telling everyone how it should be written. This does not mean that they actually know:

> ... You must send for the herb-master of this House. And he will tell you that he did not know that the herb you desire had any virtues, but that it is called Westmansweed by the vulgar, and Galenas by the noble, and other names in other tongues more learned, and after adding a few half-forgotten rhymes that he does not understand, he will regretfully inform you that there is none in the House, and he will leave you to reflect on the history of tongues.
>
> Aragorn's speech (on pipeweed) to Master Meriadoc
> in the Houses of Healing, Minas Tirith
> J.R.R. Tolkien (1955). *The Lord of the Rings*. George Allen & Unwin

[1] At least the Web is starting to be indexed reasonably efficiently, if not to the degree envisaged by Ted Nelson. The popular search sites WebCrawler, Lycos and Yahoo provide both keyword search and hierarchical classifications of URLs. Indexing will certainly improve as commercial publishers 'add value' by selling organized views of the Web for particular subject areas, professions and activities.

Those who dabble daintily in the subject of hypertext classify it into two main kinds, **chunky** and **creamy**. This does not mean that they are all academic pussyfoots fussing over their dinners. The terms describe two opposing ways of organizing information.

Chunky hypertext comes in chunks, which for our purposes generally means screen-sized pieces, give or take a line or two. (The Theatre example is purely chunky.) You navigate between screens by clicking on the images which function as buttons, or on the words or phrases which are marked (with `<A HREF="...">` tags) as hypertext anchors. Since the chunks predetermine what kinds of navigation are possible, thorough design is needed to avoid confusing the reader.

By contrast, **creamy hypertext** comes in large dollops, and you frequently have to wade through it by scrolling smoothly up or down until you find the place you want. Of course, it must have some buttons or hypertext anchors somewhere amongst all its smoothness. If you want to locate a particular word or phrase, it will often be in the document you have loaded, so a database-style text search can be effective.

It is best not to mix the two styles in one hypertext, because your readers will naturally expect the style to be consistent. There are certainly exceptions to this; for instance, you could present a chunky hypertext summarizing a lot of scientific papers in your area, with, at the bottom, a row of buttons giving access to the full texts of those papers in creamy style – in other words, more or less one paper to one document, with very few anchors.

A bad mix.

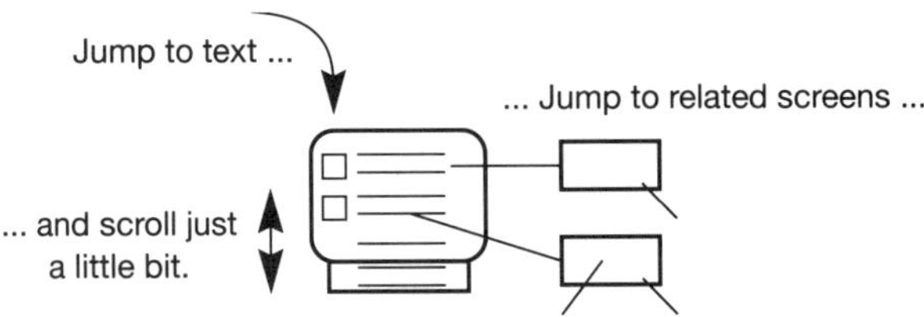

Users accustomed to jumps may easily miss that extra little bit of information 'off the bottom of the screen'. They are annoyed because the design misleadingly mixes 'chunky' with 'creamy'.

Much of the Web is made up of chunky text, because it makes the individual files that have to be fetched over the Internet as small and quick to fetch as possible. Large items are generally at the end of search or index branches, to minimize the risk that readers will fetch them unnecessarily and bombard the authors with hate mail. (The issue also applies to graphics.)

The definition of 'large' depends on the speed of the Net and the bandwidth of individual users' links to their providers, so you can be sure that document sizes will grow in the next few years. For now, small and chunky means under about 20 kilobytes, large and creamy means more than about 100 kilobytes, and in between it is up to your skill and judgement. If you are lucky enough to be in an institution which gives you a permanent free high-speed connection, remember to spare a thought for those who are less fortunate.

A good mix.

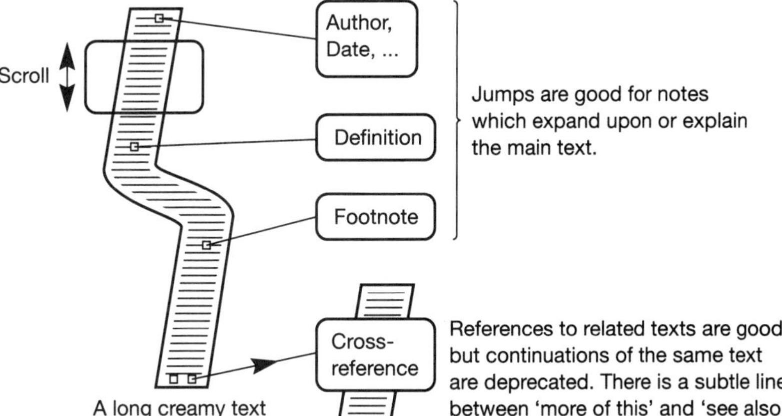

Scroll
Author, Date, ...
Definition
Footnote
Jumps are good for notes which expand upon or explain the main text.
Cross-reference
References to related texts are good, but continuations of the same text are deprecated. There is a subtle line between 'more of this' and 'see also'.
A long creamy text

The trouble with excessive chunkiness is that it makes it very difficult to fetch whole documents such as magazine articles: you don't want to do 100 HTTP fetches and 100 Save As operations to retrieve a 100-paragraph article. Some commercially minded authors publish their stuff in hundreds and hundreds of little files, apparently in the hope that people will buy their books rather than spend hours downloading all of the little pages!

The trouble with excessive creaminess is that it makes it very slow, and expensive in connection time, if you get hundreds of kilobytes of unwanted guff while you are searching for something else. We suggest that you start your hypertext design on the assumption that HTML is a language for screen-sized chunky texts. If, later, you find that you need large creamy texts, go ahead and use them.

5.3.3 Different patterns of hypertext: Trees, nets, stars and lists

Many patterns of hypertext documents are possible: gone are the days of nothing but sequences with one page after another (as if books ever were really like that).

Trees

The basic pattern for hypertexts on single subjects is the tree. The top page gives a quick summary and introduction, and contains links (`<A HREF=...>`

anchors in HTML) to pages covering the main topics. These in turn link to more detailed pages, so the structure branches into a tree. Trees are ideal for many purposes, but can result in slow navigation if the reader is way down one branch and needs to go to another. Navigation aids are therefore useful, and an index of some sort is generally necessary.

Tree.

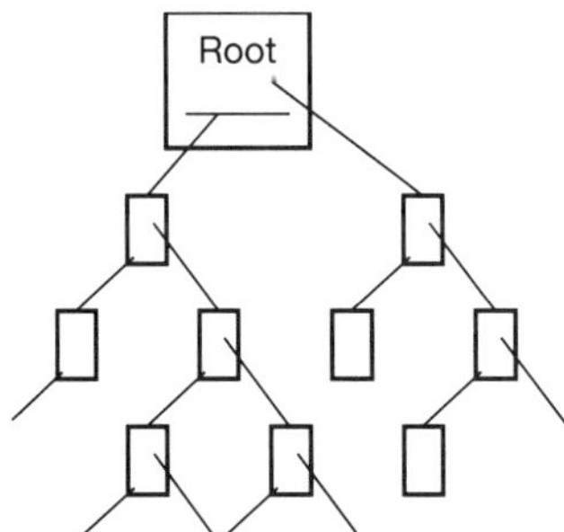

- Good for explanations, magazines
- Quick overview, more detail at lower levels
- Navigation aids useful (top, index buttons)
- Allows DIY story – reader chooses own path
- Allows teach yourself, multi-choice answers

The colour section shows the glorious pages of the University of California at Berkeley's Museum of Paleontology (`http://ucmp1.berkeley.edu`). These pages are an informative delight, and it would take many hours to study all of them. The layout of the UCMP pages, using tables, is discussed in Chapter 12. Here, we will focus on the hypertext design, the relationship of the pages to each other.

The Welcome page branches out to seven main topics, ranging from the vigorous sculptures used as icons, through the details of the Web server,

The UCMP Welcome Page.

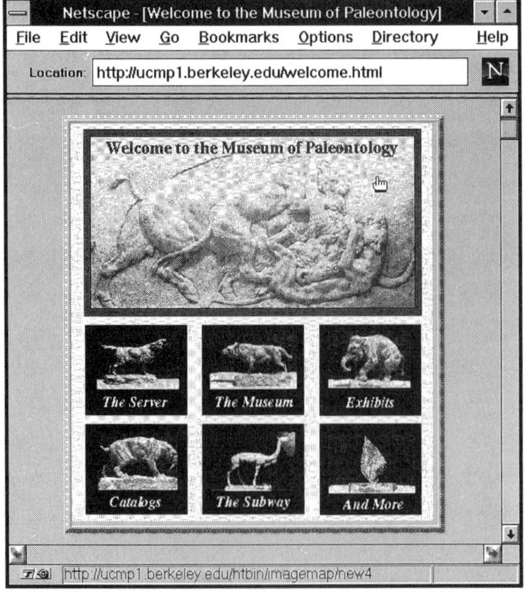

a puff for the Museum itself, and only then to the exhibits (see illustration below), which are what everyone presumably came to see. The principle is well known to supermarkets – you put the most desirable goods at the back, so that visitors have plenty of time to notice the other goods on the way there.

The catalogues are more serious and less visual means of finding what you want to study. Then comes the subway (see below) and the 'And More' section, a bit of a ragbag of miscellaneous topics.

Each of these half-dozen branches itself branches into a further half-dozen possible paths for the museum visitor to explore: the whole structure is a tree.

The UCMP Exhibits Page.

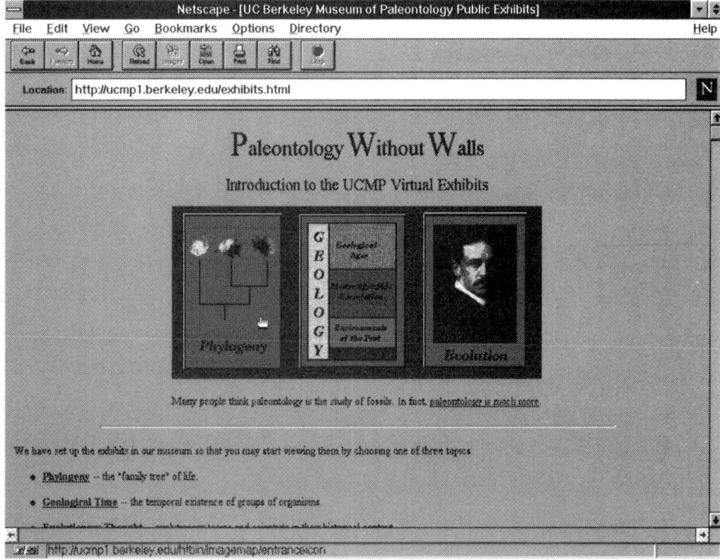

The Exhibits page leads to[2] phylogeny, the study of the origins and connections of species; to a wonderfully rich display on the subject of geological time, the 'UCMP Time Machine' (see p. 95); and to an interesting exhibit on evolutionary thought.

The Subway (see illustration) consists of a large image map to appeal to visitors old and young, in the form of a paleontological subway route-map.

You just click on the 'station' you want to go to, and there you are: paleontology is much more than dinosaur fossils, is the lesson.

The Museum has managed to be both adventurous and cautious in its hypertext design: the subway is accompanied by a simple list of link anchors (blue underlined text under the map) for text-only visitors.

[2] Notice that links are provided both graphically and textually to give all users access to the exhibits, though it would be a shame to visit UCMP without a graphics browser.

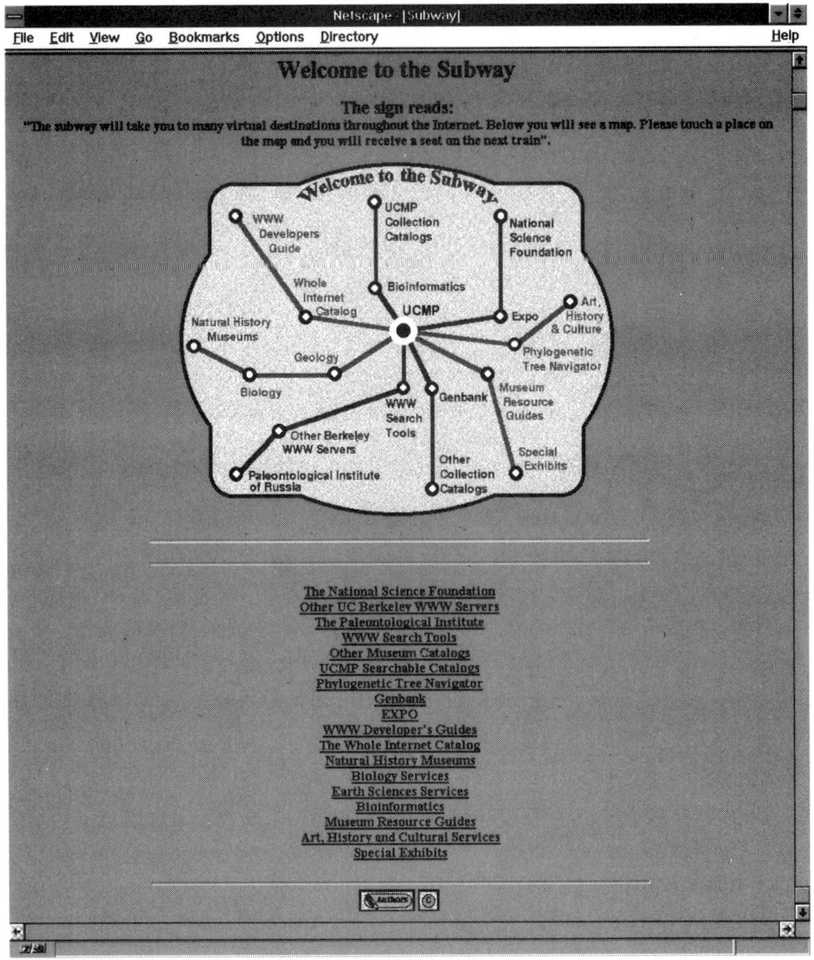

The UCMP Subway Page.

Similarly, despite the attractive subway-map concept, the plan of the hypertext is just a hierarchy with rather few cross-links. This simplicity of design is well worth imitating.

With the 'Geological Time Machine', UCMP has had the conceit of representing the fossil record very naturally as a sequence of time stages, and the visitor as a time traveller in a Tardis (see illustration). A scrolling list in an HTML <FORM> lets the visitor set the time controls, and the Submit button, wittily renamed 'Ride the Web Geological Time Machine...' starts the time travel.

The page gives access to several dozen topics. In general we would advise against such a large choice, but here it seems quite natural. An alternative would have been to set the coarse time control (Precambrian, Paleozoic, Mesozoic, Cenozoic) and then the fine, but the Museum reckoned, probably correctly, that direct access was more exciting. This kind of decision is the stuff of hypertext design.

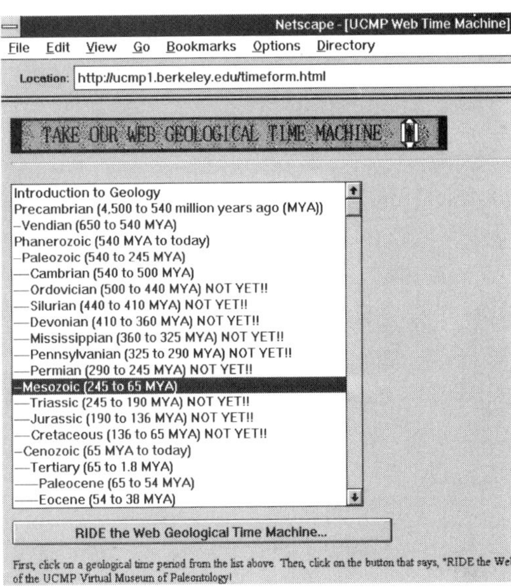

The UCMP Time Machine Page.

At the bottom of the main Exhibits page, which as we've seen leads to a wealth of material, is a Navigation Toolbar. This provides three kinds of index, which the Museum calls 'lifts' (that is, time- and space-travel elevators) enabling the visitor to search for any taxon (classification), any geological period, or any topic described in the Museum's pages.

As these 'lifts' are similar in design, we'll illustrate just one of them.

The Taxon lift is a hierarchically indented list, again implemented using an HTML <FORM>, with a renamed Submit button.

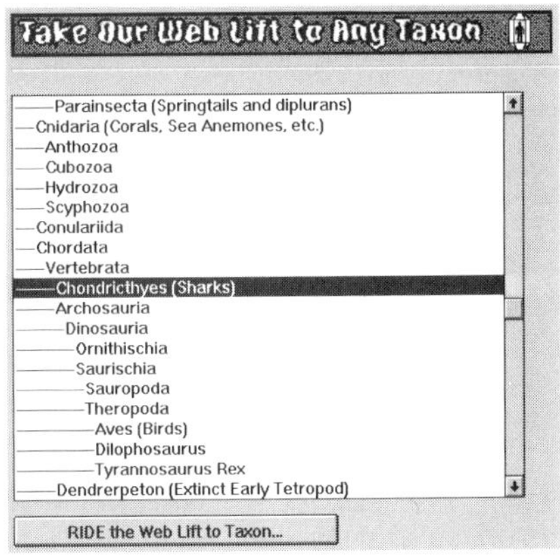

The UCMP 'Web lift'.

Since this is provided as a short cut for quick navigation, some knowledge on the part of the visitor can reasonably be assumed. The use of a Latin hierarchy, in which *Aves (Birds)* are seen to be *Theropods*, which are *Vertebrates* which are *Chordates*, is thus appropriate here, whereas it would be quite unreasonable as the primary means of access to these exhibits. Of course, the hierarchy also has some didactic value on its own as a guide to evolutionary history.

By these means, the Museum's enormous range of material is made readily accessible: indeed, it is now open to all Web users, not just people who live near Berkeley, so the pages must be reckoned to have greatly increased the Museum's outreach.

We can't resist giving a glimpse of the UCMP time machine itself, a set of pages which one might be proud of, even without the rest of the Museum's hypertext. Apart from the actual geological periods, there is a beautiful introduction to stratigraphy at the 'entrance' to the Museum:

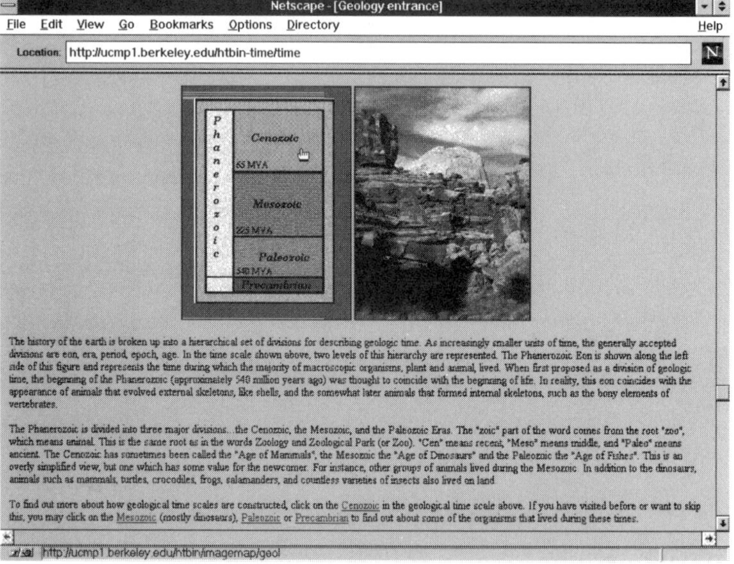

Doors naturally lead from there to the various geological ages, or you can simply click on the age in which you are interested (the cursor shows a pointing hand ☞ in Netscape when over something clickable). For instance, dinosaur-lovers will at once travel to the Mesozoic age.

The Mesozoic summary page gives access, with a search field, to suitably exciting Mesozoic animals, and via the buttons to detailed exhibits on Stratigraphy, Fossils of this Time, and to Fossil Localities. There is also another chance to ride the time machine.

The UCMP pages repay detailed study both for the intrinsic interest of the material, and for their elegant and highly accessible structure. It is not easy to construct such a useful and informative hypertext.

The diagram below summarizes this tour of `http://ucmp1.berkeley.edu/`, UCMP's Web site, showing how, despite its size, it has more or less a simple tree structure (though small fragments of net and star structure also occur). Perhaps simplest really is best.

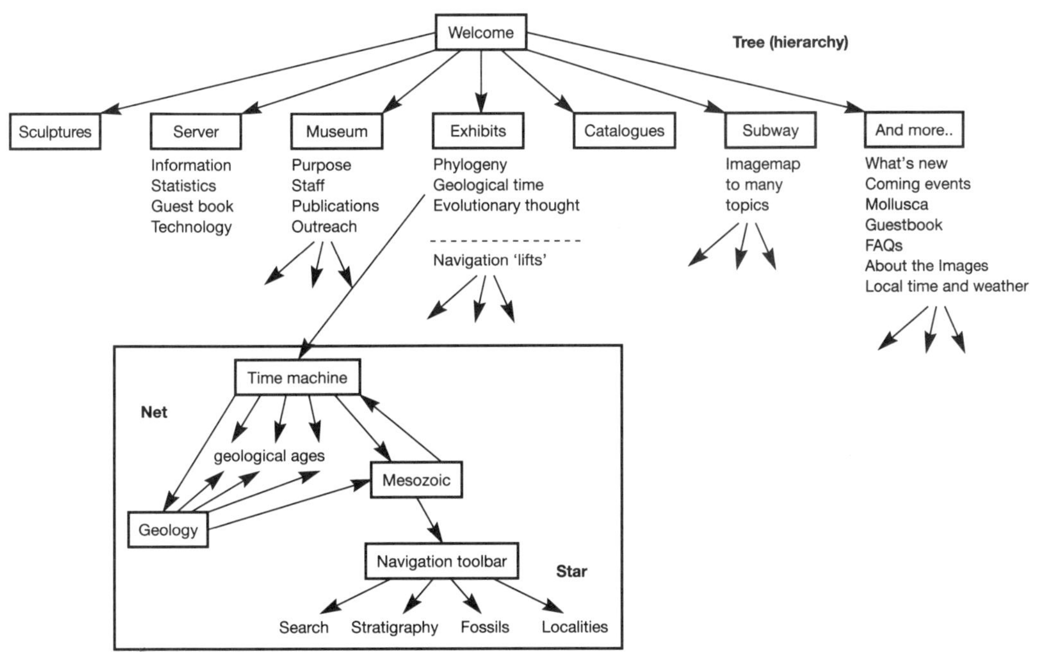

Nets

Richer patterns of interconnection turn naturally into networks. These allow unlimited freedom, with which comes, inevitably, the possibility of getting lost or going wrong. A partial cure is to provide a default path through the net with Forward and Back buttons; another approach is to put a little map on screen showing where the current page fits into the broader picture.

Network.

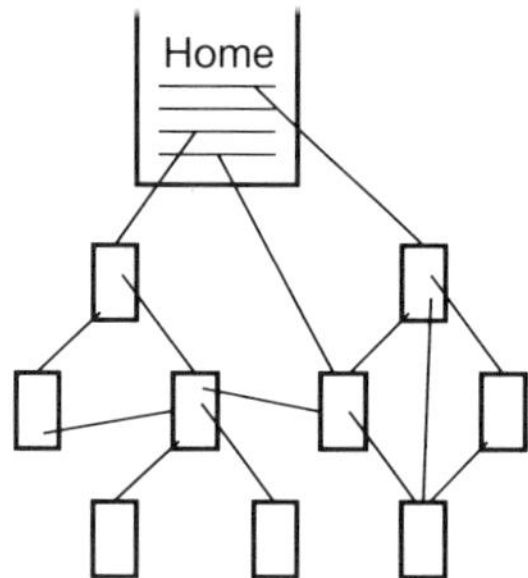

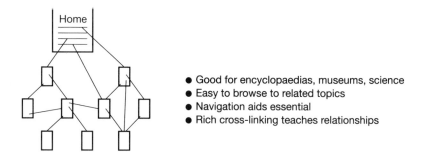

- Good for encyclopaedias, museums, science
- Easy to browse to related topics
- Navigation aids essential
- Rich cross-linking teaches relationships

Networks vary enormously, from beautifully structured encyclopaedias to rambling tangles of linked pages. The Web has come in for a lot of criticism because of the number of unstructured sites and the confusing connections between them. Help to defeat the critics by making your pages orderly and satisfying to read. If you draw a diagram like the figure to show how your pages fit together, you will probably spot several immediate structural improvements that you could make with little effort.

The ultra-hip magazine *Wired* has its own decidedly wacky Web pages on `http://www.hotwired.com/` (see illustration).

Once you have recovered from the shock of the imagery, though, you can see that the page is mostly a list of links to other pages, so the structure is probably tree-like.

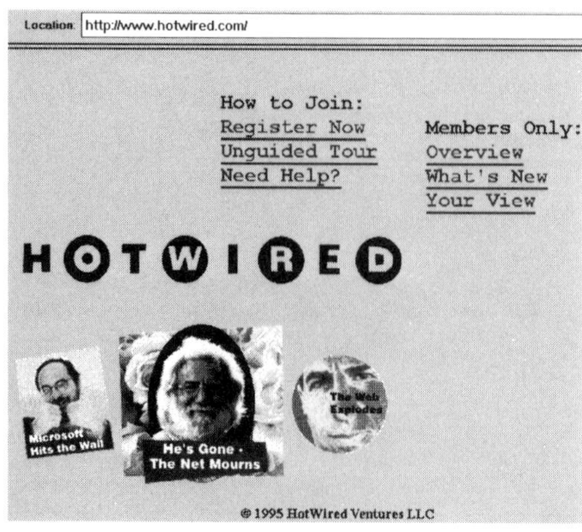

The authors, fearless explorers of the Web, strapped on their Sola Topis, spread on their mosquito repellent, and unsheathed their machetes, to discover just how the HotWired pages are organized.

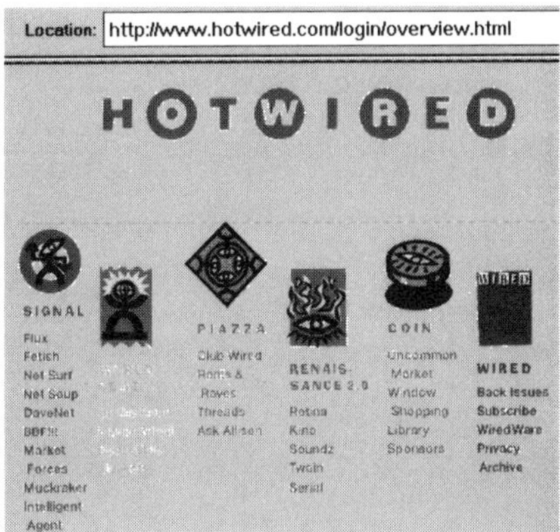

The Overview looked a promising place to start (see illustration). The whizzy iconography and clashing colours (purple/yellow harmonies, primary blue, red, . . .) disguise the rather conventional tree structure. Each of the main items – Signal, World Beat, Piazza, Renaissance 2.0, Coin, and Wired, gives access to a colourful list of topics and articles. These may be unintelligible to the squarer reader, but the structure is as straight and true-blue as Big Blue.

The second item under Signal is called Fetish. Spraying on a little more jungle juice, and sharpening our machetes to a dangerous degree, we ventured in.

Fetish seemed, at the time of visiting, indeed to contain items of apparel and things to buy, but nothing that would shock your maiden aunt. (Only the colours . . . .)

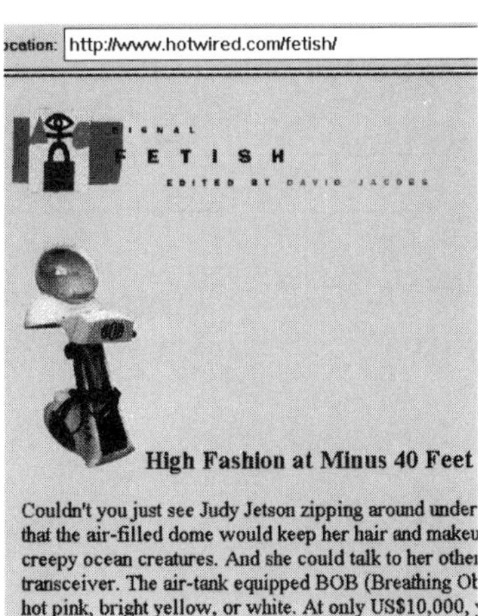

At the foot of the page was a conventional Navigation Toolbar (yes, you can imagine its appearance) with buttons labelled Search, Help, and Threads (of discussion by readers). These are in fact provided on all or most of the HotWired pages. In addition, links give immediate return access to the Overview, What's New, and Your View pages, making this a simple network structure.

The Unguided Tour (from the home page) offers a description of each of the regular features (Signal, and so on) which HotWired calls channels, by analogy with radio (see illustration). Each of these contains a link to the Register Now page, so once again this is a simple network.

If you want to create unconventional and exciting pages, then, the lesson from HotWired is to select strange and novel material, draw

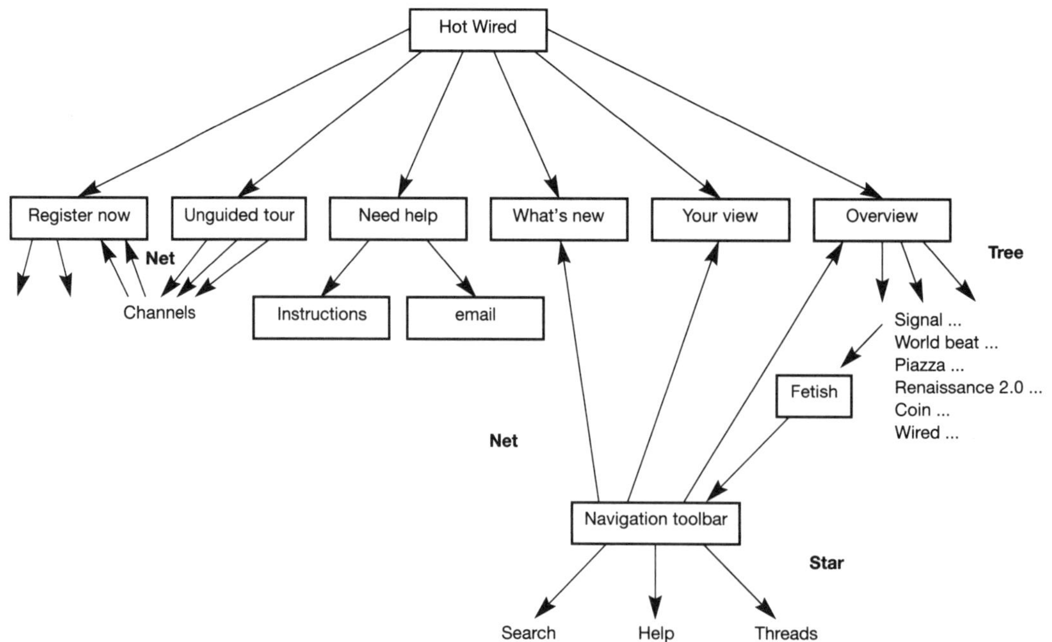

interesting graphics, and use a very plain network structure for easy navigation. Your readers may be disorientated by your subject matter, but there is no excuse for losing them in a jungle of hypertext.

HotWired have also used exemplary Navigation Toolbars, showing that even these can be made interesting to look at. The presence of the Unguided Tour, Need Help, and Instructions pages makes it quite clear that they have taken the need for comprehensible navigation very seriously, however wild and woolly their surface image.

The structure of the HotWired hypertext is summarized in the diagram at the bottom of p. 100.

As usual, it is largely a **tree** (hierarchy), but with **star**-like Navigation tool links and regularly laid out jumps to other interesting places in the **network**.

Stars

Less confusing than an unrestricted network is the star, giving direct access from one page to a whole lot of others directly. This in fact is a very common pattern, when you consider that an Index, Navigation Toolbar, or top-level Contents page automatically converts any structure into some kind of star. For simple structures it is quite good on its own.

Star.

Index

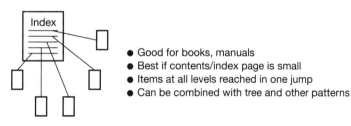

- Good for books, manuals
- Best if contents/index page is small
- Items at all levels reached in one jump
- Can be combined with tree and other patterns

An attractive set of examples of the star in practical use can be found on the Mystic Fire pages (`http://mosaic.echonyc.com/mysticfire/`) where various philosophers are presented, with forms which you can use to order books and cassettes for further study. For instance, Alan Watts, a philosopher of the 1960s, has his own home page, shown below. He was sufficiently enamoured of the east to want to show that you could tell stories using ideograms, long before everyone started to use icons for everything:

'This simple tale hardly needs translation:' from *TAO, The Watercourse Way*, Alan Watts, 1975

Each Mystic Fire page (see illustration overleaf) contains a short biography, a photo or two, and links to snippets of the philosopher's work

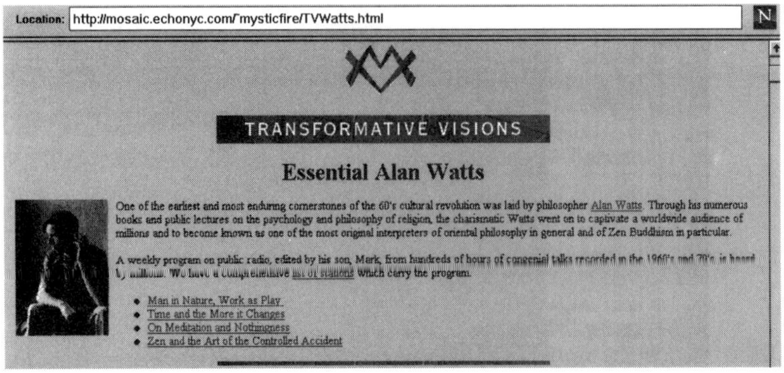

Location: http://mosaic.echonyc.com/~mysticfire/TVWatts.html

TRANSFORMATIVE VISIONS

Essential Alan Watts

One of the earliest and most enduring cornerstones of the 60's cultural revolution was laid by philosopher Alan Watts. Through his numerous books and public lectures on the psychology and philosophy of religion, the charismatic Watts went on to captivate a worldwide audience of millions and to become known as one of the most original interpreters of oriental philosophy in general and of Zen Buddhism in particular.

A weekly program on public radio, edited by his son, Mark, from hundreds of hours of congenial talks recorded in the 1960's and 70's, is heard by millions. We have a comprehensive list of stations which carry the program.

- Man in Nature, Work as Play
- Time and the More it Changes
- On Meditation and Nothingness
- Zen and the Art of the Controlled Accident

to illustrate the main themes. This star-shaped plan is quite general in application.

This page can be seen to branch starwise to four sections of Watts' work, which are actually sections of the same HTML file as the page shown. The anchor 'Alan Watts' paradoxically branches back to the main Mystic Fire index of philosophers, which is itself a star with a ray leading to each person's home page.

A third star pattern occurs (as is very common on the Web) in the rather good-looking navigation tool at the bottom of each home page, including Watts':

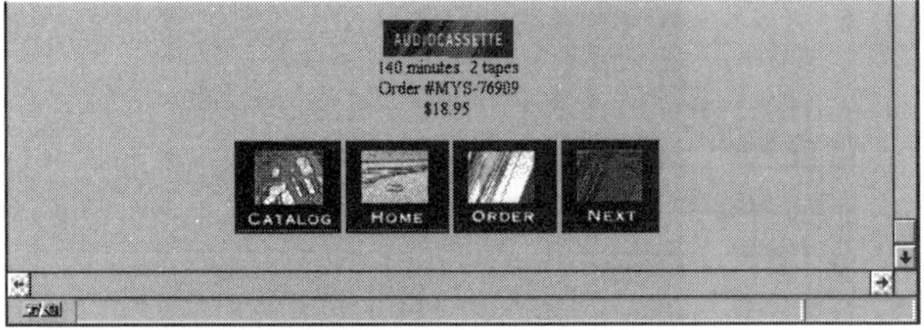

As you'd expect, the Catalog button takes you to the main catalogue of books you can buy, the Home button takes you back up to the Mystic Fire home page, the Order button gives you a form, and the Next button subverts the structure into a List (see below) by stepping to the next philosopher in line.

The structure of the Watts pages is illustrated at the top of p. 103.

When does a cluster of stars turn into a tree? This may sound like a how-long-is-a-string question, but there is a useful criterion in practice: when the branching structures are best seen as a single, homogeneous structure. In the example shown here:

- The *NI People* star is essentially a reference list or index; each philosopher is dealt with in a discrete page, which fans out in a beautiful star to text items which lead no further.

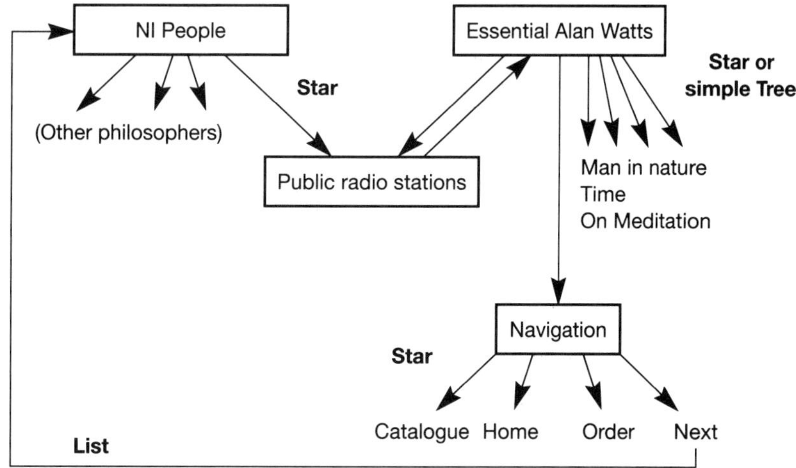

- The *Essential Alan Watts* structure could equally well be treated as a very simple tree (of depth 1) or a star, it makes no difference. The designers have kept things simple, which has the good results of making the structure easy to browse and quick to maintain.
- The *navigation toolbar* (which is provided for all philosophers, regardless of creed) is also a typical star, whose structure is visually, and in practical use, quite separate from the hierarchy of pages forming a normal tree.

Whatever the academics may think of such a simplistic approach, we find it useful, and we think it will help you to design better hypertexts too.

Lists

Lastly, we must mention the oldest structure of them all, the list. It has its uses, such as for scanned-in books. You can of course make the list branch just a little bit by putting in some links to images.

A list structure is illustrated on the Alan Watts diagram above, where the Next button at the end of each philosopher's page steps to the next

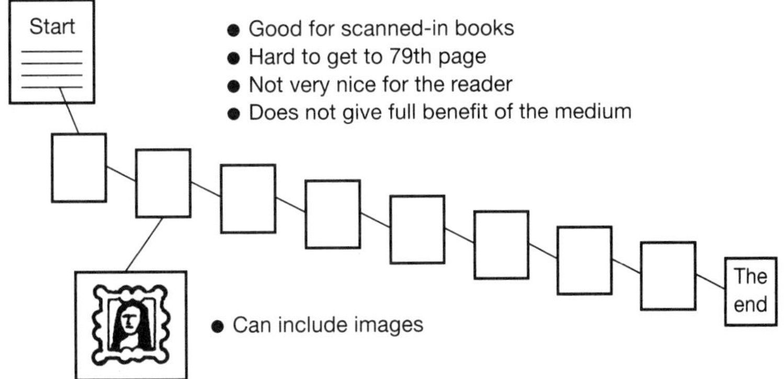

philosopher. Of course, if you are interested in the Tao and Confucianism, the fact that the Next Philosopher in alphabetic order is a Vienna Positivist may not help you much. Since books are to a large extent sequential lists (of pages, of chapters, ...), the list structure is quite familiar, but this example makes clear its inherent limitations.

5.4 Tagging up – manually or with assistance

Only now, with a solid set of requirements behind you and a decently worked-out design, can you safely go ahead 'with soldering iron and wire-wrap gun' (Fred P. Brooks).

5.4.1 WYSIWYG editors for HTML

Tagging up a set of documents is not difficult (especially with a book like this to help you), only tedious. Some of the tedium is relieved if you use a tool such as SoftQuad's HoTMetaL (which now supports many HTML 3 tags) or Harawitz' HTML Assistant: these can at least shove in the basic tags at the touch of a button. Netscape 2.0 includes a WYSIWYG editor for HTML, and given their enormous user base, this tool may become the most common way of preparing hypertext from scratch.

Quite a different kind of product is Microsoft Assist. This allows you to use Word 6 as a very smooth editor for HTML. Since Word comes with a battery of import formats, as well as live links (Object Linking & Embedding) to spreadsheets, databases and other sources of information, Word/Assist may be the easiest route from existing documents to HTML for many corporate users. Assist is actually free, though you need Word to make use of it; it consists of a set of macros for Word 6 which configure the screen and enable you to view and export documents as HTML. Someone has a corporate policy aiming to capture Web business ... (and to get you to buy a new copy of Word). You can download Assist from `ftp.microsoft.com`.

5.4.2 Automatic generation from a database or software tool

If you need to construct frequently updated lists, tables or groups of similarly structured headings and paragraphs, you probably have a candidate for automatic generation of HTML from a database or other software tool. You will very likely be able to save a large amount of repetitive and error-prone effort by working out a system for organizing your information in a database, say. You can then invest in a one-off effort to build some macros or scripts to

Hypertext can be generated automatically from most databases, using macros.

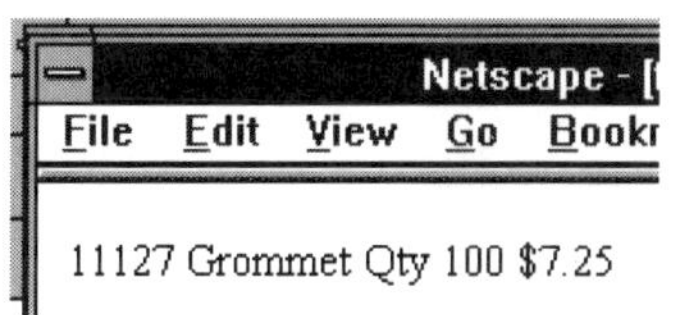

generate HTML, and to test these programs thoroughly. You may want to delegate this job to a specialist.

Ever after, when you need to update your hypertext – each week or month – you just run your macros and the job is done. Of course you still have to enter the data into the database and verify it, but if your tables are sensibly designed this is easy to do, and far less error-prone than writing everything by hand. You are still free to make finishing touches to your hypertext by hand, if you want.

5.4.3 Working systematically

It helps if you have text and graphics ready-named as a complete set of (un-marked-up) `.HTML` files before you start tagging. Other people like the feeling of composing at the organ, and insist on writing text while editing graphics while inserting tags while creating URLs (...while playing the drums, tuba, and cymbals between their knees). We commend to you the dentist's maxim:

> 'Stay with each tool as long as possible.'

It is far more satisfactory to create all the images, then to insert all the tags, and then to test them all, than to switch continually from one tool to another. This is because if you have, say, your graphics tool running, it is no trouble to make another image, but it is slow and wasteful to have to change to the word processor, only to change back to graphics a moment later. Also, if you do all the images together, you will probably give them a more harmonious and uniform style than if you make them in separate sessions, as your mind will be focused on the visual task.

A handwritten check-list is helpful when constructing hypertext pages.

	Layout	Links	Text	Problems
Theatre	ok	ok	ok	
Programme	sort out priority	ok		typefaces too complicated
Current		ok		
Future				images? provisional dates?
Bookings		ok	ok	firm vs enquiries
Reservations		ok		
Pricing				
Company		ok		
Actors				

You should at least choose your own style consciously, and find your own way of being systematic. We find a check-list on a piece of paper very helpful. The figure above shows a simple handwritten example of a kind that we find helpful, for the Theatre example (see Colour plates). Ruled columns are useful because they make it obvious when an item has been missed out. If you start by simply listing the pages and add comments as you go along (links ok, image needs redesign) then there is really no extra work involved in making a list – on the contrary, the list will save you effort time and again.

5.5 Testing and debugging

Once your *Chef d'Oeuvre* is declared complete, you absolutely **must** check it out.

> Life is one darn thing after another
>
> President Coolidge

Just when you think your URLs are all sorted out, darn if half the list items aren't showing up .... It is easy to make mistakes. The *only* way to be sure your HTML is correct is to go through all of it, and to check that everything works as intended. Even if you checked it already.

> – *Aw, mom, we did that yesterday!* –
> – *Adapt, Wilbur: this is for your own good.* –

You need to start at the beginning, without any preconceived notions of what has and has not been done: by definition, you do not know what you have forgotten! This is so difficult to do on a large system that conventional wisdom deploys a completely independent team to do the testing. You will be fine checking your own HTML as long as you maintain a sort of detached concern, like a traditional hospital doctor on the ward round: oh, that's an interesting problem .... There is absolutely no future in blame, whether attached to yourself or to others. **If a tag is wrong, note it down and get it fixed**. End.

5.5.1 Testing approaches

Any approach that checks everything is fine. You may like to do something like this:

(1) Make a list of all your HTML documents. Rule a dozen columns.

(2) Spell-check them all. Tick them off as you go.

(3) View the documents in your browser. Check that all the text is visible and paragraphed.

(4) Check that header levels and character-level mark-up look appropriate.

(5) Check that figures, forms, tables and anchors are correctly formatted and fit their context. Extra space or breaks, or conversely more careful flow of text, can make a big difference.

(6) Fill in all form fields and submit them. Check that the right messages are sent.

(7) Follow every link. Check that all of them go where they should.

(8) Try out every hotzone on clickable images. Check the links work as intended.

(9) Look at the system again from the beginning, as a reader. Are more links needed to make the system usable or comprehensible? Are navigation aids needed?

(10) Finally, look at each document in the system, as a designer. Does it look worthy of your efforts? Could the graphic design or page layout benefit from a little more effort?

(11) View your hypertext with a different browser. Sometimes pages which look great in one browser are horrible in another. (Spare a thought for non-Netscape users, too.)

Once you have cleared your HTML through this process, it may not be perfect, but it will be tough and usable.

5.5.2 Some common mistakes

HTML is not a devious and tricky language like C or APL ('x/+^%='), nor does it growl at you with incomprehensible messages, as a C programming language compiler does:

```
syntax error at line 658: unknown identifier
```

HTML's very friendliness, though, can give you trouble: the browser silently goes crazy, offering you no obvious clue as to what was wrong. Maybe the noisily raving C compiler is, after all, preferable. There are several tools such as HoTMetaL now available (look on the Web with Yahoo (`http://www.yahoo.com`) or W3 (`http://www.w3.org`) for the latest details) which can check your HTML in the same way that a compiler checks a computer program. HAL offer an HTML validation service which does the same thing. They will undoubtedly pick up some mistakes that you did not notice.

Examples which we have enjoyed include:

- invisible text
- case sensitivity
- unclosed tags
- swapped filenames
- omitted quotation marks
- squashed text
- PC/UNIX incompatibilities.

Here are some hints to help you spot these sorts of problem.

Invisible text

The famous invisible text is easily created: just put it inside a tag! For instance:

```
<H3 I wanted this to be my title></H3> <!--no good-->
```

In fact the line should have read

```
<H3>I wanted this to be my title</H3>
```

Case sensitivity

Text in URLs is often case sensitive, so that

```
<A HREF="fred.html#f1"> <!--no good-->
```

is not at all the same thing as

```
<A HREF="fred.html#F1">
```

and indeed the links didn't work if the labels were in the 'wrong' case. Your browser very probably has different tricks up its sleeve. Sensitivity to case, to white space (present or absent), to supposedly optional tags, or to recent features of HTML 3 are all likely candidates for small bugs. Note that UNIX **is** case sensitive.

Unclosed tags

What is wrong with

```
<H2>Another Section<H2> <!--no good-->
```

– you spotted it at once? You need a closing </H2> tag with a '/'. It is also quite easy to end up (after a little manual editing and rearrangement) with HTML such as

```
<H2>Another Level 2 Section</H3> <!--no good either!-->
```

which is unlikely to work: most browsers do not assume that a wrong-level closing tag should close a heading. Look through your text with a browser (or better, two different browsers) for suspicious signs, such as whole sections in bold face....

People often forget the whole closing tag, too. For instance, if most of a document appears in *italics, you need to put in an* </EM> *or* </I> *somewhere close to where the italicizing started!*

Swapped filenames

Everyone has written

```
<LINK HREF="topform.html"> <!--no good-->
```

when they meant

```
<LINK HREF="formtop.html">
```

and then wondered what was going wrong. If you keep a **printed listing** of your files this shouldn't happen often. Similar chaos readily breaks out when moving files to new directories or servers, unless you are very careful to use purely relative addressing and a fixed structure.

Omitted quotation marks

Different browsers have varying reactions to missed quotation marks.

`<A HREF=myfile.htm>` or `<A HREF="myfile.htm>`

may or may not work (Netscape is forgiving of both, actually). Quotes are necessary in multi-word identifiers, and you can't expect your browser to cope with:

```
<H3 ID="multi-word identifier>MWI</H3> <!--no good-->
```

Squashed text

It is really very easy to forget some <P> or <BR> tags. Your browser blithely ignores your 'invisible mark-up' in the form of carriage returns in your documents! For instance:

```
<P>
I wanted this to be line 1. <!--no good-->
And this to be line 2.
I hoped this would be line 3.
```

Unfortunately, this would be shown on screen as:

> I wanted this to be line 1. And this to be line 2. I hoped this would be line 3.

It worked on my PC

Personal computers running DOS/Windows are insensitive to case, allow the use of underscores in filenames and use three-character file extensions. So

```
<A HREF="DOS_file.htm">Some DOS text</A> <!--no good-->
```

is quite legal on a PC, and when you test your HTML, your DOS/Windows browser will succeed in finding the right file. But when you install it on a UNIX server, the link fails, for three reasons. You need to put

```
<A HREF="portable.html">Some portable text</A>
```

You should write filenames in URLs:

- in lower case,
- with no underscores, and
- with the four-character extension '.html'.

It worked in UNIX

UNIX allows you to use long file names, as do other operating systems like Apple's and new versions of Windows. While DOS/Windows browsers remain in wide use, it is best to use short file roots (up to 8 characters) so that there is no risk of ambiguity. For instance,

```
<A HREF="thisfileisverylongindeed.html">
```

and

```
<A HREF="thisfileisshort.html">
```

both appear to DOS when used locally on a DOS/Windows browser as if they were

```
<A HREF="THISFILE.HTM">
```

Since not many people develop on a UNIX workstation and publish on a PC, this is not generally a serious problem, but it is annoying to people who want to navigate offline through your hypertext, using their PC.

5.6 Rollout and maintenance

Finally the great day arrives. You ship the whole set of documents and images to your providers, wait anxiously as they load it up, and spot a fresh typographic error on your home page, in a small change which you inserted 'after testing was complete'. According to teachings associated with the Koran, prayer rugs should never be perfect lest God be offended. Actually, no one ever managed to weave a fault-free carpet of any size.

Rollout is the start of a maintenance process, not the end of the cycle. You will always need to make updates in style and content. If you tested carefully, you will not need many changes in mechanism.

It is sensible to include a form for recording mistakes or suggestions, or at least a '`mailto:`' URL with your return address:

```
<A HREF="mailto:author@feedback.acoustic.com">Send Feedback to Author</A>
```

This calls up a mail tool using the configuration you set up in your browser, from a normal-looking hypertext link anchor:

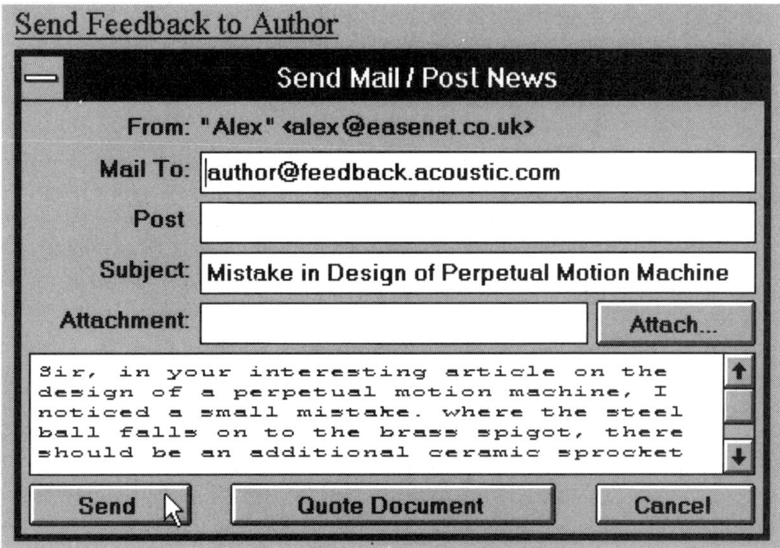

This enables your readers to give you their feedback. It is the most important part of the whole process! Don't treat comments as a nuisance; responding to comments with further development is the only way that you can hope to give your readers what they want. If you get a heap of comments, this means that plenty of people are reading your hypertext!

Incidentally, the use of a mail alias, like the 'author' of the example, or the widely-used 'webmaster', is advisable, as these names can stay constant whereas people change jobs. Aliases also make it easy when you need to filter your mail: you can separate out all webby mail from your personal letters, for instance.

5.7 Summary of HTML life cycle

The approach to HTML development described in this chapter can be summarized as:

(1) Understand what kinds of hypertext are possible. (Look at good examples on the Web.)

(2) Specify what you want.

(3) Design your HTML structure before you build it. (Use tools for large structures.)

(4) Tag up your documents systematically.

(5) Test and debug them.

(6) Roll out the product, expecting feedback from users.

(7) Keep on improving.

THE TIMES
FRONT PAGE
BRITAIN
WORLD
BUSINESS
OPINION
January 19 1996
BRITAIN
SEARCH
INTERACTIVE TIMES
Attempt to cool leadership fever
Major opens up debate on EU policy
BY PHILIP WEBSTER AND NICHOLAS WOOD
JOHN MAJOR pleased the Tory Euro-sceptics yesterday by bowing to pressure for a White Paper laying out the Government's position on Europe in the run-up to negotiations on the future of the European Union.
The move, which took ministers and MPs by surprise, came amid a ministerial drive to calm a renewed bout of leadership fever sparked by suggestions that previously loyal backbenchers have been plotting against Mr Major.
The White Paper was announced after Mr Major took his sharpest sideswipe yet at Baroness Thatcher over her attack last week on One Nation Conservatism. Pointing to his record in cutting inflation, mortgage rates and unemployment, he declared: "That is what she, when Prime Minister, sought to achieve. It is what we have delivered."

(*Top left*) **The Times.** This is the online version of the newspaper *The Times*. The tabs along the side are an image, as are the words 'The Times'. The lines across the page beneath this main title are horizontal rules and the date and the word 'Britain' are placed in their respective positions by using a small table.

(*Bottom left*) **Insect drawings on the Web.** Notice the use of clickable images. The Netscape browser currently shows these with a blue outline although you can turn this off (see Chapter 9). The idea is that users click on the small version image to see a larger complete version only if and when they want to (the larger image may take several seconds to download). The small images are items in an unordered list, hence the bullets.

(*Bottom right*) **Insects in detail.** This is the result of selecting a small picture shown in the preceding screen. The insect drawings are downloaded in about 30 seconds from a low bandwidth connection.

Insect Drawings at Illinois
Below are a series of original drawings used some 50 to 60 years ago as teaching aids for entomology at the University of Illinois. They were rescued from Harker Hall, the old Law, then Chemistry, and later Entomology building, during its recent renovation. The original drawings are on canvas, approximately 1.0 by 1.5 meters and were drawn as a WPA project during the Depression. Many of them seem to be based (sometimes closely) on drawings found in "Destructive and Useful Insects" by C.L. Metcalf and W.P. Flint. The images below are mainly overviews of several of the more common insect orders (The taxonomic purist will note that some of the panels contain more than one order as we recognize them today. Errata are listed here). The images you see have been electronically "cleaned". Click on the opened icon (or the order name) to see the full image (or another page of choices). Also included are links to the Tree of Life at the University of Arizona by David and Wayne Maddison for those who want taxonomic information on each of the orders. Click on the tree icon to jump to these sites.
Last updated 2/1/95
Collembola (Springtails) (60K)
Thysanura (Silverfish) (124 K)

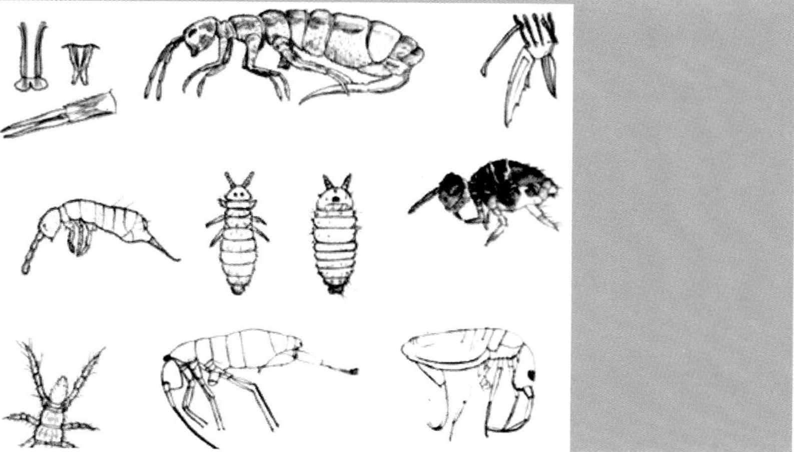

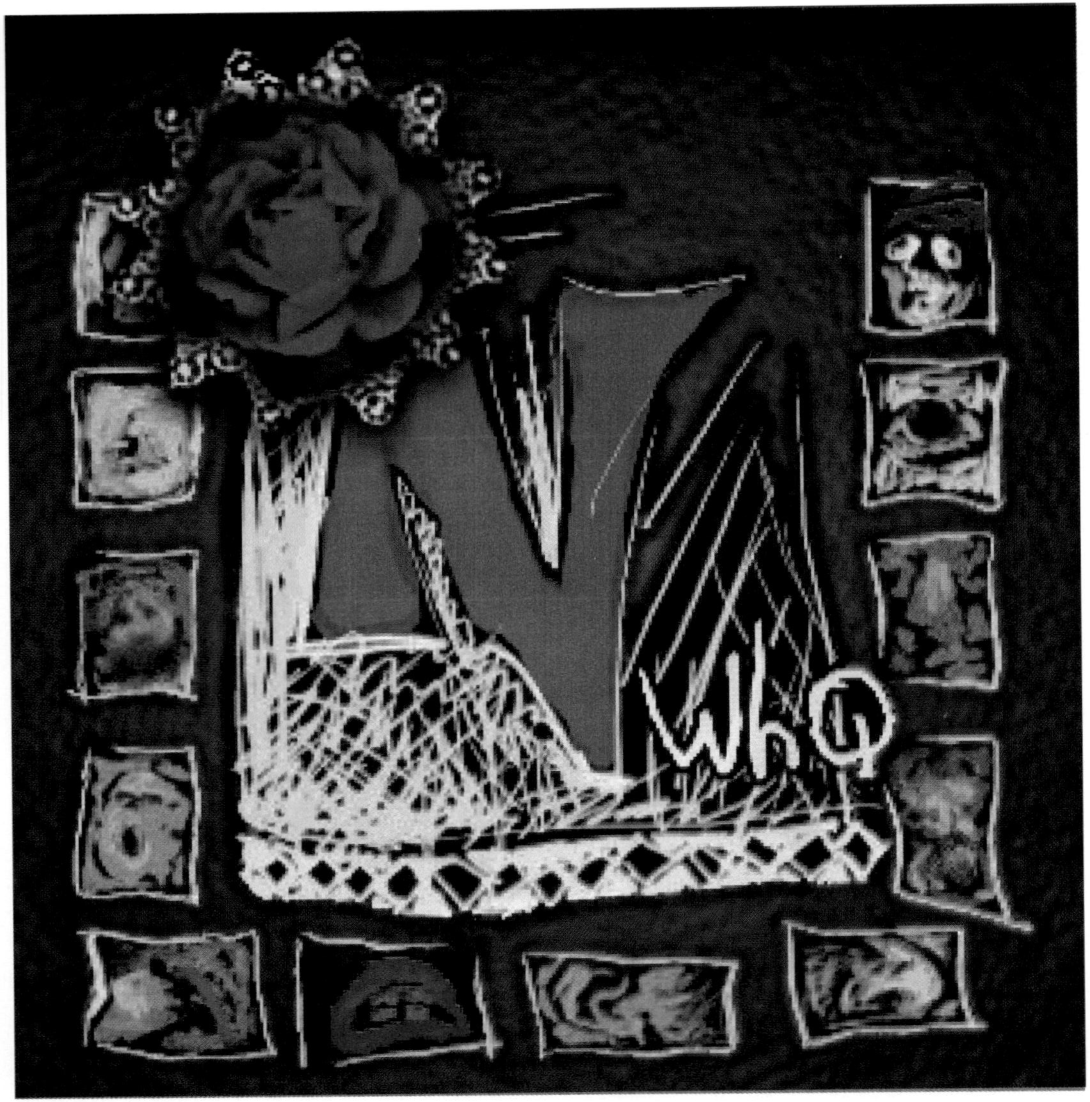

Imaginative example of an image map.
Each of the constituent graphics is secretly a hypertext link to a piece of artwork or piece of creative writing.

Artwork on the Web. This is what appears when you click on the rose in the preceding screen.
Image by Elizabeth Fischer.
Reproduced courtesy of NWHQ, http://www.knosso.com/NWHQ.

flow9.gif flow10.gif flow11.gif

flow12.gif flow13.gif

pansy1.gif pansy2.gif pansy3.gif

(*Top*) **Clip art for the Web.** The flowers can be used to decorate your own Web pages. You click on the name of the GIF file next to your favourite flower arrangement and it is transmitted sweetly down the wire to your chosen location on your hard disk. There it waits ready to be incorporated into a Web page by using `IMG` in the usual way (see Chapter 11 and try http://cameo.softwarelabs.com/gini/index.htm).

(*Right*) **At Christmas we searched on 'guinea-pig' and this appeared.** Each link gives rise to a delightful photograph of a guinea-pig and as fellow 'pig enthusiasts' the authors couldn't resist this simple but effective Web page!

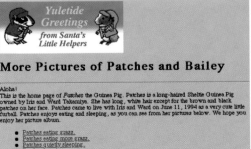

Yuletide
Greetings
from Santa's
Little Helpers

More Pictures of Patches and Bailey

Aloha!
This is the home page of *Patches* the Guinea Pig. Patches is a long-haired Sheltie Guinea Pig owned by Iris and Ward Takamiya. She has long, white hair except for the brown and black patches on her face. Patches came to live with Iris and Ward on June 11, 1994 as a very cute little furball. Patches enjoys eating and sleeping, as you can see from her pictures below. We hope you enjoy her picture album.

- Patches eating grass.
- Patches eating more grass.
- Patches quietly sleeping.
- Patches begging.
- Patches running.

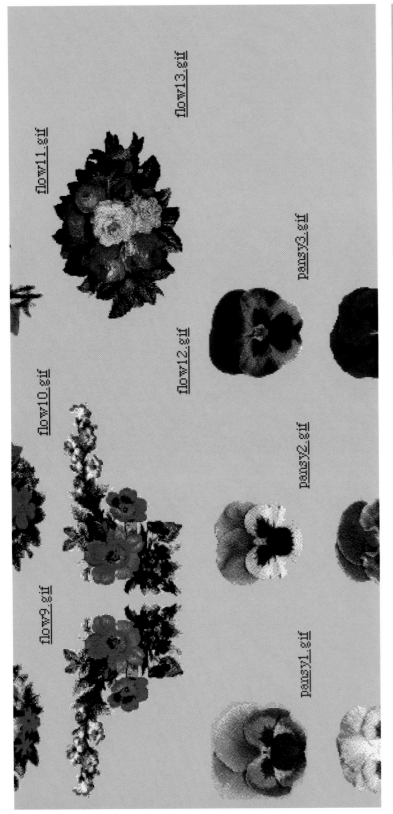

(*Top left*) This is one of many search programs available on the Web.

INDIA WORLD
Namaste. Welcome to IndiaWorld, India's first daily electronic news and information service.
Preview Subscribe Today's Additions Gifting
Headlines India Daily BSE Quotes Busybee Laxman
India Today Kalnirnay Movies Cricket Quiz
[Free Pages | Subscribe | Today's Additions | Cricket | News Headlines]

(*Bottom left*) **IndiaWorld electronic news on the Web.** The choice of topics is presented as an image map with matching textual hypertext links underneath for those readers operating from text-only browsers.

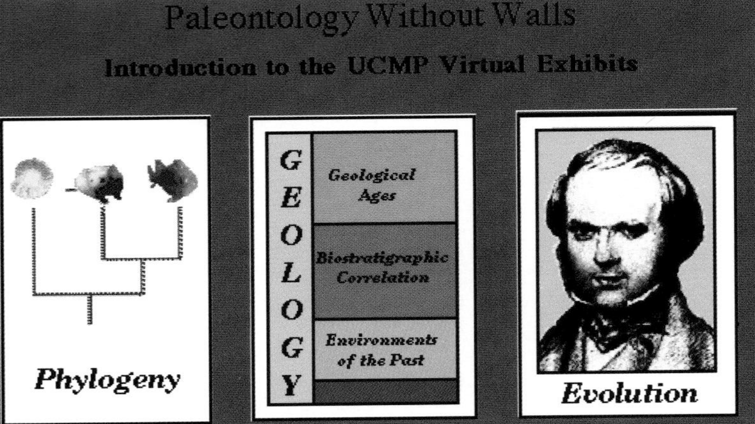

The Phanerozoic is divided into three major divisions...the Cenozoic, the Mesozoic, and the Paleozoic Eras. The "zoic" part of the word comes from the root "zoo", which means animal. This is the same root as in the words Zoology and Zoological Park (or Zoo). "Cen" means recent, "Meso" means middle, and "Paleo" means ancient. These divisions reflect major changes in the composition of ancient faunas, each era being recognized by its domination by a particular group of animals. The Cenozoic has sometimes been called the "Age of Mammals", the Mesozoic the "Age of Dinosaurs" and the Paleozoic the "Age of Fishes". This is an overly simplified view, but one which has some value for the newcomer. For instance, other groups of animals lived during the Mesozoic. In addition to the dinosaurs, animals such as mammals, turtles, crocodiles, frogs, salamanders, and countless varieties of insects also lived on land. Additionally, there were many kinds of plants living in the past that no longer live today, and many ancient floras went through great changes too, but not always at the same time that the animal groups changed.

To find out more about how geological time scales are constructed, click on the Cenozoic in the geological time scale above. If you have visited before or want to skip this, you may click on the Mesozoic (mostly dinosaurs), Paleozoic or Precambrian to find out about some of the organisms that lived during these times.

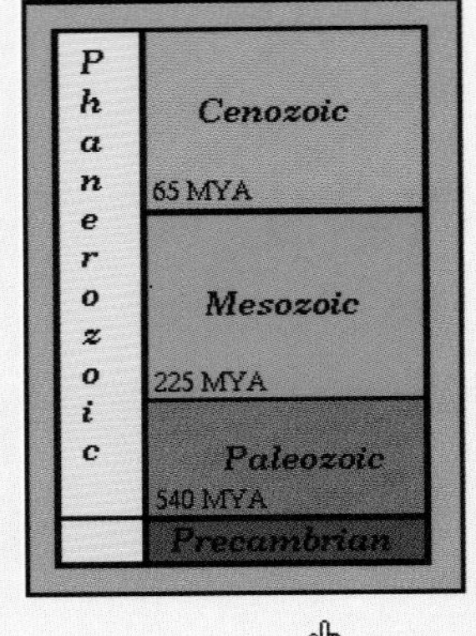

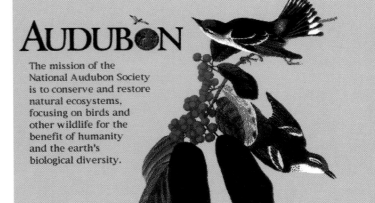

AUDUBON

The mission of the National Audubon Society is to conserve and restore natural ecosystems, focusing on birds and other wildlife for the benefit of humanity and the earth's biological diversity.

By noting the relationships of different rock units, Nicolaus Steno in 166
The first stated that sedimentary rocks are layed down in a horizontal m
rock units were deposited on top of older rock units. To envision this lat
a wall. The oldest layer was put on first and is at the bottom, while the n
concept was introduced by James Hutton in 1795, and later emphasized
idea that natural geologic processes were uniform in frequency and mag
been referred to as the "law of uniformitarianism".

Steno's principles allow
begin to recognize rock
locally described by the
between rock sequence
It was the use of fossils
to correlate between ge
contribution was possil
of the earth's crust.

For the next major con
to William Smith, a can
1815 Smith produced a
successfully demonstra
succession. This princi
definite order in which

(Top left and right; Bottom right) **Paleontology without walls.** This Web site is described in Chapter 5 on Designing your Web Project.

(Bottom left) **The opening Web page of the Audubon Society.** You can read about the Audubon Society on www.audubon.org/index.html.

Gilbert and Sullivan Archive

- WHAT'S NEW

- Introduction
- Gilbert and Sullivan Files
- Savoy Operas of the 1890's
- MIDI files -- listen to the music.
- The Opera Schedule Server
- Search the Librettos
- G&S Festivals
- Major G&S Organizations and Resources

The Sorcerer (November 7, 1877; Opera Comique; 178 performances)
With the help of a love philter. everyone in the village is in love -- with the wrong person.

- **Plot Summary**: Text or WordPerfect version.
- **Libretto**: Text or WordPerfect version.

H.M.S. Pinafore , or *The Lass That Loved a Sailor* (May 28, 1878; Opera Comique; 571 performances)
The captain's daughter and a common sailor on his ship fall in love. The first smash hit G&S opera, and one of the Big Three today.

- **Plot Summary**: Text or WordPerfect version.
- **Libretto**: Text version.

The Pirates of Penzance The Pirates of Penzance, or *The Slave of Duty* (April 2, 1880; Opera Comique; 363 performances)
A young pirate just out of his "indentures" in love with Mabel, Major General Stanley's ward, while the rest of the pirate crew want to marry the general's other wards. Also one of the Big Three G&S operas.

- **Plot Summary**: Text or WordPerfect version.
- **Libretto**: Text, WordPerfect or Word for Windows version.

(Top left) **A page with a contents list consisting of pointers to other information.** The contents list is a series of hypertext links included as list items in an unordered list.

(Bottom left) You can download the lyrics of Gilbert and Sullivan songs from the Web in various commonly used formats.

(Top right) **Information on obscure beers available in English and Dutch.** The Web site allows you to scan tables of facts about beer and advertises the Bierjaarboek. Here the layout is achieved by using a table to organize the structure of the page with BLOCKQUOTE used to generate italic indented text to the left. An image has been inserted into a table cell. See Chapter 10.

The Complete Guide to Belgian, Dutch and Luxemburg Beers available in Dutch!!).

As the blurb says:

> *Ten years ago Peter Crombecq Peter Crombecq published his first Beer Tasters' Pocket Guide. In the meantime, the Beer Annual as it is now called has become the essential guide to Benelux beers. In this especially bulky jubilee edition, Crombecq provides a survey of the developments on the beer domain of the past 10 years. Once again he presents us with clear and up to date information on the taste of the hundreds of beers that are being brewed in the Benelux countries. This is a book no beer lover should go without.*

The Beer Annual (all 496 pages of it) contains more information than these beer pages can show. The preface describes the evolution of the beer world during the last decade. The first three chapters deal with the brewing process and the influence of the different stages in this process on the taste of the beer; they also provide an extensive vocabulary to describe a beer's taste, hints on how to best store beers, on pouring, and on tasting. Chapter 4 presents a survey of the Benelux countries's active beer taster societies. The beer lists in chapter 5 contain all beers that have been on the market during the last ten years (some 3,600), and are not restricted to those still available. Moreover there is a description of the tastes of over 1,000 beers, and all beers have been categorized according to 70 types and 469 tastes. The beer lists also list special labels (beers which already exist under another name) and a reference to the original. Where possible, the date of first and last brew have been included. The lists per country (chapters 6, 7 and 8) do not only contain the addresses of breweries, alehouses and beer traders, but breweries are also grouped according to their holding companies and according to size, and finally there is

70s_marble.gif

***** If Greg Brady were making a homepage today, he'd pick this background. Looks like an oil slick on pavement.**

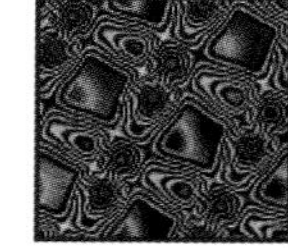

acid.jpg

***** Looks like jewelry or a kaliedoscope gone mad.**

(Bottom right) **JPEG and GIF images for backgrounds are available on the Web.** These are available from MacDaddy's Background Sampler. In many cases you can select an image, download it and save it to a file on your computer and then reference it in a Web page by using the BODY BACKGROUND tag described in Chapter 11. Some background images are free. Others require payment.

These are just some of the technical people involved in developing the Web. There are many, many others and those included are merely those known particularly well to the authors and whose photo was easily available. Apologies to all those who feel they would like to have made an appearance!!

Håkon Lie works for the World Wide Web consortium in France at INRIA. He is currently developing the CSS style sheet language.

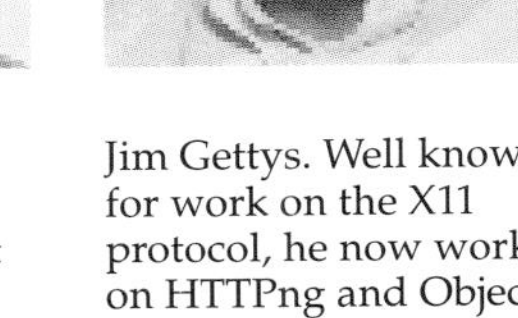

Jim Gettys. Well known for work on the X11 protocol, he now works on HTTPng and Object-oriented Web (OOPS).

Henrik Frystyk Nielsen is best known for his work on libwww, a public domain library for accessing the Web.

Jim Miller has led efforts to define PICS, in addition to working on security and electronic payments.

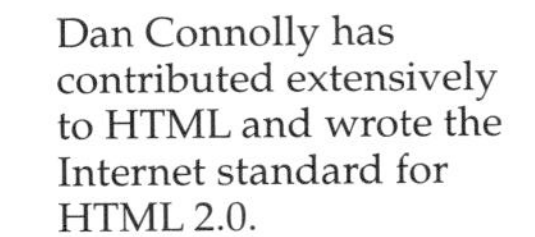

Dan Connolly has contributed extensively to HTML and wrote the Internet standard for HTML 2.0.

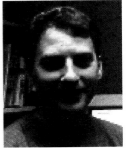

Bert Bos works for W3C at INRIA near Nice in France on style sheets and related layout issues.

Roy Fielding has contributed vastly to the development of HTTP and standards for relative URLs.

Dave Raggett has worked on HTML+ and HTML 3, writing the Arena browser. Dave coined VRML and set up the IETF working group for HTTP.

Tim Berners-Lee invented the Web and now directs the World Wide Web consortium.

Lou Montulli, the developer of the Lynx browser which provides terminal-based access to the Web.

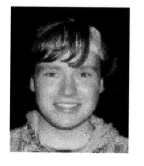

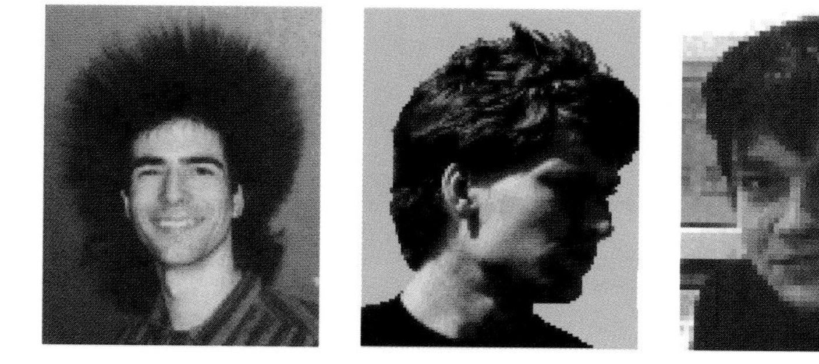

Eric Bina wrote X-Mosaic together with Marc Andreessen when at NCSA.

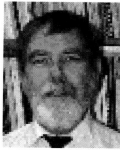

Anselm Baird-Smith works for the World Wide Web consortium on the Java implementation of a new public domain HTTP server.

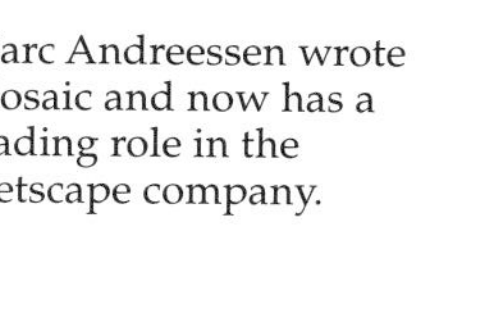

Marc Andreessen wrote Mosaic and now has a leading role in the Netscape company.

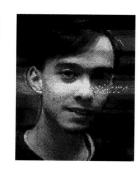

Chris Lilley works for the World Wide Web consortium on graphics and fonts.

Brian Behlendorf plays a strong role in the Web standards effort and is a member of several IETF and World Wide Web consortium workgroups.

Tom Green is responsible for the World Wide Web consortium newsletter to members and also plays an administrative support role.

Mark Peche is largely responsible for the development of VRML together with Tony Paresi.

Kevin Hughs is a graphic designer who has played a key role in developing the Web and VRML.

Arthur Secret works on the library of software resources for the Web. He has recently moved from CERN to the W3 consortium in Boston.

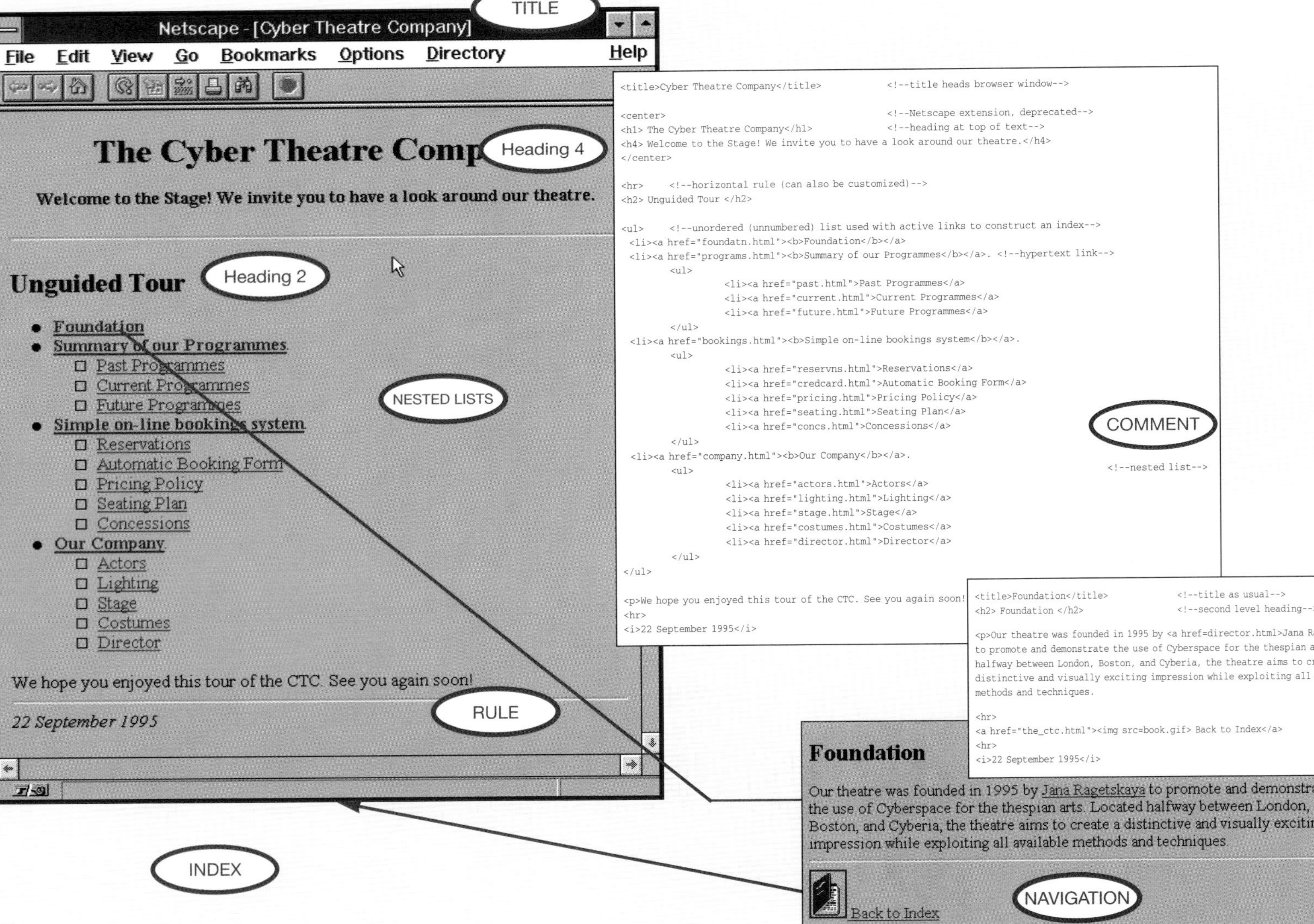

TITLE
Netscape - [Cyber Theatre Company]
File Edit View Go Bookmarks Options Directory Help
The Cyber Theatre Comp
Heading 4
Welcome to the Stage! We invite you to have a look around our theatre.
Unguided Tour
Heading 2
Foundation
Summary of our Programmes.
Past Programmes
Current Programmes
Future Programmes
Simple on-line bookings system.
Reservations
Automatic Booking Form
Pricing Policy
Seating Plan
Concessions
Our Company.
Actors
Lighting
Stage
Costumes
Director
NESTED LISTS
We hope you enjoyed this tour of the CTC. See you again soon!
RULE
22 September 1995
INDEX
COMMENT

```
<title>Cyber Theatre Company</title>          <!--title heads browser window-->

<center>                                      <!--Netscape extension, deprecated-->
<h1> The Cyber Theatre Company</h1>           <!--heading at top of text-->
<h4> Welcome to the Stage! We invite you to have a look around our theatre.</h4>
</center>

<hr>    <!--horizontal rule (can also be customized)-->
<h2> Unguided Tour </h2>

<ul>    <!--unordered (unnumbered) list used with active links to construct an index-->
  <li><a href="foundatn.html"><b>Foundation</b></a>
  <li><a href="programs.html"><b>Summary of our Programmes</b></a>. <!--hypertext link-->
       <ul>
              <li><a href="past.html">Past Programmes</a>
              <li><a href="current.html">Current Programmes</a>
              <li><a href="future.html">Future Programmes</a>
       </ul>
  <li><a href="bookings.html"><b>Simple on-line bookings system</b></a>.
       <ul>
              <li><a href="reservns.html">Reservations</a>
              <li><a href="credcard.html">Automatic Booking Form</a>
              <li><a href="pricing.html">Pricing Policy</a>
              <li><a href="seating.html">Seating Plan</a>
              <li><a href="concs.html">Concessions</a>
       </ul>
  <li><a href="company.html"><b>Our Company</b></a>.
       <ul>                                                        <!--nested list-->
              <li><a href="actors.html">Actors</a>
              <li><a href="lighting.html">Lighting</a>
              <li><a href="stage.html">Stage</a>
              <li><a href="costumes.html">Costumes</a>
              <li><a href="director.html">Director</a>
       </ul>
</ul>

<p>We hope you enjoyed this tour of the CTC. See you again soon!
<hr>
<i>22 September 1995</i>
```

```
<title>Foundation</title>          <!--title as usual-->
<h2> Foundation </h2>              <!--second level heading-->

<p>Our theatre was founded in 1995 by <a href=director.html>Jana Ragetskaya</a>
to promote and demonstrate the use of Cyberspace for the thespian arts. Located
halfway between London, Boston, and Cyberia, the theatre aims to create a
distinctive and visually exciting impression while exploiting all available
methods and techniques.

<hr>
<a href="the_ctc.html"><img src=book.gif> Back to Index</a>
<hr>
<i>22 September 1995</i>
```

Foundation
Our theatre was founded in 1995 by Jana Ragetskaya to promote and demonstrate the use of Cyberspace for the thespian arts. Located halfway between London, Boston, and Cyberia, the theatre aims to create a distinctive and visually exciting impression while exploiting all available methods and techniques.
Back to Index
NAVIGATION

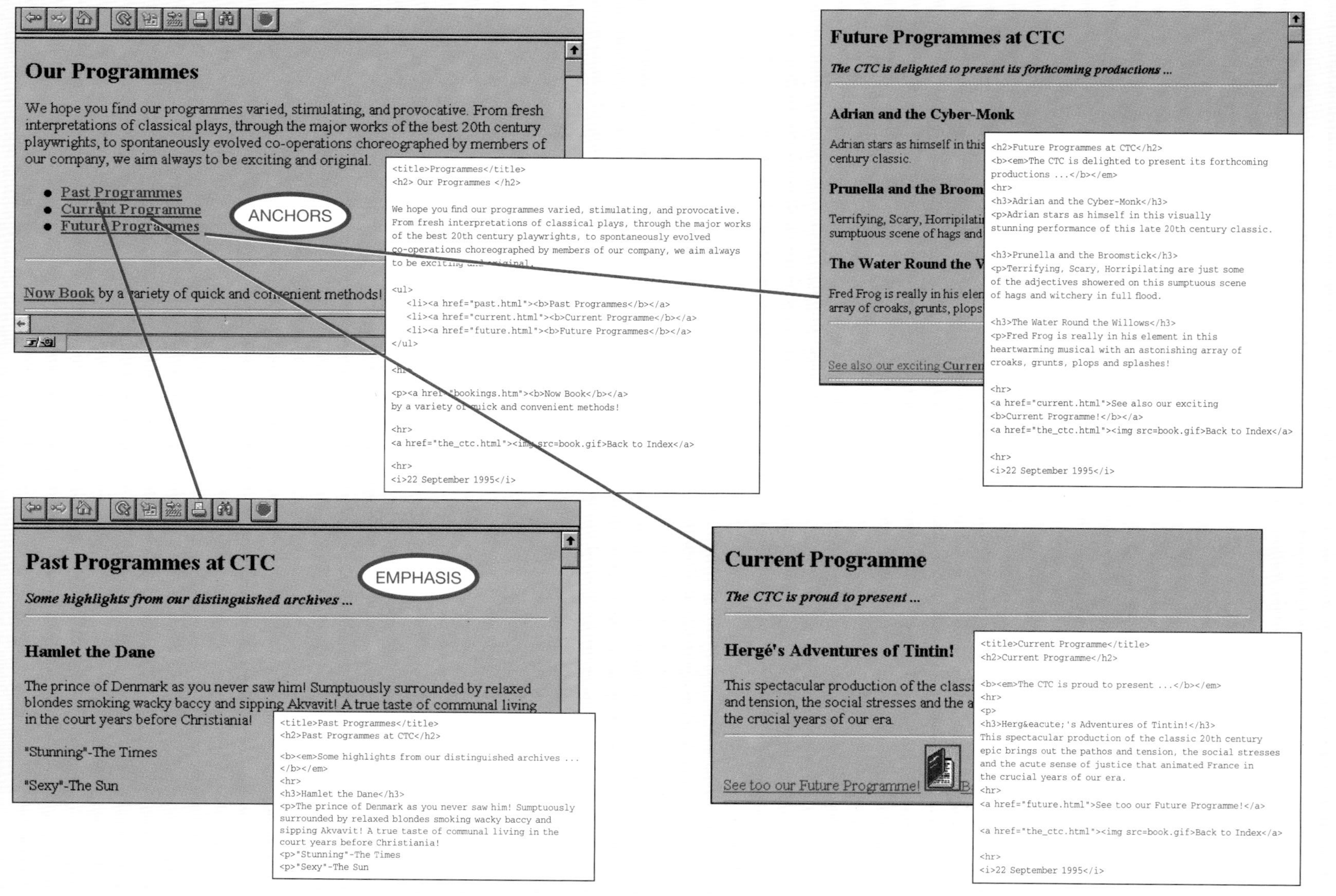
Our Programmes
We hope you find our programmes varied, stimulating, and provocative. From fresh interpretations of classical plays, through the major works of the best 20th century playwrights, to spontaneously evolved co-operations choreographed by members of our company, we aim always to be exciting and original.
Past Programmes
Current Programme
Future Programmes
ANCHORS
Now Book by a variety of quick and convenient methods!
<title>Programmes</title>
<h2> Our Programmes </h2>
We hope you find our programmes varied, stimulating, and provocative.
From fresh interpretations of classical plays, through the major works
of the best 20th century playwrights, to spontaneously evolved
co-operations choreographed by members of our company, we aim always
<ul>
<li><a href="past.html"><b>Past Programmes</b></a>
<li><a href="current.html"><b>Current Programme</b></a>
<li><a href="future.html"><b>Future Programmes</b></a>
</ul>
<hr>
<a href="the_ctc.html"><img src=book.gif>Back to Index</a>
<hr>
<i>22 September 1995</i>
Future Programmes at CTC
The CTC is delighted to present its forthcoming productions ...
Adrian and the Cyber-Monk
See also our exciting
<h2>Future Programmes at CTC</h2>
<b><em>The CTC is delighted to present its forthcoming
productions ...</b></em>
<hr>
<h3>Adrian and the Cyber-Monk</h3>
<p>Adrian stars as himself in this visually
stunning performance of this late 20th century classic.
<h3>Prunella and the Broomstick</h3>
<p>Terrifying, Scary, Horripilating are just some
of the adjectives showered on this sumptuous scene
of hags and witchery in full flood.
<h3>The Water Round the Willows</h3>
<p>Fred Frog is really in his element in this
heartwarming musical with an astonishing array of
croaks, grunts, plops and splashes!
<hr>
<a href="current.html">See also our exciting
<b>Current Programme!</b></a>
<a href="the_ctc.html"><img src=book.gif>Back to Index</a>
<hr>
<i>22 September 1995</i>
Past Programmes at CTC
EMPHASIS
Some highlights from our distinguished archives ...
Hamlet the Dane
The prince of Denmark as you never saw him! Sumptuously surrounded by relaxed blondes smoking wacky baccy and sipping Akvavit! A true taste of communal living in the court years before Christiania!
"Stunning"-The Times
"Sexy"-The Sun
<title>Past Programmes</title>
<h2>Past Programmes at CTC</h2>
<b><em>Some highlights from our distinguished archives ...
</b></em>
<hr>
<h3>Hamlet the Dane</h3>
<p>The prince of Denmark as you never saw him! Sumptuously
surrounded by relaxed blondes smoking wacky baccy and
sipping Akvavit! A true taste of communal living in the
court years before Christiania!
<p>"Stunning"-The Times
<p>"Sexy"-The Sun
Current Programme
The CTC is proud to present ...
Hergé's Adventures of Tintin!
the crucial years of our era
See too our Future Programme!
<title>Current Programme</title>
<h2>Current Programme</h2>
<b><em>The CTC is proud to present ...</b></em>
<hr>
<p>
<h3>Hergé's Adventures of Tintin!</h3>
This spectacular production of the classic 20th century
epic brings out the pathos and tension, the social stresses
and the acute sense of justice that animated France in
the crucial years of our era.
<hr>
<a href="future.html">See too our Future Programme!</a>
<a href="the_ctc.html"><img src=book.gif>Back to Index</a>
<hr>
<i>22 September 1995</i>

Bookings

Reservations can be made by telephone, personal visit, or by credit card over the Internet.

Here is a table of our Pricing policy, with seating plan and concessions.

We look forward to seeing you in our audience, and to meeting you after the performance in the theatre bar.

Back to Index

Reservations

There are 3 ways of reserving seats at CTC:

1. Personal Visit
2. Telephone
3. Credit Card over the Internet

If you choose to visit us personally, you may be assured of a warm welcome. You can enjoy a coffee while you peruse our latest programme. Our specially-trained staff will be happy to assist you.

You may telephone us on the day and collect your tickets up to 30 minutes before the performance. Just call

0123 456 - 7890 and ask for Cynthia.

PARA

Or you can decide which performance you wish to see by looking through our on-line Programmes, and then book immediately by Credit Card.

HTML codes omitted for clarity.

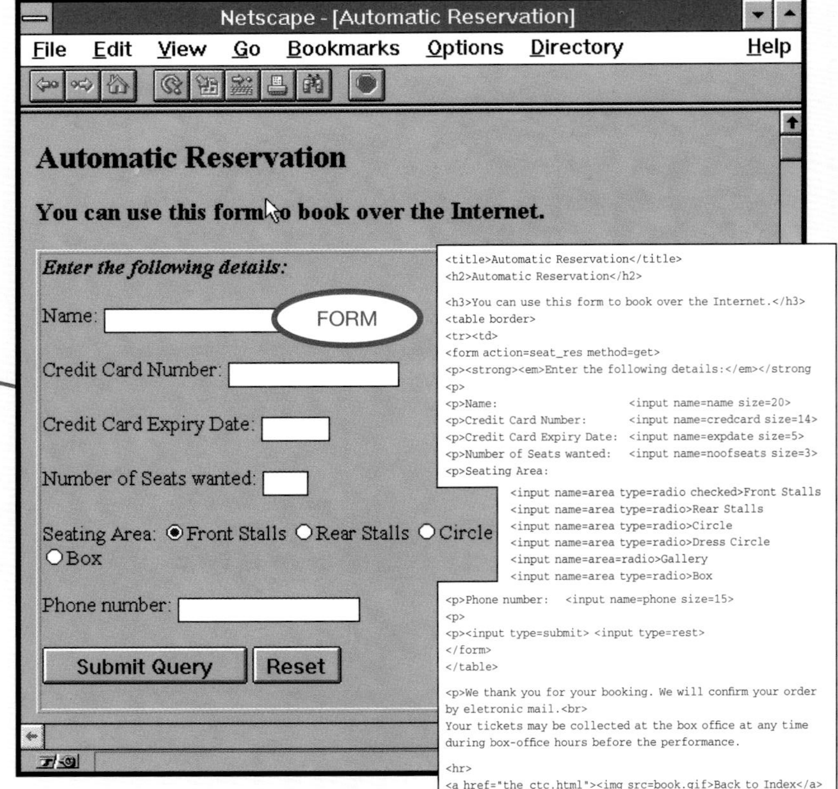


```
<title>Automatic Reservation</title>
<h2>Automatic Reservation</h2>

<h3>You can use this form to book over the Internet.</h3>
<table border>
<tr><td>
<form action=seat_res method=get>
<p><strong><em>Enter the following details:</em></strong
<p>
<p>Name:                  <input name=name size=20>
<p>Credit Card Number:    <input name=credcard size=14>
<p>Credit Card Expiry Date: <input name=expdate size=5>
<p>Number of Seats wanted: <input name=noofseats size=3>
<p>Seating Area:
        <input name=area type=radio checked>Front Stalls
        <input name=area type=radio>Rear Stalls
        <input name=area type=radio>Circle
        <input name=area type=radio>Dress Circle
        <input name=area=radio>Gallery
        <input name=area type=radio>Box
<p>Phone number:   <input name=phone size=15>
<p>
<p><input type=submit> <input type=rest>
</form>
</table>

<p>We thank you for your booking. We will confirm your order
by eletronic mail.<br>
Your tickets may be collected at the box office at any time
during box-office hours before the performance.

<hr>
<a href="the_ctc.html"><img src=book.gif>Back to Index</a>

<hr>
<i>22 September 1995</i>
```

Our Pricing Policy

ANCHOR

We want our productions to be enjoyed by all. Accordingly we offer a range of prices to suit all pockets, with generous concessions for those in need. Our Seating Plan shows the layout of the theatre, with our standard prices.

Special Concessions are available to the disadvantaged, to groups, and to individuals booking matinees in advance.

You can book by a variety of quick and con... details.

```
<title>Pricing</title>
<h2>Our Pricing Policy</h2>

We want our productions to be enjoyed by all. Accordingly
we offer a range of prices to suit all pockets, with
generous concessions for those in need.

Our <a href="seating.html">
<b>Seating Plan</b></a> shows the layout of the theatre,
with our standard prices.

<p>
Special <a href="concs.html">
<b>Concessions</b></a> are available to the disadvantaged,
to groups, and to individuals booking matinees in advance.
<hr>
```

Our Concessions

We offer generous concessions for those in need.

1. **Unwaged, Disabled, Pensioners, Students**

   35% of standard rates on production of ID, either booked at least 24 hours in advance, or standby. Available for all performances Monday - Thursday and all matinees.

2. **Groups**

   75% of standard rates for groups of 8 - 20 people, booked at least 1 week in advance.

   60% of standard rates for groups of more than 21 people, booked at least 2 weeks in advance.

3. **Advance Matinee Bookings**

   60% of standard rates, book...

```
<title>Concessions</title>
<h2>Our Concessions</h2>


We offer generous concessions for those in need.
<p>
<OL>
 <LI> <b>Unwaged, Disabled, Pensioners, Students</b><p>
        35% of standard rates on production of ID,
        either booked at least 24 hours in advance,
        or standby. Available
        for all performances Monday - Thursday
        and all matinees.<p>

 <LI> <b>Groups</b><p>
        75% of standard rates for groups of 8 - 20 people,
        booked at least 1 week in advance.<p>
        60% of standard rates for groups of more than 21
        people, booked at least 2 weeks in advance.<p>


 <LI> <b>Advance Matinee Bookings</b><p>
        60% of standard rates, booked at least 1 week
        in advance.<p>

</OL>
```

Seating Plan & Prices

Our seating is among the most modern and comfortable in the world. All seats have an unsurpassed view and acoustic whether the theatre is full or not. Our choice of materials and our wide gangways make for total convenience and safety.

Click for seat prices & availability

Balcony
Circle
Dress Circle
Dress Circle
Dress Circle
Rear Stalls
B
B
Front Stalls

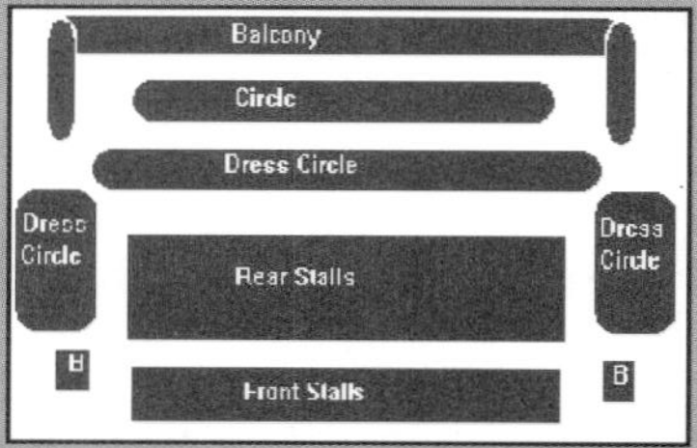

IMAGE MAP

Our Pricing Scheme

Our standard prices cover the full range from elegant boxes for that special party to simple but good seats in the balcony. Group discounts and Concessions are available for all performances. We hope everyone will enjoy themselves at CTC.

LIST

- Box £100
- Back Stalls £50
- Front Stalls, Dress Circle £25
- Circle £10
- Balcony £5

```
<title>Seating Plan</title>
<h2>Seating Plan & Prices</h2>

Our seating is among the most modern and comfortable in
the world. All seats have an unsurpassed view and acoustic
whether the theatre is full or not. Our choice of materials
and our wide gangways make for total convenience and safety.
<hr>

<table><tr>        <!--table used to lay out the document-->

<td><H3>Click for seat prices & availability</H3>
<A HREF="noseat.html">
   <IMG SRC="seatplan.gif"
        ALT="a clickable seatplan goes here"
        width=300
        height=200
        units=pixel
     ISMAP>
</A>

<td><p><h3>Our Pricing Scheme</h3>
Our standard prices cover the full range from elegant
boxes for that special party to simple but good seats
in the balcony. Group discounts and <a href=concs.html>
Concessions</a> are available for all performances.
We hope everyone will enjoy themselves at CTC.
<ul>
<li>Box £100
<li>Back Stalls £50
<li>Front Stalls, Dress Circle £25
<li>Circle £10
<li>Balcony £5
</ul>

</table>
```

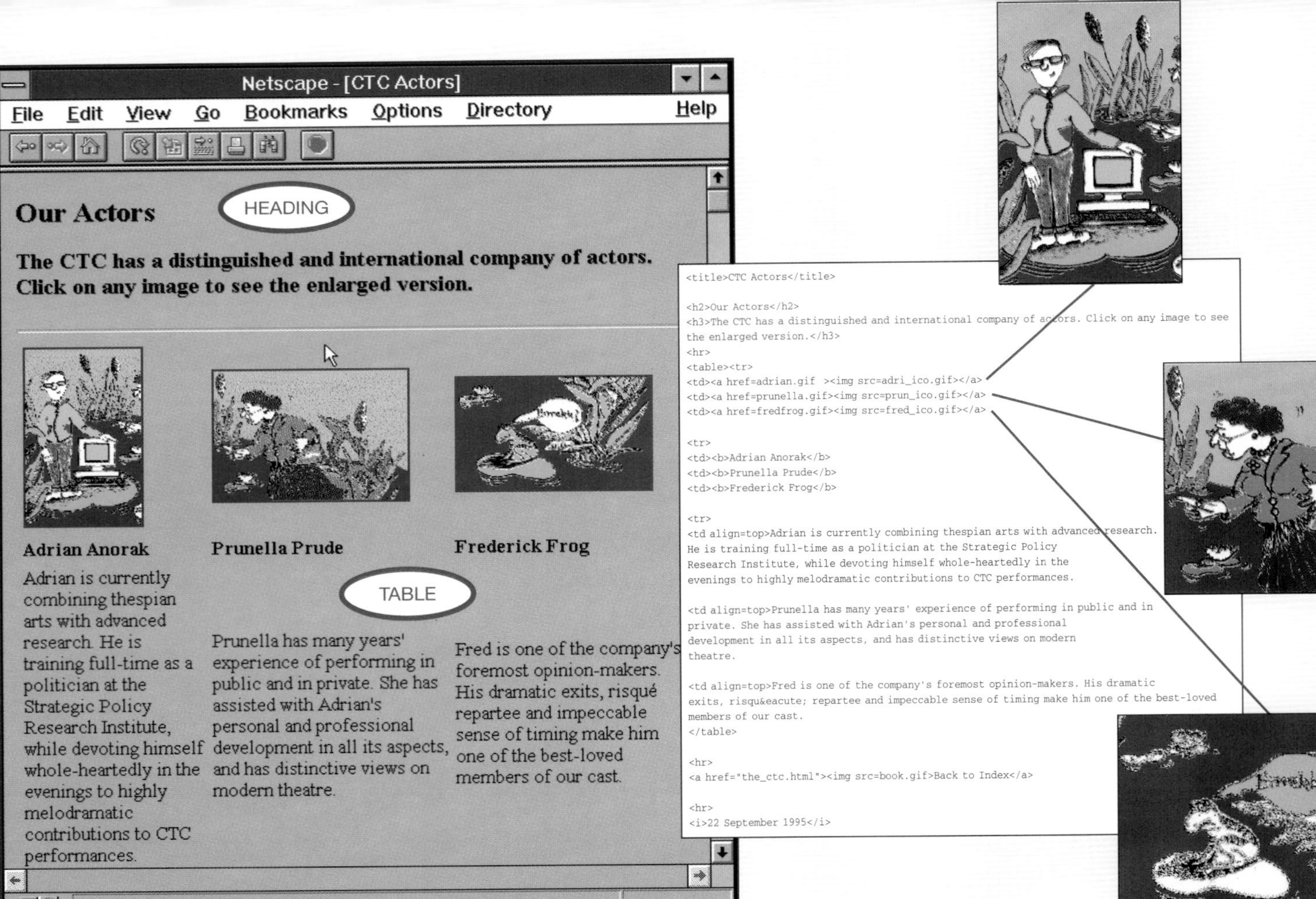

Netscape - [CTC Actors]
File Edit View Go Bookmarks Options Directory Help
Our Actors
HEADING
The CTC has a distinguished and international company of actors. Click on any image to see the enlarged version.
Adrian Anorak
Prunella Prude
Frederick Frog
TABLE
Adrian is currently combining thespian arts with advanced research. He is training full-time as a politician at the Strategic Policy Research Institute, while devoting himself whole-heartedly in the evenings to highly melodramatic contributions to CTC performances.
Prunella has many years' experience of performing in public and in private. She has assisted with Adrian's personal and professional development in all its aspects, and has distinctive views on modern theatre.
Fred is one of the company's foremost opinion-makers. His dramatic exits, risqué repartee and impeccable sense of timing make him one of the best-loved members of our cast.
<title>CTC Actors</title>
<h2>Our Actors</h2>
<h3>The CTC has a distinguished and international company of actors. Click on any image to see the enlarged version.</h3>
<hr>
<table><tr>
<td><a href=adrian.gif ><img src=adri_ico.gif></a>
<td><a href=prunella.gif><img src=prun_ico.gif></a>
<td><a href=fredfrog.gif><img src=fred_ico.gif></a>
<tr>
<td><b>Adrian Anorak</b>
<td><b>Prunella Prude</b>
<td><b>Frederick Frog</b>
<tr>
<td align=top>Adrian is currently combining thespian arts with advanced research. He is training full-time as a politician at the Strategic Policy Research Institute, while devoting himself whole-heartedly in the evenings to highly melodramatic contributions to CTC performances.
<td align=top>Prunella has many years' experience of performing in public and in private. She has assisted with Adrian's personal and professional development in all its aspects, and has distinctive views on modern theatre.
<td align=top>Fred is one of the company's foremost opinion-makers. His dramatic exits, risqué repartee and impeccable sense of timing make him one of the best-loved members of our cast.
</table>
<hr>
<a href="the_ctc.html"><img src=book.gif>Back to Index</a>
<hr>
<i>22 September 1995</i>

Our Company

The CTC company is completely democratic. Equal weight is given to the stage lighting technicians as to the direction or cast. Since roles are, in any case, shared evenly between members of the company, traditional distinctions are completely broken down in a direct demonstration of the CTC's free and open spirit.

Our Actors are involved in design and scripting as well as performance.

Our Lighting & Sound are vital and creative elements in all our productions.

Our revolutionary Stage Management is world-famous.

Jana's Costumes, Hats, Shoes, & Properties are as functional as they are visually distinctive.

Our Director is taking us to a new tomorrow.

Back to Index

```
<title>Our Company</title>
<h2>Our Company</h2>

<h3>The CTC company is completely democratic. Equal weight is given
to the stage lighting technicians as to the direction or cast.
Since roles are, in any case, shared evenly between members
of the company, traditional distinctions are completely broken
down in a direct demonstration of the CTC's free and open
spirit.</h3>

<hr>
<p>Our <a href="actors.html">
<b>Actors</b></a> are involved in design and scripting as well as
performance.

<p>Our <a href="lighting.html">
<b>Lighting & Sound</b></a> are vital and creative elements in
all our productions.

<p>Our revolutionary <a href="stage.html">
<b>Stage Management</b></a> is world-famous.

<p>Jana's <a href="costumes.html">
<b>Costumes,  Hats, Shoes, & Properties</b></a> are as functional
as they are visually distinctive.

<p>Our <a href="director.html">
<b>Director</b></a> is taking us to a new tomorrow.


<hr>
<a href="the_ctc.html"><img src=book.gif> Back to Index</a>

<hr>
<i>22 September 1995</i>
```

Lighting & Sound

The CTC is justly famous for Dave Ragetsko's innovative approach to stage lighting and sound effects. Every aspect of modern technology is dramatically exploited to make our theatre one of the most sought-after places for stage technicians.

Stage Management

Set Design has always been kept to a minimum at CTC. While not espousing outdated Method-Acting Minimalism, Jana believes that backdrops ought never to upstage the action on set.

Famous sets have included Ragetsko's black stage, lit with the latest black floodlights while the auditorium was brilliantly illuminated. Critics marvelled while Ragetsko was heard to mutter

"Get th

Costumes

Costumes for all CTC productions are designed and handmade by Jana herself, assisted by Prunella. Jana is an expert needlewoman and likes nothing better than a weekend by the fireside running up a complete set of costumes for a traditionally Tudor rendering of Shakespeare's Plantagenet plays.

Direction

The CTC is directed by its founder Jana Ragetskaya.

Jana eschewed training at traditional theatrical centres like RADA and the RSC, preferring instead to develop her own methods by *dynamical interaction* with the theatre company, allowing the ferment of ideas, movements, and emotions to determine the form of any particular piece.

This revolutionary approach has been the dynamo which has driven the CTC ever onward, with many exciting new companies following in its wake.

Jana has led many workshops and seminars on her methods, and is well-known in drama circles for her trenchant criticism of method acting and blind pursuit of technique.

IMAGE

Back to Index

```
<title>CTC Director</title>
<h2>Direction</h2>
The CTC is directed by its founder Jana Ragetskaya.
<hr>

<table>
<td><IMG SRC="director.gif">
<td>Jana eschewed training at traditional theatrical centres like RADA
and the RSC, preferring instead to develop her own methods by
<em>dynamical interaction</em> with the theatre company, allowing the
ferment of ideas, movements, and emotions to determine the form of any
particular piece.
<p>
This revolutionary approach has been the dynamo which has driven the
CTC ever onward, with many exciting new companies following in its wake.
<p>
Jana has led many workshops and seminars on her methods, and is
well-known in drama circles for her trenchant criticism of method
acting and blind pursuit of technique.
</table>

<hr>
<a href="the_ctc.html"><img src=book.gif>Back to Index</a>

<hr>
<i>22 September 1995</i>
```

(Top right) **Bonsai trees on the Web.** This is one of many sites displaying interesting graphics on the Web. In this case you can even download certain 'trees' to your own computer for your own pleasure.
Courtesy of the Online Bonsai Icon Collection
http://www.neosoft.com/~hav/tobic.html

(Bottom right) **The SFRaves Home Page.** This layout is achieved by inserting images and text into an HTML table (see Chapter 10). The bookcase is an image map (see Chapter 9). You click on a book to see more information, photographs and so on. There is also a clickable calendar.

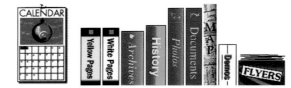

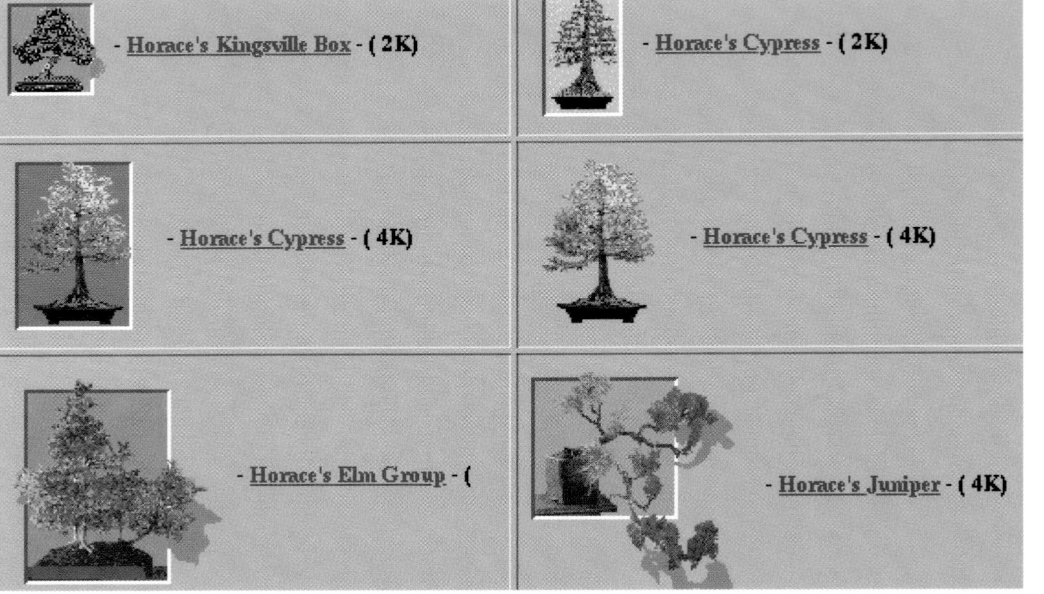

The SFRaves Home Page
http://www.hyperreal.com/raves/sf/

SFRaves is an electronic virtual community of ravers, networking together around the clock, sharing information and ideas, and even planning our own parties. The mailing list started in 1992 and has over 300 members from all parts of the community and all parts of the world (although the focus of the discussion is on San Francisco). Below is information about SFRaves itself as well as information about the entire San Francisco scene.
NEW! Shockwave version of this page!

6 MARKING UP PARAGRAPHS AND HEADINGS

In this chapter:

- Simple paragraph mark-up including discussion of word-wrap, non-breaking space characters, alignment and paragraph styles. The elements: `P`, `NOWRAP`, `BR`, `NOBR` and `WBR` are discussed (Section 6.2)
- Horizontal tabs. This involves the HTML 3 element `TAB` (Section 6.3)
- Headings. The heading elements `H1` to `H6` are discussed, also the use of style sheets and `SEQNUM` and `SKIP` to control numbering of headings in a document (Section 6.4)
- Preformatted text. This is done using the `PRE` element (Section 6.5)

- Quotations, both inline and longer quotations using: BQ, BLOCKQUOTE and Q (Section 6.6)
- Footnotes using the HTML 3 element ID (Section 6.7)
- Notes: cautions, warnings and admonishments. These are accomplished with the HTML 3 element NOTE (Section 6.8)
- Structuring a document into chapters, sections, appendices and so on. This involves a discussion of style sheets and DIV (Section 6.9)
- Information about the author of a document: the ADDRESS element (Section 6.10)

6.1 Introduction

This chapter focuses on how to write paragraphs, quotations, footnotes and headings in HTML. It also covers the use of tabs and preformatted text and touches upon style sheets which give you finer control over the rendering of the elements discussed. We assume you have read Chapter 3 which gives an overview of HTML and that you understand what an element is, know how to insert tags and are acquainted with the general rules for putting attributes in a document.

6.2 The paragraph element

6.2.1 Introduction

The paragraph is a fundamental structural unit of an HTML document. Paragraphs are block-level elements, which means to say that they can include any of the 20 or so character-level elements which you will find described in the next chapter. They can also include the ubiquitous IMG element for inlined graphics and the anchor element for hypertext links. Within a paragraph you can tag the text to embolden it, to make words appear italic, larger than normal, smaller than normal, as subscripts, superscripts and so on. The possibilities are endless.

6.2.2 Marking up paragraphs

Each paragraph must begin with the familiar <P> start tag. All text up to the next <P> is then considered by the browser to be part of the same paragraph and you can simply type paragraph after paragraph in succession. You don't need to put your own line breaks in between paragraphs – the browser does this for you. Paragraphs do not need an end tag, something which some HTML authors still don't realize. Of course you *can* put an end tag in if you like but this is really not necessary – you can always leave the end tag out. The browser is clever enough to infer the end of a paragraph from context.

Here are three simple paragraphs:

```
<P>Poems are made of words.<P>The poet chooses certain words rather than
others and places them in a particular order; the words combine to produce
an effect on those that read them.<P>It is clear that some study of a
poet's choice and use of words is essential if we are to understand the way
poetry works.
```

These are displayed as:

> Poems are made of words.
>
> The poet chooses certain words rather than others and places them in a particular order; the words combine to produce an effect on those that read them.
>
> It is clear that some study of a poet's choice and use of words is essential if we are to understand the way poetry works.

Although it is common for people to try to do so, you can't put extra space in by inserting 'blank' paragraph tags to pad things out. Even if you try to force a line by inserting lots of extra paragraph tags like this:

```
<P>First line
<P>
<P>
<P>
<P>
<P>Second line
```

the browser will render the text as though those extra paragraph tags simply weren't there. If you do want more (or less) space between paragraphs, the best way to accomplish this is to allocate the paragraph a style, an idea which we will come to later.

6.2.3 Word-wrap

Normally a paragraph will be wrapped round from one line to the next, as happens in most word-processing packages. As the window in which the paragraph is displayed becomes narrower, so the lines are wrapped more frequently to accommodate them; as the window is expanded, so the lines are wrapped less.

6.2.4 Controlling line breaks

There are various ways of controlling line breaks in HTML. One of the simplest is the BR element which comes in handy for creating short lines of text in a paragraph. This tends to be used a great deal for poetry on the Web, for example:

```
<P>I sing of a maiden<BR>That is makeless;<BR>
King of kings<BR>To her son she ches.<BR>
<P>He came all so still<BR>There his mother was<BR>
As dew in April<BR>That falleth on the grass
```

which is rendered:

I sing of a maiden
That is makeless;
King of kings
To her son she ches.

He came all so still,
There his mother was,
As dew in April
That falleth on the grass

> Those who read the latest Netscape updates will realize that BR has recently been expanded. Netscape have added the CLEAR attribute to BR to enable you to control the way that text flows around a left- or right-aligned IMG element in a document. This idea is explained in Chapter 5 which includes various examples to show the effects you can achieve.

Netscape 2.0 uses the NOBR element to mark up sections of text which must not be broken. Text between the start tag <NOBR> and the end tag </NOBR> will not have a line break inserted by the browser at all, for word-wrap is effectively switched off. If, for example, you wanted to keep all this on the same line:

Where are the songs of Spring? Ay, Where are they?

you could use NOBR. The result would be a long unbroken line of text which would not wrap even when the window was made smaller. Now if you know where you would *like* to break the line (that is, if it *has* to be broken, which you hope it won't) then you can use Netscape's WBR (WordBReak) element. For example, below we suggest to the browser that, if necessary, it can break the line after the word 'spring':

```
<P><NOBR>Where are the songs of Spring?<WBR>Ay, Where are they?
</NOBR><BR>
Think not of them, thou hast thy music too
```

This is rendered appropriately:

> Where are the songs of spring? Ay, Where are they?
> Think not of them, thou hast thy music too

Or, less appropriately in a narrow window:

> Where are the songs of spring?
> Ay, Where are they?
> Think not of them, thou hast thy music too

`WBR` corresponds to the conditional breaking space entity of HTML 3, `&cbsp;`. Conditional breaking spaces behave as ordinary spaces but indicate a good place to break the line. Unfortunately the `&cbsp;` entity has not yet been implemented by Netscape.

6.2.5 Preventing a word from being split in the middle between lines

HTML 3 also gives you the option of using a non-breaking space entity ` ` to make sure that the line is not broken at a crucial point in the text. You simply insert the entity at the point where you want the non-breaking space to be. For example:

```
Rolled round in earth's diurnal course
```

If the words 'diurnal course' fall at the end of a line, they will not be split apart. The use of ` ` is implemented in Netscape 1.1 and 2.0.

6.2.6 Hyphens

Another useful HTML 3 entity is `` which defines a soft hyphen. A soft hyphen indicates a place normally invisible but which is a good point to break the word if need be. For example:

```
hyphen&shy;ated
```

will appear as:

> hyphenated

or, at the end of a line, it may be split onto the next:

> hyphen-
> ated

A hard hyphen, by contrast, is one which is a visible hyphen joining two parts of a word. For English documents, browsers will assume hard hyphens to be good places to break regardless of whether word-wrap is on or off.

6.2.7 Alignment of paragraphs

Paragraphs can be aligned with the `ALIGN` attribute which is used to specify the horizontal alignment of the text:

- `<P ALIGN=left>` means that the paragraph is rendered by the browser as flush left. This is the default alignment and is used if the `ALIGN` attribute is not inserted into the mark-up.
- `<P ALIGN=center>` means that the paragraph is centred.
- `<P ALIGN=right>` means that the paragraph is rendered flush right.
- `<P ALIGN=justify>` means that the paragraph is justified by the browser where practical; otherwise the paragraph is displayed left-aligned.

The ultimate shape that a paragraph assumes on the screen is naturally also a function of window size. Netscape 2.0 allows you to align paragraphs left, right or centred but not (yet) justified.

6.2.8 Paragraph styles

In desktop publishing you work with a number of paragraph styles which are kept in a template. The idea of paragraph styles in HTML is something relatively new and is accomplished with the aid of style sheets. A style sheet is the HTML equivalent of a template. It is written in a simple language and is attached to a document via the `LINK` element in the document head. The list of styles to apply can be included in the `STYLE` element. The styles in this example specify paragraphs with a drop-cap initial and small-caps text:

```
<HTML>
 <HEAD>
  <TITLE>Gothic influences</TITLE>
  <STYLE NOTATION=CSS>
   P  : text-effect=drop-cap
   P  : font-size=12pt
   P  : first-font-size=24pt
   EM : font-style=small-caps
  </STYLE>
 </HEAD>
<BODY>
  <P><EM>The late</EM> eighteenth and nineteenth century interest in the
Gothic (all things medieval and mysterious) influences Keats in the Eve of
St Agnes
 </BODY>
</HTML>
```

The above could be formatted as:

> THE LATE eighteenth and nineteenth century interest in the Gothic (all things medieval and mysterious) influences Keats in the Eve of St Agnes

This is just a taste of what is to come. Style sheets are an important and developing area of HTML 3 and are demonstrated by the Arena browser. The use of style sheets makes many of the fussy stylistic extensions to HTML 2.0 and 3 unnecessary. Mark-up is much simpler – you don't, for example, have to resort to such fiddly elements as `FONT` to get the effects you want. Style sheets are the subject of Chapter 14.

6.3 Tabs

6.3.1 Introduction

People familiar with desktop publishing packages will also be familiar with the concept of left tabs, right tabs, decimal tabs, centre tabs and so on. The main reason for introducing the `TAB` element into HTML 3 is to simplify importing documents prepared from DTP packages. Also, although it is possible to produce similar effects to tabs by using tables, this is a very cumbersome approach. The `TAB` element is much more convenient.

In conventional DTP packages tab stops tend to be associated with a particular paragraph style in the document. The tab stops are positioned in terms of so many millimetres or tenths of inches from the left-hand margin. In HTML where you don't know how wide the window is, or what size of font will be used to display the paragraph, this approach is impractical. Since the window varies in size and since the font is unknown to the author, the whole way in which tabs are done is quite different. The approach taken by HTML is to allow the author to specify how far along into the text line the tab should appear. You say 'let's have a tab *here*' and define it *in situ*. You give it a name, and reuse the same tab stop again and again in the document.

This in contrast to a DTP package where, if you define a tab for a given paragraph, that tab is available for that paragraph only. In HTML you can set named tab stops which can then be used for the rest of the document. This idea will become apparent when you look at the example below.

> A tab can be put any place where you can put the `BR` element. `TAB` is a character-level element.

6.3.2 Simple example

```
<P><B>noct<TAB ID=t1>ambulant</B> - walking at night<BR>
<TAB TO=t1>(from Latin: <I>NOX NOCTIS</I> night + <I>ambulare</I> walk)
```

which is rendered as:

> **noctambulant** – walking at night
> (from Latin: *NOX NOCTIS* night + *ambulare* walk)

The tab has been set to a position along the line corresponding to after 'noct' and before 'ambulant'. The position of a tab is where you define it. This idea is borrowed from the text processing language Latex and is really rather nifty.

This tab is identified for future use by giving it an `ID`, in this case `t1`. The tab `ID` should be unique within the document and composed of an initial letter followed by letters, digits or hyphens.

- `ID` is used to name a new tab stop at the current position.
- `TO` specifies a previously defined tab stop.

6.3.3 Aligning text on a tab

The `ALIGN` attribute can be used to explicitly specify the horizontal alignment.

- `ALIGN=left` (the default) causes all text after the tab to left align until a new tab is encountered or a line break occurs.
- `ALIGN=center` causes following text up to the next tab stop or line break to be centred on the designated tab stop. If the `TO` attribute is missing, it centres the text between the current left and right margins.
- `ALIGN=right` causes text up to the next tab stop or line break to be rendered flush right to the designated tab stop. If the `TO` attribute is missing, it renders the text flush right against the current right margin.
- `ALIGN=char` The following text is searched for the first occurrence of the character representing the decimal point. The text up to the next tab or line break is then aligned such that the decimal point (or character) starts at the designated tab stop.

The `CHAR` attribute is used to specify the character to be used with `ALIGN=char`, for example `CHAR="."` (the default) or ','. The default depends on the language as set by the `LANG` attribute. The French and Germans use ',' while the English use '.'. See also Chapter 10 on tables: alignment within a table cell is done in much the same way. This use of CHAR must be combined with use of the TO attribute.

6.3.4 Splitting a line into a left and right component using tabs

Sometimes, you may want to make the remainder of the line flush right while leaving the earlier words unmoved. You do this also with the ALIGN attribute. This is very difficult with tables and this method works much better. For example:

```
Left part of line<TAB ALIGN=right>and right part of line.
```

which is rendered as:

Left part of line   and right part of line.

6.3.5 When not to use tabs

If you want detailed control of a paragraph and realize that you need to use lots of tabs in complex ways, you should ask yourself whether a table is needed. If you want this kind of effect:

nuts	oil	eggs
flour	salt	sugar
pepper	apple	milk

then use a table, and not tabs. Tabs are there for simple things. Another alternative to using tabs is to use a style sheet. If you want, for example, to indent the first line of each paragraph, you can reference a predefined style by using perhaps <P CLASS=indent> in your mark-up. See Chapter 14.

6.4 Headings

6.4.1 Introduction

Headings are easy to insert in HTML and, although you will probably only want headings as far as level 3, HTML defines six levels of headings in all. A heading element simply tells the browser what kind of heading you would like: the browser determines all the font changes, paragraph breaks before and after, and any white space necessary to render it on the screen. The heading elements are H1, H2, H3, H4, H5 and H6 with H1 being the highest (or most important) level and H6 the least.

Heading elements have the same content model as paragraphs, that is, text and character-level mark-up such as character emphasis, inlined images and math.

6.4.2 Example of the six levels of headings

These are the six levels of headings as they were rendered on the Netscape browser. The headings were marked up quite simply as:

```
<H1>Major Rumple</H1>
<H2>Captain Haddock</H2>
<H3>Lieutenant Klein</H3>
<H4>Sergeant-Major Jones</H4>
<H5>Lance-Corporal Smith</H5>
<H6>Abbie-the-Cat</H6>
```

Major Rumple

Captain Haddock

Lieutenant Klein

Sergeant-Major Jones

Lance-Corporal Smith

Abbie-the-Cat

6.4.3 Alignment of headings

Headings are usually rendered flush left. The `ALIGN` attribute can be used to explicitly specify the horizontal alignment:

- `ALIGN=left` which renders the heading flush left (the default);
- `ALIGN=center` which does as you would expect and centres the heading on the screen;

- `ALIGN=right` which renders the heading flush right;

- `ALIGN=justify` which renders the heading justified where practical, otherwise this gives the same effect as the default `ALIGN=left` setting.

6.4.4 Numbering headings in HTML 3

The combination of style sheets together with new HTML 3 attributes allows headings to be numbered. Whereas previously headings played a relatively simple role in document mark-up, now that they can be numbered, they become all the more important in specifying the hierarchical structure of a document. HTML 3 also provides facilities for authors to specify a custom graphic for a heading.

The role of the style sheet in numbering headings

Each heading may be given a style in the style sheet by using the CLASS attribute. For example:

```
<H2 CLASS=numbered-simple>
```

Styles in the style sheet may in turn specify:

- whether or not a heading has a number;
- which style is used for that number: whether Arabic, upper roman, lower roman, upper alphanumeric or lower alphanumeric, or a numbering scheme appropriate to the current language;
- whether the parent numbering is inherited, in other words whether for an H1 heading numbered 2, the H2 headings are numbered 2.1, 2.2, and so on, and the H3 headings 2.1.1, 2.1.2 and so on;
- the positioning of the number and the font used to portray it on the screen.

The role of HTML in numbering headers

HTML 3 provides two attributes which can override the default treatment of header sequence numbers. These are:

(1) SEQNUM which is used to set the sequence number associated with the header level of the current element to a given number. For example, SEQNUM=9 starts the sequence at 9.

> The numbering sequence is usually set to 1 at the beginning of the document and then incremented after each heading element. It is reset to 1 by any element of a higher level, so that a Heading 1 element resets the sequence numbers for H2 to H6. In practice this means, for example, that if you had:
>
> H1 numbered as 1
> H2 numbered as 1.1
> H3 numbered as 1.1.1
>
> a second H1 element would increment all as follows:
>
> H1 to 1
> H1 to 2
> H2 to 2.2
> H3 to 2.2.1

(2) SKIP which allows you to do two things:

(a) It allows you to say that you want certain numbers skipped out of the heading sequence. For instance, rather than 1, 2, 3, 4... you want 1, 2, 6, 7... For example:

```
<H1 CLASS=numbered>Soup</H1>
<H1 CLASS=numbered>Cauliflower cheese</H1>
<H1 CLASS=numbered SKIP=3>Chocolate Mousse</H1>
<H1 CLASS=numbered>Fruit</H1>
```

which might be rendered:

1 Soup
2 Cauliflower cheese
6 Chocolate mousse
7 Fruit

SKIP has been used to increment the heading number after 'cauliflower cheese'.

(b) It allows you to miss out a heading from the numbering sequence. Here you need to use SKIP in a slightly different way.

First you need to mark up the element with a style which specifies an unnumbered heading. This should be present in the style sheet. Having done this, you insert SKIP=-1 immediately after the unnumbered heading in your document. Why? Because the browser insists on counting all the headings regardless of whether or not they are numbered on the screen:

```
<H1 CLASS=numbered>Soup</H1>
<H1 CLASS=unnumbered SKIP=-1>Cauliflower cheese</H1>
<H1 CLASS=numbered>Chocolate mousse</H1>
<H1 CLASS=numbered>Fruit</H1>
```

which would result in:

1 Soup
Cauliflower cheese
2 Chocolate mousse
3 Fruit

Without the SKIP=-1 inserted, you would get:

1 Soup
Cauliflower cheese
3 Chocolate mousse
4 Fruit

6.4.5 Using a graphic with a heading

With HTML 3 you can associate a graphic with a heading. The DINGBAT attribute specifies an iconic image to appear preceding the header. The icon is specified as an entity name. A list of standard icon entity names for HTML 3 is given in Appendix H. The attribute SRC specifies an image to appear preceding the header. The image is specified as a URL.

6.4.6 Other attributes which can be used with headings

These are:

- NOWRAP which is used when you don't want the browser to automatically wrap lines. You can switch word-wrap off for a header element and then use BR to insert line breaks.
- MD to specify a message digest – see Chapter 4.
- CLEAR which allows you to control whether a heading is placed alongside or below a graphic or a table in the margin – see Chapter 4.

6.5 Preformatted text

6.5.1 Introduction

Preformatted text, which is specified using the <PRE> and </PRE> tags, is rendered using a fixed-pitched font. In preformatted text, white-space characters (principally space, line feed and carriage return) and also <BR> tags are treated literally. This means that each space you insert when authoring the text is exactly depicted on the screen when the text is displayed. This is in contrast to other tags for which repeated white-space characters entered are collapsed to a single space character, and line breaks are introduced automatically by the browser.

6.5.2 Simple example

One of the things you find on the Web is lyrics of songs. These are almost invariably written using preformatted text which is hardly surprising because it's a simple way of getting round the problems of getting indents and line breaks in the right places. The text and white space in the PRE element come out more or less exactly as you put them in. It's a bit of a giveaway that the result is rendered in a fixed-width font like Courier, but this is unimportant for those who simply want the words of songs rather than an especially beautiful presentation. Here's the first verse of the chorus in Carl Orff's *Carmina Burana* which is no doubt 'somewhere on the Web':

```
<PRE>
O fortuna
Velut luna
stratu variabilis
semper crescis
aut decrescis
vita detestabilis
nunc obdurat
et tunc curat
ludo mentis aciem
egestatem,
potestatem
dissolvit ut glaciem.</PRE>
```

It comes out just as you type it in:

```
O fortuna
Velut luna
stratu variabilis
semper crescis
aut decrescis
vita detestabilis
nunc obdurat
et tunc curat
ludo mentis aciem
egestatem,
potestatem
dissolvit ut glaciem.
```

In preformatted text, carriage returns and line feeds within the text are rendered as a move to the beginning of the next line, with the exception of line breaks immediately following the starting PRE tag, or immediately preceding the ending PRE tag. These should be ignored by the browser.

Here is an entire 'table' done with the PRE element, taken from some Web pages telling you about forthcoming concerts in California. There can be no doubt that PRE does the job, although a real HTML table might have been a better choice. The information is there anyway, which is by far the most important thing!

```
<PRE>
TU OCT  3 OPEN MIKE - at Morgan's Coffee and Tea, sign up at 7pm, 7:30pm
           show.  373-1479 This has become the hottest open mike in the
           area -- often more artists than there is time to hear them
           all.  Every Tuesday night at Morgan's.

TH OCT  5 BOX SET - at Morgan's Coffee and Tea, 8pm,  373-1479
           Box Set has been a big favorite at music festivals this
           Summer.  This show is the acoustic duo version of the group,
           they also have an electric, 5 person band.
```

```
FR OCT  6 BARBARA KESSLER - at Morgan's Coffee and Tea, 8pm 373-1479
            Barbara has been receiving a great response from fans around
            the country.  Her song, "The Date" was featured on the
            Martha's Vineyard Songwriter's album.</PRE>
```

6.5.3 Avoid...

The <P> tag should be avoided in preformatted text, but for robustness, browsers normally treat these tags as line breaks. Block-level elements such as headers, lists, FIG and TABLE should be avoided in preformatted text.

6.5.4 You can include...

Anchor elements for hypertext links may be included in preformatted text, also the character-level elements described in Chapter 3 and FORM elements.

6.5.5 Attributes used with the PRE element

These are ID, LANG, CLEAR and CLASS, all of which are described in Chapter 4.

6.6 Quotations

6.6.1 Introduction

HTML needs to cater for two kinds of quotations: simple inlined quotations of a few words long, and longer quotations of perhaps several lines – extended quotations.

6.6.2 Short inlined quotes

Short inlined quotes a few words long can be included with the character-level element Q. This has the simple effect of placing the relevant characters in quotes using the quote marks appropriate to the language – different quote marks would be used for, say, Spanish than English.

An example of the Q element to mark up a quote:

```
<P>The guinea-pig squeaked loudly. <Q>He's hungry</Q> said Jack.
```

which might be rendered:

> The guinea-pig squeaked loudly. 'He's hungry' said Jack.

This element is also discussed in Chapter 7.

6.6.3 Longer quotations

The BLOCKQUOTE element is currently implemented on browsers such as Netscape. The HTML 3 equivalent is the shorter BQ which is similar in function but with a quicker name to type. BQ also has a CREDIT element to allow the source of the quotation to be credited, for example as follows:

```
<BQ>
<P>To study history one must know in advance that one is attempting
something fundamentally impossible, yet necessary and highly important. To
study history means submitting to chaos and nevertheless retaining faith in
order and meaning. It is a very serious task, young man, and possibly a
tragic one.
<CREDIT>Hermann Hesse<BR>
The Glass Bead Game<BR>
</CREDIT>
</BQ>
```

6.6.4 Attributes which can used with BQ

You can use the ID attribute together with BQ so that you can jump to a quote from somewhere else in the same document or even from another document.

- LANG, CLASS, CLEAR and NOWRAP are also proposed as attributes for BQ in HTML 3. The BR element can be used in the usual way to control line breaks with NOWRAP.

6.7 Footnotes

6.7.1 Introduction

HTML 3 includes an element FN for inserting footnotes into a document. The intention is that footnotes should not be placed at the bottom of the page as in a paper document (there is no general concept of 'bottom of the page' as such) and that instead, browsers should either display footnotes in pop-up boxes or place all footnotes at the end of the document.

6.7.2 Simple example of footnotes

To define a footnote, you use the FN element. In the example from a Shakespeare play below, we want the footnote to explain the meaning of the phrases *inoculate, relish of it* and *indifferent honest*:

```
<DL><DT>Hamlet: <DD>You should not have believed me, for virtue cannot so
<A HREF="#fn1">inoculate</A> our old stock but we shall <A
HREF="#fn2">relish of it</A>. I loved you not.
<DT>Ophelia: <DD>I was the more deceived.
<DT>Hamlet: <DD>Get thee to a nunnery. Why wouldst thou be a breeder of
sinners? I am myself <A HREF="#fn3">indifferent honest</A> . . . </DL>
<FN ID=fn1><I>inoculate</I> - graft</FN>
<FN ID=fn2><I>relish of it</I> - smack of it (our old sinful nature)</FN>
<FN ID=fn3><I>indifferent honest</I> - moderately virtuous</FN>
```

The text would be rendered something like this:

Hamlet: You should not have believed me, for virtue cannot so inoculate our old stock but we shall relish of it. I loved you not.

Ophelia: I was the more deceived.

Hamlet: Get thee to a nunnery. Why wouldst thou be a breeder of sinners? I am myself indifferent honest

Then, as footnotes:

inoculate – graft
relish of it – smack of it (our old sinful nature)
indifferent honest – moderately virtuous

The first footnote is inserted as follows:

```
<FN ID=fn1><I>inoculate</I> - graft</FN>
```

The start tag is <FN ID=fn1> or 'this footnote's ID is fn1'. The word to associate with the footnote is then highlighted by using italics; finally </FN> completes the footnote.

Other footnotes are defined in a similar manner:

```
<FN ID=fn2><I>relish of it</I> - smack of it (our old sinful nature)</FN>
<FN ID=fn3><I>indifferent honest</I> - moderately virtuous</FN>
```

Note: REL=footnote is recommended especially if footnotes are in a different file. This is used by the browser to get pop-up behaviour.

In each case the attribute ID has been assigned a value which determines which footnote should be displayed if the reader clicks on a chosen word.

Once you have defined one note by using FN and ID combined as above, you can of course map other words in the text to the same footnote. You can also link a word in a different file to the footnote and it is thus possible to use footnotes to build up a kind of glossary of terms for a complete publication distributed across more than one server.

6.7.3 Attributes associated with FN

Apart from ID which has been dealt with above, these are LANG and CLASS, explained in Chapter 4.

6.8 Cautions, warnings and other admonishments

6.8.1 Introduction

Cautions, warnings and admonishments of the sort you see in technical documentation are introduced in HTML 3 by using the NOTE element. The NOTE element instructs the browser that it should render the element in a side-note, in a box, or in some other appropriate way. In a DTP package, you would normally invent your own style for each kind of note: HTML 3 aims to provide the author with ready-made styles for the purpose.

6.8.2 The use of CLASS to determine the style of rendering

The NOTE element uses the CLASS attribute to tell the browser which type of note is involved. The CLASS specifies a style which includes the icon to display, together with any other preferences for rendering it. In other words, each type of note should have a different CLASS so that it is portrayed on the screen in its own idiosyncratic manner. For example:

```
<NOTE CLASS=caution> Do not attempt to disconnect your husband's computer
while he is accessing the Web over a modem link, by picking up the phone.
```

might be rendered as follows:

Do not attempt to disconnect your husband's computer while he is accessing the Web over a modem link, by picking up the phone.

Similarly,

```
<NOTE CLASS=warning> Rabbits will eat through electric cables if let loose
near a computer.
```

might be rendered as follows:

Rabbits will eat through electric cables if let loose near a computer.

In fact you would probably use a standard warning icon for this kind of note, but there would be no reason why a style sheet could not specify any icon of your choosing!

6.8.3 An alternative approach

An alternative treatment of notes is simply to use CLASS with P. For example:

```
<P CLASS=caution>
```

In other words the note is a function of a particular style of paragraph.

6.9 The DIV (division) element

6.9.1 Introduction

The DIV element is an HTML 3 element used for structuring documents. It is used to provide a means of giving 'containers' – chapters, sections, appendices, abstracts, and so on – different styles. DIV has a general content type which means that it can include a series of elements, such as paragraphs, tables, lists, headings and so on. From a stylistic point of view these can then be treated as a single unit by the browser. For example, an 'abstract' could have all its paragraphs and tables displayed in a different font from a 'chapter'. A 'side bar' could have all its paragraphs enclosed in a border, and so on.

6.9.2 DIV and style sheets

Stylistic differences for structural units of documents are achieved by associating each DIV element with its own style, The style – such as italic text in a chosen colour, or text of a particular size – is specified by using the CLASS attribute and the functionality of DIV is thus intimately woven with style sheets. For example:

```
<DIV CLASS=border>
...
</DIV>
```

would give all elements between the start and end tags a style which included a border.

6.9.3 Simple support of DIV by Netscape

Netscape currently supports very simple use of DIV to allow you to left-align, right-align, or centre a section of a document:

```
<DIV ALIGN=right>
...
...
</DIV>
```

All elements between the DIV start and end tags will be aligned to the right. Thus paragraphs, lists, tables, and so on will all be right-aligned between the start and finish of DIV.

6.9.4 Attributes used with DIV

These are: LANG, CLASS, ID, NOWRAP, ALIGN and CLEAR. See Chapter 4 for more information on those not described in this chapter. The ALIGN attribute in HTML 3 has the values left, right, justify and center.

6.10 The ADDRESS element

This is a rather old element which is a little vague in its use. The ADDRESS element is intended to contain information about the author of the document, such as name and address. It can also be used for including 'mailto' links, special links that start an email program on some servers and let the user send email to the Web page owner. The most general way of providing your email address is inside the ADDRESS element.

An example:

```
<ADDRESS>
The Editor<BR>
45, Bridge Street,<BR>
Acton-in-the-Woods<BR>
Berkshire<BR>
RG56 34T<BR>
Tel: +144 (123) 456 789
</ADDRESS>
```

7
CHARACTER EMPHASIS

In this chapter:

- 'Presentation' tags which attempt to control directly the appearance of text (Section 7.2)
- 'Informational' tags which indicate the meaning or purpose of marked-up text (Section 7.3)
- Tags using elements you have defined yourself (Section 7.4)

7.1 Introduction

As explained already, you the author do not have control over the display devices other people use to view your documents. You are writing something which has a surprising property: you do not know its appearance to your readers, but you do have control over what you say and mean. If you want better control, you will want to use an HTML 3 style sheet: the alternative is the proliferation of complicated tags in response to your pleadings – some such tags can unfortunately already be found in this chapter.

In the case of character mark-up, we can divide the tags into two groups:

- those few tags which actually say how text is to be presented, if possible (Section 7.2);
- the rest of the character-level tags, which give information on the purpose of the mark-up, leaving the device (or a style sheet) to choose the display style (Section 7.3).

7.2 Character-level presentation tags

HTML does allow you direct control over some text renderings, using tags to put text into **bold face**, to $_{\text{subscript}}$ it, and so on. These generally only make sense for visual display though `<BIG>` could be rendered in speech, for instance, by a louder voice.

In contrast, researchers have developed consistent ways of rendering informational mark-up as complicated as mathematical subscripts in speech. Equally, it is possible to adopt speech styles which handle quoted text, emphasis, and other informational mark-up in ways readily intelligible to blind users, even if generated automatically by a speech synthesizer.

Most of these presentation styles will be familiar to you through their popularity in word processor programs. These tags are discussed here (in alphabetical order), with mark-up and rendering examples. Remember that tags are not case sensitive; you can write your mark-up in upper or lower case.

7.2.1 <B> bold

Bold face is very widely used to distinguish items under discussion, and for many kinds of emphasis. Since HTML provides explicit tags for headings (such as `<H3>...</H3>`) and many other document structures, you should consider whether simple bolding is really what you want.

HTML: `Come all you <B>sailors bold</B> and draw near!`

Rendering: Come all you **sailors bold** and draw near!

7.2.2 <BIG> big print

Big specifies that the font used for the enclosed text should be larger than usual. See also `<SMALL>`.

HTML: `<BIG>O</BIG>nce upon a time,`

Rendering: Once upon a time,

7.2.3 <I> italics

Italics are useful for many purposes, and are conventionally employed to draw the reader's attention to a word or short phrase that is not as the reader might have expected.

HTML: ... but it was during the <I>Italian renaissance</I> that ...

Rendering: ... but it was during the *Italian renaissance* that ...

7.2.4 <S> strikethrough

Strikethrough directly reduces the legibility of text. Its traditional use is to indicate suggested deletions or to record actual deletions, so that reduced legibility is not a major problem (and may be desirable). The recording of deletions implies a rather formal style of document management, which might be better handled using the <INS> and <DEL> elements, accompanied by some kind of automatic change control and configuration management.

HTML: <STRIKE>mistake</STRIKE> message

Rendering: ~~mistake~~ message

7.2.5 <SMALL> small print

Small specifies that the font used for the enclosed text should be smaller than usual. See also <BIG>.

HTML: whereas <SMALL>whispered</SMALL> conversation seems sibilant.

Rendering: whereas whispered conversation seems sibilant.

7.2.6 <SUB> subscript

Subscripting is necessary in much mathematical and engineering work. For short equations or individual symbols, it is probably easier than using HTML 3's <MATH>, and it is available on existing HTML 2.0 browsers. A disadvantage is that such symbols would be missed by a search for <MATH> tags. For instance:

HTML: pH = -Log₁₀(H)

Rendering: $pH = -Log_{10}(H)$

7.2.7 <SUP> superscript

Superscripting, like subscripting, is very useful for many scientific applications. Again, it may be easier than using <MATH> for short equations (and <MATH> will not be available immediately).

HTML: `e=mc<SUP>2</SUP>`
Rendering: $e = mc^2$

7.2.8 <TT> fixed-width 'teletype-style' font

Teletype font is very helpful when you want to show the reader that text is typed. Since it is also fixed-pitch, it can be useful for simple formatting of characters.

HTML:
```
<P>Jane typed:
<TT> I am learning to type </TT>
with grandpa's Imperial.
```
Rendering: Jane typed: `I am learning to type` with grandpa's Imperial.

7.2.9 <U> underlined (RARELY SUPPORTED)

Underlining used to be used in many places where bold and italics are now more popular. Mechanical typewriters and line-printers were able to apply underlining by simple overstriking with the underline key. Since underlining affects readability when the line crosses descenders of letters such as p, q and g, we can perhaps suggest that underlining ought to be a rare means of emphasis. It is currently not widely supported by browsers.

HTML: `<U>Potamogeton fluitans</U>`
Rendering: Potamogeton fluitans

Scientific (Linnean) names of species, as in this example, are nowadays widely printed in italics, so <I>. . .</I> may be more appropriate as well as being more likely to be supported by your readers' browsers.

7.2.10 Extension tags which control presentation

Netscape have introduced a few elements specifically to enable authors to control presentation, and are proposing that these be introduced as HTML 3. Other enterprises are implementing the same elements, so they may become *de facto* standards. Microsoft is also making extensions here.

<FONT SIZE=value> relative or absolute font sizing

Font sizes and colours are best set in style sheets.

Netscape browsers can be instructed to change the size of the font used for any part of a paragraph with the FONT element and its SIZE attribute.

The SIZE attribute is treated as absolute if a digit in the range 1 to 7 is supplied: 1 means the smallest Netscape font, 7 means the largest. (Exactly what these are depends on the configuration of the browser.) So, for instance, <FONT SIZE=2> tells the Netscape browser to use the second-smallest font.

The SIZE attribute is treated as relative to the document's Netscape BASEFONT if a sign is attached to the digit. So, for instance, <FONT SIZE=+2> tells the browser to increase the size of the font by two Netscape size steps, such as from the BASEFONT size 3 (the default) to size 5.

HTML:

```
Little fingers need <FONT SIZE=+3>Big building
blocks.</FONT>
```

Rendering: Little fingers need Big building blocks.

Another attribute is COLOR for drawing the text. For example COLOR=Red or COLOR="#c00000" using the RGB format. See Section 11.3 for details.

Microsoft's contribution similarly chips away with attributes which might be better in style sheets. <FONT FACE=Arial>, for example, specifies that browsers should attempt to use a Swiss typeface such as Arial, Geneva or Helvetica if any such is available to them, and if no local setting for typeface has been made. The problems inherent in this approach are evident.

<BASEFONT SIZE=value> base font sizing

The extension <FONT SIZE=value> tag operates when in relative mode with respect to the BASEFONT, which is by default size 3. It can be changed to any value in the range 1 to 7. The effect is to change the sizes of text in the document. To get default (size 3) text with BASEFONT set to 1, for instance, you have separately to specify a size of +2:

HTML:

```
<BASEFONT SIZE=1>Three blind mice!
                         <!--new default-->
<FONT SIZE=+2>See how they run!
                         <!--temporarily normal again-->
```

Rendering: Three blind mice! See how they run!

It is undesirable to set BASEFONT more than once in a document.

<CENTER> text centring

There is an extension to HTML to centre text on the page. Whereas HTML 3 treats centring as a paragraph attribute (<P ALIGN=center>), the deprecated extension <CENTER>...</CENTER> applies only to the text included within it, so it is effectively a character mark-up element.

HTML: `<CENTER>Madam,<BR>I'<BR>m "Adam"</CENTER>`

Rendering:

Madam,
I'
m 'Adam'

Note that the approved way to centre text in HTML is to use `<DIV ALIGN=center>...</DIV>`, or the `ALIGN` attribute in headers (`<H3 ALIGN=center>`) or paragraphs.

<MARQUEE> **animated text**

Microsoft's Internet Explorer, free for Windows 95, includes its own extensions to HTML. If these become popular they will presumably be taken up by other browsers. One such is `MARQUEE`, which animates text in the manner of a sign advertising a musical on Broadway. This is a zippy feature whose designers have really let their hair down, judging by the number of attributes, mostly unique to the element. We'll try to cover them briefly; if anything makes the case for a tightly controlled standard, this is it.

`<MARQUEE ALIGN=top>` makes the scrolling text align with the top of the marquee. Other values are `middle` and `bottom`.

`BEHAVIOR=scroll` is the default. The text scrolls on to the display (from the left) and then scrolls off it (to the right). `BEHAVIOR=slide` scrolls in and sticks there. `BEHAVIOR=alternate` bounces horribly back and forth.

`BGCOLOR=Fuchsia` lets you specify the background colour for the marquee, either as a lump of hexadecimal such as `BGCOLOR=#FF0000` or using a tastefully named colour. The code means red-green-blue, with FF meaning level 255 (maximum) for red, and 00 meaning level 0 (nothing) for green and for blue; you can use any hexi-levels in between. The example therefore indicates red (max), green (none), blue (none) which results in bright red. See Section 11.3. The named colours which you can use with the `BGCOLOR` attribute are: `Black`, `Maroon`, `Green`, `Olive`, `Navy`, `Purple`, `Teal`, `Gray`, `Silver`, `Red`, `Lime`, `Yellow`, `Blue`, `Fuchsia`, `Aqua` and `White`. Don't cringe.

`DIRECTION=right` makes the text scroll from right to left instead of the usual left to right. The values might have been better named `LTR` (left to right) and `RTL` (right to left) in line with the `DIR` attribute which controls the direction of display of (static) text.

`HEIGHT` and `WIDTH` let you size the marquee either in pixels or as a percentage of the screen height or width respectively. For example, `<MARQUEE HEIGHT=50% WIDTH=80%>`.

SCROLLAMOUNT sets the size of the step in pixels from one redrawing of the marquee text to the next. If you make it large the marquee effectively seems to move more quickly but also more jerkily.

SCROLLDELAY sets the delay in milliseconds before the marquee starts its next cycle.

HSPACE and VSPACE set the left/right and top/bottom margins respectively in pixels, for example HSPACE=5.

For example:

```
<MARQUEE BGCOLOR=lime BEHAVIOR=alternate SCROLLAMOUNT=3 SCROLLDELAY=50
HEIGHT=40% VSPACE=20 LOOP=666>A programmer's approach to HTML.</MARQUEE>
```

7.3 Character-level informational tags

The alternative to the presentation approach just described is the **informational** approach, where the tags are associated not with a desired appearance but with an intended purpose.

NEW standard HTML 2.0

A simple instance of HTML's informational approach comes with the tags <EM> and <STRONG> to emphasize text. For example:

```
I <EM>specially</EM> like <STRONG>dark</STRONG> chocolates.
```

Most browsers choose to render this example as something like:

I *specially* like **dark** chocolates.

<EM> is typically italic, though you should not assume this. <STRONG> is typically bold, but you should not assume that either. A very simple screen handler with only one font option might instead render the example as:

```
I _specially_ like *dark* chocolates.
```

Lynx, one of the best-known text-only browsers, ignores both <EM> and <STRONG>.

If you have a high-resolution screen with a width of, say, 1200 pixels, you may easily come to assume that text specially formatted for your screen will look good everywhere. Remember that on, say, an 800-pixel wide screen (typical of VGA monitors with older personal computers and many notebooks) the results may not be so attractive.

Other users may have 'dumb' terminals capable only of text (80 characters × 24 rows); blind users may have Braille or speech-output devices. Informational elements such as <EM> can be rendered appropriately on all such devices, whereas presentation elements such as <I> cannot.

The informational character-level tags are described in alphabetical order, except that the group of tags that describe fragments of computer programs (<CMD>, <ARG> and <VAR>) are described together at the end of this section. All the renderings shown are illustrative examples; browsers will certainly vary in their handling of these tags.

7.3.1 <ABBREV> abbreviation

Abbreviations are meant for standard phrases which are not acronyms. Again, the tag can be searched for, to help to ensure that all jargon used is properly explained.

HTML: `<ABBREV>e.g.</ABBREV>`
Rendering: e.g.

7.3.2 <ACRONYM> acronym

Acronyms are far too abundant in many documents nowadays, even or perhaps especially when they actually convey rather little technical information. The <ACRONYM> element helps to control the spread of undefined jargon by making it easy to identify and hence to describe all the abbreviated names used in a document.

HTML: `<ACRONYM>NASA</ACRONYM>`
Rendering: NASA

7.3.3 <AU> author's name

The author tag defines a document's author.

HTML: `<AU>Phil Penpusher</AU>`
Rendering: Phil Penpusher

7.3.4 <CITE> citation

Citations are normally used to supply references to books, journals and papers in sufficient detail to enable the reader to find them in a library. <CITE> differs from <A HREF=...> in not creating a hypertext link (which would allow the reader to find the document simply by clicking on the link anchor). Citations are useful in enabling programs to collect up references to documents, even if they are not available online.

HTML: `<CITE>Patanjali,Yoga Sutras, No. 2, India</CITE>`
Rendering: Patanjali,Yoga Sutras, No. 2, India

You can combine the use of <CITE> with <A HREF=...> to indicate that a link is also a formal or scientific document reference:

HTML:
```
<CITE><A HREF="patanj.html">
            <IMG SRC="yogafrog.gif">
            Patanjali,Yoga Sutras, No. 2, India
      </A>
</CITE>
```

Rendering:  Patanjali,Yoga Sutras, No. 2, India

7.3.5 <CODE> specimen of program code

The code tag indicates a piece of computer program code. The rendering is usually a fixed-pitch font as with <TT>, <PRE> and <KBD>, but its logical meaning is different. The use of the <CODE> tag enables filters to search for and extract the program code from documents for further processing.

HTML:
```
<CODE>For i=0 To MaxChars Do ProcessChar(i)</CODE>
```

Rendering: `For i=0 To MaxChars Do ProcessChar(i)`

You should use <CODE> instead of <CMD> and <ARG> when you have several command words to annotate. In this example, you would otherwise need to mark up each of the commands `For`, `To`, `Do` and `ProcessChar` with `<CMD>...</CMD>` which would quickly become unworkably complicated.

7.3.6 <DEL> deleted text

The deleted text tag marks the enclosed text as formally deleted from, for instance, a legal document. Browsers may render deleted text in strikethrough (like <S>) but are not obliged to do so.

HTML:
```
Plaintiff shall be understood to mean <DEL>Mr</DEL> Mrs
Jones.
```

Rendering: Plaintiff shall be understood to mean ~~Mr~~ Mrs Jones.

7.3.7 <DFN> defining instance of a term

The definition tag is intended to supply a defining instance of a term used elsewhere in a document.

HTML:
```
<DFN>flaming means (inadvisedly) attacking ad
hominem</DFN>
```

Rendering: flaming means (inadvisedly) attacking ad hominem

7.3.8 <INS> inserted text

The inserted text tag marks the enclosed text as formally inserted into, for instance, a legal document (compare with <DEL> for deleted text). Browsers may use formatting such as underscore to indicate inserted text.

HTML:
```
Plaintiffs shall be understood to mean <INS>Mr and</INS>
Mrs Jones.
```
Rendering: Plaintiffs shall be understood to mean Mr and Mrs Jones.

7.3.9 <KBD> something for the user to type in

The keyboard tag indicates text which the user can type in. It is more specific in meaning than <TT> and should be used in preference to it, if you want to indicate 'now it's your turn', rather than simply 'this is text'. Its purpose is primarily for use in instruction manuals.

The example shows a command (<CMD>) with an argument (<ARG>) and the name of a key ('<ENTER>'), together forming something for the user to type in at the keyboard. Notice the special treatment of the angle brackets (<...>), to prevent the browser from reading them as part of a tag.

HTML:
```
<KBD>
        <CMD>format</CMD>
        <ARG>c:</ARG>
        &lt;ENTER&gt;
</KBD>
```
Rendering: `format c: <ENTER>`

7.3.10 <LANG> language context

The language tag allows you to specify the language context separately, instead of having to do this repeatedly in other character-level elements with the LANG attribute (see <Q> below for illustration). The tag is especially useful when a document contains sections in several languages.

7.3.11 <PERSON> proper name

The person tag is intended to distinguish proper names. Again, this tag can readily be searched for, making it easy to construct an index of people mentioned in a text. The <AU> tag should be used in preference for authors' names.

HTML:
```
<PERSON>Shankaracharya</PERSON>
```
Rendering: Shankaracharya

7.3.12 <Q> inline quotation (in place of "..." or '...')

Inline quotations are useful for short snippets of quoted text that you want to discuss without having to put them in block quotes (<BQ>) as entire paragraphs in their own right. You may also like to use them to distinguish technical words or phrases when they are introduced for the first time. (This makes it easy to search for such occurrences, for instance to make a cross-reference table.) Text within <Q>...</Q> tags is typically shown in English-language browsers in double quotes ("...") alternating with single quotes ('...') when nesting occurs.

Displays for other languages may use other symbols, such as «...» in Spanish for "...". The language context is specified by the LANG attribute within an individual <Q> tag, or by separate <LANG>...</LANG> tags.

HTML:
```
<Q LANG="en.uk"> <Q>Yoga is the stilling of the
thoughtwaves of the mind</Q>, recited Peter.</Q>
```
Rendering: "'Yoga is the stilling of the thoughtwaves of the mind', recited Peter."

Setting the LANG attribute for a quoted piece of text does not cause it to be translated (giving, in the case of the Yoga Sutra just quoted, the Sanskrit 'Yogash Chitta Vritta Nirodhaha') – that is far beyond the capacity of any browser. The attribute only controls the rendering in so far as that is language-dependent.

At the moment there is no real support for languages such as Sanskrit which use character sets other than Latin-1. Much work is currently under way to enable a free choice of character sets which, like the elegant Devanagari script shared by Sanskrit and Hindi, are not available on many machines, and may require various kinds of special treatment.

For example, the word 'Hindi' is written हिन्दी, which actually consists of the characters ि – i, ह – h, न्द – nd (a ligature) and ी – long i. The partly-inverted character order may not matter to browsers (unless we want to have the Devanagari rendered into Latin characters), but the need for a sizeable set of 2- or even 3-letter ligatures (such as *nd* and *ndr*) is quite awkward and could be handled in a variety of ways, yet to be agreed.

One proposal to help cater for various languages is the DIR attribute, with possible values LTR (left to right) and RTL (right to left) to control the direction in which successive text characters are displayed.

7.3.13 <SAMP> sequence of literal characters

The sample tag passes any characters enclosed within it to the display. This can be useful where there is a possibility that the browser might take other actions with the characters.

HTML: `Then he said <SAMP>$@%#</SAMP> and Daisy gasped.`
Rendering: Then he said $@%# and Daisy gasped.

7.3.14 Elements for fragments of computer programs

<CMD> command (in a computer language like a UNIX shell, C or Visual Basic)

The command tag is intended only for names of commands, such as those in computer programming languages.

HTML: `<CMD>rm</CMD>`
Rendering: `rm`

<ARG> argument to a command

The argument tag is intended only for names of arguments to commands which are themselves marked up with the <CMD> tag. (Arguments contain the data, such as numbers or pieces of text, which the command is to process: they are the grist to the command's mill. Some commands need several different arguments.)

HTML: `<ARG>-r</ARG> <ARG>*</ARG>`
Rendering: `-r *`

<VAR> named variable (placeholder)

The variable tag indicates the name of a placeholder in a computer program.

HTML: `<VAR>Current_Account_Balance</VAR>`
Rendering: `Current_Account_Balance`

7.3.15 Combining tags

You can combine the use of tags in a sentence, as in:

```
<P>Here is some <B><I><U><TT>excessively NOISY script </B></I></U></TT>
```

Browsers will render the text as directed if at all possible:

Here is some ***excessively NOISY script***

Tags of various kinds can be mixed freely to combine effects. Such freedom can be very useful, though it also enables you to construct confusingly marked-up texts. For example:

```
                  informational              presentation
<P>The Swedish for <EM>buffet</EM> is <B>Sm&ouml;rg&aring;sbord</B> ,<BR>
(pronounced roughly as s-myrrh-goss-boo with a hint of a 'd' at the end).
```

This can be rendered:

> The Swedish for *buffet* is **Smörgåsbord**,
> (pronounced roughly as s-myrrh-goss-boo with a hint of a 'd' at the end).

7.4 Extending HTML with your own character-level elements

SGML (the parent language of HTML, and from which HTML inherits many behaviours) allows documents to include many other non-standard elements, such as PROPNAME for proper (personal) names. By default, HTML browsers just skip such elements and process their contents as if those tags were absent. You can instruct the browser to render such elements by associating their names with specific styles. For example:

```
<RENDER TAG="PROPNAME" STYLE="I,B">     <!--put this at top of document-->
```

The style attribute is a list of presentation tag names (I, B, U, SUP, SUB, TT) separated by commas, as in the example. The symbol P, for paragraph break, is also allowed. With the example RENDER tag at the start of a document, the following tag using the newly defined PROPNAME element is rendered as desired:

HTML:	`<PROPNAME>Dante Alighieri</PROPNAME>`
Rendering:	***Dante Alighieri***

> Definitions such as RENDER should always be grouped at the start of a document to ensure consistent behaviour by the browser.

Non-standard mark-up has its dangers, but you may find it simplifies indexing your documents. For example, you could make a recipe book with a tag for the ingredients:

```
<RENDER TAG="INGRED" STYLE="I">          <!--definition of new tag-->
...
<INGRED>Flour</INGRED> 200grams          <!--use of new INGRED tag-->
<INGRED>Milk</INGRED>  100ml             <!--another use of the tag-->
...
```

which will appear like this in your HTML 3 browser:

Flour 200grams
Milk 100ml
...

You can then organize and print out an *index of ingredients* by searching for all the <INGRED> tags with a program or macro (outside the browser) which paginates the document (ready for printing on paper) and makes a list of which (paper) page the ingredients appear on:

F
Flour 23, 26, 27, 29, 41
...

A similar job can be done using the URLs of a set of Web documents, which can be designed as (a linked-up list of) pages of a book: it can be convenient to have the same structure available on the Web as on paper.

If you want to index words which should appear as normal text, you could use a private element without defining its rendering. Browsers then simply ignore your tags, which are there only for your own use. For example, your privately defined ingredient tags:

```
<RECIPE>Flour</RECIPE>
```

are not displayed by normal browsers, so the text 'Flour' just appears to users in the ordinary paragraph font with no visible mark-up. Alternatively the arrangement

```
<RECIPE Flour>
```

will be ignored altogether by normal browsers, but your source text can be searched for all the (invisible) ingredient tags by your own indexing program or macro.

7.5 Summary

Character-level mark-up gives hypertext authors some degree of direct control (though purists consider this undesirable) over the presentation of their documents, within the limits of the presentation devices used by readers.

More importantly and more generally, character-level mark-up indicates the purpose of a wide range of textual components. With knowledge of these purposes, browsers can deliver optimized presentations of documents, and other tools can exploit that knowledge to extract features of specific interest quickly and accurately. The versatility of this kind of informational (or logical) mark-up is a major reason for the popularity of HTML as a format for portable documents.

8 LISTS

This chapter:

- describes all the HTML 3 list elements and tags, with the documented extensions that apply to them. The main constructions (with or without `LH` for list header text) are
  - `UL` with `LI` for bulleted items (Section 8.2)
  - `OL` with `LI` for numbered items (Section 8.3)
  - `DL` with paired `DT` and `DD` for defined items (Section 8.4)
- gives examples of the list tags in use
- describes how you can qualify the list tags for special purposes

8.1 Introduction

Lists in HTML are similar to the lists that you make and use every day, whether for shopping, as reminders on your desk, for business presentations, or just to organize repetitive information in documents. HTML here as elsewhere takes the common concept and formalizes it with a precise but simple syntax.

There are three main ways to set up a list in HTML (but see also the use of menus in forms, Section 12.4.9 for when you want users to select items from a list). These are:

(1) bulleted lists with UL and LI

```
<UL>
    <LI>a bullet point
    <LI>next bullet point
</UL>
```

(2) numbered lists with OL and LI

```
<OL><LH>Header for Numbered List</LH>
    <LI>first item
    <LI>next item
</OL>
```

(3) definition lists with DL and DT, DD

```
<DL>
    <DT>an item<DD>definition of this item
    <DT>next item<DD>definition of next item
</DL>
```

These constructions, the tags used in them, and many possible variations are discussed below.

8.2 Unordered lists (UL)

8.2.1 Purpose

UL creates lists with or without bullets (simple or fancy), but without any kind of sequence numbering.

Optional attributes (not yet widely supported) which control the kind of bullet used in your lists are:

PLAIN	(no bullets),
SRC	(use the specified image), and
DINGBAT	(use a predefined glyph such as a folder: 🗀).

Netscape uses instead an extension attribute TYPE, with possible values disc, circle and square. These are the same bullets used by default by Netscape browsers for successive levels of nested lists, so all you are doing is changing the sequence of levels in which the Netscape bullet-types appear. Other browsers may use other kinds of bullet.

Generic HTML 3 attributes which may be used with the UL tag include ID, LANG, CLASS, STYLE, MD, WRAP and COMPACT. Most of these are rather specialized.

8.2.2 Simple bulleted list

The simple bulleted list is the easiest to create, using the defaults set up by your browser:

```
<UL>
    <LH ID=Spice>Spices</LH>
    <LI>Aniseed
    <LI>Bay
    <LI>Cardamom
</UL>
```

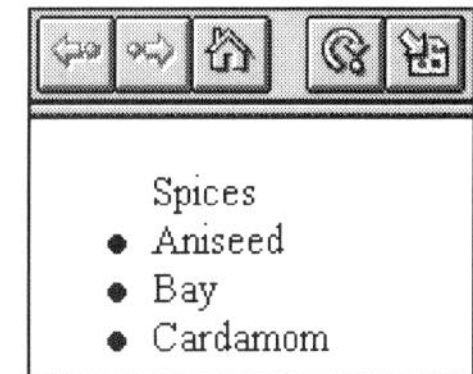

8.2.3 Plain list

HTML allows you to drop the use of bullets if you want a completely plain list for any reason. All you have to write is <UL PLAIN>, which seems satisfactorily minimalist for such an austere style. You may still need to put the list header (<LH>) into bold face (<B>) to get a clear result, though future browsers may give list headers more emphasis than the current ones do.

```
<UL PLAIN>                                  --- *** NEW in HTML 3 ***
<LH><B>Plain Unvarnished Lists</B></LH>     --- list without bullets
    <LI>Plain Jane
    <LI>Simple Sam
    <LI>Gospel Truth
    <LI>Shaker Chair
    <LI>Vanilla Flavor
</UL>
```

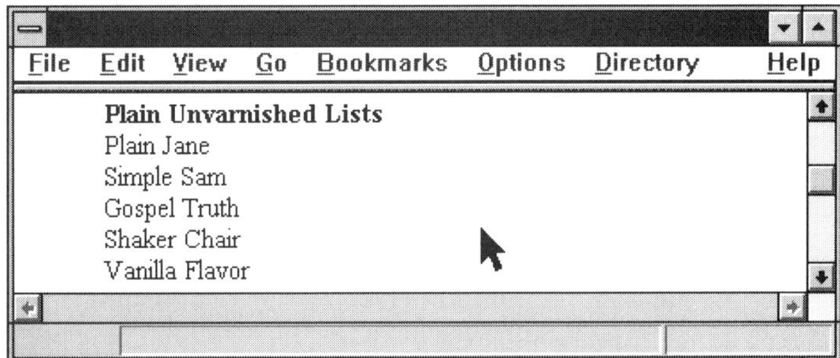

8.2.4 Images as bullets

Even the most cursory inspection of the Web today reveals a strong demand for graphical bullets. For example, the wonderfully named World Wide Weed site (`http://huizen.dds.nl/~jeroenw/index-e.htm`) in the Netherlands (where the described substance is legal) has the following implementation of a list with graphical bullets:

```
<HR>
<H3><IMG SRC="ball_gr.gif">                  <!--repetitive tags!-->
    <A HREF="links-e.htm">Softdrugs on the net</A>
<P><IMG SRC="ball_gr.gif">
    <A HREF="adam.htm">A trip to Amsterdam</A>
<P><IMG SRC="ball_gr.gif">
    <A HREF="use-e.htm">Cannabis usage</A>
<P><IMG SRC="ball_gr.gif">
    <A HREF="join-e.htm">How to roll joints</A>
<P><IMG SRC="ball_gr.gif">
    <A HREF="image.htm">Image database</A>
<P><IMG SRC="ball_gr.gif">
    <A HREF="news-e.htm">Newsgroups</A>
<P><IMG SRC="ball_gr.gif">
    <A HREF="faq.htm">The hemp FAQ in HTML</A>
</H3><P><HR>
<IMG WIDTH=50 SRC="logo.gif" BORDER=1> World Wide Weed - 1995
```

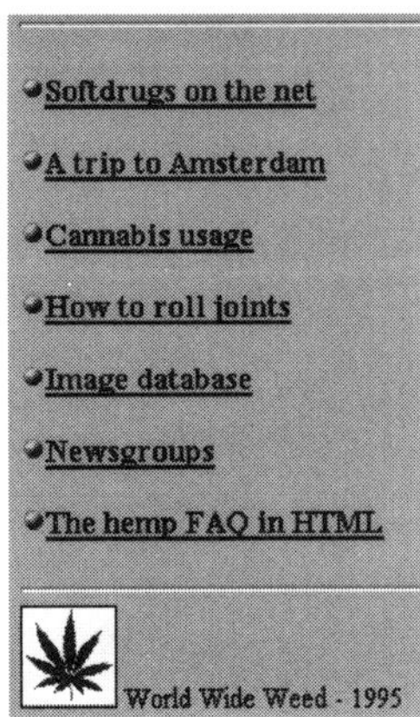

Now, whatever you may think of the substance of this page, you can surely agree that the use of `<P><IMG SRC="bullet.gif">` for every line of a list is, if not actually illegal, at least rather untidy. HTML 3 offers a cleaner alternative.

You can specify an image for bullets in HTML 3 by indicating it as a URL attribute (such as `SRC="bullet.gif"`) just once within the `UL` tag. If you use the same small image for all items in a list, the overhead of fetching the image (once) will be very small in all browsers that cache images. This mechanism enables you to create attractive special effects without causing your readers long delays. For example:

```
<UL SRC="../bullets/belemnit.gif">      <!--image for a fossil bullet-->
    <LI>antique
    <LI>ancient                         <!--same bullets for all items-->
    <LI>archaic
</UL>
```

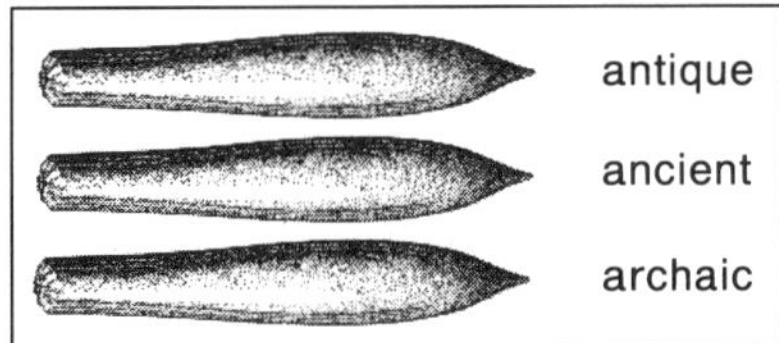

The World Wide Weed list could similarly be implemented in HTML 3 like this:

```
<UL SRC="ball_gr.gif">
    <LI><A HREF="links-e.htm">Softdrugs on the net</A>
    <LI><A HREF="adam.htm"   >A trip to Amsterdam</A>
    <LI><A HREF="use-e.htm"  >Cannabis usage</A>
    <LI><A HREF="join-e.htm" >How to roll joints</A>
    <LI><A HREF="image.htm"  >Image database</A>
    <LI><A HREF="news-e.htm" >Newsgroups</A>
    <LI><A HREF="faq.htm"    >The hemp FAQ in HTML</A>
</UL>
```

which is certainly more compact, if not what everyone would call straight.

8.2.5 Predefined dingbats as bullets

An alternative is to use one of the predefined 'dingbat' images known to HTML 3 browsers, listed and illustrated in Appendix H. These may not be as exciting as your own, but they can be loaded rapidly. Users are likely to recognize them easily, as they include familiar icons such as floppy disks, documents and folders. For example:

```
<UL DINGBAT=folder>              --- Dingbats *** NEW in HTML 3 ***
    <LI>DOCS
    <LI>IMAGES
    <LI>HTML
</UL>
```

DOCS
IMAGES
HTML

You can also use a dingbat within an individual `LI` if you want to give it a unique bullet image. Browsers typically use the icons in common use on each specific platform, so PC icons will stay different from those on the Mac.

8.2.6 Netscape bullets

Netscape provides a limited range of bullet `TYPE`s already mentioned (just `square`, `circle` or `disc` at present) which you can use in much the same way as `DINGBAT`s. These of course only work on Netscape-compatible browsers. Most other browsers display solid discs.

```
<UL TYPE=square>              --- Netscape extension
    <LI>cube
    <LI>rectangle
    <LI TYPE=disc>spheroid  --- Netscape extension
</UL>
```

cube
rectangle
spheroid

Notice that Netscape has introduced the possibility of switching the type part of the way through an unordered list, using their TYPE tag in <LI>, by analogy with their use of a VALUE tag (<LI VALUE=5>) within an ordered list (OL) to cause a jump in the numbering.

8.2.7 Wrapped lists

You should not often want to use the WRAP attribute. Nearly everyone expects lists to be in top-to-bottom, left-to-right order, which HTML calls vertical (WRAP=vert). This has one advantage over a single down-the-page list, namely that it saves space.

Very occasionally people want the other, horizontal arrangement:

```
<UL WRAP=horiz PLAIN>
    <LI>Alabama
    <LI>Amarillo
    <LI>Atlanta
    <LI>Baton Rouge
    <LI>Birmingham
    <LI>Boston
    <LI>Buffalo
    <LI>Chattanooga
    <LI>Cincinnati
    <LI>Columbus
    <LI>Denver
</UL>
```

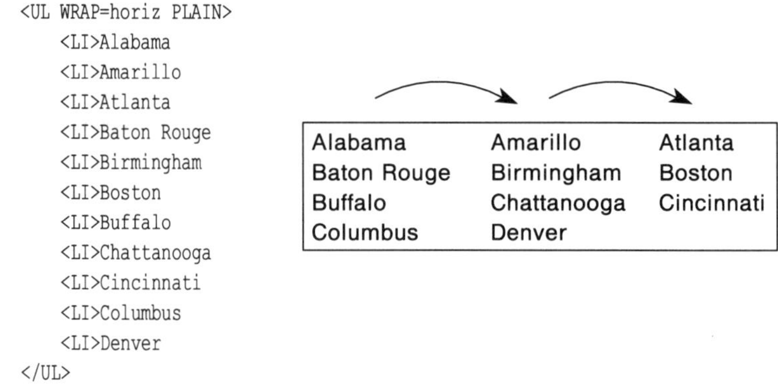

but most of us find horizontally wrapped lists totally disorientating.

It is more likely that what you are really after is a table:

Name	Family	Favourite Food
anthony	aardvark	ants
freddy	fox	rabbits
micky	mongoose	snakes
slipman	slug	lettuces
nikita	penguin	vodka

width of *my* screen gives me 3 columns...

which uses the columns to express a logical structure. In that case you should not rely on a list being formatted horizontally (with, in this case, three items per line) as you might hope, but use a proper TABLE to guarantee the formatting you want.

When users have screen widths, font sizes, or browsers with different settings from your own, the wrapping will be different from what you see in your browser. If you rely on any particular number of columns in a list, users may receive confusingly formatted information.

Note that browsers can adjust the number of columns in a wrapped list to suit the current window width, which is handy if you want to minimize the (vertical) length of your document; this naturally is not an option with tables.

To sum up, the alternatives for wrapping bulleted lists are:

```
<UL>                --- go down page in single column (like HTML 2.0)
<UL WRAP=vert>      --- go down page, then use next column (normal)
<UL WRAP=horiz>     --- across page, then next row (rare, confusing)
```

8.2.8 Keeping lists compact

The COMPACT attribute is quite problematic, as different browsers may use different tricks to save space, and the result is highly dependent on style settings. You can do better by specifying fonts and line spacings in a style sheet.

```
<UL COMPACT>        --- ask browser to try to save space between items.
```

8.3 Ordered lists (OL)

8.3.1 Purpose

OL creates a sequential list of LI items enumerated in the style you want. The default style is 1, 2, 3 but you can have a, b, c or i, ii, iii among others. What is more, you can nest ordered lists so that you get 1, 2, 2.1, 2.2, 2.2.1 and so on (though the treatment of nested ordered lists is browser-specific). Your style sheet (not HTML) describes your preferences. For example:

```
<OL>
        <LH>Library Organization</LH>
    <LI>Aeronautics
    <LI>Agriculture
        <OL><LH>--- a nested list</LH>
            <LI>Agrobotany --- might appear as 2.1 or 2:a in other browsers
            <LI>Agroeconomics --- might appear as 2.2 or 2:b, etc
            <LI>Agronomy
        </OL>
    <LI>Astronomy
</OL>
```

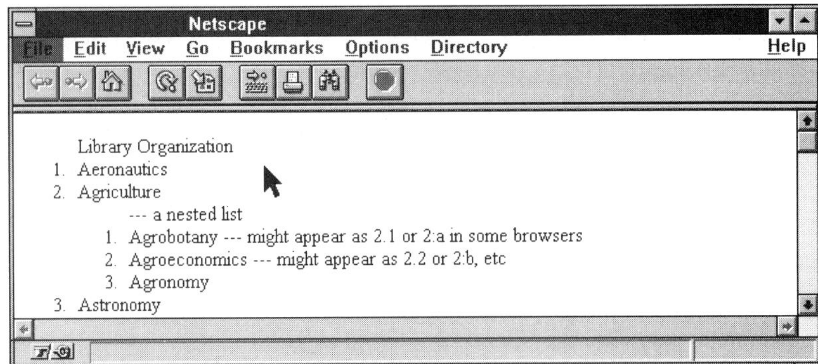

8.3.2 Netscape's sequence type

Netscape implements different numbering styles with an extension attribute, TYPE. For example, you can say <OL TYPE=i> to get small roman numerals. The permitted Netscape types work as follows:

HTML	Description	Effect
1	Arabic numerals (default)	1, 2, 3,...
A	CAPITAL LETTERS	A, B, C,...
a	small letters	a, b, c,...
I	LARGE ROMAN NUMERALS	I, II, III, IV, V,...
i	small roman numerals	i, ii, iii, iv, v,...

This selection enables you to distinguish different kinds of list in your documents, but the conventions you use are up to you – though it is best to be simple and consistent. Your first choice should always be plain arabic numerals. For example:

```
<OL TYPE=i START=5>     --- Netscape extension
    <LI>fifth column
    <LI>sixth sense
    <LI>seventh seal
    <LI>eighth army
</OL>
```

v	fifth column
vi	sixth sense
vii	seventh seal
viii	eighth army

8.3.3 Changing the whole list's sequence numbering

By default, ordered lists begin at 1 (which may be shown as i, I, a, A, or 1 depending on the style in force) and increase from there. You can, if you need to, make the sequence either continue where the previous list left off, using CONTINUE, or start at some arbitrary place in the sequence, using START. For example:

```
<OL START=7>        --- Set the starting sequence number
    <LI>Heptagon
    <LI>Octagon
</OL>
```

7	Heptagon
8	Octagon

```
<OL CONTINUE>       --- Don't restart the sequence number
    <LI>Nonagon
    <LI>Decagon
</OL>
```

9	Nonagon
10	Decagon

You can also interrupt the sequence within an ordered list, with or without starting off the list with START or CONTINUE, by modifying individual LI tags (see Sections 8.5.2 and 8.5.3).

8.3.4 Generic attributes with OL

Generic HTML 3 attributes which may be used with the OL tag include ID, CONTINUE, START, LANG, CLASS, STYLE, WRAP, COMPACT, CLEAR and NEEDS. (WRAP is discussed above in Section 8.2.7; it is probably less useful with OL than with UL.) If you really need something that looks like a list and contains items of very variable size, it may be best to format it as <P> text with <H4> or <H5> headers.

8.4 Definition lists (DL)

8.4.1 Purpose

Definition lists are used to create glossaries or other lists with a heading for each entry. The basic idea is that each <DT> item is the name of something you want to define; the following <DD> text is supposed to give a definition of the item.

The idea of 'definition' extends readily to explanation: you can use DL to show off goods on sale, to explain how things work, or to give details of the main politicians mentioned in a news bulletin. Another use of DL is to set up dialogues, with each DT naming a speaker, and each DD containing a speech. An example is given in Appendix A.

Definition lists must be bracketed with <DL>...</DL>, but within this there is no need to use the closing tags </DT> and </DD>, as the definitions are satisfactorily bounded by the next item and by the closing </DL> tag. We suggest that you never use </DT> and </DD> at all.

You can often get away with a list containing only DL or only DT, creating the effect of a plain or indented list, but this is very bad manners. Use instead UL, plain or with an appropriate bullet. You have no guarantee that wrongly constructed HTML will work on all browsers, even if it works fine on your own system.

Generic attributes which you can use with DL are ID, LANG, CLASS, STYLE, CLEAR and COMPACT.

8.4.2 A simple definition list

```
<DL ID=netizens CLEAR=40>        --- ID unique within this document
<LH>Some Famous Netizens</LH>
    <DT>Dweeb<DD>young excitable person,
        who may mature into a <EM>Nerd</EM> or <EM>Geek</EM>
    <DT>Cracker<DD>hacker on the Internet
    <DT>Nerd<DD>male so into the net that he forgets wife's birthday
</DL>
```

Some Famous Netizens
Dweeb
young excitable person, who may mature into a *Nerd* or *Geek*
Cracker
hacker on the Internet
Nerd
male so into the net that he forgets wife's birthday

8.4.3 A compact definition list

You can use the attribute COMPACT with DL as with other kinds of list. It instructs browsers to attempt to save screen space by packing terms and definitions more tightly than usual. We cannot especially recommend you to use <DL COMPACT>, as its effect is bound to vary between browsers, and in any case, the definition format is not very suitable for squashing up.

The example illustrated here shows what Netscape does with <DL COMPACT>: instead of starting each DD on a new line, it is just tabbed a short distance on the same line as the DT term. This treatment, while correct, and typical of what you can expect HTML 3 browsers to do, is not especially readable. Some browsers may typeset the DT text differently from the DD, for example using boldface.

```
<DL COMPACT>      <!-- effect varies-->
        <LH>Shortlist</LH>
    <DT>short<DD>small is beautiful
    <DT>sweet<DD>as the honeycomb
</DL>
```

Other browsers may use different fonts for DT and DD.

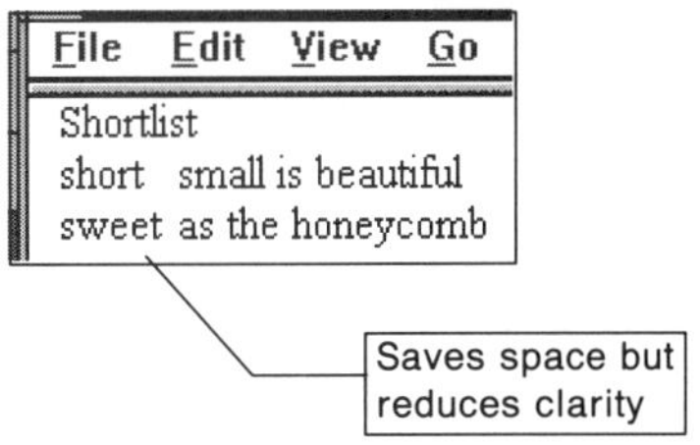

8.5 List items (LI)

8.5.1 Purpose

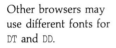

LI creates an individual list item within UL (Section 8.2) and OL (Section 8.3) lists.

You can use attributes inside the <LI> tag to control the appearance and formatting of individual list items, that is, when one item needs to be different from the other members of the same list. You should never use the same attribute in every item of a list – it is clearer, less error-prone and more efficient to specify what you want in the UL or OL tag which controls the whole list at once.

Generic attributes which may occasionally need to be used with the LI tag are CLASS, ID, STYLE, SRC, MD, DINGBAT (see Section 8.2.5 under UL for description) and SKIP (Section 8.5.2).

8.5.2 Skipping over sequence numbers

HTML 3 permits you to number lists discontinuously, though not to go back in the sequence, by skipping over some number of items. (But see Section 8.5.3 for Netscape's contrasting approach.) This can be combined with OL's START attribute, which qualifies the whole list. For example:

```
<OL START=3>
    <LI>Third Man
    <LI SKIP=2>Sixth Sense
</OL>
```

3 Third Man
6 Sixth Sense

Consider carefully the difference between <LI SKIP=2> and <OL START=3>, which could both start the whole list off at 3. The effect of the START=3 attribute (of the whole ordered list) is identical to putting <LI SKIP=2> for the first list item, though not with putting SKIP later in the list (where it might cause a jump in the numbering from 5 to 7, say). The use of START is certainly less confusing for starting a list.

8.5.3 Netscape's way of skipping

Note that Netscape uses VALUE (which resets the sequence number to a new absolute value) instead of SKIP (which increments the sequence number relative to the current place in the sequence):

```
<OL>                                       <!--Netscape extension VALUE-->
    <LI>One is one and all alone and ever more shall be so
    <LI>Two, two, the lily-white boys, cloth&eacute;d all in green, Ho Ho
    <LI VALUE=7>Seven for the symbols at your door    <!--jump to 7-->
</OL>
```

This is rendered (depending on the browser's configuration) as:

1 One is one and all alone and ever more shall be so
2 Two, two, the lily-white boys, clothéd all in green, Ho Ho
7 Seven for the symbols at your door

8.6 List headers (LH)

The list header LH is optional, for all three kinds of list. It is the nicest and most consistent way of putting a title or introductory phrase at the head of a list. For a major list, you can of course use an ordinary header (<H3>Our Departments are:</H3>); for a list which flows naturally out of the text, you can just end a paragraph with a colon (... and you can choose from:</P>), but in general the <LH> tag is the one to use.

LH was introduced to allow lists to be collapsed to just the supplied LH text, in rather the same way that the venerable Microsoft Windows 3.1 File Manager lets you collapse a directory listing down to the name of the directory (by clicking on it). To cause a list to appear folded down in this way, HTML 3 provides the FOLD attribute (for example, <LH FOLD>This is all you see initially</LH>). A click on the list header unfolds the list to reveal the list elements.

You *can* use mark-up such as <EM>, <I>, <B> in list headers, but we suggest you keep this to a minimum, and restrict yourself to emphasizing a keyword or otherwise surprising phrase. If you find you are repeatedly using the same mark-up on list header text, you ought to set it up in a style sheet. If you are repeatedly using <B>, a header such as <H3> may be more appropriate.

Permissible generic attributes of LH include ID, LANG, STYLE and CLASS. There is some case for using ID here, so you can refer to a list somewhere else; other attributes should probably be rare.

Some (separate) examples of LH are:

```
<LH>Top of The List</LH>                <!--simplest form-->
<LH>My <EM>FAVOURITE</EM> Things</LH>   <!--mark-up within list header-->
<LH ID=toplist>My List</LH>             <!--ID useful for cross-refs-->
```

8.7 Summary of lists

HTML 3 provides three kinds of list to present the reader with structured information. These are:

- the unordered list (`UL`), typically with bullets
- the ordered list (`OL`), typically numbered
- the definition list (`DL`), typically with a term on one line and its definition on the next.

There are many variations on these themes, including optional list headers (`LH`), as well as a range of possible kinds of bullet (including images and dingbats) and choices of numbering styles. (To construct lists from which the user can make a selection, see Chapter 12.) Increasingly, browsers are permitting lists to be nested for more sophisticated structuring of information.

9
HYPERTEXT LINKS

In this chapter:

- An explanation of hypertext links at layman level
- Examples of hypertext links between files in the same directory
- Examples of hypertext links to files elsewhere on the Internet
- Hypertext links to specific points in a document using `NAME` and `ID`
- URLs: basic and more technical information on their format
- Image maps: the difference between server-side and client-side processing
- Server-side image maps using `IMG` and `ISMAP`
- Client-side image maps using the `MAP` element
- Client-side image maps using the `OBJECT` element
- The `SHAPE` attribute to define regions of an image
- Combining `MAP` with server-side image maps
- Combining `SHAPE` with server-side image maps

9.1 Introduction

One of the most important aspects of HTML is that it allows you to construct hypertext links between documents. The basic concept of cross-referencing information is centuries old and predates even the printing press. Indeed in this sense hypertext links have been around for a long time. Computer technology has now made it possible for readers to follow the links effortlessly, literally at the click of a button.

Hypertext links are what make the Web more than a collection of independent files. The ability to simply click your mouse over a hypertext link to retrieve a file somewhere out there on the Web, on a different computer, in a different company, in a different country, or perhaps just somewhere on your own machine, is what makes the Web so successful. It has altered the direction of several industries: software and computing; telecommunications and cable TV; publishing and now banking and credit card associations are struggling to understand the impact of the Web, thanks to the invention of global hypertext links.

9.1.1 Advice to beginners

Even if you plan to write only simple hypertext links you will need a basic knowledge of the following:

(1) The use of filenames and directories/folders to organize files on disk. You need to know about these concepts because hypertext links reference information by naming the file and directory in which the information is found.

(2) The design principles for putting together a series of linked Web pages. Read Chapter 5 which not only gives you some advice on this subject but shows you examples of how other people have tackled the problem.

9.2 Simple examples of a hypertext link

9.2.1 Example 1: Tourist information online

We start our explanation of hypertext links on the Web with a very simple example. This consists of part of a (fictitious) online Tourist Information Leaflet on Boston. The idea is very simple: we want readers to be able to click on the words 'Boston Common' to jump to more information on this area. This is how it's done.

There are two files, which, for the sake of simplicity, *are on the same computer and in the same directory* as each other. These are a plain text file

boston.html, which contains general information on Boston marked up with HTML tags, and a second file called **common.html** containing information on Boston Common. Here they are:

boston.html

```
<P>If you are visiting Boston you will no doubt want to come and
see famous <A HREF="common.html"> Boston Common</A> which is the
oldest park in America.
```

common.html

```
<P>Boston Common was purchased in 1634 to be used as grazing land
for cattle, goats and sheep. It lies near the fashionable area of
Beacon Hill and includes a public garden displaying fine summer
flowers. Not far from the Charles River, it is centrally placed.
```

Stylistically HTML code is rendered in different ways by browsers so there are no hard and fast rules about how this code would be shown to the user on the screen. The most common way for showing hypertext links is underlined so this is how we have depicted the links in our own rendering below:

> If you are visiting Boston you will no doubt want to come and see famous Boston Common which is the oldest park in America.

When you click on Boston Common you see the file common.html displayed thus:

> Boston Common was purchased in 1634 to be used as grazing land for cattle, goats and sheep. It lies near the fashionable area of Beacon Hill and includes a public garden displaying fine summer flowers. Not far from the Charles River, it is centrally placed.

The mark-up of the hypertext link is as follows:

```
<A HREF="common.html">Boston Common</A>
```

- The `<A>` tag is the anchor element start tag; `</A>` is the corresponding end tag. These tags are used to define a hypertext link.
- `HREF` is an attribute of the anchor element. The value it takes is the destination of the link, in this case the file common.html.
- `Boston Common` is the label of the link: the words which will appear as a clickable hotword on the screen when the mark-up is displayed.

9.2.2 Example 2: Link to the *New York Times* newspaper

In Example 1 we chose to link to a file in the same directory and on the same computer, and such links are certainly not difficult to construct. However, it is more likely that you want to establish a link to a computer somewhere else on the Internet, which is inevitably more complicated. This is because you need to include in the value of the HREF attribute, information about its exact location on the many, many computers connected to the Internet.

In Example 2, we construct an imaginary link which goes from the current document you are writing to another completely different file on the Web, the home page of the *New York Times*:

```
<P>My favourite newspaper is the
<A HREF="http://www.nytimes.com/">New York Times</A>.
```

which is rendered by most browsers as follows:

My favourite newspaper is the New York Times.

The anchor element is used again and you will identify three parts to it:

(1) The **label** for the link. In this case the label of the link is `New York Times`.

(2) The `HREF` attribute to indicate the target of the link.

(3) The value for the `HREF` attribute. This long sequence of characters starting `"http..."` is the URL – **the Uniform Resource Locator**. This tells the computer from which machine on the Internet the file should be retrieved, and even (although not the case here) the directory containing it. The URL is a kind of global network address and is explained in Chapter 1 to which you should now refer if you are new to the idea.

More about URLs

A beginner's guide to URLs is given in Chapter 1; our aim here is to give you a little more information on the subject. Look at some examples of URLs:

`http://www.lcs.mit.edu/`
The Laboratory for Computer Science at MIT, in Cambridge Mass.

`http://www.hp.com/`
Access HP, the home page for the Hewlett-Packard Company

`http://www.bath.ac.uk/`
The University of Bath, in the United Kingdom

`http://www.sunday-times.co.uk/`
The *Sunday Times* newspaper in the United Kingdom

All these examples use HTTP, the HyperText Transfer Protocol, for retrieval and this explains the '`http:`' prefix at the start of the URL. The part following the '//' is the host name for the computer acting as the server for this URL. It is common for Web servers to have host names that start with 'www' although this is by no means universal. The last part of the host name gives you a clue as to the kind of organization running the server.

In the USA, URLs for universities end in '.edu', while URLs for companies end in '.com'. Non-profit organizations typically have '.org'. Outside the USA, it is common to see an abbreviation for the country name, for example '.ca' for Canada, '.it' for Italy and '.uk' for the United Kingdom. Multinational companies tend to have a '.com' suffix to avoid being pinned down to any one country. Country codes and suffixes are detailed in the appendices. You will occasionally see URLs for other kinds of protocols, for example:

`ftp://ftp.netscape.com/`
The FTP server for the Netscape Communications Company

`gopher://gopher.micro.umn.edu/1`
The Gopher server at the University of Minnesota, home of Gopher

`news:alt.privacy`
alt.privacy which deals with privacy issues in cyberspace

`mailto:dsr@w3.org`
email address for Dave Raggett at the World Wide Web Consortium

The File Transfer Protocol (FTP), as explained in Chapter 1, is often used for computer software, such as free versions of Web browsers. FTP servers tend to have host names starting with 'ftp.'. Gopher is a menu-based document retrieval protocol that predates the Web. Most Gopher sites have menu items pointing to other Gopher sites, so you can easily move around gopherspace. URLs for network news groups or articles use the 'news:' scheme. These URLs are interesting in that they don't include the host name for a server. Instead, the browser uses the 'local' news server. The 'mailto:' scheme is used for email addresses, and often appears on Web pages to allow you to contact the person or company responsible for the page.

9.2.3 Example 3: Web page for a Cat Club

This third example again uses URLs. This time the URLs are more specific and home in on particular files in particular directories of named machines on the Internet. The example also serves to illustrate how to construct a series of bulleted hypertext links as a list, a most popular method of presenting alternative paths for users to follow. The elements used in our example are `UL` for 'unordered list' and `LI` for 'list item'. The element `UL` has the effect of telling the browser to insert a bullet automatically in front of each list item. `H2` is a second-level heading. `A` is, of course, the anchor element.

This is the effect we want:

The Kenton and Preston Road Cat Fanciers Club

This Web page gives information on forthcoming events in August and September including shows, talks and meetings. Click on any item from the list below for information.

- Dates for the next months
- Cat shows on in August and September
- Entering your cat
- Parking at cat shows
- Maps of locations and useful phone numbers

Here is the HTML to do the job:

```
<H2>The Kenton and Preston Road Cat Fanciers Club</H2>
<P>This Web page gives information on forthcoming events in August and
September including shows, talks and meetings. Click on any item from the
list below for information.
<UL>
<LI><A HREF="http://kitten.rs.kenton.edu/cats/meet.html">Dates for the next
months</A>
<LI><A HREF="http://kitten.rs.kenton.edu/cats/shows.html">Cat shows on in
August and September</A>
<LI><A HREF="http://kitten.rs.kenton.edu/cats/entering.html">Entering your
cat </A>
<LI><A HREF="http://kitten.rs.kenton.edu/kitten/parking.html">Parking at
cat shows</A>
<LI><A HREF="http://kitten.rs.kenton.edu/kitten/maps.html">Maps of
locations and useful phone numbers</A>
</UL>
```

Note straightaway the use of URLs in the hypertext links. For example:

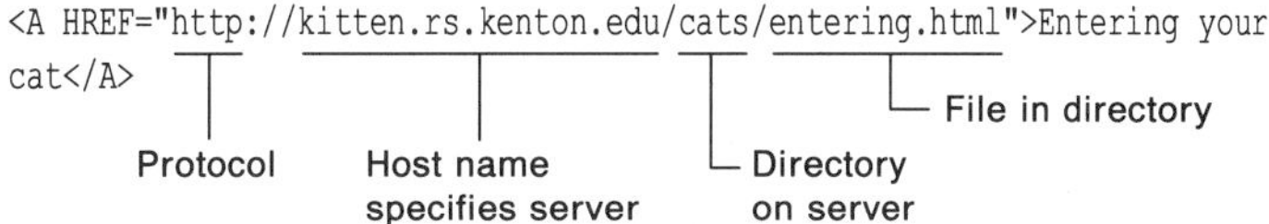

The author has placed the links in list elements, which is quite legitimate. You can equally place them in headings, credits, captions, table cells, and so on. Hypertext links can in fact be included in most elements (but not in math equations). They can be inserted within character emphasis elements and can include character emphasis themselves. Thus a hypertext link which has italic emphasis:

- *Dates for the next months*
- Cat shows on in August and September
- Entering your cat

```
<LI><A HREF="http://kitten.rs.kenton.edu/cats/meet.html"><I>Dates for the
next months</I></A>
```

will appear displayed accordingly on your screen. By and large the principle behind HTML is to impose as few restrictions on authors as possible. This is deliberately done so that it makes it easy to translate documents generated by word processors into HTML. Note, however, that hypertext links cannot themselves contain headings, lists, paragraphs or other block elements.

Relative URLs

HTTP (and FTP) support a more concise form of URLs where the network address is expressed relative to the URL for the current document. This is particularly useful when you want to link to another file in the same directory or folder as the current document, as it allows you to abbreviate the URL to just the filename of the target file. You don't have to write the full URL every time.

For instance, suppose there are two files: overview.html and products.html in the same directory. If you want to make a link from overview.html to products.html, there is no need to spell out the complete URL for the file you want to link to: this can be inferred from the context.

The examples below illustrate this point. Below is a directory tree. The files contain information about cats and dogs presented as two subdirectories of Animals, called, quite simply, Dogs and Cats. Imagine you are writing about the dog Treacle in a file called treacle.html (on the diagram) and want to link to his photo in pict1.gif (also on the diagram). The link need not include the whole long URL for that file, but rather just specify where, *relative* to treacle.html, pict1.gif is found. In the hypertext link in treacle.html, all you need to write is:

```
HREF="/DogPhotos/pict1.gif"
```

which reads: *go down a directory into DogPhotos, and then to pict1.gif.*

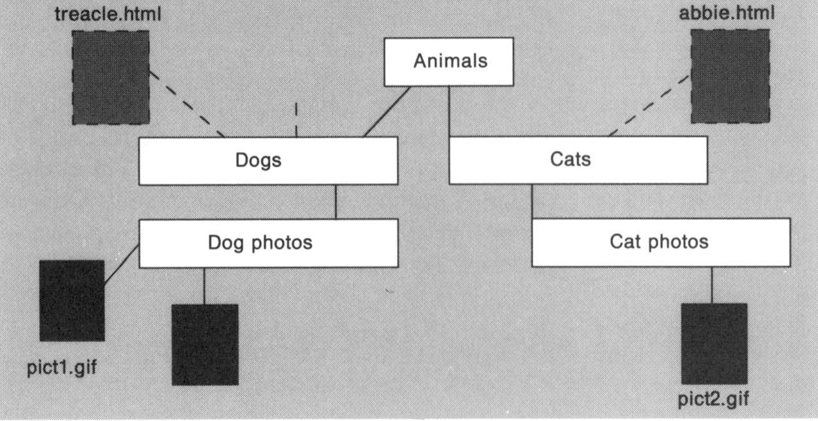

From Treacle.html to a photo of a cat:

```
HREF="../Cats/CatPhotos/pict2.gif"
```

which is: *go up to the parent directory, then into Cats, then into CatPhotos and finally into pict2.gif.*

To reference a dog photo treacle.gif from a file abbie.html in Cats you would use:

```
HREF="../Dogs/DogPhotos/treacle.gif"
```

You can see that two dots '..' are used to mean 'the parent directory' and a slash '/' is used to mean the child directory. This is UNIX notation and a basic guide to UNIX will explain more. Note that Microsoft uses slashes facing the other way ('\' instead of '/'). This is very confusing, but there you are, that's the computer industry for you!

DOS and Macintosh users: your slashes are the wrong way!!

The rule is that the UNIX '/' is used to separate directory levels, regardless of whether the server is a UNIX box, a DOS or Windows PC, or a Macintosh. This means that you have to translate the DOS and Macintosh conventions to the UNIX slash when you want to write a file path as a URL. On DOS this means '\' becomes '/', while on the Mac, ':' becomes '/'. This sleight-of-hand is required so that browsers can always apply the standard rules for interpreting relative URLs.

You are not allowed spaces in filenames either

Macintosh users are also in a pickle (as we British say) over filenames. Macintosh filenames often include spaces, which aren't allowed in URLs. The trick is to replace them by the code '%20'; for example, the filename for this chapter on our Macintosh, 'Chapter 9 Hypertext links', is written as a URL as:

```
Chapter%209%20Hypertext%20links
```

Windows 95 also supports long filenames with spaces in them. The same trick applies as for the Mac: you must replace each space character by the code '%20'.

9.3 Linking to a specific point in a document: `NAME` and `ID`

A link to a point within a document is done with a **fragment identifier** which is the technical term for a piece of HTML which singles out a unique piece of the marked-up text. The fragment identifier is a way of tagging a place in a document so that hypertext links can jump straight there on future occasions.

When would you want to jump to a particular location rather than just to the beginning of a file? Suppose you want to place a link from a table of contents to 'Chapter 5'. You use a fragment identifier to label 'Chapter 5' in some way; it is then simplicity itself to jump from the table of contents to that chapter when need be.

There are two distinct ways of accomplishing tricks of this sort. The first involves the anchor `NAME` attribute; the second uses `ID`, the HTML 3 alternative. Were this hypertext we would now suggest a leap to Chapter 4 on HTML 3 generic attributes, where both `NAME` and `ID` are explained in some detail.

9.3.1 Simple example of `NAME`

This is a simple example of the `NAME` attribute. It concerns fish. The idea is to arrange that, if the reader clicks on **Fish Lures**, a list of possible lures to attract the attention of the Emerald Mullet appears on the screen.

In the source file we have:

```
<H3><A NAME=lures>Fish Lures</A></H3>
<P>The Emerald Mullet is quite friendly and will come and investigate any
bait within minutes. Observe and marvel but do not attempt to catch the
fish, for this mullet is both poisonous and very partial to toes.
```

In the target file we have:

```
<LI><A HREF="#lures">Minced meat, lamb chops, fish fingers, corned beef.
Hamburgers and hot dogs are <EM>not</EM> taken.</A>
```

The '#' character following a URL precedes the fragment identifier. For an external link – in other words, a link to a different file – you might have:

```
<LI><A HREF="../fishing/fish.html#lures">minced meat, lamb chops, fish
fingers</A>
```

9.3.2 Simple example of the `ID` attribute: Online bird watching guide

Now for an example which uses the `ID` attribute rather than `NAME`. The subject of the example is Birds, in this case a group of birds which are similar in appearance and easy for the invariably optimistic bird-watcher to confuse.

The text is a single file held on a server. Readers can click on a bird name in the text to jump to another part of the file as required. If they click on Arctic Redpoll, the section on Arctic Redpolls is immediately displayed. If they click on Twite, the section on Twites appears.[1]

[1] Seasoned birders will notice that the birds in this example, although they do look similar, *generally* do not appear in the same place together so that the example is just a little silly. Perhaps 'small greeny brown warblers' would have been a better choice for this example. Or, 'almost identical sea gulls'. Well, maybe next time....

Twite

Adult male and female dull brown above, with dark streaking; pale buff below, shading to white on belly. In summer, male may show an indistinct red patch. May be confused with Linnet.

Linnet

The Linnet is a sociable bird which is found in open farm-land. Do not confuse the Linnet with the Twite which has a yellow beak, rather than the black beak of the Linnet.

Redpoll

Small dark finch. Adult male and female dark above, with blackish streaking. Small black bib; small characteristic red patch on forehead. See also Arctic Redpoll.

Arctic Redpoll

Small pale finch. Underparts often white and fluffy in appearance. Small black bib; red patch on forehead. Breeds on arctic tundra and willow scrub.

Here is the HTML 3 code to do the job:

```
<H4 ID="Twt">Twite</H4>
Adult male and female dull brown above, with dark streaking; pale buff
below, shading to white on belly. In summer, male may show an indistinct
red patch. May be confused with <A HREF="#Lin">Linnet.</A>
<H4 ID="Lin">Linnet</H4>
The Linnet is a sociable bird which is found in open farm-land. Do not
confuse the Linnet with the <A HREF="#Twt">Twite</A> which has a yellow
beak, rather than the black beak of the Linnet.
<H4 ID="Redp">Redpoll</H4>
Small dark finch. Adult male and female dark above, with blackish
streaking. Small black bib; small characteristic red patch on forehead. See
also <A HREF="#Arctic">Arctic Redpoll.</A>
<H4 ID="Arctic">Arctic Redpoll</H4>
Small pale finch. Underparts often white and fluffy in appearance. Small
black bib; red patch on forehead. Breeds on arctic tundra and willow scrub.
```

The links to specific headings are accomplished by giving each `H4` element in the document an `ID`. Thus in the case of the Twite, we see:

```
<H4 ID="Twt">Twite</H4>
```

Here the `H1` heading has an `ID "Twt"` which means it can be referenced by that name in future. The word `Twite` also appears because this is the text of the heading that readers will see; they will not see the `ID`. Once declared, `ID`s can be used in hypertext links. Thus while reading about Linnets, the reader can click on the word 'Twite' and trigger the link:

```
<A HREF="#Twt">Twite</A>
```

The # indicates a reference within a file. In this case, the expression "#Twt" says that the reference is to an item with an ID of "Twt". When the link is triggered, the browser finds the item with the matching ID and displays the file at that point.

Most elements can be given IDs but the most useful ones are probably captions of tables and figures, the idea being that you can jump to these from other documents as and when necessary.

When authoring a document by hand it is generally a good idea to make identifiers understandable to yourself. Be warned that identifiers are case sensitive, so sec3 and SEC3 are different! Each ID must be unique within a document.

Note: Although ID is more convenient than named anchor tags, few browsers support the use of ID in this role at the time of writing, although we are confident that this will soon change. In general, fragment identifiers are useful for HTML documents that are significantly longer than can be displayed on a single screenful, as they take the user directly to the appropriate section of the document.

Technical notes on URLs

Drawbacks of URLS

While URLs have been very effective, they do have some notable drawbacks. They are currently limited to US ASCII, making it impractical to create URLs in languages like Arabic and Japanese.

URLs with accented characters

You can include accented Western European characters from the Latin-1 character set, using an escaping mechanism, for example:

```
http://www.intermarche.fr/r%E9clame
```

for the file réclame (special offers). The '%' character acts as an escape code and is followed by two hexadecimal digits, in this case E9, which is Latin-1 for a lower case acute e. Note that host names can't be treated in this way, so I was unable to use an acute e for the last character of the company name: *Intermarché*.

Escape codes

Some of the more common escape codes are:

%09	the horizontal tab character
%20	the space character (ASCII 32)
%25	the % character (ASCII 37)

%26	the & character
%2B	the + character
%3F	the ? character
%40	the @ character

Including a query string in a URL

URLs may be followed by a query string. This is indicated by a '?' character, as in:

```
http://www.acme.com/searchindex?special%20offers
```

Such queries are generally handled by the server using special programs, typically invoked by CGI scripts. As a hangover from the early days, '+' signs in query strings are interpreted as space characters. So if you want to include a '+' sign in a query string you will need to escape this as '%2B'. Sometimes you will see complex queries such as:

```
http://guidep.infoseek.com/WW/NS/Titles?qt=fly+fishing&col=NN
```

This is a simple example of HTML form data encoded as a URL query string. The query appears as one or more field attribute=value pairs, separated by '&' characters. The example is for an Infoseek Guide query, with the text 'fly fishing' (qt=fly+fishing), on the database of network news articles (col=NN). Note the use of '+' for the space between fly and fishing. Luckily it is rarely necessary to include such complex URLs in hypertext links in actual documents.

9.4 Clickable graphics

As explained earlier in this chapter, a hypertext link contains a *label*. This is, in textual links, the word or phrase that you see on the screen ready to click. In HTML this label can be a graphic rather than just text. You click on the graphic and the link is triggered.

9.4.1 Simple example

The code below shows how a clickable graphic is generated. When the cursor is moved over the image, the browser senses that it lies over a clickable image and changes shape accordingly. Clicking the mouse button now summons up the file indicated by the HREF attribute. Here is the code:

```
<A HREF="/bug.html"><IMG SRC="/webfiles/images/bug.gif">Find out about Joe
the beetle</A>
```

and here is the result:

The link starts off with the anchor element start tag A, which includes the HREF attribute to reference the file to be fetched when the link is triggered. In this case, this is a file called bug.html. Within the confines of the anchor element is an IMG statement which refernces the graphic to be displayed as the label for the link. Most browsers will draw a coloured line around images to show you when they are part of a hypertext link.

In the next example you click on the cat to call up more information about her. If the image already invites you to click on it by the very nature of its appearance, the border is superfluous and gets in the way of the design. You can switch the border around the image off by including the attribute BORDER=0. For example:

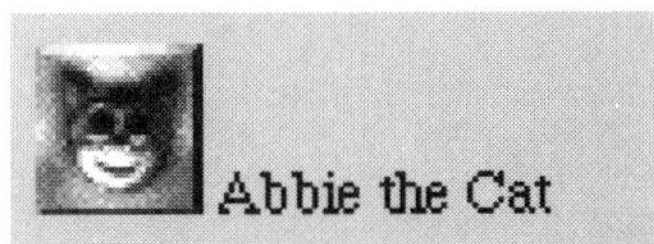

Here is the code to achieve this effect:

```
<P><A HREF="/cat.html"><IMG SRC="cat.gif" BORDER=0></A> Abbie the Cat
```

9.4.2 Using a small clickable graphic as the label for a link to a larger one

Next, the same idea, but with the hypertext link targeting a large graphic. This idea is commonly used on the Web for paintings and photographs which take a long time to download. For example:

```
<A HREF=bluejay.jpeg><IMG href=bluejay.gif> Bluejay (100k Jpeg)</A>
```

9.5 Making sure that the linked document hasn't changed

If you have written, say, a legal document and you included a hypertext link to somewhere else, the legal document may depend on that second document being unchanged. To enable authors to make sure that the document referenced in hypertext links is unchanged and is exactly as the original,

HTML 3 include means for verifying that the object – in general, a file – has not been tampered with.

Verification of this sort is done using something called a cryptographic checksum, or more commonly a **message digest**. This is a technique where every document is processed to yield a number which is a function of the document contents. This number is unique for each document: even a single-bit change in the document would change the number. To see if two documents are the same involves simply seeing if two numbers correspond. If the message digests are not equal, the documents cannot be the same. The message digest functions have been designed by the cryptographic community so that the chance of any two documents yielding the same message digest number is astronomically remote unless they are identical. The MD attribute of the anchor is used to specify the message digest for the referenced object.

9.6 The LINK element and document toolbars

In some situations you want to support the way that readers move from one page to the next and also to impart to the user some model of how your information is organized as a Web application. People have attempted to do this in the past by placing graphical buttons and navigational toolbars at the beginning or end of documents so that, as users get to the top or bottom of a long document, the toolbar takes them on elsewhere.

HTML 3 uses the LINK element in the document head to define a document toolbar which is not rendered by the browser as part of the document window as such, but is instead an extension to the standard fixtures that browsers provide. This use of LINK to define a document toolbar is explained in Chapter 13 on the document head.

Guided tours

Readers are very familiar with the idea of a linear sequence of topics, because this is like turning the pages in a book. When you design a hypertext application you may very well want to lead users through your material in a not dissimilar fashion. You as the author want to structure information in some sort of way that makes sense rather than let readers wander through a random spaghetti of hypertext: you want users to get the information out of the pages as you envisaged.

Thus the idea of a guided tour through hypertext has evolved. This is a linear sequence through a series of hypertext nodes each with a different URL on the Web. One way of doing this is to use Next and Previous buttons inserted by using LINK and guided tours are indeed another use of this element. However, although the idea seems straightforward, there are some subtleties involved. For example, you have to be careful not to confuse the functionality of the buttons 'Back' (which takes you to the chronologically previous node to be seen) and 'Forward' (which involves generally – but not always – the undo operation of back) with the ideas of 'Next' and 'Previous'. The precise meaning of 'Previous' versus 'Back' in particular poses problems.

In filling out forms, where you have done one action with side effects which cannot be undone, problems with chronological back-tracking are unresolved in a hypertext context. The situation is complicated by the fact that different users – for example, a computer expert and a secretarial assistant – will have very different expectations as to what back and forward buttons should do in these situations. You will gather that chronological back-tracking often wanders into murky waters. It should come as no surprise to learn that this area remains a place of active research in the hypertext community.

9.7 Image maps

9.7.1 Introduction

After a while, simple text-based menus get to feel slightly boring. It is time to design a visually more appealing graphical menu. A simple way to achieve this is to make different areas of an image act as different hypertext links. The active areas are called hotzones. A graphic which is divided into a number of hotzones is called an **image map**.

Image maps can be processed either by software on the server, or by the client – by the browser itself. At the time of writing, server-side image mapping is the most commonly used, but this may well soon change.

9.7.2 Server-side processing of image maps

In server-side processing, when the user clicks on the image, the location clicked (in terms of coordinates) is passed to the server. The server looks up to see which area of the image map the click corresponds to, and returns the appropriate document or other information in response. Look at the following image map. This is taken from the home page of AccessHP (`http://www.hp.com`):

This is represented in HTML as:

```
<P><A HREF="/cgi-bin/imagemap/ahp/ahpHome-B.map">
<IMG ALT="Navigation Bar" SRC=/ahp/Bottom.gif
   WIDTH=504 HEIGHT=29 ISMAP></A>
```

HTML 2.0

This is a paragraph with a hypertext link containing an IMG element. Absolutely critical is the inclusion of an ISMAP attribute within the IMG element, as this has the effect of making the browser send the location clicked to the server. Note that the click event is sent to the URL given by the HREF attribute of the enclosing hypertext link, and not the SRC attribute of the IMG element. The other attributes are icing on the cake.

HTML 2.0

The ALT attribute gives a text string for browsers which can't display images, and can be shown in place of the image. In other words, on a text-only browser like Lynx you would see a hypertext link with the label '[Navigation Bar]'.

The WIDTH and HEIGHT attributes speed up the initial display of the document, allowing the browser to continue formatting the rest of the document without having to wait for the image data specifying the image size. For more details on the IMG element, see Chapter 11.

Server-side image maps are processed as follows:

(1) When the user clicks on the image, the browser sends a request for the URL of the document associated with the area clicked.

(2) The server examines the image map file, and sends back the appropriate URL.

(3) The browser then sends the server the request for the corresponding document.

If the browser doesn't support graphics, the server has no way of knowing which choice was selected. As a result, many Web pages offer a conventional hypertext menu using text-based labels in addition to the graphical menu.

This problem, and the slow speed involved in processing the click event, has led to the development of methods that allow the browser itself to process image events without having to send them to the server. This is client-side image mapping, an approach explained later on, but first we will show you how to create a server-side image map file.

Devising a server-side image map

(1) You need to create the graphic itself: the image that will be displayed to the user.

(2) You need to create a *map file* which specifies the coordinates for each of the image's addressable regions and their corresponding URLs. To do this, you need to use a graphics package to display the image. As you position the cursor on each boundary point, the package returns its coordinates as x and y values. You write these down and then use them to create a map file using a plain text editor.

(3) There are two common file formats for image maps, originating with two popular early Web servers developed at NCSA in the USA, and at CERN in Switzerland. Both CERN and NCSA image map formats allow you to define four kinds of region. These are:

(a) Circles
(b) Rectangles
(c) Polygons
(d) Points

A map file for an NCSA server takes a general form as follows:

```
default URL
rect URL left-x,top-y right-x,bottom-y
circle URL center-x,center-y radius
poly URL x1,y1 x2,y2 x3,y3 ... xn,yn
point URL x,y
```

A map file for a CERN server brackets coordinate pairs and has the URL on the right:

```
default URL
rectangle (left-x,top-y) (right-x,bottom-y) URL
circle (center-x,center-y) radius URL
polygon (x1,y1) (x2,y2) (x3,y3) ... (xn,yn) URL
point (x,y) URL
```

Here is an example of the CERN format from MIT:

```
default http://web.mit.edu/
circle (35,25) 10
http://web.mit.edu/geninfo.html
rectangle (50,25) (100,50)
http://web.mit.edu/academics.html
polygon (25,75) (25,100) (35,125) (50,75) (25,75)
http://web.mit.edu/computing.html
```

The default URL is there so that, should users click on any part of the image which is not on the map, they still get some kind of response, even if it is simply a message explaining that the click was outside any of the hotzones defined. In both formats, x values are measured in pixels starting from zero at the left and increasing as you move to the right, while y values are measured in pixels starting from zero at the top and increasing as you move downwards.

The map file is stored on the server in a particular part of the server file system: your Webmaster will know exactly where to put it.

(4) You need a CGI script to handle the coordinate–link transformation. The name of the CERN server script for handling map files is *htimage*. It is generally in /bin/cgi but you will need to seek the advice of your Webmaster about this. The equivalent script on an NCSA server is *imagemap*, also usually in /bin/cgi.

(5) You need to write the HTML which displays the image, tells the browser that the image is a clickable one, and sends a request to the server which then executes the CGI script. For example:

```
HREF="/bin/cgi/htimages/images/maps/example.map">
<IMG SRC="images/gif/example.gif" ISMAP>
</A>
```

The first line tells the browser where the map file is and where the CGI script to use is. The second line uses the `IMG` element combined with `SRC` in the usual manner although you note that the `ISMAP` attribute is added to show that the image is a clickable map.

This is an equivalent example of the HTML for an image map to be handled on a NCSA server. It's identical apart from the name of the CGI script:

```
HREF="/bin/cgi/imagemap/images/maps/example.map">
<IMG SRC="images/gif/example.gif" ISMAP>
</A>
```

You should always supply a text-based method of going to the same locations as defined by the image map. This is needed when browsers can't download or display the image.

Don't place more than one `IMG` element with the `ISMAP` attribute inside the same anchor element, as the server will try to use the same image map file for both images, which is almost certainly not what you intended. Placing each `IMG` element in its own anchor element avoids this problem!

There are several tools around which allow you to display the image and then provide simple line-drawing tools for defining the hotzones and defining the URLs. They then allow you to generate the results as image map files in either NCSA or CERN formats. The best known of these tools are *MapEdit* for UNIX and Windows, and *WebMap* for the Macintosh. Pointers to these and other such tools can be found at `http://www.io.org/faq/www/imagemap.htm`.

9.7.3 Client-side processing of image maps

In client-side image mapping the browser uses an image map defined in HTML rather than one defined at the server end. The browser uses the locally defined image map to *map* the coordinates of the user's mouse click to a URL and then follow the corresponding hypertext link.

Why client-side image maps are useful

Client-side image maps have several advantages over the older server-side variety:

- They reduce the load on Web servers.

- They speed the resolution of links.
- The destination can be shown as the user moves the cursor over the map.
- The cursor can change its shape dynamically to indicate it's over a hotzone.
- Image maps can be used with local files, for example for documents on a CD-ROM. This is also true for other document retrieval protocols like FTP and Gopher.
- Image maps in the document are not dependent on the server, and are hence easier to deal with. There is no need for special image map files which have to be placed in special directories, and so on.

Sometimes, though, a server-side image map is more appropriate. For example, for a *Find the Ball* competition[2] a client-side image map would give the game away. In some applications the descriptions of the hotzones would be too complicated. This might be the case in a very detailed geographical map. The data to describe the map would get too cumbersome to download.

The Spyglass `MAP` element

The Spyglass company, well known for 'Enhanced Mosaic' have proposed an extension to HTML for representing client-side image maps; it can be used with `IMG` elements, and allows image maps to be placed in separate files, or embedded within an HTML document.

Note: The `MAP` element was, by and large, the work of Jim Seidman of Spyglass Mosaic Inc. Although client-side image mapping as implemented by `MAP` has been quite successful, it inevitably suffers from the limitations of `IMG`, in particular that `IMG` is not a container element. Contrast `IMG` with `OBJECT` which can contain other HTML mark-up and is therefore much more flexible.

To create a client-side image map:

(1) Add the image to your HTML document as an inline image, using an `IMG` element.

```
<IMG SRC="image.gif">
```

(2) Add the `USEMAP` attribute to the `IMG` element. This attribute specifies the image map with a URL.

```
<IMG SRC="image.gif" USEMAP="#navbar">
```

[2] These were once quite common in British newspapers. You had to mark where you thought a (hidden) soccer ball was and send it in. The nearest person won a prize.

(3) Determine the pixel coordinates of each hotzone you wish to define. This can be done using one of the commonly available image map tools.

(4) Create a map definition, for example:

```
<MAP NAME="navbar">
<AREA SHAPE=rect COORDS="24,18,143,41" HREF="prev.html">
<AREA SHAPE=rect COORDS="24,18,143,41" HREF="prev.html">
</MAP>
```

The fragment identifier on the USEMAP attribute must match the value of the NAME attribute. The MAP element can be in the same file as the IMG element, or in a separate file. The AREA element takes one of the following general forms:

```
<AREA SHAPE=rect COORDS="left-x,top-y,right-x bottom-y" HREF="URL">
```

A rectangular region defined by the pixel coordinates of upper left and lower right corners.

```
<AREA SHAPE=circle COORDS="center-x,center-y,radius-x" HREF="URL">
```

A circular region defined by the coordinates of the centre, plus the radius.

```
<AREA SHAPE=polygon COORDS="x1,y1,x2,y2,x3,y3" HREF="URL">
```

An irregular region defined by a series of (x,y) coordinate pairs.

If two or more regions overlap, then the region defined first in the map definition takes precedence over other regions. Note that there is no default URL. Instead, you can define a RECT equal in size to the image, and place it last in the list (placing it first would cause it to take precedence over all the other AREA elements).

To ensure that the document works with browsers that don't support the MAP element, you can include the ISMAP attribute, and place the IMG element in an anchor element. This way, such browsers send the mouse clicks to the server, while browsers that are MAP savvy process the mouse clicks locally instead. For example:

```
<A HREF="http://www.acme.com/cgi-bin/imagemap/maps/cs/test.map">
<IMG SRC=test.gif USEMAP="#test" ISMAP></A>

<MAP NAME=test>
<AREA SHAPE=rect COORDS="23,18,144,42" HREF=test.html>
</MAP>
```

The Spyglass MAP element and USEMAP attribute are supported by an increasing number of browser companies, including Netscape Communications Corporation.

9.8 A new idea: Client-side image maps with the OBJECT element

In Chapter 11 you will see mentioned a new element called OBJECT which is likely to be implemented by all major browser writers in the near future. This element allows graphics and all manner of other media to be referenced in Web documents and may well eventually take the place of IMG.

Apart from allowing graphics and other media to be referenced in a simple way, OBJECT, like MAP, provides the author with facilities for client-side image map processing. One of the advantages of the OBJECT element over MAP is its attribute SHAPE, which, at the time of going to press, is being proposed by the World Wide Web consortium.

To see why SHAPE is important, look at the shortcomings of the MAP element:

- Existing browsers which do not recognize MAP cannot follow the links. This is the case for many browsers.

  Note: HTML is not just for graphical user interfaces. Many people use terminal access with browsers like Lynx, or are unable to benefit from graphics through visual impairments. In the future, speech-based browsers are likely to become of increasing importance for people on the move who are unable to look away from the road, and so on. With this in mind, authors are encouraged to take advantage of HTML as a media-independent document format.

- The ALT attribute for MAP is optional and so there is no requirement for authors to provide an alternative means for users to access the links when they are working with non-graphical browsers.

- Web-page designers are forced to provide additional hypertext links to cater for non-graphical users. You often see a carefully crafted image map with a matching selection of textual links underneath it. If you are using a graphical browser, textual equivalents to image maps are unnecessary.

So how do OBJECT and SHAPE help in these matters? The OBJECT element is designed so that authors can incorporate mark-up to be used if and only if a browser displaying the document does not employ graphics. OBJECT lets the author include HTML solely for digestion by text-only browsers – graphical browsers to ignore it.

The OBJECT element contents are used when the browser is unable to render the object specified by the parameters given with the start tag.

9.8.1 Simple example of OBJECT

Here is a simple example of the OBJECT element catering for both text-only and graphical browsers:

```
<OBJECT DATA="botleycathedral.jpeg">
<P><EM>Botley Cathedral</EM> a well-known landmark to the West of Oxford,
England.
</OBJECT>
```

So long as the browser can OBJECT the photograph of the Hancock Tower, the contents of the element – the textual description of Botley Cathedral – is ignored. On the other hand, if the browser cannot display the photo, the words appear instead.

OBJECT is a new element which has been proposed by the World Wide Web consortium and major browser vendors including Netscape Communications, Spyglass Mosaic, Sun Microsystems and Microsoft. See Chapter 11 for more information.

9.8.2 OBJECT and SHAPE

Look again at the navigation toolbar from AccessHP:

Currently it has a textual equivalent underneath it for the benefit of those relying on text only rather than on graphics. Using OBJECT and SHAPE this toolbar can be respresented as:

```
<OBJECT DATA="navbar.gif" SHAPES>
   <A HREF=guide.html SHAPE=rect COORDS="0,0,118,28">Access Guide</A> |
   <A HREF=shortcut.html SHAPE=rect COORDS="118,0,184,28">Go</A> |
   <A HREF=search.html SHAPE=rect COORDS="184,0,276,28">Search</A> |
   <A HREF=top10.html SHAPE=rect COORDS="276,0,373,28">Top Ten</A>
</OBJECT>
```

On graphical browsers supporting OBJECT the toolbar appears and the various rectangular portions summon up different information when clicked on. Meanwhile, on HTML 2.0 browsers and also on those not supporting graphics, you see:

Access Guide | Go | Search | Top

You see both types of menu together, as is frequently the case with, say, IMG and MAP.

9.8.3 The SHAPE attribute

In the example above we use the SHAPES attribute and also the SHAPE attribute. Similarly named but with different functions, the SHAPES attribute tells the browser to parse the contents of the element to look for anchor elements. The anchor element (`<A HREF=...> ... </A>`) is meanwhile extended to permit the `SHAPE` attribute which serves to associate the hypertext link with a region on the image specified within `OBJECT` (in our example this is `navbar.gif`). `SHAPE` takes one of the general forms:

```
SHAPE=rect COORDS="left-x, top-y, right-x, bottom-y"
SHAPE=circle COORDS="center-x, center-y, radius"
SHAPE=poly COORDS="x1, y1, x2, y2, x3, y3 ... "
```

where x and y are measured in pixels from the left/top of the associated image. If x and y values are given with a percent sign as a suffix, the values should be interpreted as percentages of the image's width and height, respectively. For example:

```
SHAPE=rect COORDS="0, 0, 50%, 100%"
```

Note: Percentage coordinates are supported by Netscape for the `MAP` element.

The visually impaired community have argued strongly in favour of the `SHAPE`d anchor mechanism, as it forces authors to provide a way to follow the links regardless of which browser they are working with.

It's also worth noting that the `SHAPE` attribute can be used together with the `TARGET` attribute proposed by Netscape for designating the target user interface object (for example, frame) for displaying the linked document or resource.

9.8.4 Another example: Defining overlapping regions

In the following graphic, the light and dark regions are mapped to different URLs. Although the regions overlap, clicking on each region loads the appropriate document.

If two or more regions overlap, the region defined first in the map definition takes precedence over other regions. For example, in the map definition for the graphic above, the green region is defined before the blue region:

```
<OBJECT data="overlap.gif" SHAPES>
   <A HREF=green.html SHAPE="rect 66,13,186,37">Green</A> |
   <A HREF=blue.html SHAPE="rect 195,43,245,46">Blue</A>
</OBJECT>
```

9.8.5 The same example using the MAP element

This is the same as above but expressed using the Spyglass client-side image map proposal:

```
<OBJECT DATA="navbar1.gif" USEMAP="#map1">
</OBJECT>

<MAP NAME="map1">
   <AREA HREF=guide.html ALT="Access Guide" SHAPE=rect COORDS="0,0,118,28">
   <AREA HREF=shortcut.html ALT="Go;" SHAPE=rect COORDS="118,0,184,28">
   <AREA HREF=top10.html ALT="Top Ten" SHAPE=rect COORDS="276,0,373,28">
</MAP>
```

The OBJECT element references the MAP with a URL given with the USEMAP attribute. The SHAPE/COORDS attributes behave in the same way as for the SHAPEd anchor proposal. The ALT attributes can be used to provide a few words describing each choice.

MAP doesn't yet support a mechanism for designating the target user interface object (for example, frame) for displaying the linked object. An obvious extension would be to add the Netscape TARGET attribute to the AREA element for this purpose

The MAP element won't be recognized by browsers designed for HTML 2.0. Users of such browsers will be unable to follow the various links. At the time of writing this includes all Lynx browsers.

This also appears to be true for newer browsers like Netscape 2.0 when the image is inaccessible.

As the ALT attribute is optional, there is no requirement for authors to provide an alternative means for users to access the links when they are working with non-graphical browsers. This is a severe problem for visually impaired people!

9.8.6 Combining MAP with server-side image maps

The Spyglass client-side image map technique can be combined with conventional server-side image maps. The IMG or OBJECT element is given with both ISMAP and USEMAP attributes, as in:

```
<A HREF="http://www.acme.com/cgi-bin/imagemap/maps/test/test.map">
   <OBJECT DATA="navbar.gif" ISMAP USEMAP="#map1">
</OBJECT></A>

<MAP NAME="map1">
   <AREA HREF=guide.html ALT="Access Guide" SHAPE=rect COORDS="0,0,118,28">
   <AREA HREF=shortcut.html ALT="Go" SHAPE=rect COORDS="118,0,184,28">
   <AREA HREF=top10.html ALT="Top Ten" SHAPE=rect COORDS="276,0,373,28">
</MAP>
```

MAP-savvy browsers will use the client-side image map, while other graphical browsers will use the server-side image map. Users working with browsers that don't support MAP and can't show the image will be screwed!

Note that this approach increases the pain for authors as they have to create separate image map files and install them on the server in the appropriate place. They still don't meet all users' needs. Concerned authors will therefore provide separate hypertext links for non-graphical browsers.

9.8.7 Combining SHAPES with server-side image maps

You can combine ISMAP with the SHAPES attribute, for example:

```
<A HREF="http://www.hp.com/cgi-bin/imagemap/maps/hp/navbar.map">
<OBJECT DATA="navbar.gif" ISMAP SHAPEs">
   <A HREF=guide.html SHAPE="rect 0,0,118,28">Access Guide</A>
   <A HREF=shortcut.html SHAPE="rect 118,0,184,28">Go</A> |
   <A HREF=search.html SHAPE="rect 184,0,276,28">Search</A> |
   <A HREF=top10.html SHAPE="rect 276,0,373,28">Top Ten</A> |
</OBJECT></A>
```

In this case, locally defined hotzones take precedence over server-side hotzones. The browser only sends the mouse click to the server if the click is not within a region defined by a SHAPE attribute.

This allows authors to get the benefits of client-side image maps for parts of the image, for example regions that visually act as 3-D bevelled buttons, while for complex image maps, or where it is undesirable to pass the maps to the client, the mouse click is dealt with by the server, (for example, *Find the ball* competitions).

10
TABLES

This chapter describes the facilities in HTML 3 for structuring data into tables.

- It begins by introducing the concept of tables (Section 10.1),
- and shows how to construct simple but effective tables (Section 10.2).

The more advanced features are then presented in turn, showing how to incorporate:

- aligning or justifying the text within a cell (Section 10.3)
- rows of header cells (Section 10.4) to act as titles for the columns
- captions for the table itself (Section 10.5)
- controlling the table as a whole (Section 10.6), including text wrapping and table width
- making individual cells span several rows or columns (Section 10.7)
- designating header and body groups of rows (Section 10.8)

- aligning text in (groups of) columns of table cells (Section 10.9)
- understanding of inheritance of alignment attributes (Section 10.10)
- drawing a border for the table in a choice of styles (Section 10.11)
- putting other elements such as images inside tables (Section 10.12)
- helping the browser to speed up table display (Section 10.13).

We have attempted to put the more difficult and less essential attributes later in the chapter, so that the sections are roughly graded in the order in which you will need to study them.

The impressive set of table features in HTML 3 should be good for everyone:

- It enables the advanced HTML user to construct tables for almost every conceivable purpose. CALS users in particular will find many familiar features, as the designers' intention has been to simplify the importing of SGML CALS tables as far as possible.
- Netscape users will be delighted to discover that HTML 3 offers full backwards compatibility with the table model implemented in Netscape Navigator 1.1N, which is in turn an extended implementation of the earlier proposals for HTML tables.
- The good news for beginners is that you can make quite serviceable tables with just the simplest of the table elements, and then gradually add others as you become more experienced. In several cases, the more advanced features enable you to save time by working on groups of table cells rather than on each one individually.

10.1 Introduction

HTML is often used for presenting commercial, scientific and technical data, which can naturally be organized as tables. Think of railway timetables, trigonometric tables from your schooldays, theatre schedules, or even comparisons of the relative effectiveness of one soap powder against another. What you need to do to display such data sets effectively is to present them in tabular form.

Unfortunately, there is no agreement on how tables should appear. Some people like to give tables borders, others like an occasional horizontal line, others just white space. To allow for this natural variation, HTML 3 provides a robust basic mechanism for simple tables, accompanied by a set of increasingly sophisticated features for more subtle formatting when necessary.

We have tried in this chapter to make each section build on the earlier ones, so that you can start making simple tables right away. Since you will probably want to use several of the most attractive features like borders, captions and merged cells as soon as possible, we have in places introduced these things obliquely before discussing them in full later.

10.2 Simple tables

It is much easier to get started with tables than you might expect.

10.2.1 A real example

The following illustration, taken straight from the World Wide Web, shows a simple but effective use of an HTML table to list stocks and companies.

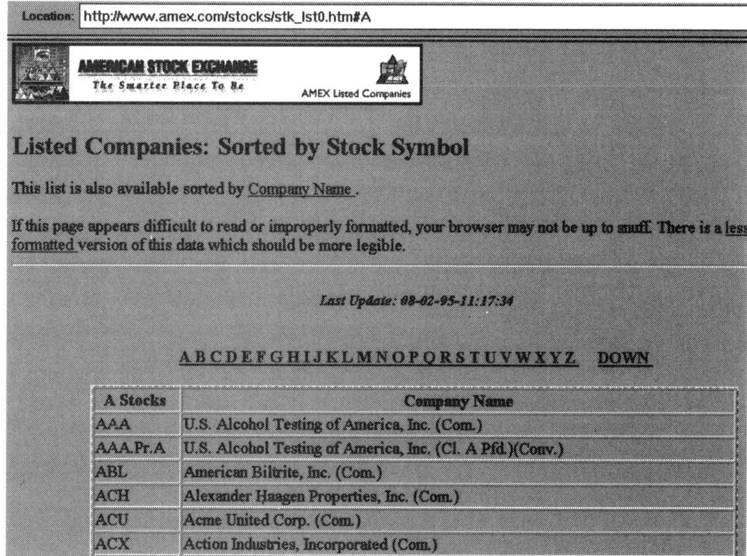

A Stocks	Company Name
AAA	U.S. Alcohol Testing of America, Inc. (Com.)
AAA.Pr.A	U.S. Alcohol Testing of America, Inc. (Cl. A Pfd.)(Conv.)
ABL	American Biltrite, Inc. (Com.)
ACH	Alexander Haagen Properties, Inc. (Com.)
ACU	Acme United Corp. (Com.)
ACX	Action Industries, Incorporated (Com.)

This illustration, prepared in Netscape 1.1N, shows the basic style of their table implementation. The raised/embossed appearance is consistent with the standard, though not demanded by it.

The AMEX page from which the illustration is taken (`http://www.amex.com`) includes the following code, which we have reformatted slightly to make it as clear as possible:

```
<TABLE BORDER=2>
   <TR><TH><B> A Stocks </B></TH><TH><B> Company Name </B></TH></TR>
   <TR><TD> AAA </TD><TD> U.S. Alcohol Testing of America, Inc. (Com.)
      <BR></TD></TR>
   <TR><TD> ABL </TD><TD> American Biltrite, Inc. (Com.)
      <BR></TD></TR>
   <TR><TD> ACH </TD><TD> Alexander Haagen Properties, Inc. (Com.)
      <BR></TD></TR>
   <TR><TD> ACU </TD><TD> Acme United Corp. (Com.)
      <BR></TD></TR>
   <TR><TD> ACX </TD><TD> Action Industries, Incorporated (Com.)
      <BR></TD></TR>
            <!--many more lines of data...-->
</TABLE>
```

The table is created by the TABLE element, qualified by the BORDER attribute to specify that a thick border should be drawn.

The first row of the table is specified as a table row <TR>, followed by two table headers <TH>.

AMEX have been ultra-cautious here (no bad thing) and ended each <TR> and <TH> with a matching </TR> and </TH>. Most probably they generated the code with a translator from a database or word-processor file, and the translation program in best belt-and-braces style followed the simple rule, 'always put in all start and end tags'.

The heading text has been emphasized with <B>...</B>. In HTML 3 this is not really necessary, as browsers (and style sheets) provide for special treatment to distinguish headers from table data.

After that it is all plain sailing, as the rest of the rows of the table have the same structure. Like the header row, they begin with <TR>. Each entry is represented as a table data <TD> item. You can see that the browser has correctly aligned all the stocks and company names into two columns.

10.2.2 Writing your own tables

If you are writing HTML 3 by hand, you can always safely omit the closing </TR>, </TH> and </TD> tags, because browsers know immediately from the following tags that the table row or item has come to an end. We can therefore rewrite the AMEX table of company stocks in HTML 3 like this:

```
<TABLE FRAME=box RULES=all>          <!--new-style attributes-->
   <TR><TH> A Stocks <TH>Company Name
   <TR><TD> AAA <TD> U.S. Alcohol Testing of America, Inc. (Com.)
   <TR><TD> ABL <TD> American Biltrite, Inc. (Com.)
   <TR><TD> ACH <TD> Alexander Haagen Properties, Inc. (Com.)
   <TR><TD> ACU <TD> Acme United Corp. (Com.)
   <TR><TD> ACX <TD> Action Industries, Incorporated (Com.)
                  <!--many more lines of data...-->
</TABLE>
```

which as you can see is considerably shorter and simpler than AMEX' own implementation.

If you don't even want to have headers above your table columns, all you need to create HTML tables is the structure:

```
<TABLE FRAME=box RULES=all>
   <TR><TD>Duck   <TD>D.     <TD>1, The Pond, Florida
   <TR><TD>Mouse  <TD>M.     <TD>3, The Hole, New York
   <TR><TD>Sailor <TD>P.     <TD>of No Fixed Abode
</TABLE>
```

This gives you a result as simple as it could be:

Duck	D.	1, The Pond, Florida
Mouse	M.	3, The Hole, New York
Sailor	P.	of No Fixed Abode

10.2.3 Floating tables

Incidentally, tables are by default centred on the page, with no text or other HTML structures on either side of them, like the simple examples above. They are in fact typical block-level elements, comparable with paragraphs or lists. But if you want a table to float against the left or right margin, with text beside it, you can make it do so with the HTML 3 attribute `ALIGN`: you write `<TABLE ALIGN=left>` or `=right` respectively. When a table is made to float left or right, subsequent HTML elements such as text and images flow around the table if there is room. `ALIGN=center` does not float.

You now know all you need to, to construct simple but useful tables in your Web pages. The rest of this chapter elaborates on this knowledge, adding a wide range of elegant and powerful features.

10.3 Aligning text in individual table cells

The simplest way to control the alignment of text in a `TH` or `TD` cell (header and data cells work the same way) is to set it individually. This gives you fine

control over the appearance of the table, but is repetitive, and makes your HTML bulky and slow to display if you need to do something to every cell. We will explain better approaches later.

10.3.1 Aligning or justifying cell contents horizontally

The approach is direct. You qualify the tag of the cell you are interested in with the ALIGN attribute. It can take the values left (the default for TD), center (the default for TH), right, justify or char. For example:

```
<TABLE FRAME=box RULES=none ID=just>
<TBODY ALIGN=center>          <!--overridden by lower-level align-->
  <TR><TD ALIGN=justify>
  We would like to explain exactly why we have elected to take
  the action that we did, given that it appears that certain
  members feel that it was less than appropriate.
  <TR><TD ALIGN=right>
  In our circumstances we feel that a ragged left boundary
  is better than no boundary at all.
</TABLE>
```

Justified text is made to fit both left and right boundaries of the cell. The last (or if the text is short, the only) line of the text is not stretched to fit against the right boundary (the effect looks amateurish), so the line is effectively left-justified.

The example creates the following table:

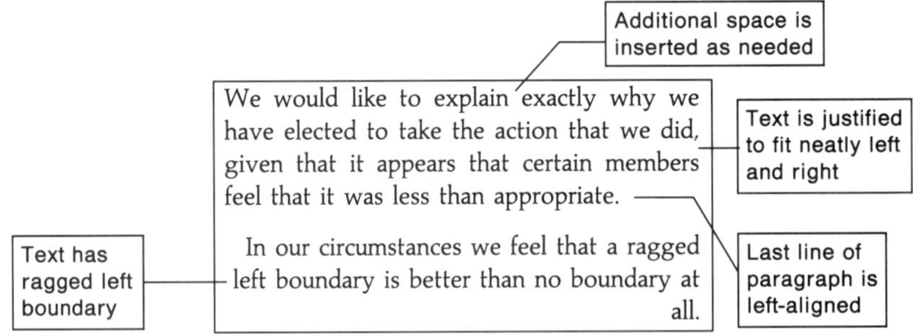

Incidentally, this example uses a frame-style border, with no lines between table cells.

10.3.2 Aligning cell contents vertically

Similarly, you can directly control the vertical alignment of the contents of any table cell, using VALIGN. It can take the values top, middle (the default), bottom or baseline. These have their common meanings, but baseline needs some explanation. All cells in a baseline row should have their first line of text on a common baseline; subsequent lines of text are unconstrained.

For example:

```
<TABLE FRAME=hsides>
   <TR><TD VALIGN=top>Soprano<TD>a two<BR>line cell
</TABLE>
```

arranges the 'Soprano' cell contents at the top of the cell, even though there is white space below:

Soprano	a two line cell

10.3.3 Using a horizontal alignment character

Something very useful for organizing forms (see Section 12.6 on Form Design) is alignment on a specific character, which you arrange to occur in all lines of text (typically separated with <BR> line breaks) within a TD cell. For example, you can align on the colon (':') character so that every prompt of the form 'Wingspan:' or 'Weight:' is neatly right-aligned with the colons forming a perfect column.

Lines that do not include the alignment character are shifted by the browser to end at the alignment position.

A cell that spans several rows or columns takes its alignment from its first row or column.

The pair of HTML attributes you need for this arrangement is

```
<TD ALIGN=char CHAR=":">
```

and you can use any character that you find convenient. Notice the repetition of the word 'CHAR'. You need to arrange to reserve that character for alignment purposes, so you normally can't use a letter or digit.

Suitable characters include:

- the colon ':' which is useful for aligning text prompts;
- the dot or period '.' which is ideal if you have a column of decimal numbers, as it aligns them at the decimal point;
- the dash '–' if you want to line up text comments, as the dash character does not look strange either before or after a piece of text.

For example, field ornithologists might use an application containing the following table/form:

```
<TABLE>
   <TBODY>                        <!--this line is optional, actually-->
   <TR><TD ALIGN=char CHAR=":">
      <FORM>
         Wingspan : <INPUT NAME="wing" SIZE="5" ><BR>
           Weight : <INPUT NAME="mass" SIZE="5" ><BR>
         Ring No. : <INPUT NAME="rnum" SIZE="12"><BR>
         <INPUT TYPE=reset>       <INPUT TYPE=submit>
   </FORM>
</TABLE>
```

This remarkably short piece of HTML 3 creates a neatly aligned form for the bird-ringers, like this:

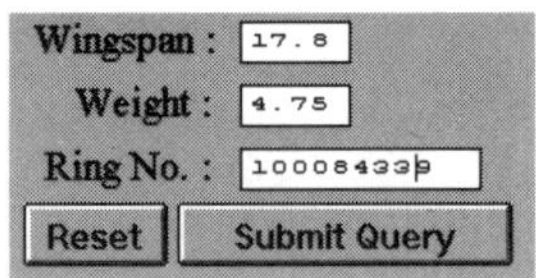

You should avoid putting further alignment attributes on the cell contents (for example, by inserting `<P ALIGN=center>` in a table cell) as such attributes would take priority over cell-level alignment and spoil the table's appearance. The rule is that low-level specifications take priority over high-level ones.

10.3.4 Setting an offset for the alignment character

If you use `CHAR` as described so far, browsers simply fit your text into table cells, aligning on the specified character. You can improve on this by telling the browser where, relative to the width of the table cell, you want the character to be placed.

The HTML attribute for this is

```
CHAROFF=50%
```

and you are free to enter any percentage between 0 and 100. The percent symbol is needed.

For example:

```
CHAR="-"
CHAROFF=70%
```

This example aligns the cell contents so that the included '–' characters are all at 70% of the width of the cell, measured from the left to the right. Depending on how much text is on either side of the character, this may cause the browser to provide additional white space on one side or the other.

10.4 Table headers

The table header acts much like a header in a printed book, except that if necessary it can be made to repeat automatically on each printed page covered by a long table, or when on screen to remain fixed while the table data is scrolled by the user.

A table header in HTML 3 consists of a single THEAD element, containing a group of ordinary table rows (TR), which in turn contain table header cells (TH). You can use the generic attributes ID, LANG, STYLE and CLASS to indicate or control the whole group. Only one header group can be specified in a table; if it occurs, it must come after the caption and column specifications (if any) and before the table body. Groups are discussed further in Section 10.8.

10.4.1 Creating table header rows

Table header rows are created by HTML code virtually identical to that for normal table rows, except that the <TD> tag is replaced by the <TH> tag. By default, the contents of header cells are centred, unlike data cells which are flush left. Browsers often do something to distinguish headers from data, for example by putting the headers into boldface type.

To create a header row, you write <TR> as usual, followed by <TH> tags to introduce each of the columns with (normally) a column title:

```
<TABLE FRAME=box RULES=all>
<THEAD ALIGN=center>        <!--but centering is header's default-->
   <TR><TH>Doric   <TH>Ionic   <TH>Corinthian
<TBODY ALIGN=left>
   <TR><TD>Simple><TD>Delicate<TD>Ornate
</TABLE>
```

This creates a table with six cells, three headers and three data:

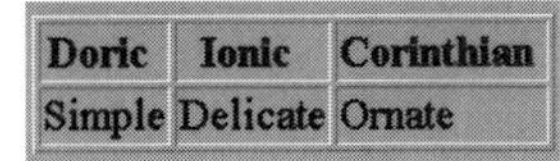

Doric	Ionic	Corinthian
Simple	Delicate	Ornate

It is up to you whether you consider this to be made up of three columns (as the cell contents suggest!) or two rows. The HTML code, as you can see, treats rows as the major units and columns as minor or implicit.

10.4.2 Controlling table header cells

You can use the generic attributes ID, LANG, STYLE and CLASS in <TH> header cells just as in <TD> data cells, so you can specify their treatment in a style sheet as usual. You can also control their alignment both horizontally and vertically in exactly the same way as for <TD> cells.

One other thing you can do (which is also available for <TD> cells) is to define what HTML 3 calls 'axes', concise text labels for the horizontal and vertical axes of the table. The AXIS attribute defaults to the cell contents, that is, any text you put inside the table cell. If you want its value to be different, you assign it a text string, such as:

```
<TH STYLE="background: blue" AXIS=time>Time in Milliseconds
```

Alternatively you can provide a list of axis names, using the AXES attribute:

```
AXES=mass, time
```

Axis names may be used by browsers:

- when rendering to speech; short names save time during speech output
- when processing a table to load its contents into a database; axis names can be used as database field names, and the table's class attribute (for example, <TABLE CLASS="readyforDB">) can signal which tables are intended for this kind of use.

10.5 Table captions

The table caption is optional. It is usual to write normal text, but the characters you use can be marked up for emphasis, and the special character entities defined in HTML can be included. You can use the generic attributes ID, LANG, STYLE and CLASS if you need them.

More surprisingly, you can put images (<IMG SRC=...>) and hypertext anchors (<A HREF=...>) into the table caption. This enables you to link your tables directly to related material, and to incorporate icons. HTML tables are integral parts of the World Wide Web hypertext.

By default, the table caption appears above the table. You can control this behaviour with ALIGN=top, =bottom, =left or =right in HTML 3.

For example:

```
<TABLE FRAME=box RULES=all>
<CAPTION ALIGN=bottom>This caption goes below its table
   <TR><TD>chippendale<TD>occasional<TD>mahogany
</TABLE>
```

creates an HTML 3 table with a caption beneath it:

chippendale	occasional	mahogany

This caption goes below its table

10.6 Controlling the table as a whole

You can use the generic attributes ID, LANG and CLASS for tables, as for most other HTML elements. Tables can also be controlled by several more specific attributes, including NOWRAP (shared by other text elements), WIDTH and FLOAT. These are discussed below.

10.6.1 Turning text wrapping off

The keyword NOWRAP is permitted as an attribute of the cell elements (TH, TD). As you would expect in this position, it switches off text wrapping for all the text in the whole table. The syntax is simply:

```
<TABLE>
   ... <TD NOWRAP> ...
<TABLE>
```

The default behaviour is for cell content text to wrap when the column widths together reach the maximum width available (slightly less than the width of the browser window or screen). If you switch wrapping off, long texts may be clipped, especially if the user makes the browser window narrow. NOWRAP may cause tables to become undesirably wide, so we recommend you use the attribute as rarely as possible.

10.6.2 Controlling table width

By default, tables are sized in accordance with the widths of their contents, and the available width of the screen or window into which they must fit. This is quite complicated for browsers, as there are several competing pressures to consider. You can specify the width you intend for your table (and for individual columns, as will be explained) but browsers may be unable to comply with this: if cell contents require a wider table, browsers will probably ignore your suggested width.

Designers are aware of the default width in pixels of Netscape's browser on the PC, so they tend to assume this. In future, style sheets will help designers avoid usage assumptions of this kind.

Widths can be supplied in any of the HTML Standard Units for Widths, which are as follows:

pt	points	(a common measure of size of print, approx. 1/72 inch)
pi	picas	(another common traditional measure, equal to 12 points)
in	inches	(one inch is 25.4 millimetres)
cm	centimetres	(one centimetre is 10 millimetres)
mm	millimetres	
em	em units	(defined as the height of the default font)
px	screen pixels	(the default if no unit is specified)

Width settings can be applied equally to individual columns, groups of columns, or to whole tables.

For example, <TABLE WIDTH=432pt>, <TABLE WIDTH=6in> and <TABLE WIDTH=152mm> are all approximately equivalent. No space is allowed between number and unit.

The equivalent width in screen pixels depends both on screen size and on the current resolution (for example, 640 × 480 pixels), and cannot be predicted. Pixels are therefore the least useful of these measures and should be avoided if at all possible. Remember in any case when setting widths that users may not have the same font settings as you. Such matters are best left to style sheets.

Finally, you can set table width as a percentage of the space between the current left and right margins, using the % symbol. For instance:

```
<TABLE WIDTH=75%>
```

10.6.3 Making the table float or flow with the text

Tables are usually treated as part of the general flow of text. If you wish, you can specify that a table is to float to the left or to the right, with the rest of the text flow continuing around it. There is no default. For example:

```
<TABLE ALIGN=right>
```

10.7 Cells spanning rows or columns

The simple approach discussed so far works very well for plain sets of data. Very often, though, you want to make the data stand out better by grouping items that apply to more than one row or column. HTML 3 uses exactly the same approach for both <TH> and <TD> cells.

To make a cell span two or more rows, you use the ROWSPAN attribute, as in

```
<TH ROWSPAN=2>        <--a header cell spanning 2 rows-->
```

The value, as you'd expect, specifies how many <TH> or <TD> cells this particular cell is to span. Similarly, to make a cell span two or more columns, you use the SPAN attribute, as in

```
<TH COLSPAN=3>        <!--a header cell spanning 3 columns-->
<TD COLSPAN=2>        <!--a data cell spanning 2 columns  -->
```

For example:

```
<TABLE BORDER>
   <CAPTION>Table with merged cells</CAPTION>
   <TR><TH ROWSPAN=2><TH SPAN=3>Length/mm
   <TR><TH>body<TH>tail<TH>ears
   <TR><TH ALIGN=left>males  <TD>31.4<TD>23.7<TD>3.8
   <TR><TH ALIGN=left>females<TD>29.6<TD>20.8<TD>3.4
</TABLE>
```

This creates a table with a header which extends across the three data columns, like this:

Table with merged cells

	Length/mm		
	body	**tail**	**ears**
males	31.4	23.7	3.8
females	29.6	20.8	3.4

There is a risk, if you apply ROWSPAN and SPAN attributes to different cells in a table, that those cells may overlap.

For example, here is the HTML definition of a table in which the cells called 'Sixth' and 'Seventh' overlap:

```
<TABLE BORDER>
   <CAPTION ALIGN=bottom>a BAD table with overlap</CAPTION>
   <TR><TD ROWSPAN=2>First<TD>Second<TD>Third<TD>Fourth<TD>Fifth
   <TR><TD ROWSPAN=2>Sixth                  <!--bad idea!-->
   <TR><TD COLSPAN=2>Seventh<TD>Eighth      <!--don't do this!-->
</TABLE>
```

The effect of this code depends on the browser. Netscape actually displays the messy consequences of the table exactly as it is specified:

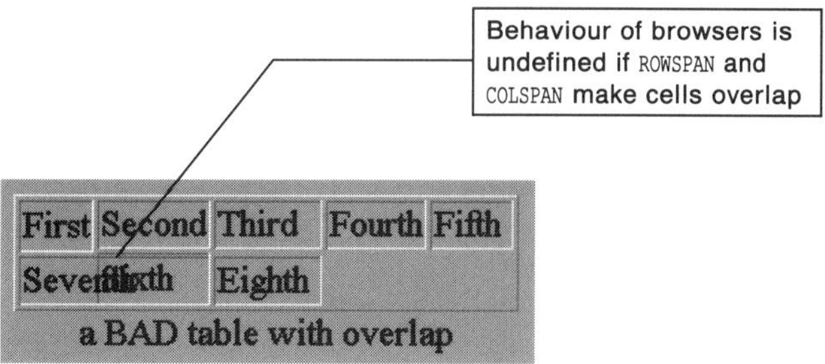

Other browsers may produce a tidier, but arguably less accurate, result by concealing the overlapped cell contents. You should clearly be careful to avoid overlaps.

10.8 Designating header and body groups

In line with the US Department of Defense's successful CALS model for tables, HTML 3 permits you to organize your table rows into header and body groups if you wish. By default, all rows are assumed to be body. You can define at most one header group. Browsers normally display the header in a fixed position at the top of the part of the table shown in the display area: if the table body scrolls, the header remains on screen.

You can put as many rows as you like into each group, but given the restricted number of rows of text that readers can display on their browsers, there is no point putting more than a few rows into headers.

You can supply any of the generic attributes `ID`, `LANG`, `STYLE` and `CLASS`, or any of the alignment attributes (`ALIGN`, `CHAR`, `CHAROFF` or `VALIGN`) for either kind of group, allowing you to control groups of rows instead of either individual rows or whole tables.

10.8.1 The header group

If you want a header group you put a `<THEAD>` tag at its start. There is no need for a `</THEAD>` tag at the end, as the following `<TBODY>` makes it quite clear where the group ends. If provided, the header group must include at least one `<TR>` table row. The (quite separate) table caption also gives you an opportunity to describe the table as a whole.

10.8.2 The body group

Tables must have at least one body. You only need to supply `TBODY` group starting tags, though, if you have specified a header group, or if you want to place ruled lines between body groups (using `<TABLE RULES=groups>`). The tag `<TBODY>` then marks off the division between groups. This is useful as it enables you to specify the alignment of the header and the body separately. For instance, you can have the header text labels centred, and the body text left-aligned. Each `TBODY` element must contain at least one `TR` (table row) element.

This ingenious model provides excellent backwards compatibility, as well as several new and useful features. For example:

```
<TABLE FRAME=box RULES=groups>
      <TR><TD>1<TD>Start of body group
      <TR><TD>2<TD>End of body group
   <TBODY>
      <TR><TD>3<TD>Another body group...
      <TR><TD>4<TD>which requires a TBODY start tag
</TABLE>
```

creates the result

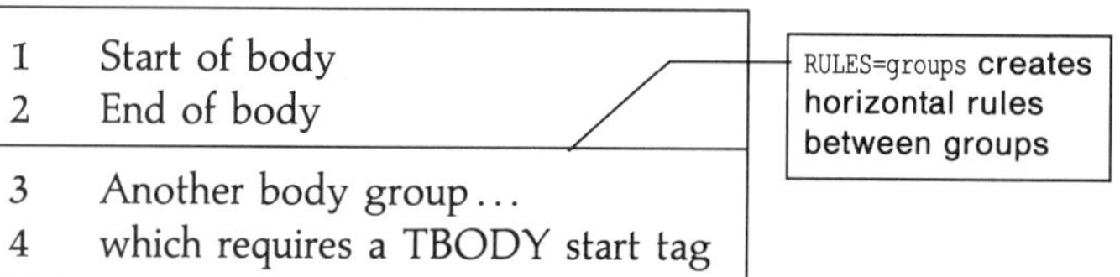

1 Start of body
2 End of body
3 Another body group...
4 which requires a TBODY start tag
RULES=groups creates horizontal rules between groups

This little table consists of two TBODY elements, both of which lack closing tags; the first lacks its starting tag as well!

10.9 Organizing by columns

So far, you have seen HTML tables as collections of rows, possibly grouped. It is also possible and useful to specify table behaviour by columns, for example to make a whole column of cells a particular width, or to align the contents of such a column vertically or horizontally. Finally, you can group columns together so as to specify their behaviour as a unit, in much the same way as a group of table rows.

10.9.1 Column widths

By default, browsers automatically adjust the widths of columns to fit both their contents and the width of the screen or window. They achieve this by scanning all the data inside the table, increasing the width of a column when a cell contents demand more space, and wrapping cell contents if the full available width is used up. You can simplify this process, possibly speed up table display, and gain greater control over the final appearance of the table by specifying the absolute or relative widths of the columns with the COL element. COL can only be used inside a table.

The attribute WIDTH allows you to set the width of the column in any of the standard width units, such as picas, points or inches (these are explained in Section 10.6.2 for setting table widths):

```
<COL WIDTH=30mm>    <!--set column to 30 millimetres if possible-->
```

By default, it gives absolute width in pixels if its value is an integer without units, for example:

```
<COL WIDTH=64>      <!--plain integer width means pixels-->
```

or relative width (compared to other such columns) if its value is a positive number followed by a star, like 2.5* or 6* – it does not have to be a whole number, though you may find it easier to use one. Incidentally, decimal fractions are allowed, but exponents such as 1.2e2 are not.

For example, in a seven-column table:

```
<COL WIDTH=4*  >    <!--CALS users will recognize the star * ... -->
<COL WIDTH=2.5*>    <!--It is there to simplify CALS table import-->
<COL WIDTH=1*  >
<COL WIDTH=2*  >
```

Absolute widths are assigned first. The remaining width is shared among the relative-width columns.

This specification lets the browser know that it is to divide the available width (already specified to be 80% of the window's width) into relative measures of 4, 2.5, 1, 2, 2, 2, and 2 (which add up to 15.5, in fact). The first column, for example, is therefore going to be

$$\frac{4 * 80}{15.5} = 20.6\% \text{ of the window's available width}$$

This may be beginning to give you a headache, as you remember your maths teacher at school doing ratios. Luckily such complexities are only for the browser. All you have to do is to specify the relative widths of the columns, in any units that you find convenient: HTML is your servant, not your master. You can avoid assigning fractional widths by doubling all the relative widths listed above to

8, 5, 2, 4 — the 4 is for each of the columns 4 to 7; the ratios are now out of 31

Notice that there is no need for a closing </COL> tag as COL does not enclose anything, but acts to modify the specification of the table as a whole.

If the browser discovers that one or more of the columns cannot be fitted into the widths you have assigned to them, it attempts to adjust the table so that everything fits. It may not succeed (especially if the window is narrow, and some columns contain long words or wide images), so your column specifications are only suggestions to the browser, though ones which it always tries to obey.

10.9.2 Groups of columns

Columns can be grouped with the COLGROUP element. By default there is one group. COLGROUP lets you put lines between groups of columns, for instance, or set the same properties for all cells in a group of columns. For example, a 7-column table can be organized into groups with just two extra lines of HTML 3:

```
<TABLE ID=spanner>
<CAPTION>Table with Grouped Columns</CAPTION>
<COLGROUP SPAN=5 WIDTH=1*>      <!--first 5 columns equal width-->
<COLGROUP SPAN=2 WIDTH=0.5*>    <!--next 2 columns half as wide-->
```

The SPAN attribute can be used in conjunction with any other attributes of COL, namely the generic ID, LANG, STYLE and CLASS; WIDTH, as shown here; and horizontal and vertical alignment. If you decide to specify groups of columns, you must do this after the table caption (if any) and before the table header or body groups.

10.9.3 Column alignment

Column alignment is specified with the same attributes used for aligning individual cells, individual rows or (thead or tbody) groups of rows. You can, as in those cases, choose to align the contents of all the cells in a column or group of columns either vertically, or horizontally, or both. For example:

```
<COL SPAN=3 VALIGN=top ALIGN=right> <!--align all cells in these 3 cols-->
```

10.10 Inheritance

You can specify the alignment properties of most of the table elements (COL, THEAD, TBODY, TR, TH and TD, but not of TABLE itself), as explained already in this chapter. Sometimes these properties could conflict, so you need to understand the rules that browsers use to decide which specification to use in cases where there is more than one possibility.

- For horizontal alignment, columns have priority over rows. For vertical alignment, rows naturally have priority over columns.
- Properties of cells take precedence over properties inherited from all higher structures such as rows or table bodies.
- Properties of elements contained within cells (for instance, if you have put paragraphs such as <P ALIGN=right>... inside cells) take precedence over cell properties.

Just occasionally, you may need to know the precise precedence order for each attribute. Since language context also affects alignment (for instance, in Arabic and other right-to-left languages, horizontal alignment assumes a default of right), the LANG attribute is included. Here are the rules:

```
        Highest priority -------------------------- Lowest priority

ALIGN:  (TH|TD) > COL > TR             > (THEAD|TBODY) > default
VALIGN: (TH|TD) > TR  > (THEAD|TBODY) > COL           > default
LANG:   (TH|TD) > TR  > (THEAD|TBODY) > COL < TABLE   > default
```

For example, this shows that given <TR ALIGN=center><TD ALIGN=left>, the cell contents will be left-aligned. There can be no conflict between TH and TD, as you have one or the other but not both; the same goes for THEAD and TBODY.

10.11 Frames, borders, rules

In place of the earlier definition of the BORDER attribute, which actually had several roles, HTML 3 uses no fewer than five TABLE attributes to control the ruled grid and outline:

- BORDER — controlling the width of the frame
- FRAME — controlling the four lines round the outside of a table
- RULES — controlling the lines separating rows or columns of table cells
- CELLPADDING — controlling the amount of space between cell wall and cell contents
- CELLSPACING — controlling the wall thickness, the space between individual cells.

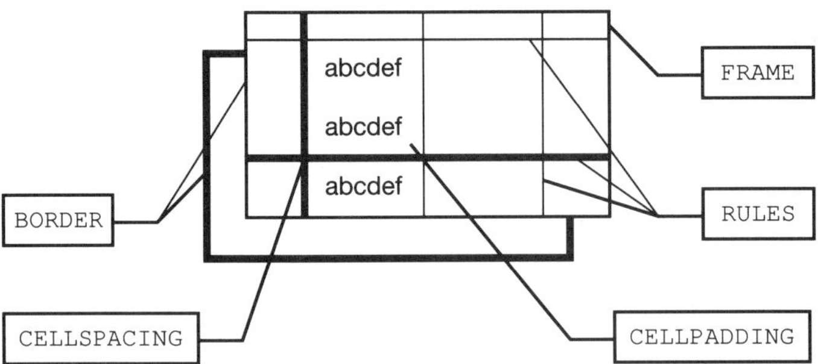

This would be quite simple, except that HTML 3 also has to maintain backwards compatibility with earlier usage, so BORDER has two sets of meanings! We earnestly recommend you to switch to the new syntax at once, as the whole picture is far less confusing than the mixture of old and new.

10.11.1 Frames

The frame is the box around the outside of a table. HTML 3 provides for a range of frame attribute values. For example, if you want a full frame, you specify

```
<TABLE FRAME=box>     <!--or =BORDER-->
   ...
</TABLE>
```

Netscape 1.1 browsers use <TABLE BORDER> to create fully bordered tables. HTML 3 browsers will treat this command as a synonym of FRAME=all together with RULES=all, which leads to the same fully bordered effect: such is the complexity imposed by backwards compatibility. Similar treatment will be given to BORDER=1 (or higher numbers), though BORDER=0 will sensibly be treated as a synonym of FRAME=none.

The default style is to draw no frame at all; you can specify this explicitly with FRAME=none. If you wish, you can also select partial frame effects with top, sides or bottom of the frame only.

The complete set of built-in FRAME attribute values (shown in a table in FRAME=box style) is:

=void	suppress frame – useful with graphics or enclosed forms
=above	top part of the frame only
=below	bottom part of the frame only
=hsides	top and bottom parts of the frame only
=vsides	left and right sides of the frame only
=box	draw all four parts of the frame
=border	draw all four parts of the frame (allowed for compatibility)

10.11.2 Rules

The RULES attribute draws the specified ruled lines between rows or columns of cells. The default is none, except that (for backwards compatibility) all is assumed if BORDER=1 or any non-zero number.

One common pattern is for horizontal rules between groups of rows. You are allowed to create several TBODY groups, and the RULES=groups attribute then separates the groups with ruled lines. RULES=rows or =cols also separates the groups in this way; many browsers will use heavier lines to distinguish group separators from row and column separators.

The complete set of built-in RULES attribute values (shown in a table in RULES=none style) is:

=none	suppress rules – useful with graphics or enclosed forms
=groups	horizontal rule between THEAD/TBODY and TBODY/TBODY groups
=rows	as basic, plus row separators
=cols	as basic, plus column separators
=all	draw borders around all cells

10.11.3 Cellpadding, cellspacing and border

Netscape 1.1 originated several attractive extensions to the rather spartan standard set of styles in HTML 3, which can all be satisfied by drawing thin black lines where necessary. New-style tables tend to have a characteristic appearance, as they are generally embossed and often have wider-than-usual borders.

Here is a table with the attribute CELLPADDING set to 10 pixels:

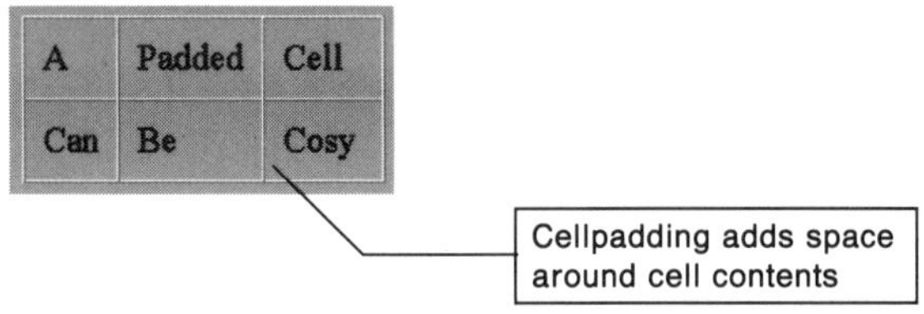


```
<TABLE BORDER CELLPADDING=10 CELLSPACING=0>
   <TR><TD>A<TD>Padded<TD>Cell
   <TR><TD>Can<TD>Be<TD>Cosy
</TABLE>
```

Style sheets should be used in preference.

One might have wanted to call this †CELLMARGIN or †CELLSPACE, since it affects the marginal space all round the cell contents, not the visible thickness of the cell walls, as one might have expected of a padded cell. CELLPADDING is measured in any of the standard width units (from picas to pixels). It is useful for ensuring that table contents are visually separate from each other and from cell walls.

† The dagger indicates that these attributes do not exist with this meaning.

Here, by contrast, is a table with the attribute CELLSPACING set to 10 pixels:

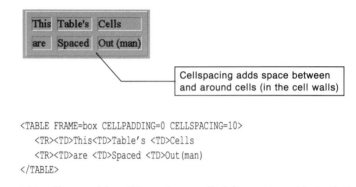

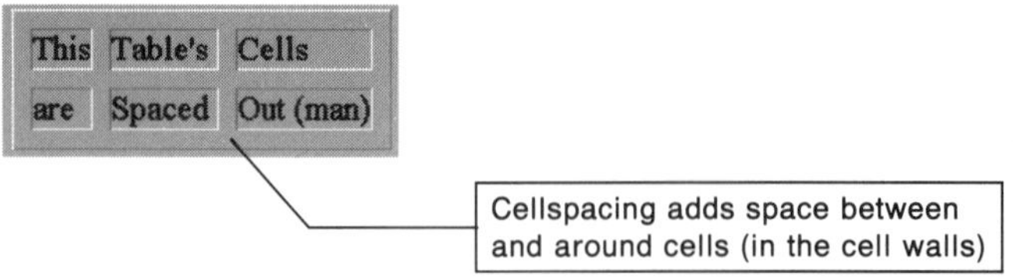


```
<TABLE FRAME=box CELLPADDING=0 CELLSPACING=10>
   <TR><TD>This<TD>Table's <TD>Cells
   <TR><TD>are <TD>Spaced <TD>Out(man)
</TABLE>
```

This effect could well have been called †PADDING, with its thick solid appearance of the cell walls, but Netscape was thinking from the perspective of the cells, and this CELLSPACING attribute does indeed space them apart. Like CELLPADDING, CELLSPACING can be measured in any of the standard width units, with pixels as the default.

CELLPADDING and CELLSPACING can be combined:

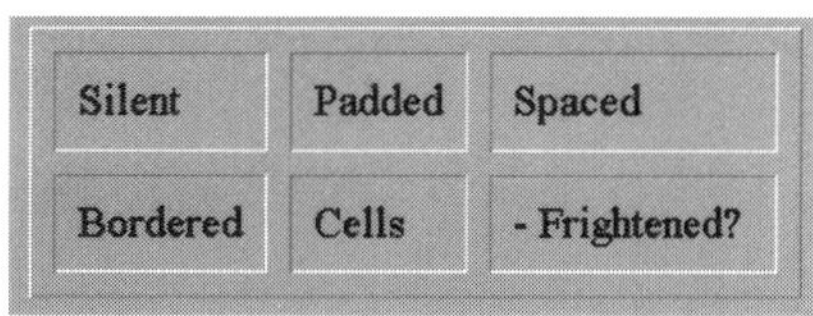

Silent	Padded	Spaced
Bordered	Cells	- Frightened?

```
<TABLE BORDER CELLPADDING=10 CELLSPACING=10>
   <TR><TD>Silent <TD>Padded<TD>Spaced
   <TR><TD>Bordered<TD>Cells <TD>- Frightened?
</TABLE>
<!--notice old-style BORDER attribute-->
```

The combination of these two attributes gives a table a strong emphasis which could be useful for many display purposes. Don't overuse 'em!

Finally, you can also give tables a wide border (which should really have been called †FRAMEWIDTH), again measured in standard width units: the default is pixels. This is typically designed to give a chamfered or bevelled appearance, as if a carpenter had carefully planed off the edges to 45°.

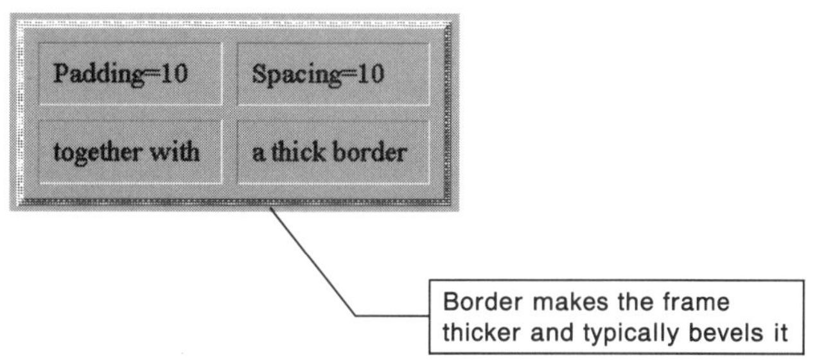
Padding=10
Spacing=10
together with
a thick border
Border makes the frame thicker and typically bevels it

```
<TABLE BORDER=5 CELLPADDING=10 CELLSPACING=10>
   <TR><TD>Padding=10    <TD>Spacing=10
   <TR><TD>together with <TD>a thick border
</TABLE>
```

Separately or together, and combined with alignment of cell contents, these attributes for table borders offer an interestingly wide range of special effects for displaying data.

You can also use character-level control of font sizes in your tables for additional emphasis, but remember that not all your readers will be able to experience the effects you are creating.

10.12 Putting other elements inside tables

There are few restrictions on what you can put inside table cells. Essentially you can include anything that can go into normal and marked-up text (see Section 10.2.1), namely headers (<H3> etc.), paragraphs (<P>), lists (<UL> etc.), form elements (see below, Section 10.12.2), images, link anchors, and even arbitrarily nested tables.

10.12.1 Marked-up text

Text in table cells can be marked up as usual. For instance:

```
<TABLE FRAME=all>
   <TR><TD COLSPAN=3>Non-Periodic Table of Chemists
   <TR><TD>K&eacute;kul&eacute;<TD><B>Faraday</B><TD>Haber
</TABLE>
```

This is normally rendered with accents and emboldened text (if the browser can manage them) just as you'd hope:

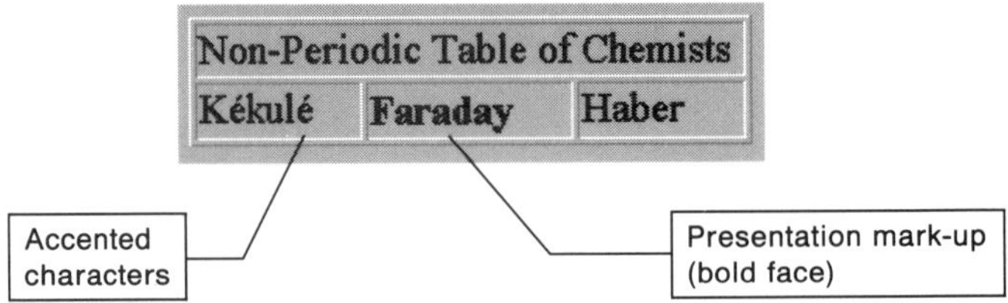

If the results of such formatting are strange, that is your problem. HTML allows you this fine degree of control of table text; it is up to you to make sensible use of it.

10.12.2 Forms

The chapter on forms (Chapter 12) includes several suggestions on layout, including putting a form inside a table. It is then quite easy to achieve neat and efficient layouts that help the user fill in your forms quickly and correctly.

Here is a classic example of a form/table as viewed by Netscape:

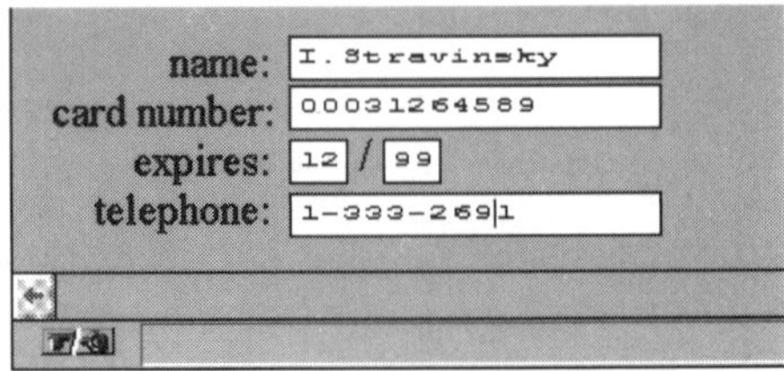

And here is the frameless table used to lay out the text labels and the form:

```
<TABLE FRAME=none>
<TR><TD ALIGN=right>
        name:<BR>
        card number:<BR>
        expires:<BR>
        telephone:<BR>
   <TD ALIGN=left><BR>
     <FORM>
        <INPUT NAME="name"          SIZE=18><BR>
        <INPUT NAME="cardnum"       SIZE=18><BR>
        <INPUT NAME="expires-month" SIZE= 2> /
        <INPUT NAME="expires-year"  SIZE= 2><BR>
        <INPUT NAME="phone"         SIZE=18>
     </FORM>
</TABLE>
```

A whole form embedded in a table

10.12.3 Nested tables

It is sometimes useful to be able to put tables inside table cells. You might think this would slow down the display hopelessly, but this isn't so. The task force which developed HTML showed that the time taken to display big or nested tables increases only linearly with their size, so that if it's twice as big it takes only twice as long to display – which is very impressive. As for the visual appearance, you will recall that you can display tables without borders. If you make the outer table borderless, various cells can contain forms, other tables, or just text. The end result is something like a newspaper layout into rows and columns of diverse items. The layout and contents are up to you.

In other words, putting tables (and other things) inside a page-sized table is a simple and direct way of organizing an HTML page so as to make full use of the two-dimensional space available. We expect that as authors get used to the idea, the mechanism will become very popular.

10.12.4 Using tables for layout

Attractive examples are starting to appear on the Web of the use of tables for layout. A site we much admire, the Paleontology Museum at the University of California at Berkeley (see the colour section for further examples, and Chapter 5 for a discussion of the structure of their hypertext), contains both simple and more elaborate uses of tables.

The Evolutionary Thought page contains two Darwinian images framed together. This elegant appearance is created by the simple Netscape HTML table code:

```
<TABLE BORDER=5>
   <TR>
      <TD ALIGN=center>
         <IMG SRC=http://ucmp1.berkeley.edu/images/exhibit/darsmall.gif>
      </TD>
      <TD ALIGN=center>
         <IMG SRC=http://ucmp1.berkeley.edu/images/exhibit/darwincol.gif>
      </TD>
   </TR>
</TABLE>
```

The table has just one row, containing two cells, each with a GIF image centred within itself.

It is quite safe to omit the </TD> and </TR> tags. Notice the need to use ALIGN=center in each row; this rather annoying repetition (required in Netscape 1.1N) can be replaced by a table style, or by a single alignment applied to the whole table body, in HTML 3.

The page has here been sized to show off the images to best advantage. The table sizes itself automatically to fit the GIF images, which in this case are much narrower than a high-resolution screen. If the page is made wide, the images remain small but more grey-space (if that is the word) appears on both sides of them, as both the table and the text are enclosed in Netscape <CENTER>...</CENTER> tags.

For a more elaborate example, the UCMP 'Museum' page, part of the hypertext structure discussed in Chapter 5, is dominated by a large table,

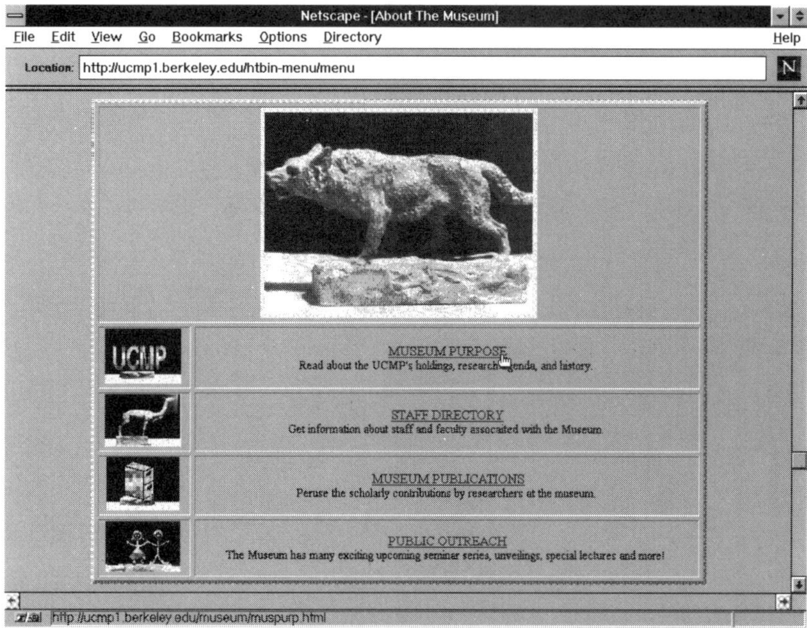

illustrated here. The page actually incorporates two other uses of tables, though these are less spectacular.

It is made up of two kinds of row, the first row – containing the wolf image, centred in the table – being visibly different from the rest.

The relevant part of the page's HTML, slightly reformatted to emphasize its structure, runs as follows. We have dropped the </TD> and </TR> tags for conciseness.

First the table is declared, using a thick border and plenty of spacing and padding. The whole structure is centred on the page.

```
<TABLE WIDTH="80%" BORDER=4 CELLPADDING=1 CELLSPACING=5>
```

Then the wolf image appears, centred, in a cell spanning two columns. Without the COLSPAN=2 attribute, the cell would appear centred in the first column. Notice that browsers assume that a cell (such as the <TD> here) must be part of a row <TR>, so the first row tag can actually be omitted, as it is here.

```
<TD ALIGN=center COLSPAN=2>
   <IMG SRC=http://ucmp1.berkeley.edu/images/direwolf5.gif>
```

Then follow four rows, identical in structure. Each contains an image, centred in column 1, and a text label centred in column 2, consisting of a hypertext anchor in a font one size larger than usual <FONT SIZE=+1>, and then on the line below (that's what the <BR> is for) a short description of the item. The second row's tags are pointed out with callout boxes.

```
<TR>
<TD ALIGN=center><IMG SRC=http://ucmp1.berkeley.edu/images/muspurpico.gif>
<TD ALIGN=center><FONT SIZE="+1">
<A HREF=http://ucmp1.berkeley.edu/museum/muspurp.html>MUSEUM
   PURPOSE</A></FONT>
<BR>Read about the UCMP's holdings, research agenda, and history.<BR>
```

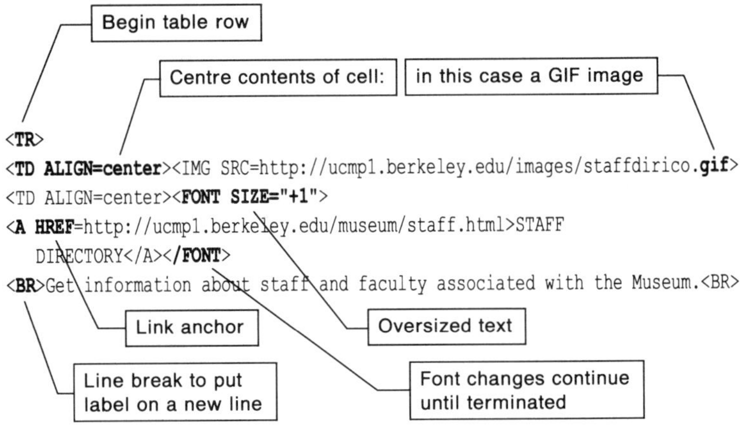

Begin table row
Centre contents of cell:
in this case a GIF image

```
<TR>
<TD ALIGN=center><IMG SRC=http://ucmp1.berkeley.edu/images/staffdirico.gif>
<TD ALIGN=center><FONT SIZE="+1">
<A HREF=http://ucmp1.berkeley.edu/museum/staff.html>STAFF
   DIRECTORY</A></FONT>
<BR>Get information about staff and faculty associated with the Museum.<BR>
```

Link anchor
Oversized text
Line break to put label on a new line
Font changes continue until terminated

The remaining lines work in exactly the same way:

```
<TR>
<TD ALIGN=center><IMG SRC=http://ucmp1.berkeley.edu/images/muspubico.gif>
<TD ALIGN=center><FONT SIZE="+1">
<A HREF=http://ucmp1.berkeley.edu/museum/muspub.html>MUSEUM
   PUBLICATIONS</A></FONT>
<BR>Peruse the scholarly contributions by researchers at the museum.<BR>
```

If HTML 3 had been available when the UCMP pages were written, the repetition in these formatting instructions could have been avoided. The museum could have chosen to use styles, or to have specified column formats just once at the top of the table.

```
<TR>
<TD ALIGN=center><IMG SRC=http://ucmp1.berkeley.edu/images/puboutico.gif>
<TD ALIGN=center><FONT SIZE="+1">
<A HREF=http://ucmp1.berkeley.edu/museum/pubout.html>PUBLIC
   OUTREACH</A></FONT>
<BR>The Museum has many exciting upcoming seminar series.
```

Finally, the table is closed.

```
</TABLE>
```

The table code does not greatly increase the length of the HTML here; it enables text and images to be combined more easily than using flow commands; and it is the only sensible way to get borders. The simplicity and regularity of UCMP's code makes a striking contrast with the often contorted HMTL written when graphics (GIF and JPEG images) were seen as the only way to obtain attractive effects.

10.13 Speeding up display

You can make the browser's life easier, and keep your readers' tempers cooler, by hinting to the browser how wide the table is going to be, relative to the window in which it is to be displayed. This enables the browser to start displaying the table even before all the table data has arrived. Otherwise, the browser has to read all the data to discover the minimum widths of all the cells, and hence of all the columns, and hence of the table itself ... and if that is too wide, then it has to decide to clip some of the cells' contents. That could lead to an empty screen for quite a few seconds.

You can set the table's width directly, using a percentage for the WIDTH attribute, for example:

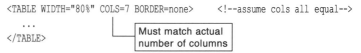

```
<TABLE WIDTH="50%">
```

The number of columns, specified in the COLS attribute, is up to you, but if you allow about 5–10 characters per column, you can't hope for many more than a dozen columns on average screens capable of displaying 80 characters per line. (The use of Braille restricts table width even more severely.) By default, tables specified in advance in this way have columns of equal width; you can improve on this by setting individual or group column widths with COL.

These pieces of information at once save you a lot of work, and enable the browser to set up the basic structure. The browser may still not be able to comply exactly with your specification, as this depends on what you have inside the cells of the table, but it will do its best.

For example:

```
<TABLE WIDTH="80%" COLS=7 BORDER=none>      <!--assume cols all equal-->
   ...
</TABLE>
```

Must match actual number of columns

10.14 Summary of tables

HTML 3's tables provide a sophisticated but easy-to-use mechanism for formatting data into rows and columns. The use of built-in defaults, inheritance of attributes and automatic sizing to fit table contents allow authors to construct tables with very few HTML instructions. More elaborate tables can be given captions and headers, and their contents can be aligned horizontally and vertically. It is possible to specify alignments for groups of cells, such as all header or all body cells, and to control columns of cells as if they were separate entities. Cells can also span rows or columns, and they may contain other HTML elements such as headings, paragraphs, lists, forms, images, hypertext anchors and even (nested) tables.

11 GRAPHICS AND OTHER MEDIA FOR YOUR DOCUMENT

In this chapter:

- Basic concepts for the beginner
- Simple examples of how to use `IMG` to insert graphics into a document
- Control of text flow with `CLEAR`
- Horizontal and vertical alignment with `ALIGN`
- Inserting borders and white space with `BORDER`, `VSPACE` and `HSPACE`
- Clickable graphics and thumbnail images
- Providing text-only browsers with alternative mark-up to graphics
- Use of `OBJECT` to insert graphics
- `OBJECT` for inserting Java applets, OLE objects, AVI files and other objects

- Decorative effects on Web pages: horizontal rules, background texture and colour, text colour
- Banners

A wizard from W3
Got stuck by his beard in a tree
He cast a strange spell
In best HTML
And with a hypertext flash
He was free

11.1 Introduction

This chapter looks at the HTML needed to insert graphics, Java applets, video clips, multimedia and a variety of other objects into your document. If you want to know about graphic formats, colour and size of graphics for fast downloading you should read Chapter 16 which tells you how to create your own artwork for the Web.

The chapter starts with a discussion of graphics on the Web, primarily using the `IMG` tag. We then go on to describe how to insert graphics with `OBJECT`, and then to how other media can be referenced with this element.

Decorative effects such as creating a background colour and pattern and using horizontal rules across pages are discussed right at the end of the chapter.

Graphics may have many roles in documents

Toolbars as navigational aids.

Decorative bullets for lists.

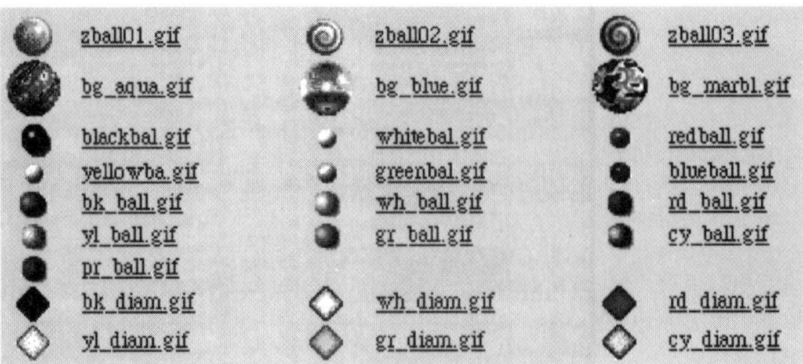

Rules across the page.

Photos and illustrations.

Text in special fonts and unusual layout.

Clickable graphics for hypertext links.

Thumbnail images to click on and download larger ones.

Backgrounds for your Web pages.

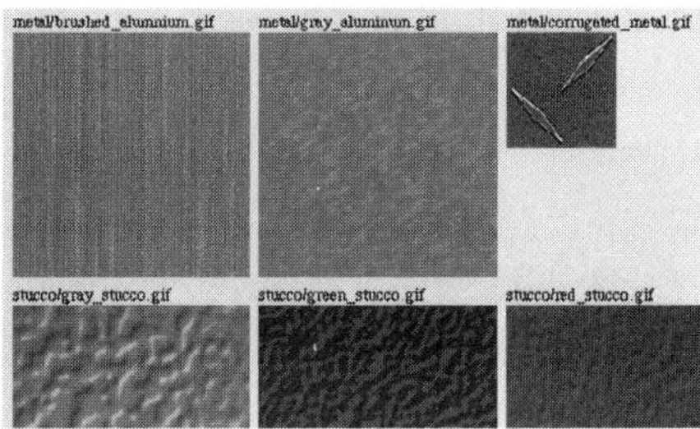

Web clip art – perfect even for the beginner!

Before we begin to discuss the ways in which HTML can be used to insert graphics, a note for the beginner. Although you may want to construct your own graphics (see Chapter 16 which explains much about this) you may prefer to use existing icons, backgrounds and other decorative features available as clip art *on the Web*. Enthusiasts all over the world have carefully assembled pages full of GIF images and all you have do is tune in, and copy and paste. There seems to be every conceivable icon, every imaginable zany bullet, every type of background design, all there just waiting for you to copy and paste them. An enormous library of clip art is available across the Internet: it's just a matter of finding what you want. To do this, we recommend that you call up an Internet search program (an easy way of doing this is simply to select Internet Search from the Directory menu if you are using the Netscape browser) and then search on the keywords *graphics* and *icons*, or perhaps *graphics* and *backgrounds* and similar combinations. All sorts of references to graphic material turn up. Delving into a list of referenced icon libraries, we found literally hundreds of icons at a single Web location including 'hot dog', 'hula girl', 'champagne', 'valentine hearts' and 'silhouette of woman with mixing bowl'. Quite extraordinary.

To copy a graphic from a Web page you generally click on it with the shift key held down, and, from the menu resulting, you choose Save As. You choose a place and a name to save the graphic and behold it is copied from its distant point of storage onto your own hard disk. Do check if there are any copyright restrictions or whether any payment is involved; on the whole there are not because people actually *want* you to use their graphics. Look under the 'comments' associated with the image. Here are some stars and balls for adorning Web pages which we found on Chris's World on `http://www.cbil.vcu.edu`:

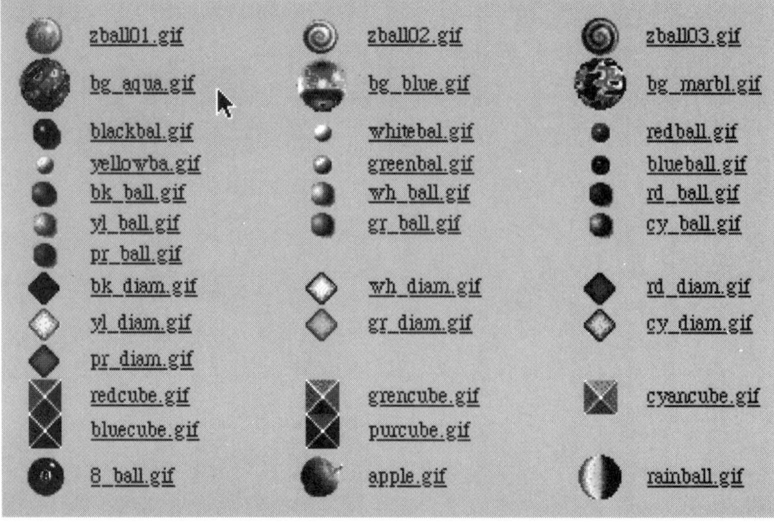

What if someone wants to use your own graphics images? You may not mind, but if you do, graphics formats such as GIF, PNG and JPEG have a facility for sticking text messages as part of the image data. Use this to include a copyright message and consider including an email address in the possibility that someone would like to re-use your image.

11.2 IMG and OBJECT for inserting graphics and other media – an overview

The two elements you are likely to use for inserting graphics, and also other media, are IMG and OBJECT. We will deal with IMG first because it's the one most commonly used today. OBJECT is new and up-and-coming.

11.2.1 The IMG element

HTML 2.0

IMG stands simply for 'IMaGe' and is primarily for incorporating graphics in the form of small pictures and icons. Use of IMG is really remarkably easy which accounts, in part at least, for the profusion of graphics on the Web today. Judicious use of IMG can leave the reader gasping at the professional look of your Web pages but remember not to overdo it. Large images which take a long time to download can drive people quite mad. See Section 16.2 for advice on the size of images you insert.

The concept of inline images

If you are a beginner, some concepts and terminology may come in useful. You may have heard that the images inserted into the Web using the IMG element are said to be embedded or *inline*. What this means is that the images are inserted as part of the document rather than displayed in their own separate window, as are external images. Inlined images are retrieved automatically with the document when it is downloaded across the Internet. External images on the other hand are displayed by a separate viewer program which is started up by the browser when needed, and must be specifically requested by triggering a hypertext link.

When you save a Web document to a file, the inlined images referenced by IMG are *not* saved too: you only get the text of the document without the images incorporated.

How does a browser lay out a page with inlined images? Inlined images are treated rather like a word in a paragraph. This is because the IMG element itself is a character-level element, a concept which is explained in Chapter 3. As a consequence of this character-level status, an image referenced by IMG may appear in the middle of a paragraph, just like a word. If you specifically want an image to stand by itself you may need to manipulate its position by using other elements such as `BR` (which breaks a line so that the image starts on a fresh line), a method which we explain in this chapter.

`IMG` has an empty content model

`IMG` has an empty content model which means that it cannot include any other elements within its bounds. So, you cannot include a hypertext link within `IMG` nor can you include lists, paragraphs or any other HTML elements. That said, you can of course include an `IMG` in other bits of HTML. You can, for example, insert an `IMG` in a list item (unfortunately the bullet for the list item is drawn as well as the image!) and in a table cell. The latter is a trick employed by many Web page designers to achieve layout effects and is best illustrated by the very creative pages of David Siegel which are really worth looking at. They are on `www.siegel.com`. We return to `IMG` in the context of a table later in this section.

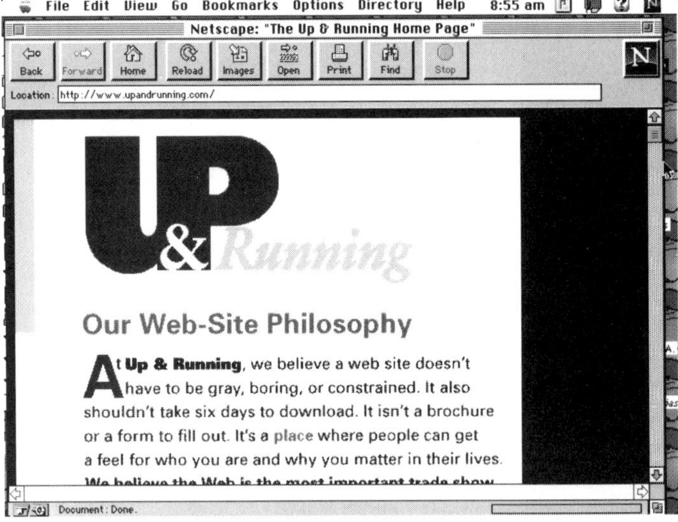

`IMG` images are specified relative to the baseline

`IMG` images are displayed relative to the **baseline**. This is the line upon which the browser writes text: ascenders go above the line and the descenders go below the line. The `ALIGN` attribute which enables you to specify the vertical position of an image uses the baseline as a reference.

The `SRC` attribute is used to reference the image by its URL

The `IMG` element has the mandatory attribute `SRC` which allows authors to specify the file containing the image to be inlined in terms of its URL. Most browsers support GIF images with 256 colours and also JPEG as a graphic format. Browsers are also soon to support PNG, a new graphics format for publishing on the Internet. Chapter 16 explains the various graphics formats and when to use them.

11.2.2 The OBJECT element – new at the time of writing

The OBJECT element is new at the time of writing. Proposed by the World Wide Web consortium in conjunction with major browser vendors, OBJECT is likely to become the standard HTML element for inserting all manner of graphics and other media into documents. While the IMG element has certainly proved worthwhile, the trouble is that it is restricted to inserting photographs, diagrams, drawings and other images into documents. Now that richer and richer media have found their way onto the Web – spreadsheets, animation, multimedia, and so on – it is essential to develop an element which can cope with all of these at once.

If you keep astride of developments in HTML, you may realize that, in the absence of a standard element for the purpose, developers have invented their own tags for referencing other media on the Web. For example, you may have come across Microsoft's DYNSRC attribute for video and audio, Netscape's EMBED tag for compound document embedding, and Sun's APP and APPLET tags for executable code. These are briefly explained, with examples, in Section 11.4.

Everyone's HTML does it differently.

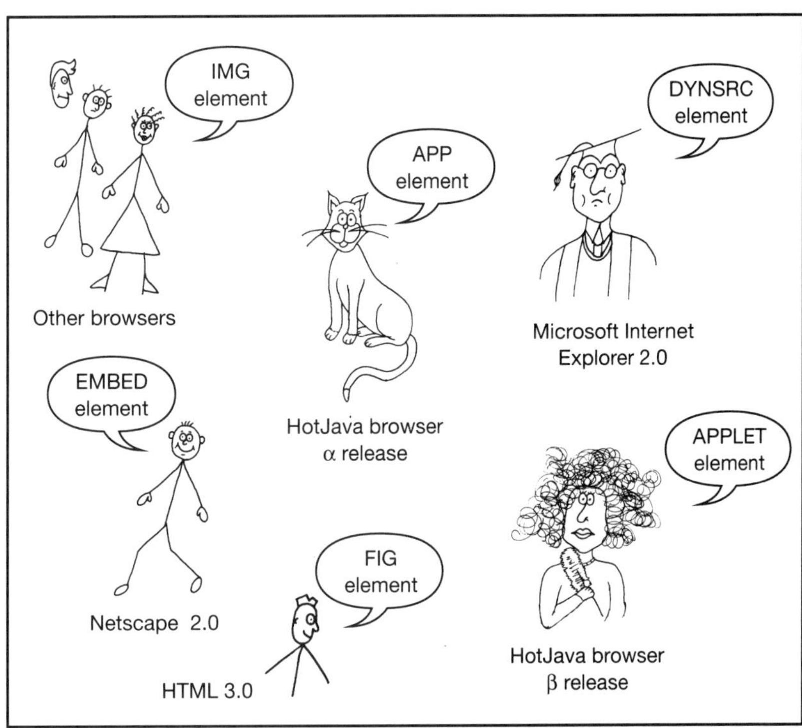

What's wrong with these non-standard tags?

The development of new tags by browser vendors is all well and good but the problem is that it leaves HTML documents incompatible. After all, if you want to use DYNSRC to insert a video clip, there is no saying that Netscape's browser will understand it even if Microsoft's browser will. Each of these proposed solutions also attacks the problem of inserting different media from a slightly different perspective. As a result each new tag invented looks very different, which is rather confusing.

The World Wide Web consortium to sort out the muddle

The World Wide Web consortium, aiming to help standardize HTML to everyone's benefit, looked at the diversity of new tags, and decided that it was not too far-fetched to devise a single HTML extension that addressed everyone's current needs. The OBJECT element was the suggestion, the idea being that it would subsume the role of the IMG tag and provide a general solution for dealing with new media, with effective backwards compatibility with existing browsers. Far from easy to negotiate, meetings with all browser vendors have been (and are being) held and it is generally hoped that all will come away satisfied and convinced.

What is the proposal?

The OBJECT element currently proposed enables authors to insert images in much the usual way. Additionally it allows you to specify the data, including persistent data and/or properties/parameters for initializing objects to be inserted into HTML documents, as well as the code that can be used to display/manipulate that data. Here, the term object is used to describe the things that people want to place in HTML documents. In practice objects are: graphics, videos, applets, plug-ins, media handlers, and so on.

The data can be specified in one of several ways: via a universally unique object identifier (uuid), a file specified by a URL, inline data, or as a set of named properties. In addition, there are a number of attributes that allow authors to specify standard properties such as width and height. The code for the object is also specified in several ways: indirectly by the object's uuid, by information included as part of the object's data, and the combination of an object class name and a network address.

11.3 Down to business

Having given a little information about IMG and OBJECT we can now go on to see how they work. IMG is by the far the more commonly used of the two, so it makes sense to begin with this element, although we give examples using both IMG and OBJECT during the course of discussion. Our account is aimed at the non-technical reader at the beginning, with later sections for a more advanced readership.

11.3.1 Using IMG to insert graphics into documents

Simple example of IMG

Here is an example of an image inserted using IMG. You can see that the image is itself referenced by the SRC (SouRCe) attribute which is critical and essential to include. The SRC attribute can take as its value either a simple filename or a URL. This means that you can reference images found elsewhere on the Internet. Chapter 9 on hypertext links explains something about URLs and you should refer to this if you are a beginner. There is also a short discussion on this subject for the novice in Chapter 1.

```
<P>This is an image referenced using the HTML IMG element.<BR>The
attribute you use to reference the image is SRC which stands for "source".
<IMG SRC="flower.gif">
```

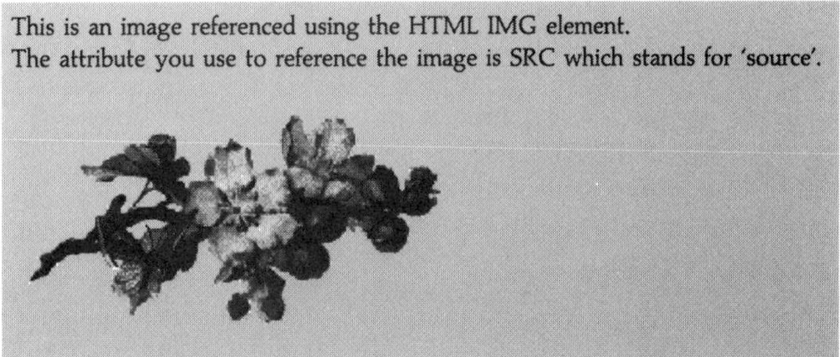
This is an image referenced using the HTML IMG element.
The attribute you use to reference the image is SRC which stands for 'source'.

In this simple example the idea is to include the image flower.gif in a document. The assumption is that the flower picture is in the same directory as the HTML file itself rather than held elsewhere on disk. The flower is inserted after the paragraph of text by adding an IMG element in the appropriate place. An IMG element has no end tag and no content. This means that you do not have to add </IMG> (and indeed you must not!) and also that you cannot insert other elements into IMG because this is not allowed.

Notice the use of the BR element in this example. This is to cause a break after the first line, forcing the rest of the text to a new line and the image to appear left-aligned in what would be the equivalent of the third line of the paragraph. You will find BR very useful in this context.

Remember that IMG images are treated at character level and in that sense occupy space along the line, just like a word or phrase. If you don't put a BR in, look what happens:

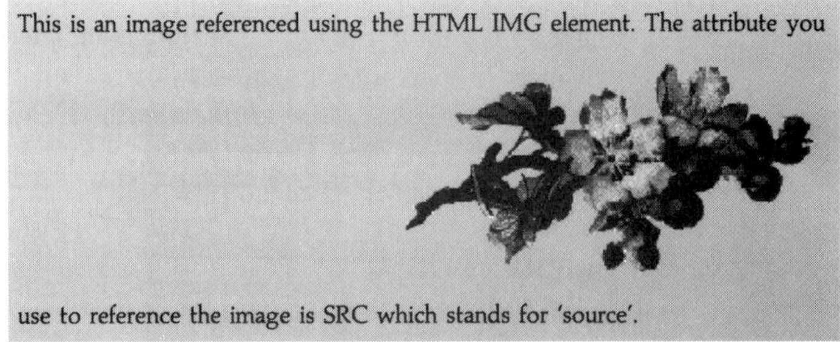

The image is now positioned in the second line but, because it is so big, it has forced the two lines apart and a less satisfying layout results. If you made the image smaller the space between the two lines would be less. Why is the image to the right rather than to the left as in the previous example? Because it has been right-aligned (see Section 11.1.4 on horizontal alignment). You will have gathered that positioning images with IMG requires a certain amount of patience if you are fussy about the exact effect you want to get.

Vertical positioning

It is possible to control the vertical positioning of the image by using the ALIGN attribute. Alignment is relative to the baseline, the line upon which text is placed by the browser as it displays words and phrases on the screen.The most common uses of ALIGN are:

```
<IMG SRC="url" ALIGN=bottom>
<IMG SRC="url" ALIGN=middle>
<IMG SRC="url" ALIGN=top>
```

Bottom alignment is the default and you can see this in the first case below where the flower is sitting on the baseline with the bottom of the image aligned on it.

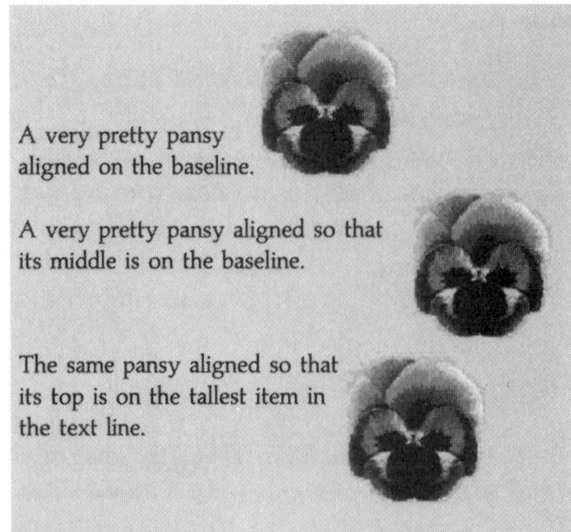

A very pretty pansy
aligned on the baseline.
A very pretty pansy aligned so that
its middle is on the baseline.
The same pansy aligned so that
its top is on the tallest item in
the text line.

Netscape has implemented all sorts of other flavours of ALIGN for vertical alignment. We recommend that you stick to the simple ALIGN values rather than using the more esoteric ones.

ALIGN=top	aligns the image with the top of the tallest item in the baseline.
ALIGN=texttop	aligns the image with the tallest text in the baseline (this is usually but not always the same as ALIGN=top).
ALIGN=middle	aligns the baseline of the current line with the middle of the image.
ALIGN=absmiddle	aligns the middle of the current line with the middle of the image.
ALIGN=baseline	aligns the bottom of the image with the baseline of the current line.
ALIGN=bottom	is identical to ALIGN=baseline.
ALIGN=absbottom	aligns the image with the bottom of the current line.

Horizontal alignment

Horizontal alignment of IMG is done using ALIGN=left and ALIGN=right. The general syntax is:

```
<IMG SRC="url" ALIGN=left>
<IMG SRC="url" ALIGN=right>
```

Note that text flows around a left- or right-aligned image by default. If you want to prevent text flowing around a graphic specified using IMG, you need to use CLEAR in conjunction with BR.

You can get an image to align centrally by using the CENTER tag. For example:

```
<P>
<CENTER>
<IMG SRC="pig.gif"
```

Style sheets will offer much better control over position on the screen. Tags like CENTER are to some extent frowned on by HTML purists because HTML elements are *not* supposed to govern the layout of the text. Netscape 2.0 implements CENTER as a simple shorthand for <DIV ALIGN=center>. Spyglass Mosaic 2.1 will centre between the left and right margins anything between the <CENTER> and </CENTER> tags.

Controlling text flow

BR (Break) has an attribute called CLEAR which on some browsers (for example, Netscape's) can be used to control text flow around images. In the example below the second paragraph is pushed clear of a left-aligned image. Without `CLEAR` this text would simply flow around the image rather than always start underneath it.

You need to use `CLEAR=left` to clear a left-aligned image, `CLEAR=right` for a right-aligned image and `CLEAR=all` if you want both margins to be clear. See also Chapter 4.

```
<P><IMG SRC=flower.gif ALIGN=left>It was a bright morning in the early part
of summer, the river had resumed its wonted banks and its accustomed pace,
and a hot sun seemed to be pulling everything green and bushy and spiky up
out of the earth towards him, as if by strings.
<BR CLEAR=left><P>The mole and the Water Rat had been up since dawn very
busy on matters connected with boats and the opening of the boating
season...
```

It was a bright morning in the early part of summer, the river had resumed its wonted banks and its accustomed pace, and a hot sun seemed to be pulling everything green and bushy and spiky up out of the earth towards him, as if by strings.

The mole and the Water Rat had been up since dawn very busy on matters connected with boats and the opening of the boating season...

Image scaling with `WIDTH` and `HEIGHT` attributes

As Netscape Navigator is laying out a new document, it pauses at each inlined image and goes over the network to discover the height and width of the image before it can continue laying out the document. The height and width are expressed as attributes of the `IMG` tag. The units are normally pixels. For example, if you are inlining an image that is 300 pixels wide and 100 pixels high, the `IMG` tag would look like this:

```
<IMG SRC="flower.gif" WIDTH=300 HEIGHT=100>
```

With Netscape, the width and height will be used to scale the image automatically to fit a 'box' that size. For example, if you have an image that is actually 200 pixels wide and 100 pixels high, but you create a document that inlines the image as follows:

```
<IMG SRC="flower.gif" WIDTH=400 HEIGHT=150>
```

the image will be scaled to fit the newly specified dimensions. Both GIF and JPEG images can be scaled this way. Browsers that do not have support for the `WIDTH` and `HEIGHT` attributes of the `IMG` tag will simply ignore them and the image will be displayed as its real GIF (or JPEG) image size, and no smaller or bigger than that.

This image has been reduced by using:

```
<IMG SRC="flow3.gif" WIDTH=100 HEIGHT=70>
```

If the height is reduced further and the width made larger, the image comes out 'squashed':

```
<IMG SRC="flow3.gif" WIDTH=120 HEIGHT=50>
```

Controlling the white space around an image

You can control how far away from the text an image will be by using VSPACE and HSPACE. Here is an example.:

```
<P><IMG SRC=cat.gif WIDTH=50 HEIGHT=50 ALIGN=left HSPACE=30 BORDER=2>Abbie
the cat lives in Oxford in a house on the Botley Road. She is quite small
and black with a loud purr which has many a time travelled along a
transatlantic cable to Boston.
```

The HSPACE attribute has been used to create a gap between the image and the text. The VSPACE attribute could be used to push the text down to a new position if required. Careful use of VSPACE and HSPACE can be used to produce all sorts of layout effects. The Web page author David Siegel creates a tiny 'blank' GIF image to insert white space into documents for various layout effects. By using VSPACE and HSPACE he expands this image to the required dimensions thus inserting more or less white space as desired. Some of his pages have text which appears cleverly indented from the margin and lines which are spaced much further apart than usual. Blank GIF images often do the job, but you would never guess. Below is one of David Siegel's pages which uses these ideas.

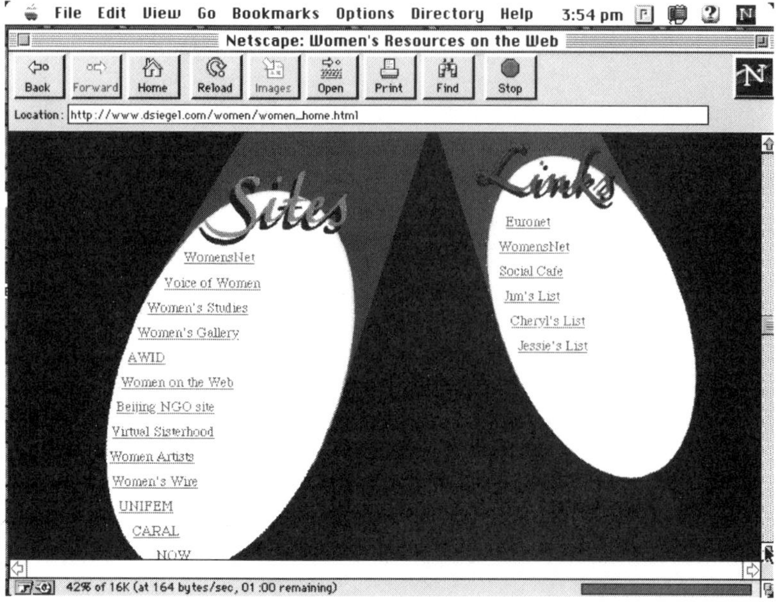

Borders around images

A border around an image can be inserted using the `BORDER` element which takes a numerical value to indicate the width of the line to be drawn. This is a Netscape 2.0 extension and borders will not necessarily be drawn on every browser. Borders are really a stylistic issue and in future will be done by, for example, using the `STYLE` attribute with `IMG` to specify not only the thickness but also the rendering and colour for the border. You can see `BORDER` in use in the example about Abbie the Cat, above.

Clickable images with `IMG`

One of the popular things to do on the Web is to make graphics 'clickable'. In other words you arrange that clicking on the graphic sets off a hypertext jump to perhaps another location on the Internet. To understand how this idea works you should read Chapter 9 on hypertext links. Here you will find examples of simple clickable images and also, more complicated, how to include 'hotzones' in an image, each of which references a different URL.

The general idea of a clickable graphic is shown below. If you look at the example code you will see that you need both the anchor element, `A`, to define a hypertext link, and the `IMG` element to insert a graphic as the label:

```
<A HREF="info.html"><IMG SRC="/gifs/arrow.gif"></A>
```

One way of understanding what is going on is to contrast this with the HTML for a textual link:

```
<A HREF="info.html">Further information</A>
```

In the graphical link the label is **arrow.gif**; in the textual link the label is **Further information**. Clicking on either would cause the file info.html to be fetched. The cursor changes shape (on Netscape to a hand) when it passes the clickable image to show the user that it is the label of a hypertext link.

Thumbnail images

Quite often you want to give the user the choice of whether or not to download a rather big file which may take some time to display. Why not have a small clickable icon-like picture as a taster of what's on offer? This is the idea of the thumbnail sketch or thumbnail image. The Louvre uses it, for instance, in its online gallery. An example:

```
<A HREF=largeimage.gif><IMG ALIGN=middle SRC=smallimage.gif></A>
```

The large image is referenced once the link is triggered.

`IMG` for fancy bullets in lists

You can import 3-D balls for bulleted lists (very popular – they are available on the Web if you search on 'graphics' and 'bullets') or any other small GIF or JPEG image for the purpose. What you do is to use `IMG` to specify the graphic. This idea is explained in Chaper 8 on lists.

`IMG` in tables for more complicated layouts

If you want to see the full potential of `IMG` in tables we cannot but recommend again David Siegel's pages on `www.siegel.com`. The layout of these pages really is quite different from others on the Web. Nowhere else have we seen such creative and elaborate use of HTML's rather limited repertoire. The page below, for example, is carefully built up by using a table. The white outline around each 'cell' is done by assembling long, thin rectangular GIF images. See also Chapter 10 on tables.

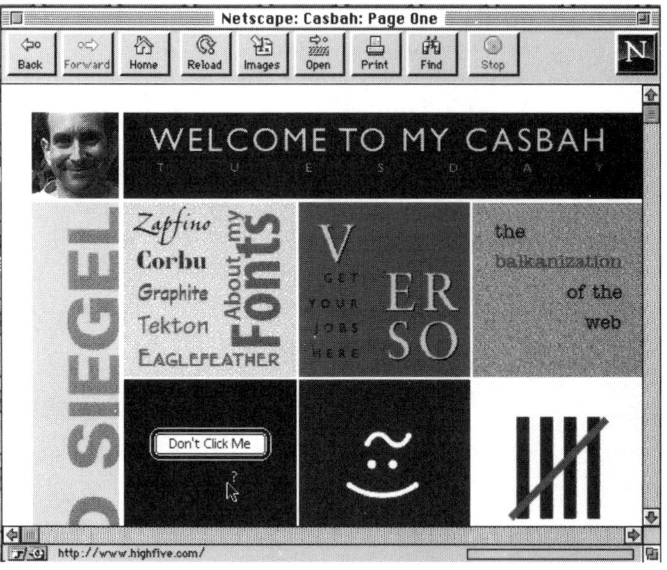

11.3.2 Using OBJECT to insert a graphic or other media in a document

As explained earlier, OBJECT is a new element proposed for referencing graphics and other media on the Web. Here are some examples of its use. The section following gives a more formal specification of OBJECT attributes.

OBJECT to insert an image in a document

You might want to use OBJECT to include an image in a document, which is very easy:

```
<OBJECT DATA=boston.gif WIDTH=60 HEIGHT=60></OBJECT>
```

This is OBJECT at its simplest. The WIDTH and HEIGHT attributes have been added for faster loading. OBJECT has a number of attributes to control the position of the graphic on the screen, namely ALIGN, WIDTH, BORDER, HSPACE and VSPACE, all of which are described at a later point in this chapter. They are used in a similar way to their IMG counterparts.

OBJECT to provide alternative text for non-graphical browsers

You can also use OBJECT to provide alternative mark-up to be displayed should the browser not be able to display the image referenced:

```
<OBJECT DATA=boston.jpeg>
<P>A photograph of Boston taken from the <EM>Hancock Building</EM>
</OBJECT>
```

From this example you will see that OBJECT can contain other mark-up within its bounds, in this case a paragraph of text. This is quite unlike IMG which cannot contain other elements.

Here is another example of OBJECT catering for those who cannot display graphics. The idea is to give instructions on changing a flat tyre. The procedure is documented using a diagram in diagram.gif. But what if you can't display the diagram on the screen? Fortunately a list of actions is included as text and these will appear displayed instead.

```
<OBJECT DATA="pics/diagram.gif">
<H1>Changing a flat tyre</H1>
<OL>
<LI>Apply the hand-brake
<LI>Find the spare tyre and tyre lever
<LI>Use the tyre lever to remove the hub-cap
<LI>Loosen the nuts
<LI>Find a safe place to jack the car up
<LI><B>Failure to insert the jack in the right place can lead to damage of
the car bodywork</B>
<LI>Jack up the wheel
<LI>Remove nuts from the car
<LI>Remove wheel and replace with spare
<LI>Tighten nuts
<LI>Let the car down
<LI>Replace hub-cap
</OL>
</OBJECT>
```

If you use IMG you are more restricted as all alternative text must be condensed into a single value for ALT: you cannot even include a hypertext link to summon up some other text.

```
<IMG SRC="/pics/flat_tyre.gif" ALT="Refer to other literature">
```

Inserting a video clip with OBJECT

Next is a more complicated use of OBJECT to insert a small video clip. In this example the author has to cater for a wide range of browser capabilities: he knows that many browsers can only display images, and showing video clips is not always possible. By using OBJECT the author has graciously catered for lesser browsers able to display graphics but not video, and grander browsers which can cope with both:

```
<OBJECT DATA=Garden.avi TYPE="application/avi">
<PARAM NAME=loop VALUE=infinite>
<IMG SRC=garden.gif ALT="The garden">
</OBJECT>
```

The first line contains the OBJECT start tag and the attribute DATA to reference the video in question. TYPE merely gives the Internet type for OBJECT's data.

The attribute can be used to allow browsers to quickly skip media they don't support, and instead to render the contents of the OBJECT element.

The general rule is that, if the object specified by DATA (or CLASSID) cannot be displayed on the screen, the OBJECT contents are used by the browser.

In our example, the browser looks at the value of DATA and the Internet Type and finds that a video is to be downloaded. Knowing that displaying videos is beyond its capabilities, the browser resorts to the OBJECT content to see what to do. The OBJECT content has an IMG element included which points to a GIF image. The browser retrieves this file and the reader is shown a photograph of a garden on the screen as an alternative to the video.

How is it that OBJECT can contain the IMG element? This luxury is by virtue of the way that OBJECT is officially defined in the DTD (Document Type Definition). The OBJECT content can range through hypertext links, paragraphs, lists, tables, and so on, and has the same content model as the HTML BODY element with the only difference being that one or more optional PARAM elements can be placed immediately after the start tag to initialize the object. All sorts of mark-up can be included for the benefit of browsers not able to display the primary file referenced.

The PARAM element allows a list of named property values (used to initialize an Active-X control, plug-in module or Java applet) to be represented as a sequence of PARAM elements. PARAM is an empty element and should appear without an end tag. The NAME attribute defines the property name (case sensitivity of the name is dependent on the code implementing the object). The VALUE attribute specifies the property value and is an opaque character string whose meaning is determined by the object based on the property name.

The DECLARE attribute is used to indicate that the object is to be declared but not instantiated until needed by something that references it (that is, late binding). Each binding typically results in a separate copy of the object (this is class dependent). In other words, OBJECT DECLARE is treated as a declaration for making an instance of an object.

Many people use browsers which can't display graphics

As time goes by more and more people are getting access to the Internet with sufficient bandwidth to handle the graphics. However, the need remains to support text-only output, first of all for people who access the Web via cellular modems for which the bandwidth is inadequate for graphics, secondly access for visually impaired people, thirdly hands-off operation for small devices which will use speech output. Many people using very old equipment who cannot afford to upgrade are also still using computers without enough memory and power to run Windows. Instead of graphic browsers such as Netscape and Mosaic, they use text-only browsers such as Lynx: it is estimated that roughly 10% of browsers are text-only.

Providing backward compatibility with other browsers

The mechanism whereby content of the `OBJECT` element is displayed on the screen when the object specified by the `DATA`, `CODE` or `CLASS` attributes can't be rendered provides for backwards compatibility with existing browsers. This is essential with browser versions and capabilties changing so fast on the Web.

The Internet Media Type. When a file is retrieved by the browser it arrives down the wire over the HTTP protocol. The data travels accompanied by a number of HTTP headers which tell the browser about the nature of the file being transferred. One of these headers is the content type, a field which conveys a code called the Internet Media Type (also known as the MIME content type) and which the browser uses to find out what kind of file has been sent.

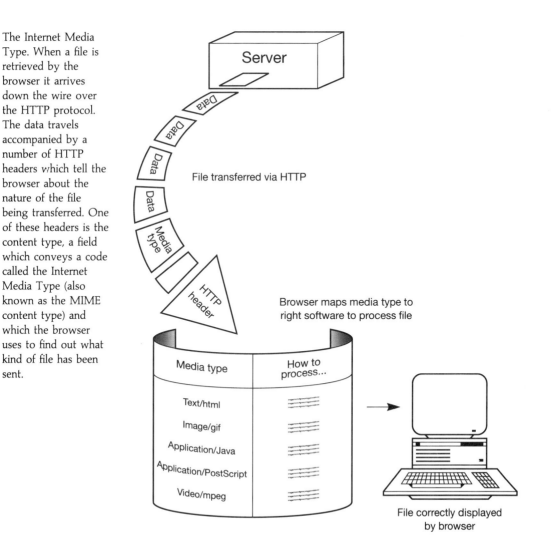

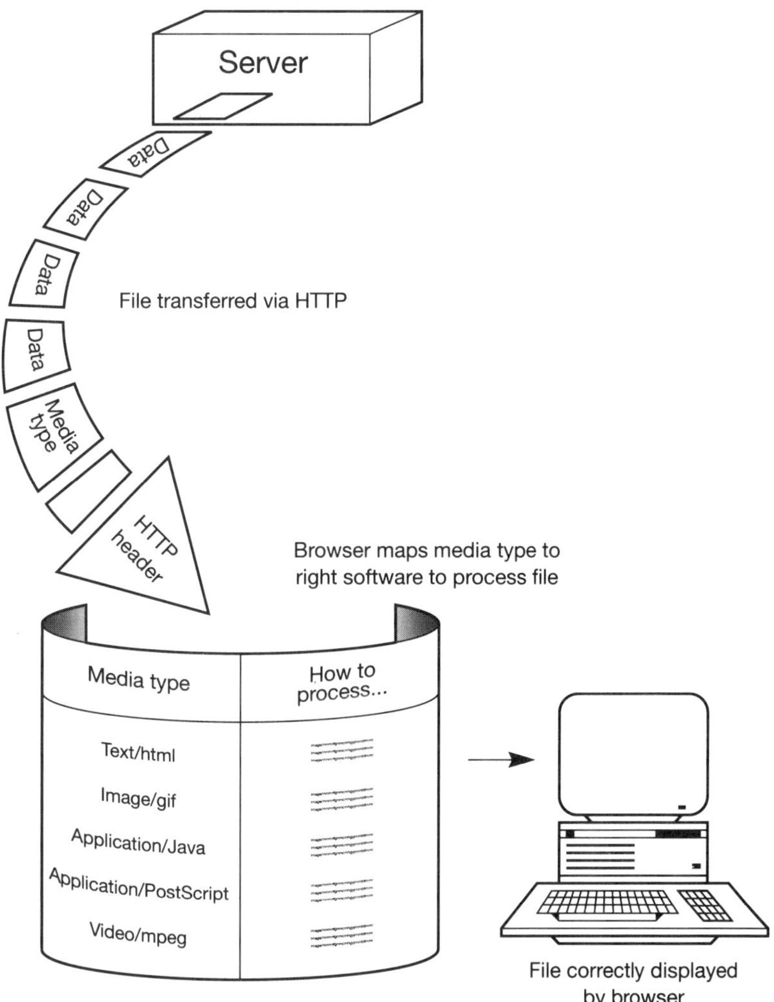

Captioned figures with FIG and OBJECT

This example shows the use of the FIG element (proposed in the original HTML 3 Internet draft but not implemented in its original form) and CAPTION with OBJECT. The combination of these three elements can be used to give a graphic or other item a caption as shown here:

```
<FIG>
<CAPTION>Harrow on the Hill</CAPTION>
<OBJECT DATA=harrow.gif
</OBJECT>
</FIG>
```

OBJECT for plug-ins, Java applets and multimedia

OBJECT can be used to insert many different kinds of file. Apart from graphics, Java applets, plug-ins, multimedia and so on can be inserted into documents using the DATA attribute to do the job. The OBJECT element includes zero or more optional PARAM elements which may be placed immediately after the start tag and used to initialize the inserted object.

Inserting data in AVI format

A simple example of using OBJECT for inserting AVI data is as follows:

```
<OBJECT DATA=TheEarth.avi TYPE="application/avi">
   <PARAM NAME=loop VALUE=infinite>
   <IMG SRC=TheEarth.gif ALT="The Earth">
</OBJECT>
```

Here the browser would show an animation if it supports the AVI format, otherwise it would show a GIF image. The IMG element is used for the latter as it provides for backwards compatibility with existing browsers. The TYPE attribute allows the browser quickly to detect that it doesn't support a particular format, and hence avoid wasting time downloading the object. Another motivation for using the TYPE attribute is when the object is loaded off a CD-ROM, as it allows the format to be specified directly rather than being inferred from the file extension.

OBJECT to insert Active-X data

This next example inserts an Active-X control for a clock:

```
<OBJECT
   ID=clock1
   CLASSID="classid:663CFEF-1EF9-11CF-A3DB-080036F12502"
   DATA="http://www.acme.com/ole/clock.stm"
>
</OBJECT>
```

The URL scheme `CLASSID` gives a globally unique ID for an Active-X control. This is enough in its own right to locate the implementation. `DATA` merely points to some data stream.

The Active-X loader looks at the beginning of the Active-X data stream to find the classid which can then be used by the loader to find the Active-X control. Active-X data streams include a class identifier that can be used to find an implementation in the absence of the `CLASSID` attribute. The `CODEBASE` attribute can be used to give a URL as a hint to the Active-X loader on where to find an implementation for this class.

For speedy loading of objects you can inline the object's state data using the new URL scheme "`data:`", for example:

```
<OBJECT
   ID=clock1
   CLASSID="classid:663CFEF-1EF9-11CF-A3DB-080036F12502"
   DATA="data:application/x-oleobject;base64, ...base 64
   data..."
>
</OBJECT>
```

Inline data is only recommended for small amounts of data.

Java and `OBJECT`

Here is an example of inserting a Java applet:

```
<OBJECT
   CODETYPE="application/java-vm"
   CLASSID="java:myapplet/main; jar=cool.jar"
   CODEBASE="http://java.acme.com/applets"
   WIDTH=400
   HEIGHT=75
>
</OBJECT>
```

The `CLASSID` attribute specifies `main` as a class name: this is called to invoke the applet. `jar` meanwhile is a parameter which names the Java compressed archive files containing the classes. Finally you need the

CODEBASE attribute to give the URL to specify where exactly to find the archive file.

11.3.3 OBJECT attributes: A more formal description

- The **DATA attribute** to specify a URL

  The DATA attribute specifies a URL referencing the object's data.

  In many cases the media type or the data itself contains sufficient information to identify what code is needed to initialize the object. Note that an object's data can even be included inline for super-efficient loading. A new URL scheme "data:" is proposed. The rest of the URL is a Base64 encoded character string that specifies the object's data as an opaque byte stream.

  On its own, this would be meaningless. If the DATA attribute appears without a CLASSID attribute, then a TYPE attribute may be sufficient to interpret the data. For instance a Microsoft COM object can be asked to write its state using the WriteClassStream procedure. This inserts the object's class identifier as the first 16 bytes of the stream. If the TYPE attribute indicates that the data is in the COM persistent stream format, then the class identifier can be retrieved from the DATA attribute and used to find the code implementing the object's behaviour.

- The **CODEBASE attribute** for referencing the code to implement the object's behaviour

  The CODEBASE attribute is not applicable if you are merely referencing a simple graphic in GIF or JPEG format, for example: it is used where OBJECT references a program or some other application. CODEBASE is used in URL schemes to identify implementations that require an additional URL to define the implementation. CODEBASE allows you to specify that URL. CODEBASE is required always, for example, in the case of Java applets in an object element.

- **CLASSID** to specify a unique object identifier

  CLASSID is used to specify a universally unique object identifier (uuid). This allows effective use of caching, as the browser can use simple string comparison to check whether two objects are the same, independent of their location. The CLASSID attribute value takes the form of a URL-style prefix separated by a colon from the character string defining the uuid. The prefix is used to identify the global name space for the uuid, for example CLASSID="uuid:{663C8FEF-1EF9-11CF-A3DB-080036F12502}" gives the uuid for a Microsoft COM object, using the uuid name space.

The CLASSID attribute may be sufficient for the browser to locate the code implementing the object. However, the CODE attribute can also be used with CLASSID to provide a hint as to where to look for this code. Note that the value specified with CLASSID takes precedence over values derived from the object's data stream.

The CLASSID attribute can be used to override the default implementation as implied by the DATA attribute. For example, you may have the pickled data for an Excel spreadsheet but want to view it with the SuperGraph package. You would then use the DATA attribute to point to the Excel spreadsheet data, and the CLASSID attribute to point to the SuperGraph plug-in.

- The **TYPE attribute** to specify the Internet type

This specifies an Internet media type (see RFC 1590) for the object's data. The attribute can be used to allow browsers to quickly skip media they don't support, and instead to render the contents of the OBJECT element. It is also useful when loading objects off local drives as it allows the media type to be specified explicitly rather than being derived from the file extension.

The following grammar for media types is a superset of that for MIME because it does not restrict itself to the official IANA and x-token types.

```
media-type     = type "/" subtype *( ";" parameter )
type           = token
subtype        = token
```

where token is defined by:

```
token          = 1*<any (ASCII) CHAR except SPACE, CTLs, or
                  tspecials>
tspecials      = <one of the set> ( ) < > @ , ; : \ " / [ ] ? =
```

Parameters may follow the type/subtype in the form of attribute/ value pairs.

```
parameter      = attribute "=" value
attribute      = token
value          = token | quoted-string
```

The type, subtype, and parameter attribute names are case-insensitive. Parameter values may or may not be case-sensitive, depending on the semantics of the parameter name. White-space characters must not be included between the type and subtype, nor between an attribute and its value.

If a given media-type value has been registered by the IANA, any use of that value must be indicative of the registered data format. Although HTML allows the use of non-registered media types, such usage must not conflict with the IANA registry. Data providers are strongly encouraged to register their media types with IANA via the procedures outlined in RFC 1590.

All media types registered by IANA must be preferred over extension tokens. However, HTML does not limit applications to the use of officially registered media types, nor does it encourage the use of an 'x-' prefix for unofficial types outside of explicitly short experimental use between consenting applications.

- The **`ID` attribute** in conjunction with `OBJECT`

  The `ID` attribute is used to define a document-wide identifier. This can be used for naming positions within documents as the destination of a hypertext link and by style sheets for rendering an element in a unique style. See Chapter 4 on generic attributes.

- The **`CLASS` attribute** for applying a pre-specified style to an `OBJECT` element

  The `CLASS` attribute enables you to attribute a chosen style from a style sheet to the `OBJECT` element. You might use this to make the border around the object inserted a thin blue line, say, or display it on a red background. You would use the `CLASS` attribute when you had a number of different cases of `OBJECT` which all needed to have, for one reason or other, a particular 'look and feel'. For a one-off change of style, the `STYLE` attribute is more appropriate.

- The **`STYLE` attribute** for giving the `OBJECT` element a style 'once off'

  The `STYLE` attribute allows you to specify the style of an element. The style is generally written using the notation of the CSS style sheet language described in Chapter 14. Contrast `STYLE` with `CLASS` above. See Chapter 14 for more information.

- **`DIR`** to specify the direction that characters are written

  Human writing systems are grouped into scripts, which determine, among other things, the direction the characters are written. Elements of the Latin script are nominally left to right, while those of the Arabic script are nominally right to left. These characters have what is called strong directionality. Other characters can be directionally neutral (spaces) or weak (punctuation).

  The `DIR` attribute specifies an encapsulation boundary which governs the interpretation of neutral and weakly directional characters. It does not override the directionality of strongly directional characters. The `DIR` attribute value is one of `ltr` for left to right, or `rtl` for right to left, for example `DIR=rtl`.

- Vertical alignment of images and other object with **ALIGN**

  The ALIGN attribute determines where to place an object inserted with OBJECT. The ALIGN attribute allows objects to be placed as part of the current text line, or as a distinct unit, aligned to the left, centre or right.

  - For ALIGN=top, the top of the object is vertically aligned with the top of the tallest text for the current line.
  - For ALIGN=middle, the middle of the object is vertically aligned with the position midway between the baseline and the x-height for the text line in which the object appears. The x-height is defined as the top of a lower-case x in western writing systems. If the text font is an all-caps style then use the height of a capital X. For other writing systems, align the middle of the object with the middle of the text.
  - For ALIGN=bottom, the bottom of the object is vertically aligned with the baseline of the text line in which the object appears.
  - For ALIGN=center, the object is moved down to the next line and centred between the left and right margins. Subsequent text starts at the beginning of the next line.
  - For ALIGN=left, the object is moved down and over to the current left margin. Subsequent text is flowed past the right-hand side of the visible area of the object.
  - For ALIGN=right, the object is moved down and over to the current right margin. Subsequent text is flowed past the left-hand side of the visible area of the object.

- The **WIDTH** attribute

  Gives the suggested width of a box enclosing the visible area of the object. The width is specified in standard units.

- The **HEIGHT** attribute

  Gives the suggested height of a box enclosing the visible area of the object. The height is specified in standard units.

- The **BORDER** around the object

  The BORDER attribute applies to the border shown when the object forms part of a hypertext link, as specified by an enclosing anchor element. The attribute specifies the suggested width of this border around the visible area of the object. The width is specified in standard units. For BORDER=0 no border should be shown. This is normally used when such a border would interfere with the visual affordances presented by the object itself. For instance, the object could render itself as a number of bevelled buttons.

- **HSPACE** and **VSPACE**

  The HSPACE attribute gives the suggested width of the space to the left and right of the box enclosing the visible area of the object. The width is specified in standard units. This attribute is used to alter the separation of preceding and following text from the object.

  The VSPACE attribute gives the suggested height of the space to the top and bottom of the box enclosing the visible area of the object. The height is specified in standard units.

Standard units for lengths

Several attributes specify lengths as a number followed by an optional suffix. The units for lengths are specified by the suffix: pt denotes points, pi denotes picas, in denotes inches, cm denotes centimetres, mm denotes millimetres, em denotes em units (equal to the height of the default font), and px denotes screen pixels. The % sign indicates that the value is a percentage of the current displayable region; for widths, this is the space between the current left and right margins, while for heights, this is the height of the current window or table cell and so on. The default units are screen pixels. The number is an integer value or a real valued number such as '2.5'. Exponents, as in '1.2e2', are not allowed. White space is not allowed between the number and the suffix.

11.4 Proprietary tags for inserting other media

Netscape's EMBED element

The EMBED element has three attributes, SRC, WIDTH and HEIGHT, and may also contain optional parameters that can be sent to the plug-in handling the embedded data type.

- SRC=<url> is the URL of the source document.
- The WIDTH attribute specifies the width of the embedded document in pixels:

```
WIDTH=<size in pixels>
```

- The HEIGHT attribute specifies the height of the embedded document in pixels:

```
HEIGHT=<size in pixels>
```

- There can be an infinite number of parameters passed to a plug-in:

```
PARAMETER_NAME=<PARAMETER_VALUE>
```

Examples of parameters are PLAY_LOOP=true, or CONTROLS=false. Parameters are specific to each plug-in. For example:

```
<EMBED SRC="didcot.mov", WIDTH=150, HEIGHT=250 CONTROLS=true>
<EMBED SRC="DoomGame.ids", WIDTH=400, HEIGHT=300 SPEED=slow LEVEL=12>
```

Netscape's LOWRES attribute

Netscape 2.0 adds another extension, called LOWSRC, to IMG. This is as follows:

```
<IMG SRC="highres.gif" LOWSRC="lowres.jpg">
```

Browsers that do not recognize the LOWSRC attribute cleanly ignore it and simply load the image called "highres.gif". Netscape Navigator, on the other hand, will load the image called "lowres.jpg" on its first layout pass through the document. Then, when the document and all of its images are fully loaded, Netscape Navigator will do a second pass through and load the image called "highres.gif" in place. This means that you can have a very low-resolution version of an image loaded initially; if the user stays on the page after the initial layout phase, a higher-resolution (and presumably bigger) version of the same image can 'fade in' and replace it.

You can freely mix and match GIF (both normal and interlaced) and JPEG images using this method. You can also specify width and/or height values in the IMG tag, and both the high-res and low-res versions of the image will be appropriately scaled to match.

Microsoft's DYNSRC

Microsoft Internet Explorer 2.0 allows you to embed .AVI (Audio Video Interleave) video clips into HTML pages. This is done by adding several new and non-standard attributes to the IMG element, notably DYNSRC which is functionally similar to IMG. Indeed DYNSRC can be used *with* IMG:

```
<IMG DYNSRC="special.avi" SRC="simple.gif">
```

the idea being that the older browsers see the file referenced by SRC and newer ones the file referenced by DYNSRC. This approach is all well and good until a yet newer version of the Internet Explorer comes out with a newer range of features enabling the browser to deal with yet more file formats. A new attribute for the benefit of the most up-to-date browser could then be added, giving three different attributes for three different alternative resources, but this seems a rather inefficient way of doing things.

In this slightly more complicated example you can see some of the other attributes used with DYNSRC:

```
<IMG DYNSRC="video.avi" SRC="image.gif" WIDTH=60 HEIGHT=60 LOOP=infinite
ALIGN=right>
```

Generally DYNSRC=url specifies the address of a video clip or VRML world to appear in the document. START=fileopen is used to specify that the video should start playing as soon as it's downloaded; START=mouseover, on the other hand, means that the video will start playing only when the cursor is moved over the animation.

An attribute CONTROLS produces a set of video controls on the screen under the video clip. To control how many times you see the video clip there is LOOP=n and LOOP=infinite. These can be used with LOOPDELAY=n which gives the time to delay before replaying the video.

Background music is done with an element called BGSOUND which has an attribute SRC=url to specify the address of the sound to be played and also LOOP=n and LOOP=infinite to specify how many times the sound should be played.

Java's APP and APPLET

Java has its own special HTML element for referencing Java code. The alpha release version of HotJava used the HTML element APP to incorporate Java applets into documents. However, with the beta release of the browser, a new element had to be introduced which had a different set of features. This was suitably named APPLET.

The syntax for APP was comparatively simple:

```
<APP SRC=path CLASS=classname PARAM=value>
```

whereas the syntax for the APPLET tag is more complicated:

```
<APPLET
CODEBASE=codebaseURL]
CODE=appletFile
ALT=alternateText
NAME=appletInstanceName]
WIDTH=pixels HEIGHT=pixels
ALIGN=alignment
VSPACE=pixels HSPACE=pixels>
<PARAM NAME=appletAttribute1 VALUE=value>
<PARAM NAME=appletAttribute2 VALUE=value>
</APPLET>
```

CODEBASE=codebaseURL specifies the base URL of the applet – the directory that contains the applet's code. If this attribute is not specified, then the document's URL is used.

CODE=appletFile is a required attribute which gives the name of the file that contains the applet's compiled Applet subclass. This file is relative to the base URL of the applet. It cannot be absolute.

ALT=alternateText is an optional attribute which specifies any text that should be displayed if the browser understands the APPLET tag but is unable to run Java applets.

NAME=appletInstanceName is an optional attribute which specifies a name for the applet instance. This makes it possible for applets on the same page to find (and communicate with) each other.

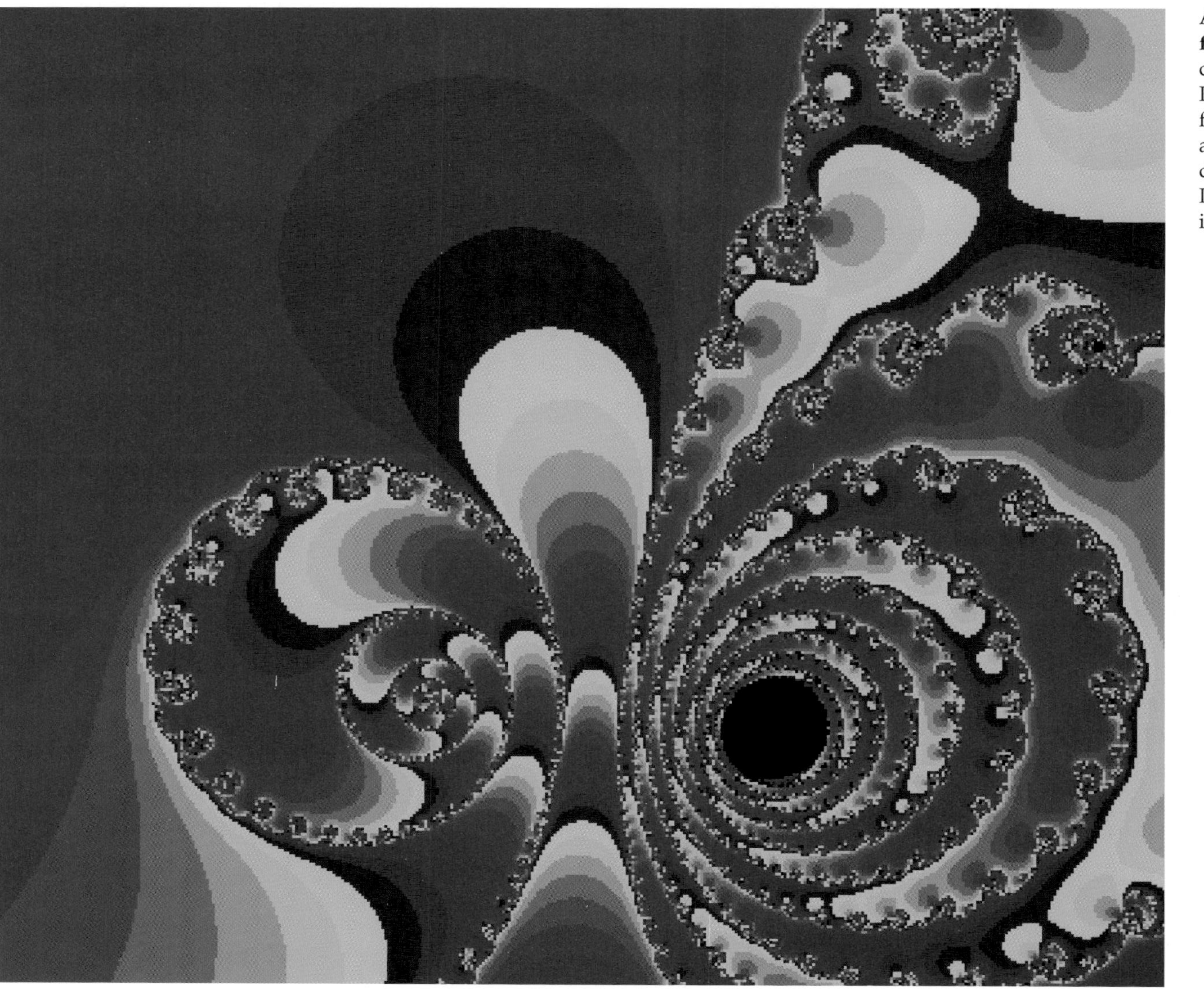

A fractal image gleaned from the Web. This one comes from Randy D. Ralph's brilliant pages full of icons and other artwork to use to decorate Web pages. It's on http://www.infinet/~rdralph/.

Our Web-Site Philosophy

At **Up & Running**, we believe a web site doesn't have to be gray, boring, or constrained. It also shouldn't take six days to download. It isn't a brochure or a form to fill out. It's a place where people can get a feel for who you are and why you matter in their lives.

(Top left) **One of David Siegel's pages on the Web.** A professional typographer and designer, David Siegel finds HTML extremely limiting because it does not allow you to control the precise layout and font. It is hoped that style sheets will make amends in this area and provide the layout artist and typographer with the right tools for designing Web screens. Look on www.seigel.com.

(Right) **An example of how you can order items over the Web.** The fill-out form is not dissimilar to a paper equivalent but uses a drop-down menu for selecting 'Size' and radio buttons to indicate 'Country'. Notice also the hypertext link to the list of country codes. HTML fill-out forms are described in Chapter 12.

David Siegel T-shirt Order Form

NOW AVAILABLE!

7 oz. 100% preshrunk super heavy cotton T-shirt. Oversized cut with double-needle stitching at neck, armholes and hem. Available in Large and Extra Large. White only. Front shown, with URL on back. $20

Ordering is easy!

Just call (800) 997-1299 from anywhere in the US, or follow the 5 easy steps below and press the SUBMIT button.

VISA MasterCard DISCOVER NOVUS

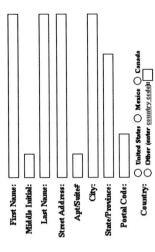

1. Choose size and quantity

Size: L **Quantity:**

2. Enter shipping address

First Name:

Middle Initial:

Last Name:

Street Address:

Apt/Suite#

City:

State/Province:

Postal Code:

Country: ○ United States ○ Mexico ○ Canada ○ Other (enter country code):

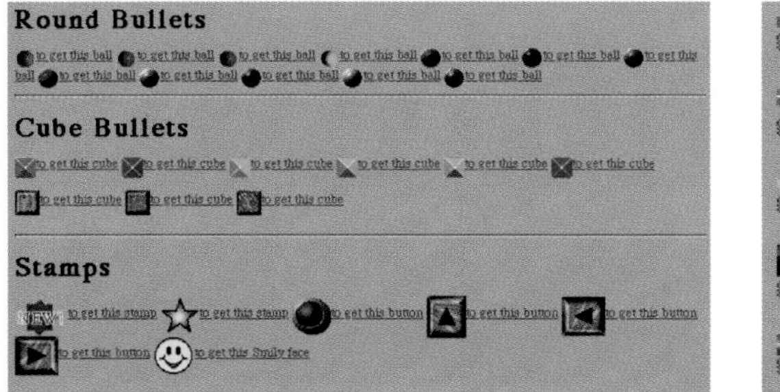

(*Top left*) **Clip art from 'Chris' World'.** A good source of graphics for your Web pages. You click on any of the graphics to download them and they can then be stored on your own computer's disk. At a future date you can incorporate the graphic into your own Web page. With all clip art, check the copyright details first – some people are only too glad for you to use their images, but it is wise to make sure.

(*Right*) **More clip art from 'Chris' World'.** This time horizontal bars to place across your Web pages. Choose from marble, luminous amber, rainbow and opalescent finishes.

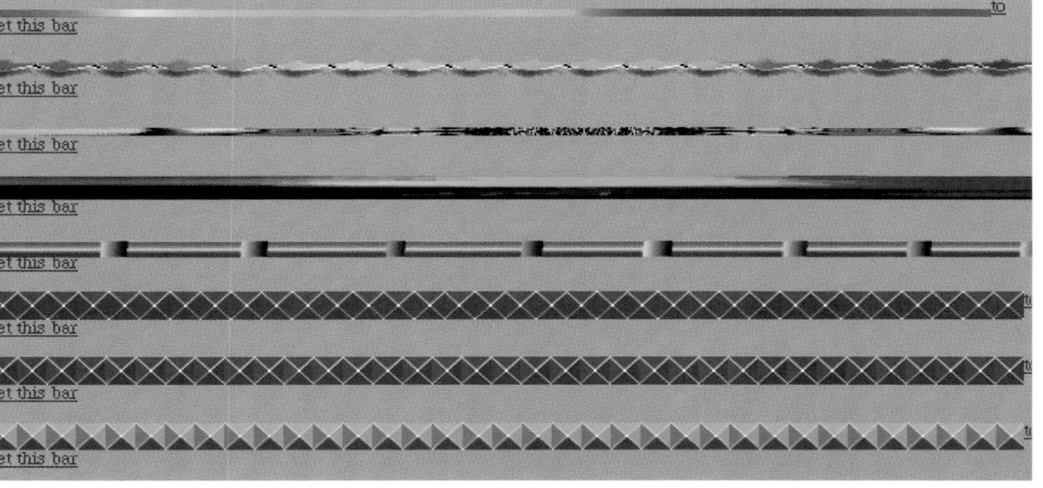

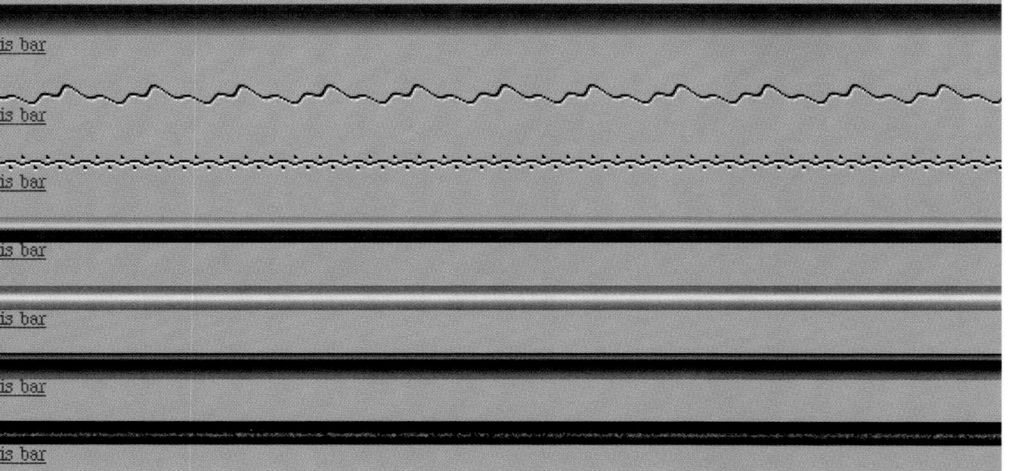

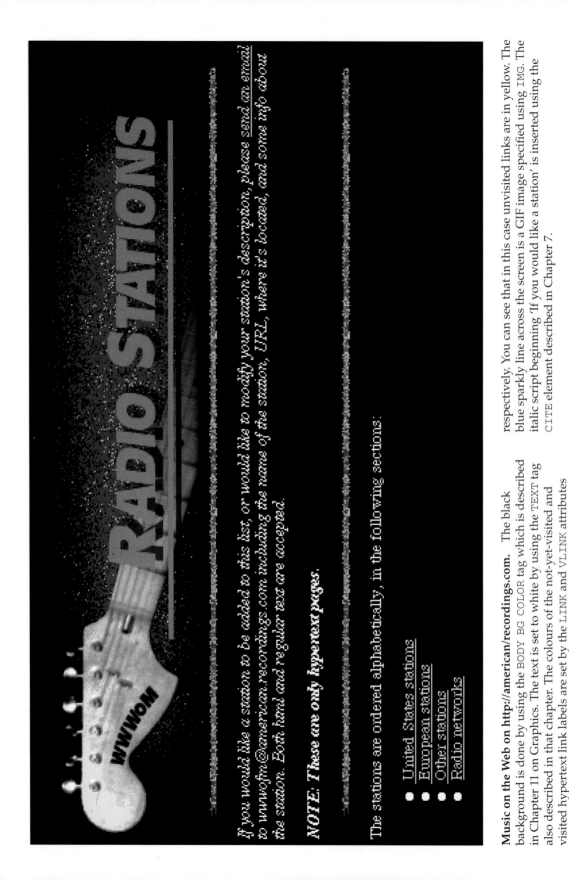

Music on the Web on http://american/recordings.com. The black background is done by using the `BODY BG COLOR` tag which is described in Chapter 11 on Graphics. The text is set to white by using the `TEXT` tag also described in that chapter. The colours of the not-yet-visited and visited hypertext link labels are set by the `LINK` and `VLINK` attributes respectively. You can see that in this case unvisited links are in yellow. The blue sparkly line across the screen is a GIF image specified using `IMG`. The italic script beginning 'If you would like a station' is inserted using the `CITE` element described in Chapter 7.

Bird Watching

Introduction

Birding is a sport that everyone can enjoy. All you really need is a pair of binoculars and a good field guide to help you identify the different varieties of birds you will find protected in our park. For a really close look at birds and other wildlife a spotting scope is recommended. A Checklist of Birds Found in Banff National Park is available from Park Information and Visitor Centres.

Cave and Basin Marsh

The Cave and Basin Marsh is located 2 km. west of Banff townsite on the south side of the Bow River from Cave Avenue. Parking is available at the Cave and Basin National Historic Site and from there several footpaths will take you through the forest to the marsh and marsh boardwalk. The Cave and Basin marsh is a large wetland area separated from the Bow River by a levee. It is fed by hotsprings that normally permit some open water areas throughout the winter. Tall willows grow in dense tangles throughout the marsh and the edges are lined by spruce and pine forest.

Late March to early May:

Song Sparrows and Red-winged Blackbirds are often found here before they appear elsewhere in the park. Throughout the willows you may find other early migrants such as Ruby-crowned Kinglets, Orange-crowned Warblers, and Dark-eyed Juncos. Waterfowl are abundant.

Late May to mid July:

(Top left) **Birding from http://vertex.webworld.com.** The large font is achieved by using the `FONT` element which is described in Chapter 7. With style sheets (Chapter 14) you will be able to control the font closely in a separate language for controlling the precise layout of HTML documents. The image is left-aligned and specified using `IMG`. Note how the text flows around it.

(Top right) **This is also from the bird-watching site.** The photograph of the red-winged blackbird is a GIF image inserted using `IMG` and is right-aligned. The heading 'Cave and Basin Marsh' is an `H3` element; 'Late March to early May' is achieved by using the `<STRONG>` tag. The blue background is done by specifying `BODY BACKGROUND="sky.jpg"` which causes the small graphic sky.jpg to be repeated in such a way that it covers the background of the screen. See Chapter 11.

New England Aquarium in Boston, http://www.neaq.org. This is a fine example of an image map. When the reader clicks on the graphic, the coordinates of the click are sent to the server which then sends the appropriate file back – different files are returned according to the coordinates of the click. See the end of Chapter 9.

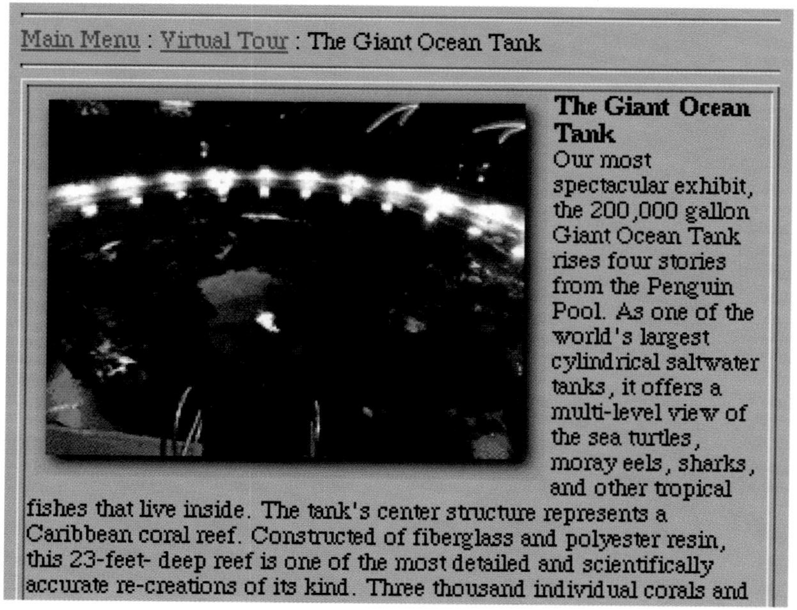

Main Menu : Virtual Tour : The Giant Ocean Tank

The Giant Ocean Tank
Our most spectacular exhibit, the 200,000 gallon Giant Ocean Tank rises four stories from the Penguin Pool. As one of the world's largest cylindrical saltwater tanks, it offers a multi-level view of the sea turtles, moray eels, sharks, and other tropical fishes that live inside. The tank's center structure represents a Caribbean coral reef. Constructed of fiberglass and polyester resin, this 23-feet- deep reef is one of the most detailed and scientifically accurate re-creations of its kind. Three thousand individual corals and

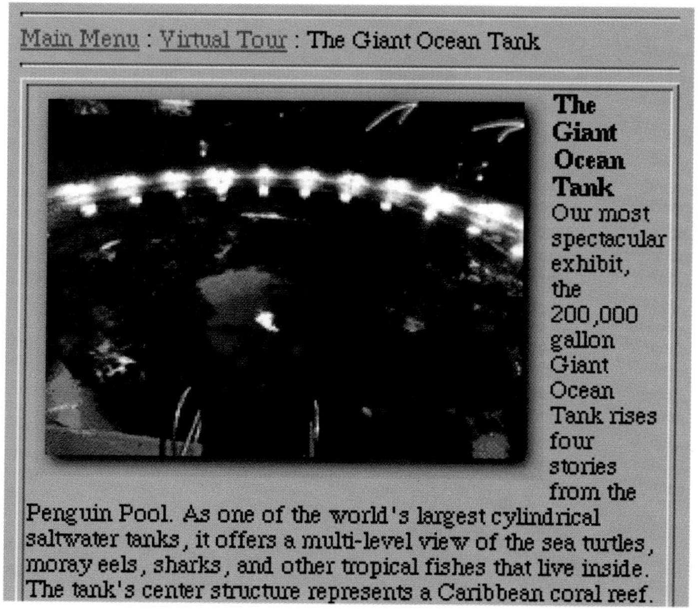

Main Menu : Virtual Tour : The Giant Ocean Tank

The Giant Ocean Tank
Our most spectacular exhibit, the 200,000 gallon Giant Ocean Tank rises four stories from the Penguin Pool. As one of the world's largest cylindrical saltwater tanks, it offers a multi-level view of the sea turtles, moray eels, sharks, and other tropical fishes that live inside. The tank's center structure represents a Caribbean coral reef.

(Top left) **Also from the New England Aquarium.** This screen should be compared with the one on the right which is exactly the same Web page but viewed in a narrower window. The text flowing around the photograph has become squashed into a small column and would eventually be pushed underneath if the space next to the image were made any smaller. Note that the image is not scaled as the window size decreases; future browser writers will allow proper scaling of images to take place.

(Top right) **Text flow around an image.** With Netscape's browser, text currently flows around an image imported with `IMG` unless the author specifies otherwise. The `CLEAR` attribute explained in Chapter 4 can be used to control text flow and to push all the text under an image rather than letting it flow alongside.

Location: http://www.cs.ubc.ca/elements/tab/periodic-table

Periodic Table of the Elements

1a	2a	3b	4b	5b	6b	7b	8			1b	2b	3a	4a	5a	6a	7a	0
H 1																	He 2
Li 3	Be 4											B 5	C 6	N 7	O 8	F 9	Ne 10
Na 11	Mg 12											Al 13	Si 14	P 15	S 16	Cl 17	Ar 18
K 19	Ca 20	Sc 21	Ti 22	V 23	Cr 24	Mn 25	Fe 26	Co 27	Ni 28	Cu 29	Zn 30	Ga 31	Ge 32	As 33	Se 34	Br 35	Kr 36
Rb 37	Sr 38	Y 39	Zr 49	Nb 41	Mo 42	Tc 43	Ru 44	Rh 45	Pd 46	Ag 47	Cd 48	In 49	Sn 50	Sb 51	Te 52	I 53	Xe 54
Cs 55	Ba 56	La 57	Hf 72	Ta 73	W 74	Re 75	Os 76	Ir 77	Pt 78	Au 79	Hg 80	Tl 81	Pb 82	Bi 83	Po 84	At 85	Rn 86
Fr 87	Ra 88	Ac 89	Rf 104	Ha 105	?? 106												
Lanthinide Series		Ce 58	Pr 59	Nd 60	Pm 61	Sm 62	Eu 63	Gd 64	Tb 65	Dy 66	Ho 67	Er 68	Tm 69	Yb 70	Lu 71		

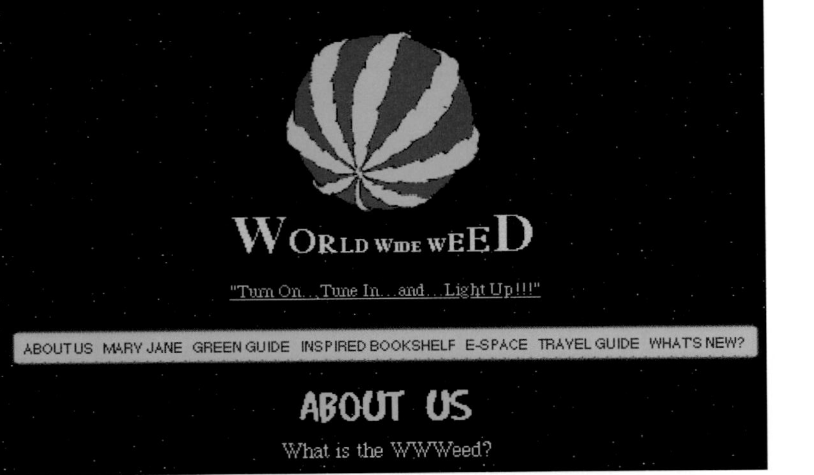

(Top left) This Web page shows the Periodic Table (the bottom lines scrolled off the screen). The whole thing is presented as an HTML table with hypertext links in many of the cells. You click on the link to see more information on the element in question. Tables are explained in Chapter 10.

(Bottom left) Extraordinary graphics for an extraordinary site!

(Opposite page) **A graphical HTML form.** The user selects a chemical compound from the list (which is only partially visible here), the representational style required, and whether the crystalline structure or molecular structure is to be displayed. A three-dimensional rendering of that compound then appears, although you do have to have the correct VRML (Virtual Reality Modelling Language) software.

Goto: http://fact.jicst.go.jp/cr-vrml.html

JICST Crystal Structure Database

SUBMIT You will need a VRML browser such as WebSpace.

Display Model

◉ Ball and Stick

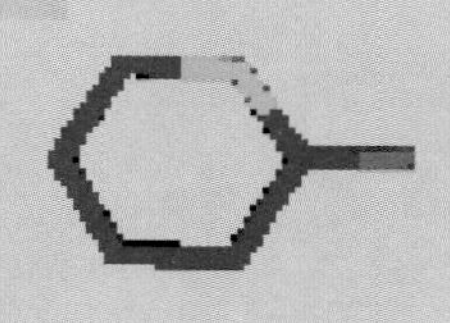

○ Stick

○ Space F

Display Object

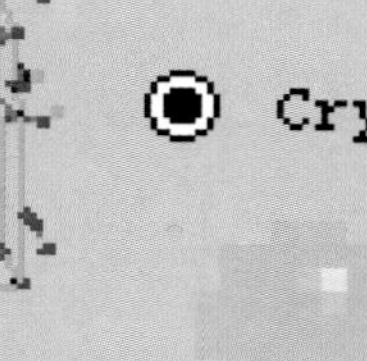

◉ Crystal

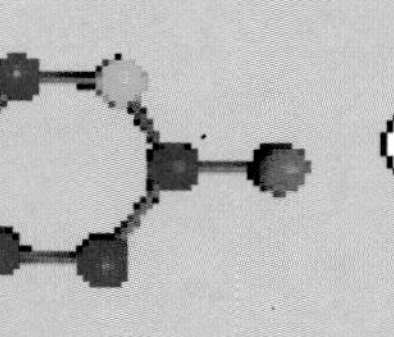

○ Molecule

Substance

```
cr860707: C9H7NO, 2-quinolone
cr860726: K3Fe(CN)6, potassium ferricyanide
cr860727: K3Fe(CN)6, potassium ferricyanide
```

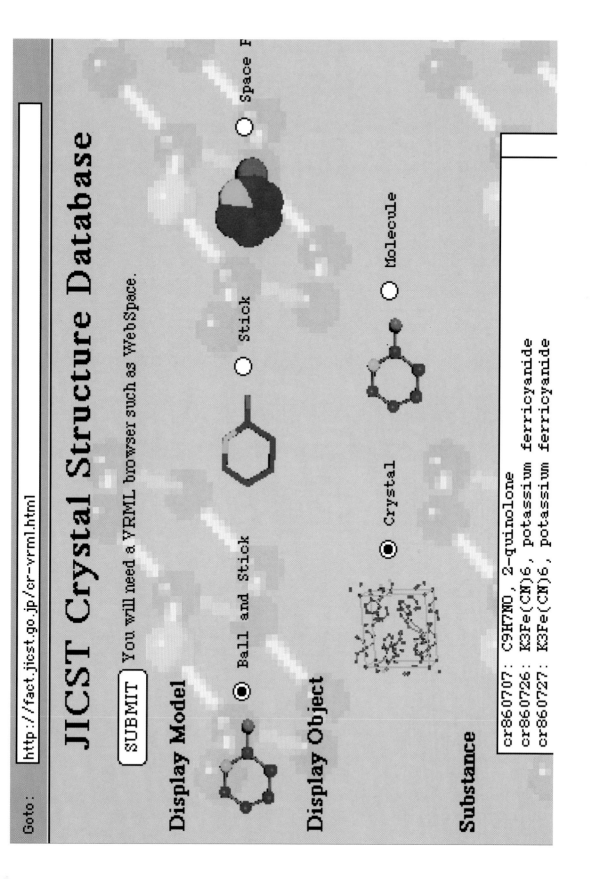

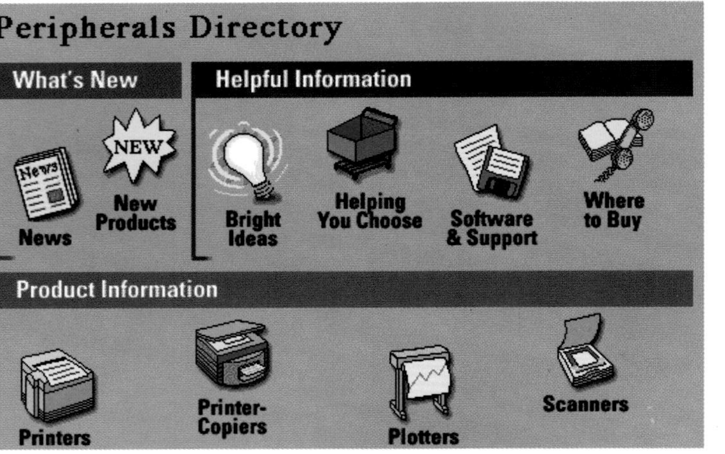

(Top left) **Product information on the Web from Hewlett-Packard via http://www.hp.com.** This is the opening screen in a series concerned with product information. Hundreds of HP products are listed and described online. The menu bar consists of an image map.

(Bottom left) **Visual menu bar.** You click on one of the product categories to move to the next screen.

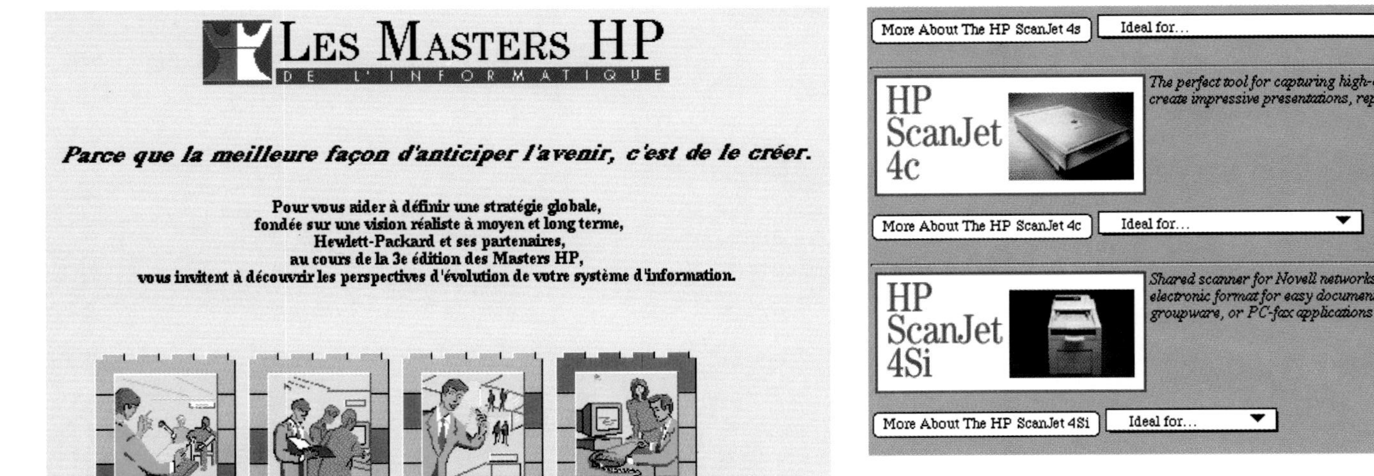

More About The HP ScanJet 4s
Ideal for...

HP ScanJet 4c
The perfect tool for capturing high-quality color and monochrome images to create impressive presentations, reports, and promotional materials.

More About The HP ScanJet 4c
Ideal for...

HP ScanJet 4Si
Shared scanner for Novell networks quickly converts printed information to electronic format for easy document distribution, sharing, and filing via e-mail, groupware, or PC-fax applications.

More About The HP ScanJet 4Si
Ideal for...

(Top left) **Simple use of colour.** A screen from the French Hewlett-Packard pages which we liked.

(Top right) **Homing in on the information you want.** There are drop-down menus to click on, and links to more information if you need it.

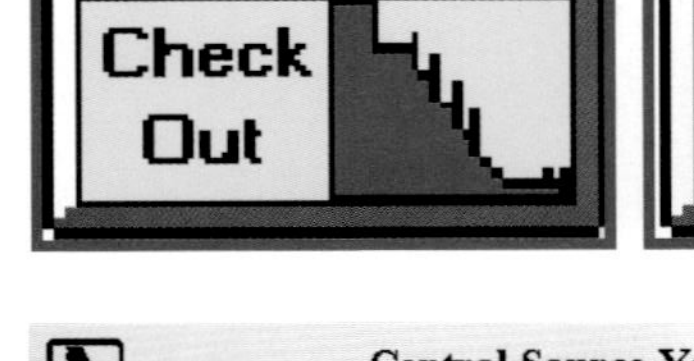

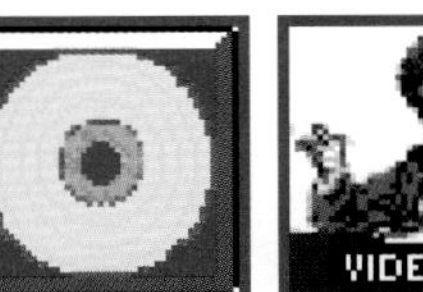

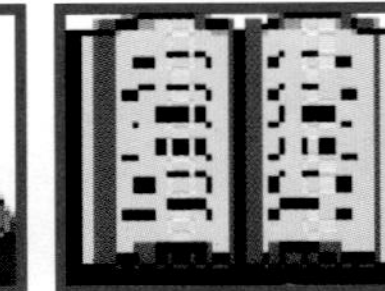

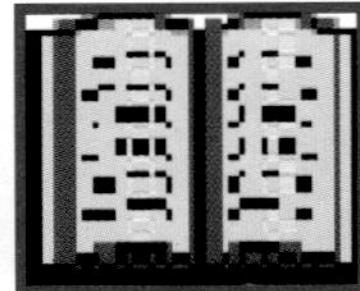

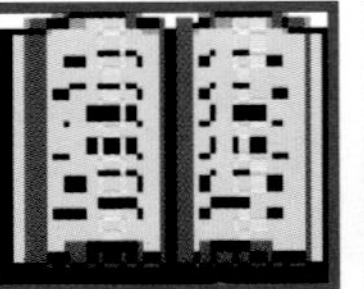

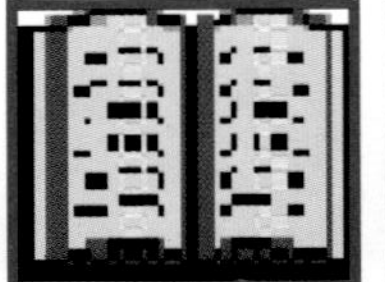

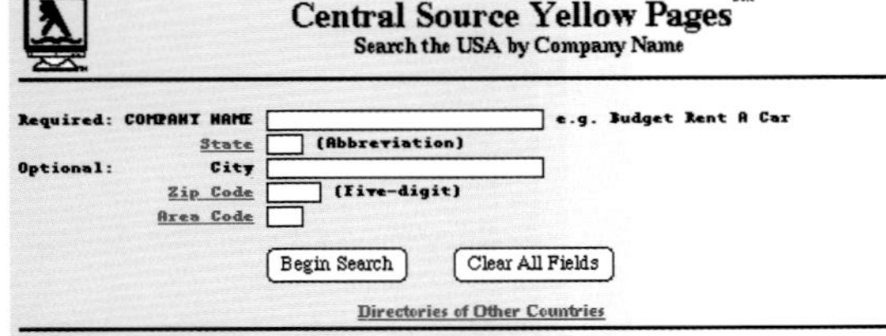

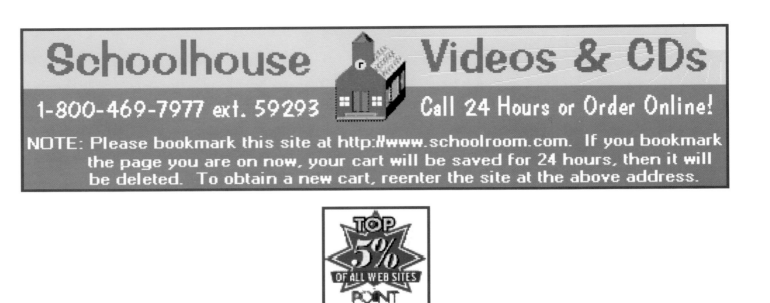

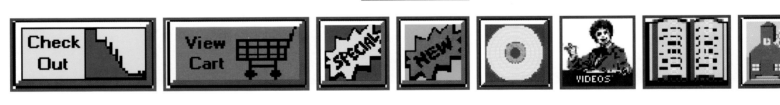

(Top) **Purchasing goods on the Web.** You use an imaginary 'cart' (a shopping trolley to British readers) and go through a 'check-out' when you have finished loading up during your wanderings through the various Web pages of the online 'shop'. The process of ordering involves filling in a form.

(Left) **Yellow Pages on the Web.** Self-explanatory, this uses an HTML form to initiate a search.

Music M@estro !

Het is leuk toeven in cyberspace, maar een goede soundtrack maakt surfomzwervingen nog veel hallucinanter. Zet misschien je radio 's op, ja? Je lijf, leden en brein zullen bijzonder opkikkeren van volgende FM-frequenties:

```
Leuven.....................88.0
Gent.......................94.5
Brabant...................100.6
Antwerpen.................100.9
Limburg...................101.4
Oost- & West-Vlaanderen...102.1
```

Elke andere frequentie brengt je radiotoestel blijvende schade toe. Niet alleen je radiotoestel trouwens.

Slak rustig je gangetje

Wil je als onverbeterlijke internetter nog 's dat bijzonder genoegen proeven een lekker ouderwetse brief naar ons te sturen? Dat kan. Stuur je

(Top left) **Information about radio stations in Belgium.** The PRE tag and FONT SIZE=+1 are used to give the larger Courier-type font. The indent is achieved by using BLOCKQUOTE. See Chapter 11 for details about setting background and text colour.

(Top right) **Example of a scrolling menu.** This is from the WeatherLinks USA on www.ngww.mall.com/frontier/vortex. See Chapter 12 to see how forms like this one are constructed.

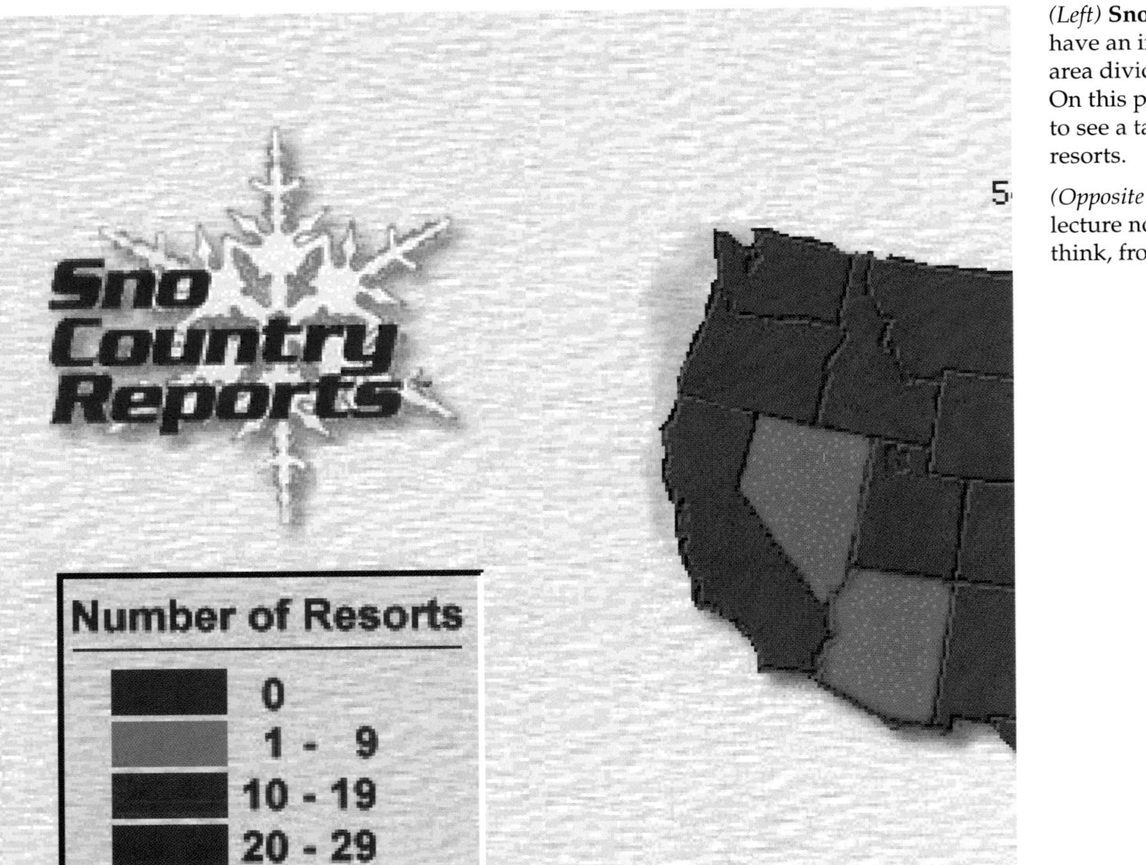

(Left) **Snow reports on the Web.** Quite a few sites have an image map consisting of a geographical area divided into a number of clickable regions. On this page you click on an image map of states to see a table listing the snow conditions of various resorts.

(Opposite page) **Course notes on the Web.** These lecture notes are presented as images derived, we think, from slides.

Physics 150

Fall 1995

Slides: Lecture 21, Schrodinger & Heisenberg, 11/13/95

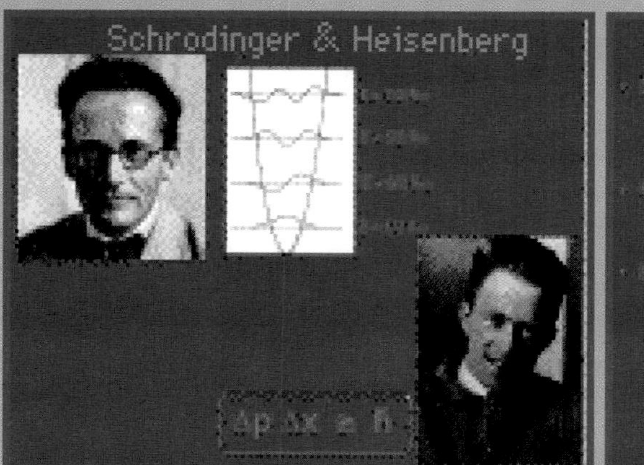

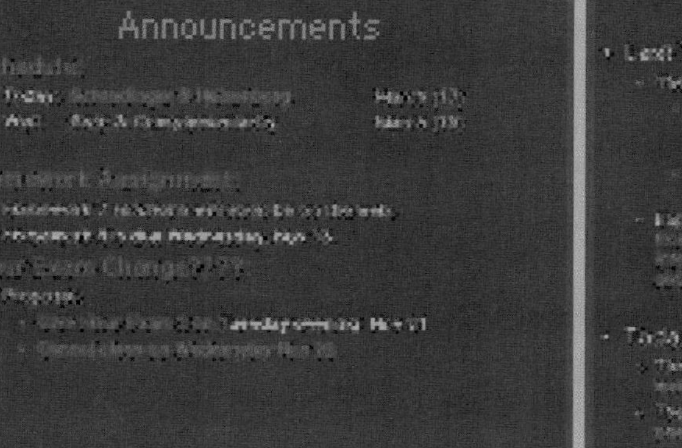

Introduction

The Schrodinger Equation

Example : The Harmonic Oscillator

Mass attached to a spring

Example : Hydrogen Atom

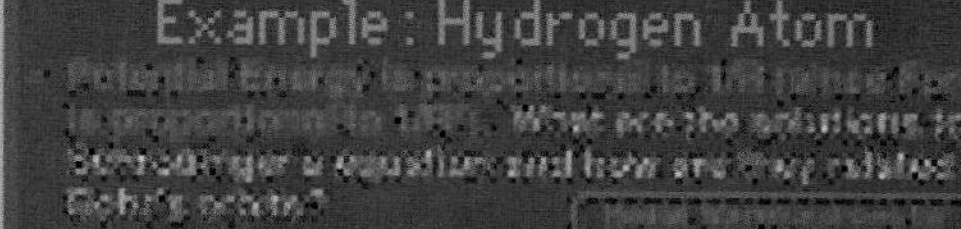

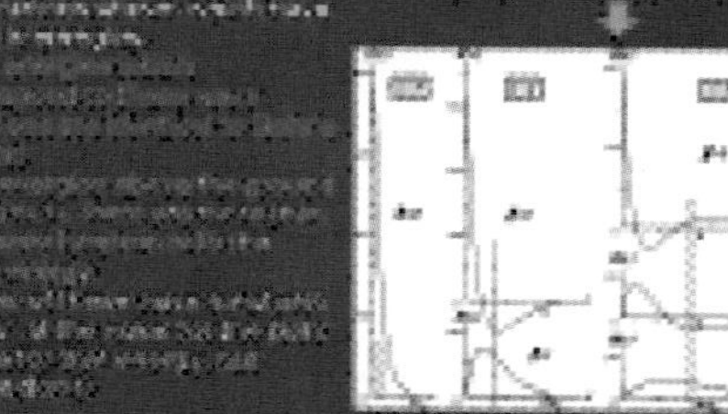

(Top left) The World Wide Web consortium happily combines work with relaxation.

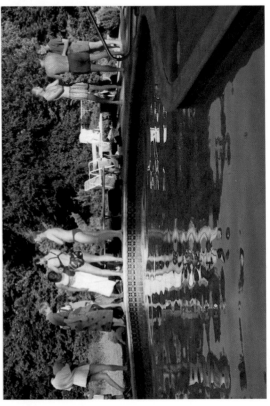

(Bottom left) Cool at the pool: a pleasant summer party for the World Wide Consortium. To the right of the photo, three gentlemen are obviously engrossed in discussion. A closer look reveals …

(Right) … none other than author Dave Raggett and two colleagues in eager debate about HTML style sheets!

`WIDTH=pixels HEIGHT=pixels` are required attributes giving the initial width and height (in pixels) of the applet display area, not counting any windows or dialogs that the applet brings up.

`ALIGN=alignment` is a required attribute which specifies the alignment of the applet. The possible values of this attribute are the same as those for the `IMG` tag: `left`, `right`, `top`, `texttop`, `middle`, `absmiddle`, `baseline`, `bottom`, `absbottom`.

`VSPACE=pixels HSPACE=pixels` are optional attributes which specify the number of pixels above and below the applet (`VSPACE`) and on each side of the applet (`HSPACE`). They're treated the same way as the `IMG` tag's `VSPACE` and `HSPACE` attributes.

`<PARAM NAME=appletAttribute1 VALUE=value>` is used to specify an applet-specific attribute. Applets access their attributes with the `getParameter()` method.

11.5 Background textures for your Web pages

A background for your Web page is very easy to construct from a GIF or JPEG image. Backgrounds are an exciting part of design which afford great possibilities for tasteful expression and equally for injudiciously colourful proclamations.

Inserting a background is accomplished by using the `BACKGROUND` attribute of the `BODY` element. All you do is put a statement like:

```
<BODY BACKGROUND=marble.gif>
```

in the head of your document (many current Web documents make this the first line) and then Bob's your Uncle (as we say in Britain): the GIF file is repeated across the screen *by the browser* (you do nothing) to add a subtle and complementary texture on which to superimpose your text. The smaller the image, the more repetitions.

Any number of backgrounds are available over the Web ready-built. If you search on the words *graphics* and *backgrounds* you should come up with lots of references to these 'libraries' of GIF files. Every effect is available: marble, cumulus cloud, parchment, carpet, virtual recycled paper (most odd, that one), sandpaper, formica, cardboard, tree bark, and so on. The list of possibilities is as varied as taste allows.

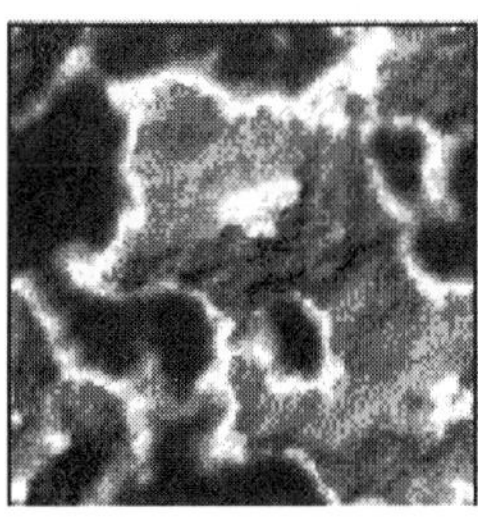  

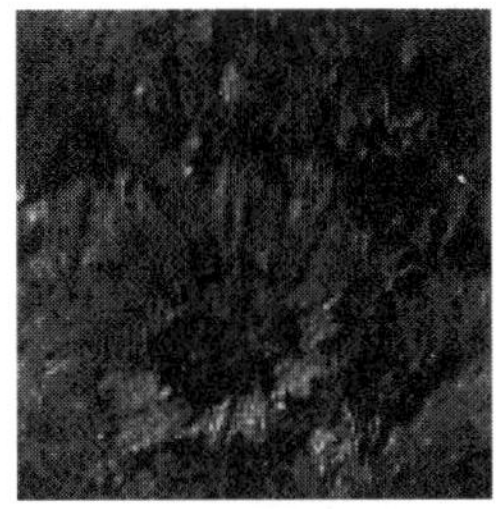

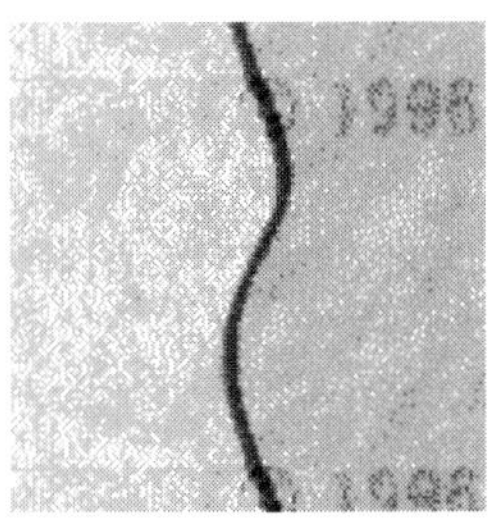

Make sure your backgrounds don't take too long to download

The smaller the graphic, the more repetitions of it there will be when the background is tiled. Small images arrive faster than larger ones, meaning that a large tile may take a long time to download. Larger images which compress very well are fine and flat untextured areas of colour indeed do well on this count. You can use flat colours to generate 3-D effects. For example, you might want to use three shades of grey for a bas-relief corporate logo in a pattern which repeats wallpaper fashion. Bear in mind that the browser clips tiles when you resize the window.

Make your own background effects

You can create your own background material. Scan in some paper with a nice texture and then clip it so that it is a perfect square say about an inch wide. Convert it to the appropriate GIF or JPEG format. You can also scan in patterns to tile but getting the edges to line up is difficult.

11.6 Colour of text and background

In Chapter 2 we explained that the whole point of HTML was that it concerned itself with the structural aspects of a document and not the nitty gritty of how the text was rendered on the screen. It is thus with some reticence that we talk about the HTML elements and attributes introduced by certain browser writers concerning colour and font.

For Netscape browsers, the colour of the background is specified in the `BODY` element by using the `BGCOLOR` attribute. The colour will overlay a background texture so that you might end up with a blue marble background, or, at the drop of a hat, a green one simply by changing the `BGCOLOR` attribute.

Netscape lets you specify the colour of text by using the `TEXT` attribute, again in the `BODY` element. Here are the opening chords in a thoroughly modern HTML document for displaying using Netscape. The HTML will work on Microsoft's Network Explorer too.

```
<BODY BGCOLOR="#000015" TEXT="#000020" LINK="#000050" VLINK="#000050"
ALINK="#000050">
```

These lines specify information as follows:

- BGCOLOR= is the background colour
- TEXT= is the main text colour – you can only have one colour for this
- LINK= is the normal colour of a hypertext link prior to visiting
- VLINK= is the colour of a visited link
- ALINK= is the colour of an active or being visited link.

You don't have to specify all of these – in fact you can specify none at all. All five attributes are optional.

What are these funny codes used to specify colours? Where do they come from and how do you know which one to choose? They are hexadecimal codes of RGB (Red-Green-Blue) values. Remember that graphics packages allow you to fiddle with the amount of red, green and blue components to produce the colour of your choice. Well, when you have generated a colour that you like the look of, you can find out its equivalent hexadecimal value using the graphics package and write this down for future reference. Note that the hexadecimal value will not always generate an identical colour on any Web browser used to view that colour as the codes are not 'gamma corrected'.

There are charts available which tell you what code results in what colour. You can try http://www.interport.net/~giant/COLOR/hype_color.html which should give samples of colours and corresponding codes.

Here are some examples of colour codes. The first column shows the RGB values to create the colour. Then comes the name (these are not standard names in any way!) and the hexadecimal code. This is made of a mixture of numbers 1–9 and the letters A–F.

RGB value	*Colour name*	*Hexadecimal code*
255, 250, 250	Snow	FFFAFA
255, 235, 205	Blanched almonds	FFEBCD
255, 250, 205	Lemon chiffon	FFFACD
240, 255, 250	Mint cream	F0FFFA

Microsoft's Internet Explorer allows you to insert real words for colours instead of these peculiar codes. For example:

```
BODY BGCOLOR="olive" TEXT="navy" LINK="teal" VLINK="fuchsia"
```

As you can see the names of colours – there are 16 in all to choose from – reflect current fashions in ladies' outdoor clothing.

11.7 Horizontal rules with HR

Horizontal rules are either simply useful lines across the page, or wonderful three-dimensional additions to your document which impart that air of professionalism or fussiness, depending on your point of view, and of course, your browser. Not all browsers show the elaborate Netscape-type rules.

Horizontal rules across the page are accomplished with the HR element. This element has no content, that is, it cannot contain other elements, and no end tag. Netscape, in accordance with current fashions for all things three-dimensional, draws nice sculptured rules as shown below. Other browsers will draw horizontal rules differently. As the author, you have control over the width of the rule across the page and also the thickness of the rule in terms of the line drawn. The width across the page is controlled with the WIDTH attribute while the thickness of the line is a function of the SIZE attribute. Both these attributes are extensions to standard HTML; in HTML 3 the rendering of a horizontal rule is style-sheet controlled rather than specified in the mark-up.

Here are some samples of horizontal rules as they appear on the Netscape browser:

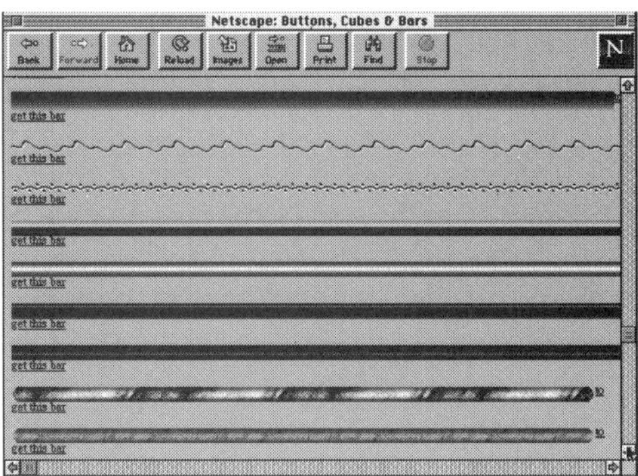

This is the code to create them:

```
<HR>
<HR SIZE=2>
<HR SIZE=4>
<HR WIDTH=50%>
<HR WIDTH=30% ALIGN=left>
<HR WIDTH=30% ALIGN=right>
```

Concise description of HR element for Netscape 2.0

<HR>

The HR element specifies that a horizontal rule of some sort (the default being a shaded sculptured 3-D line) should be drawn across the page.

`<HR SIZE=number>`

The `SIZE` attribute lets the author say how thick the horizontal rule is to be.

`<HR WIDTH=number|percent>`

The default horizontal rule is always as wide as the page. With the `WIDTH` attribute, you can specify an exact width in pixels, or a relative width measured as a percentage of document width.

`<HR ALIGN=left|right|center>`

This attribute allows the author to specify whether the rule should be pushed up against the left margin, the right margin, or centred on the page.

`<HR NOSHADE>`

If you really want a solid bar, the `NOSHADE` attribute lets you specify that you do not want any 3-D shading of your horizontal rule.

11.8 BANNERs across the page

HTML 3 suggested that the `BANNER` element be used for corporate logos, navigation aids, disclaimers and other information which shouldn't be scrolled with the rest of the document. It provides an alternative to using the `LINK` element in the document head to reference an externally defined banner.

12
FILL-OUT FORMS

In this chapter:

- A general introduction to forms on computer screens, and why you need them (Section 12.1)
- An overview of how HTML handles forms (Section 12.2)
- An analysis of HTML 3's form elements (Section 12.3)
- A description of how to submit forms to the server (Section 12.4)
- A general discussion of the principles of forms design, with practical tips (Section 12.5)

The chapter (and this book) does not cover the creation of server-side scripts to handle incoming HTML forms data, though it briefly explains their use.

12.1 Introduction

12.1.1 What is a form?

A form is a group of input controls which appear on the screen of the browser when a user loads the HTML document containing the form. Unlike the other HTML elements like headers and paragraphs, forms are designed to let your users send information *back to you*. This means that your server (computer sending out your HTML) has to process all this returned information in some way that is useful to you. It also means that forms are more complicated to set up than, say, lists or tables, because they only work in the context of matching specially written software running on your server. If you are not a programmer, then you need to find someone who can make your forms work for you on your server. Script programming is outside the scope of HTML, and this book.

So, whereas a simple HTML document is just like a book or magazine in which the author (you) tells the reader something, an HTML document with a form is like a book with a detachable reply-paid coupon for the reader to fill in. It gives the reader a chance to interact, if not with you personally, at least with a program running on your server. And, of course, it enables you to collect information from your readers.

A paper form contains a title, some printed instructions, and a lot of various boxes for you to fill in. Sometimes you have to write your name or various numbers in these boxes; sometimes you can just put a single letter (like 'M' for Married) in a small box, and sometimes all you need to do is to check (British readers: tick) the box to say 'yes, this one'. All of these mechanisms are available in HTML 3's forms in the shape of fields, checkboxes, radio buttons, selection menus, and so on.

One advantage over the paper variety is that the on-screen form is guaranteed to be legible, as all the words are typed rather than hand-written.

Another and more significant advantage is speed: as soon as your readers have filled in their forms, they can press a button to send the form data straight to you (or at least, to your server). Everything they put into the form is sent to your server for processing.

12.1.2 How forms are handled behind the scenes

Your server has to run a program to handle all the incoming user information: for example, it might save it to a file or to a database. Or, if you are very ambitious, you might have an automatic reply service, to allow your customers to book tickets for forthcoming concerts, for example. The program on your server could confirm bookings by sending your customers unique booking reference numbers, and then print out the tickets to be mailed as soon as possible. You can see that many different levels of sophistication (and expense) are possible.

The diagram shows an example of what happens behind the scenes when a user completes a form. In the example, once the data has been stored, anything may happen. Usually some sort of confirmation is quickly sent back to the user; a log is kept of changes; management reports are prepared monthly; and the system reserves the seats, prints and mails the

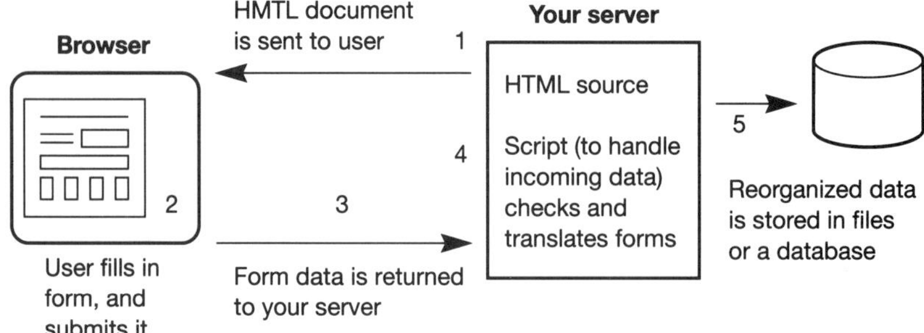

tickets, and records the user's address for the next concertgoers' mailshot. The HTML is, in fact, the placid surface which covers a torrent of activity by other systems.

12.2 Why would you want information from users?

HTML forms, then, together with their server scripts, make your documents truly interactive: your users can talk back. There are many possible reasons why you might want to enable them to do this:

- to let users give you comments and feedback on your document or the products it describes
- to enable users to find out more about your products or services
- to enable prospective customers to discuss technical issues with you directly
- to allow actual customers to order products or services from you
- to find out who is interested in your document, ideas, products or services
- to enable users to search for and retrieve information from other search engines.

12.2.1 Business traffic

All of this has a pretty commercial flavour. It is no secret that the growing ability of HTML to handle business traffic, from advertisements to serious enquiries to orders (and even, in the case of documents, music, images and software, actual deliveries of goods) is causing an unprecedented spurt of growth in the Web and the Internet in general. HTML forms are right at the heart of this, as they are the easiest and best way for users and customers to describe precisely what they want, and for suppliers to obtain the full delivery and payment details that they need to do business.

12.2.2 Academic and schools

Non-commercial hypertexts may also be improved with forms. Academic surveys, for instance, can be performed by telling people the URL of an HTML document, and processing the returned forms data. Forms can serve as quiz or even exam templates: maybe students in the Australian Outback will send in their homework like this, and their teachers will prepare for lessons by writing HTML!

12.2.3 Improved information sharing

The Internet developed mostly for government and academic information sharing. Many databases full of detailed technical information exist in relatively hard-to-access formats. HTML 3 forms make it quite easy for organizations with such data to display some Web pages containing very specific and helpful explanations of what is available, combined with easy-to-use forms which let users conduct searches and retrieve the information they need.

The process of sharing information from an existing database is very similar to the normal use of HTML forms. The only real difference is that your server needs an interface to the database. This may need some programming but is not usually difficult.

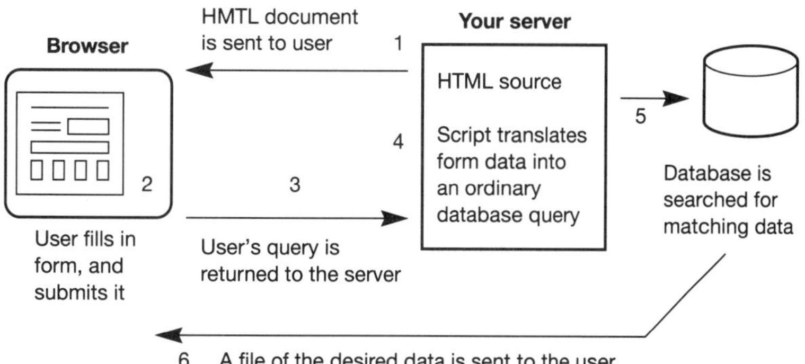

For example, data on Atlantic fish stocks is held by the European Commission, the United States Government and the Canadian authorities. The full picture is available only by detailed study of many information sources. Suitable querying of the existing databases using HTML forms could improve understanding of the problems and help to secure international agreements on conservation of the remaining fish. Of course the various authorities all need to provide their own forms. HTML 3 offers a new, uniform and internationally agreed mechanism for the purpose, which should make things easier for everyone.

MAILTO: Using HTML without forms

The use of forms to set up a dialogue with your readers is a relatively advanced topic, and you will be able to create effective HTML documents for many purposes without ever using them. We suggest that you set up your Web pages without forms, and then work out carefully whether you need the more sophisticated interaction that forms alone can provide. If all you need is to allow readers of your pages to mail you comments, you do not necessarily have to use forms: you can simply

- state your email address, preferably using an alias like 'webmaster' (so that readers can write to you, or your successor in your HTML-writing job, independently), or
- use the 'MAILTO:' keyword to connect readers' browsers to their mail tools directly.

Most browsers now handle the 'MAILTO:' mechanism, provided that their human users have remembered to fill in their email addresses and the directory paths of their mail tools. A typical use of this simple mechanism is:

```
<A HREF="MAILTO:pete@www.yourco.com">Mail to pete@www.yourco.com</A>
```

which causes a predefined mail form to appear; when filled in and submitted, an ordinary email message is sent to the address given in the HREF. An example of MAILTO: is illustrated in Section 5.6.

We think this is well worth knowing, as it may save you the trouble and expense of setting up the server mechanisms you would otherwise need to handle forms. That said, email is no substitute for the power and convenience of a properly configured forms system.

12.3 Overview: how HTML 3 handles forms

12.3.1 Your first form

HTML 3's handling of forms is quite sophisticated, and incorporates several changes for the better over HTML 2.0. Luckily, you can still write a form in just a line or two. Don't worry about the details for now: the example here is just to show you that a little HTML can be very useful. The following snippet tells your server to run a script called 'savezip' when it receives the form data, which in this case consists of a zip (British readers: post) code. It might be handy for an anonymous survey, for example:

```
<FORM ACTION="savezip">
   <P>Zip or post code: <INPUT NAME="zipcode" SIZE="9">
   <P> <INPUT TYPE=submit>
</FORM>
```

This little piece of HTML displays an input field, with a standard Submit button:

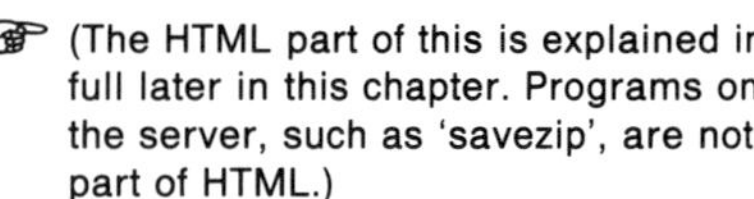
(The HTML part of this is explained in full later in this chapter. Programs on the server, such as 'savezip', are not part of HTML.)

Most of the other form constructs are no more complicated than this, but there are often several ways of achieving a result. For example, you can use lists such as <UL PLAIN> to format columns of input fields, or tables, or decimal alignment: each method has its own advantages.

12.3.2 More sophisticated forms

HTML 3's FILE widget lets users upload a file. Other novelties still under discussion include SCRIBBLE (on an image) widget, customizable images on SUBMIT and RESET buttons, and graphical SELECTion menus (using SHAPEs within OPTIONs). Work is also in progress on a script attribute.

It is permissible to have more than one form in a document, though this may be confusing to authors and readers. Forms may not, however, be nested (unlike tables).

Netscape are working on JavaScript; Microsoft on VBScript. These will make it far easier to write scripts for forms.

This chapter introduces the various form elements one by one, with worked examples of useful types of form. Other elements (such as TABLEs and UL or DL lists) which you will often need to use when building forms are incorporated in the examples; these elements are explained in detail in their own chapters. Once the basic elements have been explained, the chapter concludes by showing how they can be combined in forms design to yield practical forms ready to have scripts written for them and finally to be installed on a server.

12.4 HTML's form elements

HTML 2.0

Of the FORM element itself, there is little to write. You always put:

```
<FORM ACTION="http://myserver.cobweb.com/doform">
   ...fields go here...
   ...mixed with any body-content text and tables you like...
   <P> <INPUT TYPE=submit> <INPUT TYPE=reset>
</FORM>
```

The form tag itself can be qualified with an HTTP METHOD (=post or =get) attribute, to tell the browser which HyperText Transfer Protocol method the server supports. get is the default. For example:

```
<FORM METHOD=post ACTION="http://www.acme.co.uk/forms/register">
```

The `ACTION` attribute, as illustrated above, tells the browser where to submit the form to; the default is the URL of the document itself, which usually isn't what you want.

The `ENCTYPE` attribute tells the browser which MIME contents type to use when encoding form data. Its default is `"application/x-www-form-urlencoded"` which we hope you never need to change.

Work is in progress on adding client-side scripting of forms. A script can do things such as initializing and cleaning up forms (on entering and leaving); processing mouse clicks and drags, and keyclicks. Scripts can look up the time and date and user's name. They are expressly forbidden to do anything dangerous which might spread viruses, like sending messages or writing files. Unfortunately the script language and individual browsers' script interfaces are not defined in the HTML standard, so scripts are not yet portable across browsers. The miserable best we can do is to tell you to read your Java user manual for more details.

The rest of this section presents the form elements one by one, as shown in the overview diagram.

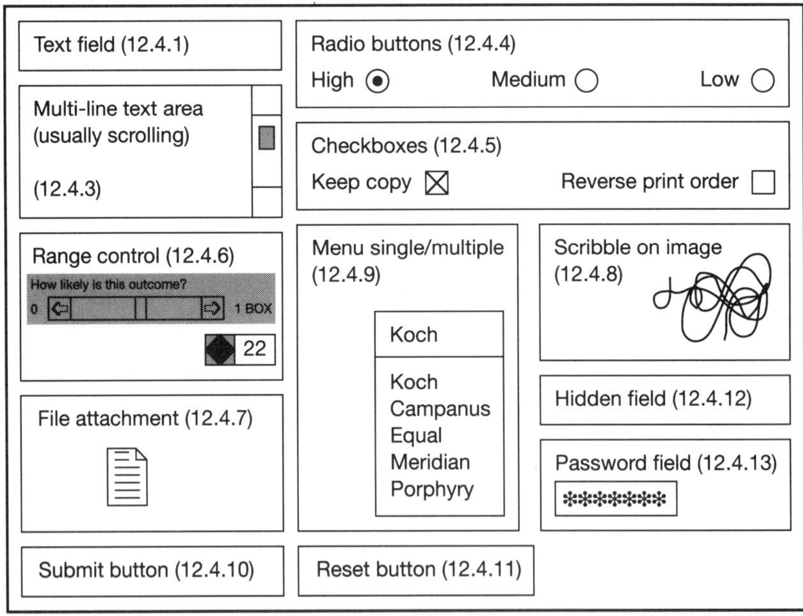

12.4.1 Simple text fields

The most general form element is `INPUT`. Its simplest use is as a simple text field. Like the other form elements, it is only allowed inside `FORM` tags. As text is the default type, you need only give the field name and size. Notice the use of ordinary formatting of text:

```
<H3>Please fill in the following details for your enquiry:</H3>
<P>Surname : <INPUT NAME="surname" SIZE="20">
```

Please fill in the following details for your enquiry:
Surname : Blenkinsop-smythes

This shows the simplest kind of formatting, namely left alignment hard up against the field prompt. This is less than ideal if there are several fields to consider.

When the form is submitted (the user presses the Submit button, see Section 12.4.10, below), the browser returns each field's name with its currently entered value.

An issue which you have to be aware of when designing forms is the probable width of the window in the browser. It is nice to group related fields (for example, surname, initials) on to a line, but you have to remember that users will not necessarily see them displayed like that.

Text fields (like range and hidden fields) can be given default VALUEs:

```
<INPUT NAME="surname" SIZE="20" VALUE="your surname">
```

These appear in the field when first displayed, or when the Reset button is pressed (see below). Two other attributes are necessary in most uses of text (and password) fields:

SIZE	for fixed-pitch fonts (the default), the number of characters to display. For variable-pitch fonts, the number of en units (half the point size of the font) visible in the field.
MAXLENGTH	the maximum number of text/password characters.

12.4.2 Generic attributes of FORM elements

You can qualify any INPUT element, including TEXT, with several generic attributes. We'll list them just once, here:

NEW standard HTML 3.0

HTML 2.0

ID	identifier unique in this document. Allows hypertext links to point to this field by referencing the identifier (this is described in Chapter 9 on hypertext links).
LANG	language identifier.
CLASS	to differentiate the type.
STYLE	to add rendering instructions.
TYPE	text, in the case of an ordinary text field, but usually omitted as it's the default.

NAME	field name, returned with the field value data when submitted.
VALUE	initial value for the field.
DISABLED	field is read-only, the user can't change it. Some browsers grey out such fields. Not widely supported.
ERROR	error message saying why currently entered value in this field is wrong. Not widely supported.

Notice though, that if two fields are *mutually* inconsistent, they should *both* receive error messages.

A note on language variations

Form users are free to enter any ASCII or Latin-1 text, including any accented characters, such as are common in French, German and Swedish. If, for instance, the user types the following name into a form field:

Åke Göransson

then the browser has to send something representing all these characters back to your server. It does this by translating any accented characters into their ISO/HTML entity equivalents, which in the case of Å (pronounced 'Oh?') and ö (pronounced 'Oer') are

Å and ö

This mechanism handles European languages quite neatly. The mechanism will be extended to handle other languages such as Japanese.

12.4.3 Multi-line text fields

Multi-line text used to be handled with TEXT, but this unintentionally limited input to 1024 characters. The use of TEXTAREA gets over this, so you can make multi-line fields as big as you need. Of course, if your server is bombarded with replies, this means you will need megabytes of free storage!

HTML 2.0

The syntax is pleasantly straightforward:

```
<TEXTAREA NAME="request" ROWS=2 COLS=64>
   Please overtype this with your request.
</TEXTAREA>
```

The HTML can be read as saying:

> 'create a free-format input textarea called "request" with a viewport of two rows of 64 characters displayed on the browser screen. Prefill the text area with the words "Please overtype this with your request."'

It is important to understand that the input text is then *not limited* to 2 × 64 characters. As the user goes on typing, the text scrolls away. The specified rows and columns define what used to be called a viewport on to the text area: you are in effect looking through a small window into a much larger room, which can hold as much text as you please.

The result is a free-format input field like this:

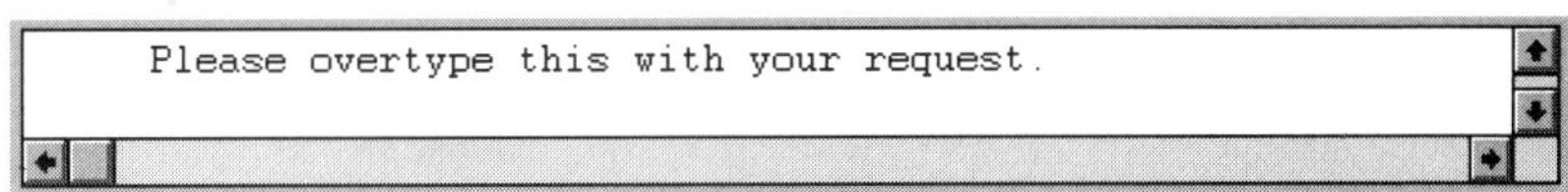
Please overtype this with your request.

You can see that the text between the TEXTAREA tags is used to initialize the field (compare this with the VALUE attribute for INPUT TYPE=text). The scrollbars make it clear that the text is allowed to extend beyond the narrow limits of the visible text area.

Netscape provide a WRAP attribute with 3 possible values. WRAP=off sends lines exactly as typed; =virtual wraps at user's own newlines only; =physical sends user's newlines and extra ones where text was wrapped by the browser.

A fixed-pitch font such as Courier is normally used in input areas for simplicity, but browsers can actually use proportional fonts like Times or Arial as long as they wrap text properly. Of course, width in characters does not have a definite meaning with proportional fonts.

The meaning of the size declared with COLS=64 therefore depends on the type of font in use:

- fixed-pitch font:

  declared number of columns = width in characters

- proportional font:

  declared number of columns = width in en units

Horizontal and vertical scrollbars, as shown in the example above, are typically provided on computers with windowed environments. Text-only browsers may allow scrolling by means of the cursor keys on the keyboard.

You should always include a NAME, as with the INPUT types. Other generic attributes (see Chapter 4) possible with TEXTAREA are ID, LANG, STYLE, CLASS, DISABLED and ERROR. These have their usual effects.

On the next page is an example from the Web of a form which consists principally of a multi-line text area. The structure is simple enough for you to guess, so we won't list the HTML. Notice that no attempt has been made to align the fields, and that the prompts for the fields and the instructions for the text area flow into each other visually instead of seeming distinct items. Also, the placing of the Submit button ('Send mail!') on the right is unusual, and the Reset button (which you press if you decide you don't want to send a message, after all) has been omitted altogether. See Section 12.6.2 below for a discussion of how to lay out forms effectively in HTML 3, and Sections 12.4.14 and 12.4.15 for the buttons.

The Library of Congress no longer uses this page.

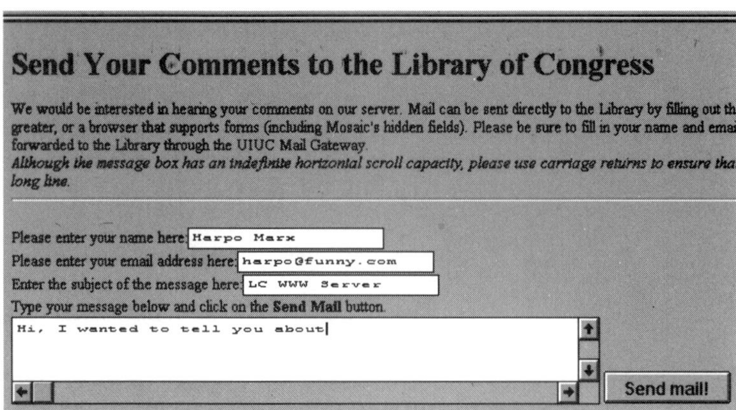

Send Your Comments to the Library of Congress
We would be interested in hearing your comments on our server. Mail can be sent directly to the Library by filling out th
greater, or a browser that supports forms (including Mosaic's hidden fields). Please be sure to fill in your name and email
forwarded to the Library through the UIUC Mail Gateway.
Although the message box has an indefinite horizontal scroll capacity, please use carriage returns to ensure that
long line.
Please enter your name here: Harpo Marx
Please enter your email address here: harpo@funny.com
Enter the subject of the message here: LC WWW Server
Type your message below and click on the Send Mail button.
Hi, I wanted to tell you about
Send mail!

12.4.4 Radio buttons

You obtain radio buttons in HTML by specifying an INPUT field with TYPE=radio. Both NAME and VALUE are mandatory for radio buttons, for reasons which should be obvious.

Radio buttons are the exception to the rule that input fields must have unique names to identify their contents, as the way that you tell the browser that these radio buttons go together is to give them the same name. Their behaviour is like a set of old-fashioned mechanical push-buttons on a radio set: when you press one, the previously pressed one pops out again. So, a set of radio buttons in a form returns just one, which is the one selected by the user. You will be relieved to hear that only the selected one's data is returned to the server.

The syntax is simple and regular. You give each button a name and supply some text for the user to read beside the button.

You must mark exactly one button as 'checked'. This button will be shown in the 'yes' state when the form is first displayed (and when the form is reset). If you mark more than one button as checked, or none at all, it is an error. The browser's behaviour is then not defined, and it may do something unpredictable like checking only the first button – or only the last one.

To help you avoid missing out anything, it is best to arrange your radio button declarations in a column (this example, like the others, must be included within <FORM>...</FORM> tags, and with SUBMIT and RESET buttons too):

```
<P><B>Which is your favourite bean:</B><P>
<INPUT TYPE=radio NAME=coffee VALUE="Java">Old Brown Java
<INPUT TYPE=radio NAME=coffee VALUE="Sumatra">Sumatra Blue Lingtong
<INPUT TYPE=radio NAME=coffee VALUE="Mocha" CHECKED>Mocha
<INPUT TYPE=radio NAME=coffee VALUE="Jamaica">Jamaica Mountain
<INPUT TYPE=radio NAME=coffee VALUE="Kenya">Kenya Peaberry<P>
```

Look and feel usually conform to the standard dialogue elements of the platform (PC, Mac, etc.).

This setup creates a beautiful row of radio buttons like this:

Notice that the CHECKED attribute is set for our favourite Mocha coffee: we supply it by default, which means initially, and when the RESET button is pressed. To repeat, you must make exactly one button the checked default.

12.4.5 Checkboxes

Checkboxes are more versatile than radio buttons, as you can have as many of them selected as you like. So if it makes sense to check two or more items, you use checkboxes not radio buttons. Alternatively you can use a multiple-choice SELECT menu. Each checkbox has just two states – checked or not checked. Most browsers use an X to indicate that a checkbox is checked.

The syntax is virtually identical to that for radio buttons:

Lining the choices up helps you to avoid mistakes

Although RFC 1866 formally requires VALUE attributes for checkboxes, in practice they can be omitted.

```
<P><B>Choose your breakfast:</B>
<P>
<INPUT TYPE=checkbox NAME="bacon"     CHECKED >Bacon
<INPUT TYPE=checkbox NAME="eggs"      CHECKED >Eggs
<INPUT TYPE=checkbox NAME="mushrooms"         >Mushrooms
<INPUT TYPE=checkbox NAME="toast"             >Toast
<INPUT TYPE=checkbox NAME="juice"             >Juice
<INPUT TYPE=checkbox NAME="cereal"            >Cereal
```

which your browser will initially display as something like this:

The user is then free to check or uncheck any or all of the boxes.

An important difference from radio buttons can be seen by inspecting the examples. As many of the checkboxes can be CHECKED (by default) as you please. In this case we have assumed that everyone will want bacon and eggs for breakfast, while the fact that they want coffee (of a variety chosen by radio button) goes without saying!

Checkboxes for variations on a theme

In this example, all the checkboxes have unique names, so the breakfast menu consists of separate items. Another use of checkboxes is for variations on a single theme. For instance, you could offer your customers a range of ice-creams rather than just one. People could have a scoop of each kind.

Your ice-cream checkboxes would be declared like this:

```
<FORM>
<H4>Please check each box for a scoop of that freshly-made ice-cream:</H4>
   <INPUT TYPE=checkbox NAME="ice" VALUE=vanilla CHECKED>Vanilla
   <INPUT TYPE=checkbox NAME="ice" VALUE=strawberry CHECKED>Strawberry
   <INPUT TYPE=checkbox NAME="ice" VALUE=pistachio>Pistachio
   <INPUT TYPE=checkbox NAME="ice" VALUE=walnut>Walnut
   <INPUT TYPE=checkbox NAME="ice" VALUE=rum CHECKED>Rum'n'Raisin
   <P><INPUT TYPE=submit> <INPUT TYPE=reset>
</FORM>
```

The effect is like this:

Please check each box for a scoop of that freshly-made ice-cream:

☒ Vanilla ☒ Strawberry ☐ Pistachio ☐ Walnut ☒ Rum'n'Raisin

[Submit Query] [Reset]

You can see that three scoops are pre-selected to encourage your customers to buy. They can uncheck them and choose just one scoop if they prefer.

The Submit button sends only the checked boxes' names and values to the server (as for radio buttons), while as you'd expect, the Reset button puts the state of all the checkboxes back to their initial states – in this case, as shown in the figure.

The ice-cream submission includes the input field name ('`ice`') together with the name of each flavour of ice-cream checked at the time the Submit button is pressed. The data sent back therefore says, for example:

'ice = Vanilla + Ice = Strawberry + Ice = Rum'n'Raisin'

A program on the server unpacks all this again into its component parts, so that the consumer's order can be processed.

12.4.6 Range fields

HTML 3 provides for a range control, allowing the user to pick any value between the specified `MIN` and `MAX` values. Ranges are useful for obtaining feedback from users, especially where an exact number is not necessarily the obvious answer. Ranges are also good in situations where you already know what values are sensible: for example, the number of scoops of ice-cream in the cornet can range between 1 and 5, but 20 scoops would fall on to the floor every time.

The standard does not say how range input is to be achieved. A text-only device could simply print the permitted range as a prompt:

[0 ... 100]:______

and validate the input as typed. It is an error if the entered value is not in the permitted range.

The way is open for browsers to implement graphical range controls like sliders (you move a slideable knob or pointer along to the position you want):

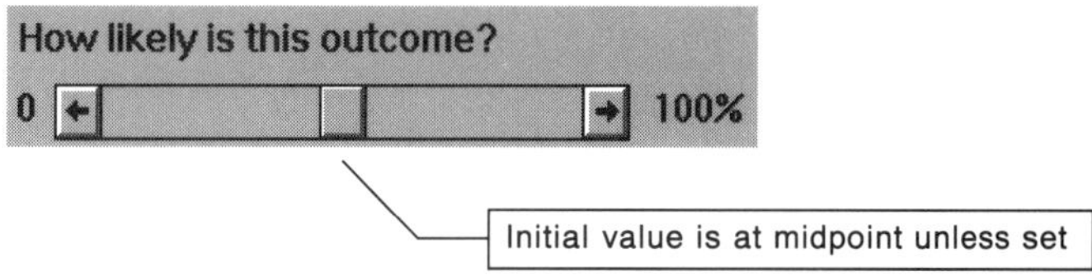

The type of range control can be governed by a style sheet or by a script.

Some browsers may use **spin buttons** like this:

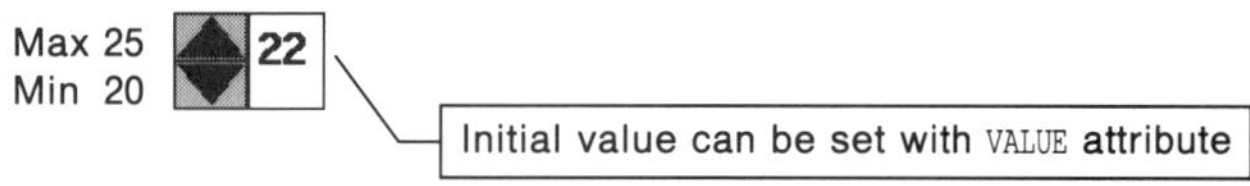

The idea is that you press the up-arrow to increase the value, or the down-arrow to decrease it. You are also free to type a number directly into the box, which can be quicker if the range is large and you are at the wrong end of it.

The syntax is

```
<P>How likely is this outcome?<BR>
0 <INPUT TYPE=range NAME=rating MIN=0 MAX=100 VALUE=22 STEP=5> 100%<BR>
```

You can use `VALUE` to initialize the field, as usual. If you do not, the default is the value halfway between the `MIN` and `MAX` values, as shown in the illustration of the slider control.

The `STEP` attribute is optional; it defines how much to jump when the valuator is adjusted one increment. For example, one click on the up-arrow of a spin button with `STEP=5` causes the old value, 22, to be replaced with the new value, 27. By default the step is 1.

Range controls can share all the attributes listed in Section 12.4.2.

12.4.7 File attachments

The file attachment mechanism lets the user attach some files to be submitted with the form. The `ACCEPT` attribute allows you to restrict the types of file

that may be attached by specifying the permitted MIME content types. For instance

```
<INPUT TYPE=file ACCEPT="image/*">
```

tells the browser to accept any registered MIME image type. Graphic browsers can use a file dialogue box to show the files chosen so far, and can treat the ACCEPT attribute as a file filter.

12.4.8 Scribble on image

The new scribble type lets the user draw with the mouse or other pointing device on the supplied image. A VALUE attribute can be provided for text-only browsers: it is ignored in graphics. The syntax is

```
<P>Explain your idea by drawing on the image:
<INPUT TYPE=scribble VALUE="describe your idea" SRC="concept.gif">
```

You can use the ALIGN attribute to locate the image, and MD to include a cryptographic checksum, so as to verify the image is unchanged.

12.4.9 Menus (single- and multiple-choice)

Menus provide a preferred alternative to input fields when the possible choices are known in advance. They use up less screen space than radio buttons (for single selections) or checkboxes (for multiple selections), so they are especially useful where much data must be gathered on a form.

Textual menus

The basic syntax is a SELECT element containing several OPTION elements:

```
<P><B>Select the kinds of music you like:</B><P>
<SELECT MULTIPLE NAME="music liked">
   <OPTION SELECTED>Jazz
   <OPTION VALUE=rocknroll>Rock
   <OPTION>Blues
   <OPTION>Folk
   <OPTION>Gamelan
</SELECT>
```

Select the kinds of music you like:

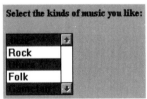

Rock
Folk

The example shows three of the options selected at once by the user. If MULTIPLE is omitted from the SELECT then only one option can be selected, that is, the menu simulates radio behaviour. Individual options can be marked SELECTED or DISABLED. Obviously you can only mark one option as SELECTED if you have specified a single-choice menu. If there is no VALUE, the value is taken from the contents of the OPTION element.

When the Submit button is pressed, the name ('music liked') is sent back with **each** of the selected options.

Graphical menus

HTML 3 offers an attractive graphical alternative for menus on capable browsers. The trick is for the syntax to enable non-graphics browsers to handle such menus adequately. The syntax is essentially the same as for textual menus, but with overlays of shapes similar to OBJECT hotzones:

```
<FORM ACTION="buyfruit">
<SELECT NAME="fruit" SRC="fruits.gif">
   <OPTION DISABLED SHAPE="circle 0.5, 0.2, 0.1"     >Apple
   <OPTION          SHAPE="circle 0.5, 0.4, 0.1"     >Orange
   <OPTION          SHAPE="circle 0.5, 0.6, 0.1"     >Peach
   <OPTION SELECTED SHAPE="rect   0.0, 0.7, 1.0, 0.9">Banana
</SELECT>
</FORM>
```

The mapping between the hotzones thus created and the visible form of the graphical menu works as shown in the illustration. Each circle is defined by the x and y coordinates of its centre, and its radius.

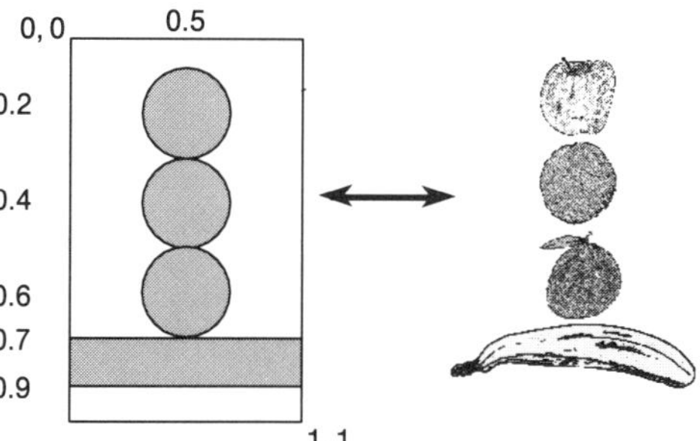

The coordinates are scaled from 0, 0 at the top left corner to 1, 1 at bottom right, for fractions. Whole numbers are taken to mean pixels (a less satisfactory choice). The system is exactly the same as for images and image maps. The image itself can be given a size in en units, where one en is equal to half the point-size of the current font.

On non-graphics browsers, the result is a single-choice menu, shown here in its closed and open states:

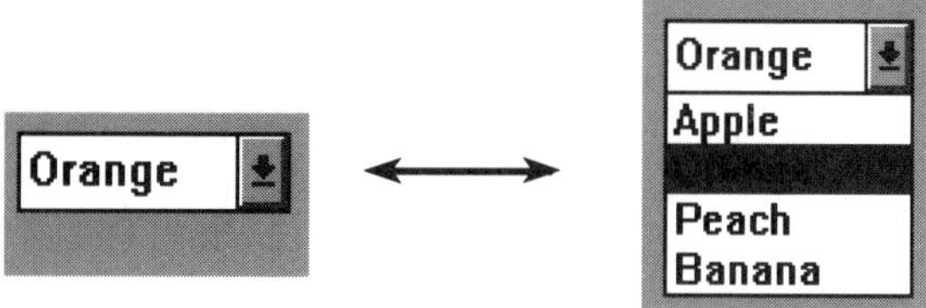

On a graphics browser, the fruits appear in full colour overlaid with hotzones of the shapes you choose. You may prefer to use larger rectangular hotzones for all the fruits, keeping the familiar idiom of a list to pick from to avoid problems from clicking on the background.

12.4.10 The Submit button

HTML 2.0

The Submit button's basic structure is

```
<INPUT TYPE=submit>
```

The default button label depends on the browser. Netscape's button is quite typical:

We suggest that you always use this structure unless you have a good reason to vary it. Ways you can ring the changes are:

`VALUE` to change the default label

```
<INPUT VALUE="Submit Query Now" TYPE=submit>
```

This may occasionally be useful, but is more likely to lead to confusion.

`NAME` to distinguish which Submit button was pressed

```
<INPUT NAME="casual" VALUE="Casual Inquiry" TYPE=submit>
<INPUT NAME="urgent" VALUE="Purchase Order" TYPE=submit>
```

which makes the zipcode example look like this:

The example suggests a context in which you *might* want to provide more than one Submit button. In general there should be exactly one – the user submits the data or not, and the server-side scripts (to handle the returned data) are as simple as possible. Prioritization is notoriously tricky, but at least where people have to decide whether to spend money, they can usually get their act together and press the right button.

It is up to the server to do something sensible with the returned name and value of the Submit button. This is incidentally the only context in which the Submit button actually describes itself.

SRC to put an image on the Submit button

```
<INPUT SRC="launch.gif" ALIGN=left TYPE=submit>
```

The specified image is fetched and used instead of the default text. ALIGN has its usual behaviour; with ALIGN=left, the image floats down to the left margin, and allows text to wrap to its right.

If you are going to use an image on the Submit button, it is probably least confusing to the user if you choose a visual idea which suggests starting or launching something, such as a ship having a bottle smashed on its bows, a rocket taking off, or an Olympic runner on the starting blocks.

TYPE=image and SRC to return a location on a Submit image

```
<INPUT SRC="launch.gif" ALIGN=top TYPE=image>
```

This slightly bizarre hangover from HTML 2.0 consists of an image which behaves like a Submit button though its type is not Submit. The location of the user's click on the image is returned. You could use this to indicate a priority of submission. It is up to your server to do something useful with the information. We do not really recommend using this device. If you want to return a choice, use checkboxes or a selection menu; if you want a range, use a range slider; if you want to distinguish casual or urgent submission, use two Submit buttons.

12.4.11 The Reset button

The Reset button's basic structure is

```
<INPUT TYPE=reset>
```

The button's action is to reset all fields in the form to their initial values (which may be blank).

It has exactly the same VALUE and SRC variations as the Submit button. There is surely no reason to display more than one Reset button on any form. We do not suggest modifying the Reset button's default appearance unless you have very good reason to do so. An inherent advantage for the default Submit and Reset buttons is that they require no image traffic between server and client. They are also highly recognizable in their standard form.

12.4.12 Hidden fields

If you need to preserve some state information, such as a transaction identifier, with the form data, then a hidden field is the way to do it.

HTTP: servers do not normally remember such state information, as it would require a lot of processing and could slow down their responses to users.

The user sees nothing special, but the contents of any hidden fields are sent with the rest of the form data. It is up to your server to do something sensible with the information, and indeed to ensure that something sensible was put in the field to start with. You need to discuss this with your server provider if you have any special requirements.

```
<INPUT TYPE=hidden NAME=transact VALUE="T 501">
```

12.4.13 Password fields

You can ask users to supply a password in an HTML 3 form:

```
<P>Your Password : <INPUT TYPE=password NAME=pwd>
```

which creates an input field like this:

Your Password : [*******]

The password type is exactly like a single-line text input, except that a star or space is echoed to the screen in place of each character of the actual password text typed in by the user. Existing HTTP sends the data in plaintext, so your users' passwords are in no way secure against sniffer programs; Secure HTTP (for example) will improve on this.

12.5 Submitting forms

The user fills in your elegant masterpiece and presses the Submit button. This sends the complete set of inputs to the URL specified by the `ACTION` attribute; and it uses the method specified in the `METHOD` attribute. The two possible methods are `get` and `post`; `get` appends the returned data to the URL, whereas `post` sends the data separately.

```
<!--call a user-written program-->
<FORM ACTION="http://www.mammon.com/programs/save_zip" METHOD=post>
```

which says that the `save_zip` handler program on your server is to process the encoded form data, which is posted separately. You have to use HTTP, incidentally.

If you do not specify a recipient with `ACTION=...`, HTML 3 simply sends the data to the document URL, which will not usually be what you want. You need to sort out with your server provider (preferably before you start designing your forms) how to deal with returned data: it is likely they have some standard software for the job. The obvious thing to do is to stick it in a file which you fetch (with FTP) or they mail to you every so often.

It is outside the scope of a book on HTML to describe how to set up a server complete with form handlers. A recent book with good and intelligible coverage of servers and scripts is *Spinning the Web: how to provide information on the Internet* by Andrew Ford, International Thomson Publishing, 1995. Ford's account of how to handle data returned from forms is necessarily a bit more technical than most of our descriptions, and demands some familiarity both with programming and with the UNIX operating system.

12.6 Form design

12.6.1 Design principles

A great deal has been written about form design, not only for user interfaces (especially with databases) but also in bureaucracies around the world. We would not want to add to the mountains of paper on the subject. Some **useful principles** to bear in mind are:

- Regularly laid-out forms are easier to understand and are more likely to be completed.
- Formatting in a single column is easy and often effective.
- It is simple to align prompts (using decimals) if they all end in ':' or another shared character.
- Related fields (title, forename, surname) should be together, for example on a line.
- Dividing lines (<HR>, table borders) and background colour can visually group related fields.

The freedom of HTML 3

HTML 3 gives you a very free choice of form layout, allowing you to use any of the mark-up elements discussed in this book. This section discusses how you can use lists and tables to organize your forms. You could take other routes: for example, forms within <PRE>...</PRE> tags can be laid out very simply with spaces and line breaks. The price you pay is that forms in PRE come out in fixed-pitch text, in place of the more usual (and attractive) proportional fonts.

Platform independence

Other forms languages typically give you a very particular language intended for use on one specific kind of computer, with one software tool, such as a database. HTML is in contrast completely portable, with browsers and servers available on numerous machines and their operating systems, and it can readily interface to almost any database or software tool.

This 'platform independence' (as the jargon would have it) is a very desirable property. If you develop your forms for a Windows NT server running on a personal computer, and find it is unable to handle all the business it generates, you can move to a fast UNIX box without changing your HTML at all! Of course, you will have to modify any scripts which depend on the operating system.

Similarly, your users can look at your forms with browsers running on UNIX workstations, Apple Macintoshes, personal computers, or even traditional ASCII-text-only terminals. Provided their browsers correctly interpret the HTML, the exact appearance on their screens is not important. They can fill in your forms and submit them as if they were all using identical machines.

Look at well-designed paper forms for ideas

If you are having trouble designing a form, have a look in your tax files: your government's revenue service goes to a lot of effort to make forms clear and effective (to encourage you to pay your tax). Feel free to copy any design ideas: you have already paid for this design effort, so you might as well benefit from it!

12.6.2 Single-column forms

Many simple form applications can be handled quite adequately using a single column of input elements (text fields, radio buttons, and so on). There are at least three ways to achieve respectable-looking single-column forms:

- using lists
- with a table using right alignment for prompt labels and left alignment for fields
- with a single table cell, using character alignment to centre the prompt characters, for example decimal points or colons.

We will demonstrate each approach in turn.

Lists

Both plain lists (`<UL PLAIN>`) and definition lists (`<DL>`) offer possibilities for arranging input fields. Here is a simple example using definition lists:

```
<FORM>
   <DL>
      <DT>Initials:<DD><INPUT NAME="initials" SIZE="5" >
      <DT>Surname: <DD><INPUT NAME="surname" SIZE="20">
      <DT>Zipcode: <DD><INPUT NAME="zipcode" SIZE="9" >
   </DL>
      <INPUT TYPE=reset> <INPUT TYPE=submit>
</FORM>
```

The result in a typical browser (Reset and Submit buttons not shown) is like this:

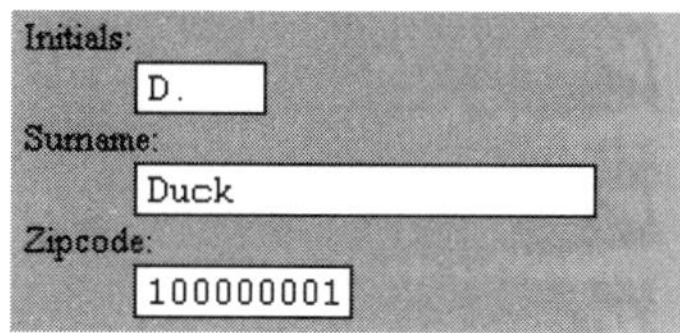

The effect is not unpleasant, but it takes up more screen space than it should, and you have no control over the positioning of the fields: in this browser, for example, the indentation is arguably too small for our purpose. You may be able to use a style sheet to organize things rather better.

Right- and left-aligned table data cells

A more powerful but messier approach is to use a table with two data cells (<TD>) for each row: the one on the left to contain right-aligned text prompts; the one on the right, left-aligned fields.

```
<FORM>
   <TABLE>
      <TR> <TD ALIGN=right>Initials:
                 <TD ALIGN=left ><INPUT NAME="initials" SIZE="5" >
      <TR> <TD ALIGN=right>Surname :
                 <TD ALIGN=left ><INPUT NAME="surname"  SIZE="20">
      <TR> <TD ALIGN=right>Zipcode :
                 <TD ALIGN=left ><INPUT NAME="zipcode"  SIZE="9" >
   </TABLE>
   <INPUT TYPE=reset> <INPUT TYPE=submit>
</FORM>
```

The effect is something like this:

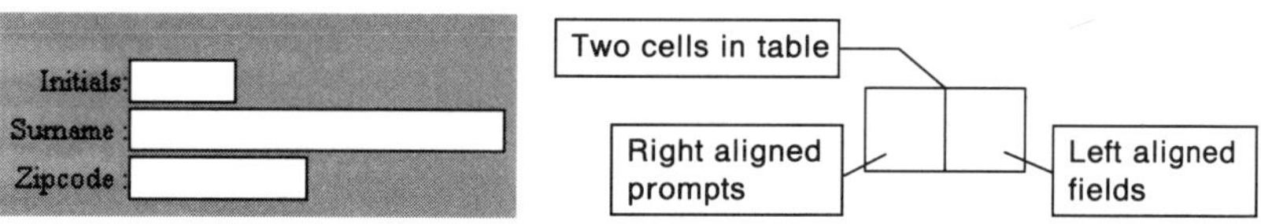

which is much more like what most database people expect from a form.

A single decimally aligned table data cell

A more compact and arguably more elegant way to achieve the same result is to align all the fields vertically within a single table cell, by specifying a convenient character to align to. This mechanism is designed for lining up decimal points with digits both sides, but is equally fine for aligning colon prompts with text one side and fields the other – it is a neat example of the generality of HTML 3. You specify 'ALIGN=char' and state that the alignment character is to be a colon (CHAR=":"). Remember to put in line breaks (<BR>) to force browsers to format the fields in a column.

For example:

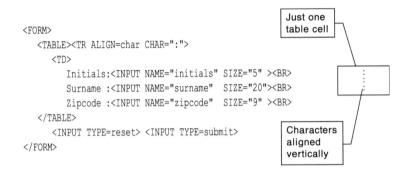

```
<FORM>
   <TABLE><TR ALIGN=char CHAR=":">
      <TD>
         Initials:<INPUT NAME="initials" SIZE="5" ><BR>
         Surname :<INPUT NAME="surname"  SIZE="20"><BR>
         Zipcode :<INPUT NAME="zipcode"  SIZE="9" ><BR>
   </TABLE>
      <INPUT TYPE=reset> <INPUT TYPE=submit>
</FORM>
```

Just one table cell

Characters aligned vertically

The effect is the same.

12.6.3 Multi-column forms

The general case is naturally a form which is too complex to fit into the single-column mould, even if that is distorted to allow 'twin' fields (like month and year) to share a line. The main problem is to align fields with the appearance of regularity although they are different sizes. Some assumption has to be made about the likely space available on the typical browser's window.

The only construct in HTML 3 which permits the required degree of precision in aligning and positioning is the table. Many cells and rows may be needed, with careful design, to achieve a visually satisfying result.

You can nest tables, so you can set up a large table which contains, in one or more of its data cells, a column-of-fields table as described above. You can then save screen space by placing two or more columns beside each other. Remember, though, that this could force some users to scroll sideways to see some of the fields. It is wise to remember that many users will have screens capable of displaying lines of no more than 80 characters.

12.7 Summary of forms

This chapter illustrated the use of forms and the HTML 3 constructs available for on-screen dialogues. These include input elements, both textual and graphical, and standard buttons to submit the form or to reset it.

Forms are not themselves difficult to write, though good visual design is a skilled art. HTML forms (running on browsers) require the support of specially written scripts on the server side. The task of writing such scripts, outside the scope of this book, is a small but specialized programming job for each form.

HTML allows an unlimited range of sophisticated forms to be created and operated, thus – with suitable scripts and secure networks – opening up the World Wide Web (and the Internet) to business interaction and commercial traffic.

13
THE DOCUMENT HEAD

In this chapter:

- The elements in the document head: HEAD, TITLE, ISINDEX, LINK, META, BASE, NEXTID, RANGE, STYLE and SCRIPT
- How LINK is used to create customized toolbars for documents
- The 'frames' idea introduced by Netscape

13.1 Introduction

As explained in Chapter 3, an HTML document formally consists of a head and a body. Broadly speaking, the head is where information *about* the document is found; and the body is where the document itself – the paragraphs, the headings, the graphics, the tables, the forms – is placed.

The aim of this chapter is to describe the elements found in the document head. The chapter is aimed at a fairly technical audience which is why we have placed it towards the end of the book. The most interesting elements from the point of view of new features in HTML are perhaps the LINK element for designing customized toolbars for documents and the STYLE element, described mainly in Chapter 14.

We include in this chapter a summary of the new *frames* idea from Netscape.

13.2 The HEAD element

The HEAD element itself has no attributes and the start and end tag can always be omitted as they can be readily inferred by the parser. Information in the HEAD element corresponds to the top part of a memo or mail message. It describes properties of the document such as the title, the document toolbar, and additional information about the document. There is no intended significance to the order of elements in the document head. Note that the TITLE element is always required. In fact, the minimal HTML 3 document consists of the TITLE element alone!

Within the HEAD element, only certain elements are allowed. These are listed in Sections 13.3 to 13.11.

13.3 The TITLE element

Every HTML document must contain a TITLE element. The title should identify the contents of the document in a global context, and may be used in a history list and as a label for the window displaying the document. Unlike headings, titles are not normally displayed in the text of a document itself.

The TITLE element must occur within the head of the document, and may not contain anchors, paragraph tags or highlighting. There may only be one TITLE in any document.

The length of titles is unlimited; however, long titles may be truncated in some applications. To minimize this possibility, keep titles to fewer than 64 characters. Also keep in mind that a short title, such as Introduction, may be meaningless out of context. An example of a meaningful title might be:

```
<TITLE>Recent Advances in Nanotechnology</TITLE>
```

13.4 The ISINDEX element

13.4.1 Introduction

This element tells the browser that the current document is an index that users may search. The ISINDEX merely informs the browser of this fact: the ISINDEX element does not magically make the document searchable.

The ISINDEX mechanism predates forms. In those days, the idea was that, if the ISINDEX was present, users could type in a line of text as a query which was sent back to the same URL from which the document was retrieved. The query consisted of a simple string to perform a keyword search. This string was constructed by adding a question mark to the end of the document URL, followed by a list of keywords separated by plus signs.

This mechanism was used initially to allow people to use the Web to look up phone numbers in a CERN telephone directory.

Although `ISINDEX` is supposed to occur in the document head many browsers allow it to be placed anywhere in the document.

Dave Raggett felt `ISINDEX` was inadequate for the needs of the Web and wanted to supplement it by a more powerful language, so that authors could provide a range of form elements for things like radio buttons, checkboxes, menus and input fields. The NCSA Mosaic team liked the idea and did all the hard work to implement forms.

13.4.2 Netscape adds the `PROMPT` attribute

Netscape's extensions to HTML 2.0 include the `PROMPT` attribute for `ISINDEX`. You can also use the `PROMPT` attribute to change the default prompt supplied by the browser, for example:

```
<ISINDEX HREF="phone.db" PROMPT="Enter Surname:">
```

13.5 The `LINK` element

13.5.1 Introduction

The `LINK` element indicates a relationship between the document and some other object. Its use is especially in the design of customized toolbars and as such will be extremely useful to HTML authors. A document may have any number of `LINK` elements in the document head. It is worth noting that the `LINK` element is empty (this means that it does not have a closing tag); it takes the same attributes as the anchor element.

13.5.2 Attributes of `LINK`

These are as follows:

`HREF` This names an object using the URL notation.

`REL` This defines the relationship defined by the link.

`REV` This defines a reverse relationship. A link from document A to document B with `REV=relation` expresses the same relationship as a link from B to A with `REL=relation`. `REV=made` is sometimes used to identify the document author, either the author's email address with a mailto URL, or a link to the author's home page.

The relationships REV and REL.

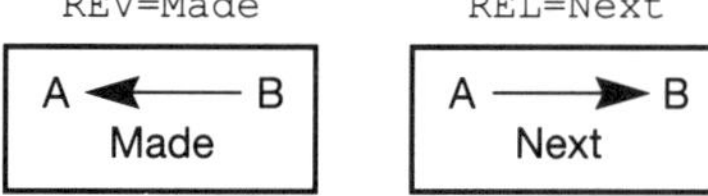

13.5.3 Using LINK to define document-specific toolbars

An important use of the LINK element is the definition of a toolbar of navigation buttons or an equivalent menu on the screen. For example:

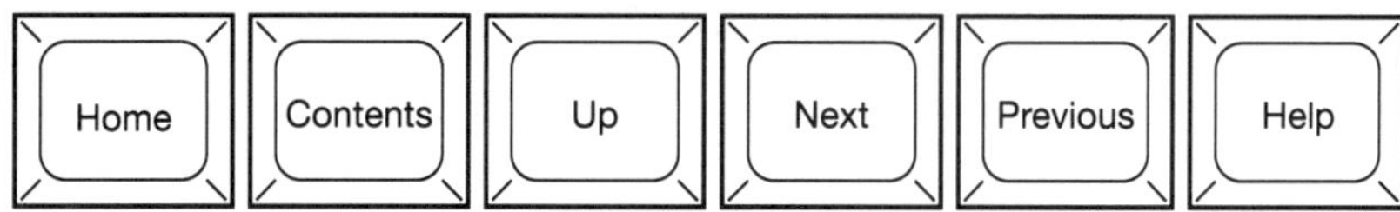

This is done using the LINK attributes REL and REV.

A graphical browser may have a customized toolbar consisting of a number of buttons. Each of these buttons may correspond to a LINK element with one of the following standard values:

REL=home REL=top	The link references a home page or the top of some hierarchy.
REL=contents REL=toc	The link references a document serving as a table of contents.
REL=index	The link references a document providing an index for the current document.
REL=glossary	The link references a document providing a glossary of terms that pertain to the current document.
REL=copyright	The link references a copyright statement for the current document.
REL=up	When the document forms part of a hierarchy, this link references the immediate parent of the current document.
REL=next	The link references the next document to visit in a guided tour.
REL=previous	The link references the previous document in a guided tour.
REL=help	The link references a document offering help, for example describing the wider context and offering further links to relevant documents. This is aimed at reorienting users who have lost their way.

The buttons themselves are not a function of HTML. They are generated by the browser: it is only what goes on when they are activated which involves HTML code. You can see that a browser could equally display a series of menu items rather than buttons, and indeed this is one option open to browsers if they wish.

The default caption for the button can be overridden by supplying a `TITLE` attribute. For example:

```
<LINK REL=glossary TITLE="Technical terms" HREF=doc36.html>
```

13.5.4 Example of `LINK` for customized toolbar

An example of the HTML for a toolbar `LINK` elements:

```
<LINK REL=previous HREF=doc31.html>
<LINK REL=next HREF=doc33.html>
<LINK REL=up HREF=doc78.html>
```

This would only allow for three buttons in the toolbar:

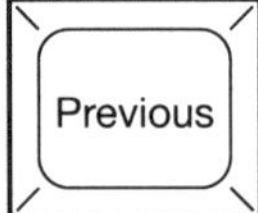

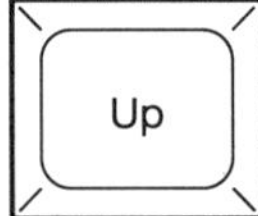

Note that the values for `LINK` have the same effect regardless of what language the document is in. Thus `REL=next` always has the same meanings to the browser even though the buttons themselves may display language-specific captions and icons. For example, in Western cultures right and left arrows could be used for next and previous but the reverse might be appropriate for languages such as Arabic and Hebrew which are read from right to left.

13.5.5 Bookmarks

In some cases the author may wish to provide a number of additional entry points into a group of documents and `REL=bookmark` is used for this purpose.

```
<LINK REL=bookmark TITLE="Order Form" HREF=doc56.html>
<LINK REL=bookmark TITLE="Further information" HREF=doc98.html>
<LINK REL=bookmark TITLE="Learn about the company" HREF=doc93.html>
```

What you do is to have a button called Bookmarks which, when you click on it, shows you a menu. The menu entries are taken from the title attributes of the `LINK` elements. In the above example there would be three titles listed.

13.5.6 Using LINK to include a document banner

The LINK element can be used with REL=banner to reference another document to be used as a banner for this document. This is typically used for corporate logos, navigation aids, and other information which shouldn't be scrolled with the rest of the document. For example:

```
<LINK REL=banner HREF=banner.html>
```

The use of a LINK element in this way allows a banner to be shared between several documents, with the benefit of being able to cache the banner separately. Rather than using a linked banner, you can also include the banner in the document itself, using the BANNER element.

13.5.7 Link to an associated style sheet

The LINK element can be used with REL=stylesheet to reference a style sheet to be used to control the way the current document is rendered. For example:

```
<LINK REL=stylesheet HREF=housestyle.styl>
```

13.5.8 The relationship between toolbars based on LINK and the Netscape frames

The Netscape concept of frames allows the author to split the browser window into a number of rectangular frames a bit like a newspaper. Each of these frames can then display a document or other object specified by a different URL. So, you could potentially have some English text in one frame, the German equivalent in another, a photograph in another frame, and an animated sequence in the last frame.

Authors can specify a frame specially for the purpose of navigational elements such as graphical toolbars. Clicking on the toolbar updates the contents of other frames. You can imagine that, if you click on Help, a frame displays the Help file as required. Or, if you click on Previous the text you looked at previously now reappears in a frame.

Typically the examples seen so far have a few frames, often just two. This is because of the limited resolution of most PCs. This is to be compared with newspapers which have maybe a dozen 'frames' on a page. So, in specifying the frames in an HTML document you are effectively building in an assumption about the resolution of the device upon which the document will be viewed. This is basically a bad idea.

Another disadvantage of frames is that they give information a superficial structure. In a newspaper, a certain amount of thought has gone into which articles should go where – articles on the same subject appear on the same page; important articles come first with less important material on the same subject following on behind and so on. By contrast the organization of material presented to the user in the frames model is more superficial and says nothing about the underlying relationships between information. It would be better to somehow represent the author's knowledge of how the information fits together rather than use such a simple one-off graphical layout with frames.

13.5.9 Printing documents: LINK makes it easier

As explained, toolbars based on LINK are useful because they make explicit a hierarchical structure of a group of related HTML nodes functioning as a larger document. This is useful for indexing software, but in particular for printing.

A large document can be split into a number of conveniently sized HTML files with the relationship between the pieces specified by the LINK element. This allows printing software to traverse the links to print out the complete document.

13.6 The META element

HTML 2.0

The META element is used within the HEAD element to embed document meta-information not defined by other HTML elements. Such information can be extracted by servers/clients for use in identifying, indexing and cataloguing specialized document meta-information.

Although it is generally preferable to use named elements that have well-defined semantics for each type of meta-information, such as title, this element is provided for situations where strict SGML parsing is necessary and the local DTD is not extensible.

In addition, HTTP servers can read the contents of the document head to generate response headers corresponding to any elements defining a value for the attribute HTTP-EQUIV. This provides document authors with a mechanism (not necessarily the preferred one) for identifying information that should be included in the response headers of an HTTP request.

13.6.1 Attributes of META

NAME	Used to name a property such as author, publication date, and so on. If absent, the name can be assumed to be the same as the value of HTTP-EQUIV.
CONTENT	Used to supply a value for a named property.

HTTP-EQUIV This attribute binds the element to an HTTP response header. If the semantics of the HTTP response header named by this attribute is known, then the contents can be processed based on a well-defined syntactic mapping, whether or not the DTD includes anything about it. HTTP header names are not case sensitive. If absent, the NAME attribute should be used to identify this meta-information and it should not be used within an HTTP response header.

13.6.2 Examples

If the document contains:

```
<META HTTP-EQUIV=Expires CONTENT="Tue, 04 Dec 1993 21:29:02 GMT">
<META HTTP-EQUIV="Keywords" CONTENT="Nanotechnology, Biochemistry">
<META HTTP-EQUIV="Reply-to" CONTENT="dsr@w3.org (Dave Raggett)">
```

the server would include the following response headers:

```
Expires: Tue, 04 Dec 1993 21:29:02 GMT
Keywords: Nanotechnology, Biochemistry
Reply-to: dsr@w3.org (Dave Raggett)
```

When the HTTP-EQUIV attribute is absent, the server should not generate an HTTP response header for this meta-information, for example:

```
<META NAME="IndexType" CONTENT="Service">
```

Do not use the META element to define information that should be associated with an existing HTML element.

Example of an inappropriate use of the META element:

```
<META NAME="Title" CONTENT="The Etymology of Dunsel">
```

Do not name an HTTP-EQUIV attribute the same as a response header that typically can only be generated by the HTTP server. Some inappropriate names are 'Server', 'Date', and 'Last-Modified'. Whether a name is inappropriate depends on the particular server implementation. It is recommended that servers ignore any META elements that specify HTTP equivalents (case insensitively) to their own reserved response headers.

13.7 The BASE element

The BASE element allows you to include the URL from which all relative links in the document are taken in the document head. In HTML 2.0 and HTML 3 the BASE element must have an HREF attribute whose value is the URL in question.

The BASE element is used, for example, where the document is on two servers or can be reached by two different paths.

Suppose http://www.nano.dr.org is the URL you use to access a document. If someone places a hypertext link in that document using a relative URL, that URL will be resolved to that location from which the document was downloaded. Now if http://www.nano.dr.org is not the *original* location for that document, the relative URL will be wrongly resolved. By using the BASE element you can specify the correct and original URL for that document and all relative URLs will be resolved using this definitive URL accordingly. For example:

```
<BASE HREF="http://www.tricks.nano.com">
```

All relative URLs will be resolved using this rather than simply the URL from where the document was retrieved.

13.8 The NEXTID element

HTML 2.0

The NEXTID element is a parameter read and generated by text editing software to generate unique identifiers. This tag takes a single attribute which is the next document-wide alphanumeric identifier to be allocated of the form z123.

When modifying a document, existing anchor identifiers should not be reused, as these identifiers may be referenced by other documents. Human writers of HTML usually use mnemonic alphabetical identifiers.

Example:

```
<NEXTID N=Z27>
```

Browsers may ignore the NEXTID element. Support for NEXTID does not impact browsers in any way.

13.9 The RANGE element

The RANGE element is used to mark a range of the document, for example for highlighting regions of the document matching some search criteria, or which are the subject of an annotation or suchlike.

```
<RANGE CLASS=search FROM=spot01 UNTIL=spot02>
```

The FROM and UNTIL attributes specify positions in the document using SGML identifiers. Most elements in the document body can define such identifiers using ID attributes. The SPOT element is useful in this regard, as it allows search software, for example, to insert IDs at random places:

```
<SPOT ID=spot01>...<SPOT ID=spot02>
```

13.10 The STYLE element

The STYLE element is all to do with style sheets which are a recent innovation in the world of HTML and which are described in Chapter 14. You should refer to this chapter to understand the STYLE element and its function in this important new area.

13.11 The SCRIPT element

The SCRIPT element allows you to include scripts in languages like JavaScript or Virtual Basic Script. Scripts allow you to change the default behaviour of an HTML document, and are particularly useful for fill-out forms. You can ensure that form fields match appropriate constraints, and provide derived fields (whose values are computed from other fields).

At the time of writing the details of scripting HTML documents are being defined with browser companies.

14
STYLE SHEETS FOR HTML DOCUMENTS

In this chapter:

- Why style sheets are needed for HTML documents
- Overview description of the CSS language for writing style sheets
- Summary of the document features which style sheets will enable you to control

14.1 An unenviable situation

Strictly speaking HTML concentrates on the structural aspects of a document, allowing authors to mark up in a relatively simple way which parts perform which functions – whether they are paragraphs, headings, lists, tables, and so on. The nuances of presentation are meanwhile not the province of HTML and indeed the minutiae of layout are not supposed to be specified by using the HTML publishing language. This may come as a surprise to authors who are familiar with an `ALIGN` attribute with up to nine different values to specify the precise alignment of images on the page, a FONT attribute to control the exact size and colour of text and all sorts of tags which deal with borders and backgrounds. Know now that such features are by and large extras, pieces of HTML which have crept in courtesy of Netscape, Microsoft and other browser writers. To date around 20 or so non-standard HTML elements and attributes are supported by various browsers, although no single browser supports them all!

14.2 HTML style sheets to the rescue

Style sheets for HTML documents will involve a separate and specialized language for specifying the layout of a document. Potentially giving almost as much control over look-and-feel of material as would a conventional desktop publishing package, style sheets should relieve HTML of its burden of non-standard extensions and free it for its proper role of structuring information.

When will style sheets be implemented? Even as we write the developers are all hard at it. Judging by the volume of email sailing between the continents, many technical points are still contentious. That said, some firm ground seems to have been established and style sheets in some form or other will be implemented in Spring 1996 by Microsoft on their browser. The World Wide Web consortium are heavily involved in style sheet development, particularly Håkon Lie and Bert Boss from INRIA in France. Their attention is on a style sheet language called CSS (which stands for Cascading Style Sheet) which forms the subject of this chapter. The brethren of the SGML community meanwhile favour a completely different language called DSSSL-Online. DSSSL has been developed by the SGML Open Consortium over a number of years as a style sheet language for SGML documents.

Note: DSSSL-Online is the new name for DSSSL-Lite. The name was changed presumably because of the associations with rather weak and dull beer!

14.3 How will you link a style sheet to a document?

There will probably be several ways of doing this. The simplest option will be via the STYLE attribute, a generic attribute which will be available on most elements. Authors will be able to specify a style for the element in question in the CSS style sheet language. Effectively, the style will be a quoted value for the attribute. For example:

```
P STYLE={ font-size: 12pt; line height: 14pt; font family: Helvetica;
font-weight: bold; }
```

Note: Netscape 2.0 does not show the contents of the style element. This means that, even if the browser cannot yet use a style sheet, it will not display the HTML associated with the style element but rather appear to 'ignore it'.

Another option is to use the `STYLE` element (quite different from the `STYLE` *attribute*) to insert a whole series of styles into the document head. These will again be written in the CSS language and may be many lines long. Examples of the `STYLE` element used to contain a style sheet in this way are given throughout this chapter. Note that older browsers *will* indeed show the contents of the `STYLE` element – the text of the style sheet will appear on the screen 'by mistake' – but it is envisaged that within six months to a year most browsers will hide the style sheet from view and implement its content as intended. Microsoft's Internet Explorer which is shipped with Windows '95 will implement the `STYLE` element.

A separate external style sheet can be referenced in two ways. Firstly, you can use the `LINK` element. Once a style sheet has been imported, the `STYLE` element can be used to override styles locally as necessary. `LINK` is described in Chapter 13 on the document head. An example of its use in this context might be:

```
<LINK REL="style" HREF="http://NYT.com/style">
```

You can also use `@import` at the beginning of the document to import a style sheet from a particular location. For example:

```
@import "http://www.style.blue.css"
```

14.4 How will style sheets work?

If you use a computer for desktop publishing you will no doubt already be familiar with the idea of the style sheet or template. In its simplest form, a style sheet consists of a number of styles like Normal, Indented, Heading 1, Heading 2, Heading 3, Footnote, and so on. As you type in a paragraph of text you can assign one of the available styles to it selected from a menu. For example:

Typical style menu.

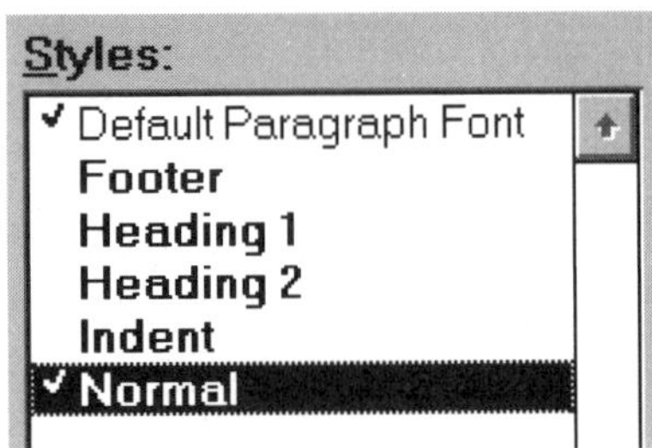

As you assign a style to a paragraph it takes on a number of properties determining everything from font size to margin settings, borders and line spacing. In HTML a similar – but not identical – idea is used.

As explained in Chapter 3, an HTML document consists of a series of paragraphs, headings, lists, tables and other elements. A style sheet used with an HTML document concentrates on these elements and, simply put, enables you to give styles to each. Thus an element such as H1 may have a style 'Times bold, red text' or one for P 'Times 12 point, blue background and black text'. The idea is not complicated.

14.5 Property lists

A style is written as a *property list*. Here is an example property list for an element H1. It is written using the notation of the CSS language:

```
H1
{font-size: 12pt;
line-height: 14pt;
font family: Helvetica;
font-weight: bold;
}
```

You can see that the syntax is relatively straightforward. The element to which the style applies is given first and the property list follows afterwards. The property list is enclosed in curly brackets and successive properties separated by a semi-colon ';'. The properties themselves meanwhile consist of a property name and value separated by a colon ':'.

If you want to allocate a number of elements the same style, you can do so like this:

```
H1, H2, H3 { font-family: Helvetica }
```

Here all three elements are given the same property list. The elements to which the property list applies are separated by commas.

If you look at this second property list above, you will see that there is essentially a left-hand side to the expression and a right-hand side. The left-hand side contains the *selectors* – to which the style applies (in this case H1, H2, H3) – and the right-hand side contains the property list. In later sections you will see how the left-hand side of an expression or 'rule' in a style sheet may contain other items to which the properties on the right-hand side apply. Specific rules take precedence over general rules. A rule involving a CLASS of element takes precedence over a rule involving an element 'straight'. A rule for a specific element will take precedence over something that is inherited.

14.6 Inheriting properties

Properties of one element may be handed down to other elements which that element contains. For example, a block-level element such as a paragraph P may contain the character-level elements EM and I:

```
<P>The computer was<EM>very</EM> <I>expensive</I>!
```

If this is the case then elements I and EM will naturally inherit many of the properties associated with P – the colour of text, the font family and so on – if they have not been given their own overriding properties. The general idea is that properties are inherited from the top-level element downwards. This means that a property such as 'background colour' placed in the HTML element would be inherited by the BODY element, by P elements and by EM elements: all would have the same coloured background.

Of course you can override inherited properties. If you want a particular paragraph to appear on red, say, rather than the blue background specified for the document as a whole in the HTML or BODY elements, this is simple to do. You locally override the blue colour by using:

```
<P STYLE="{ background=red }">
```

which uses the STYLE attribute, or you could insert a small style sheet using the STYLE element which, amongst other things, specified colour:

```
<HTML>
   <HEAD>
      <TITLE></TITLE>
      <STYLE NOTATION=text/css>
         P{ colour: pink }
         P{ letter-spacing: 0.3em }
         P{ text-align: center }
      </STYLE>
   </HEAD>
   <BODY>
      <P>A paragraph which is displayed on a red background
   </BODY>
</HTML>
```

Certain properties only apply to certain kinds of things: you would not want, for example, to put a background image behind a single character or surround a single character by a frame. Certain properties such as margin-left and margin-right apply primarily to block-level elements. In tables, lists and forms inheritance mechanisms are particularly complicated and are to date still the source of much discussion and debate.

14.7 Expressing properties in terms of other properties

CSS sometimes allows you to express the property of one element in terms of another element. For example:

```
P { font-size: 10pt }
P { line-height: 120% }
```

Here line two will set the line height (the leading) to 12 point which is 120% of the font size of 10 point. Character-level elements within the paragraph will inherit the computed line height from their parent.

14.8 Applying a style to a sub-class of an element

The HTML elements form a relatively small set and in general do not allow you to make all the structural distinctions you would like. The `CLASS` attribute allows you to extend the structural repertoire.

Take as a simple example the paragraph element, `P`. Marking up much of your text as simple HTML paragraphs may not achieve the layout effect you want or make the structural distinctions you intended. Suppose you want to say that a given paragraph is an abstract and give it a style accordingly. Or, suppose you want to say that a paragraph is a special note, devised to attract the attention of readers. What you do is to sub-class the `P` element, for example like this:

```
P CLASS=abstract
P CLASS=note
```

and then give each class you have invented, a style.

```
<HTML>
   <HEAD>
      <TITLE>Special Notice to all customers</TITLE>
      <STYLE NOTATION=text/css>
         P.note { colour: red }
         P.abstract { colour: green; font-size: 200%, margin-left: 30% }
         P.important { font-weight: extra-bold }
      </STYLE>
   </HEAD>
   <BODY>
```

Then in the mark-up you might include:

```
   <P CLASS=important>On Saturday Dec 21st we are replacing all our old
      stock with brand new
   </BODY>
```

The CLASS attribute allows you to make semantic distinctions for the structural role of particular tags. Whenever you want to reuse styles, whenever the role of the element is important in some way, then the CLASS attribute becomes very useful. The normal inheritance rules apply to classed elements; they inherit values from their ancestors in the parse tree.

14.8.1 Applying a style to an element with a particular ID

In Chapter 4 we describe the HTML 3 ID attribute. Elements with a particular ID can be given a style in the style sheets. This is done by making the ID the target, the *selector* of the style:

```
#xyz CODE { font-size: xx-large }
```

An element with the ID #xyz will be allocated an extra large font size.

14.9 Richer styles

Magazines such as *The Economist*, *Time* and *Newsweek* often have the first paragraph of the article with a drop-down initial character, and in many cases the rest of the first line is in small caps – in capital letters but in a font of reduced size. CSS allows you to specify these things using the special syntax of richer styles demonstrated below:

```
P: { color: black; font-size: 12pt }
P:initial { color: green; font-size: 200% }
P:first-line { color: blue; text-transform: uppercase }
```

In this example, the initial letter of each P element would be green with a font size of 24 pt. The rest of the first line (as formatted on the screen) would be uppercase blue text.

The use of P:first-line basically allows you to describe a style for the paragraph which applies to the first line of that paragraph only. Other properties of this sort include initial, the initial letter of the paragraph, which is generally used to define drop-down capitals in a different font, a different line height, and so on.

In the case of hypertext links, browsers since Mosaic have traditionally altered the text of the link according to whether the link has been visited or not. You can use the same kind of syntax to control this at style sheet level. For example:

```
A:link { color: red }
A:visited { color: dark-red }
A:active { color: orange }
```

Here is an example of these richer styles in use. They have been inserted into the STYLE element in the document head.

```
<HTML>
  <HEAD>
    <TITLE>Title</TITLE>
    <STYLE NOTATION=text/css>
      P         { font-size: 12pt }
      P:initial { font-size: 200%; baseline-offset: -1 line }
      EM        { text-transform: uppercase }
    </STYLE>
  </HEAD>
  <BODY>
    <P><EM>The first</EM> few words of an article in <I>The
      Economist</I>...
  </BODY>
</HTML>
```

And here is an example of the result:

THE FIRST few words of an article in *The Economist...*

A more detailed account of the mechanisms and inheritance rules that apply is given in Håkon Lie's discussion of style sheets referenced at the end of this chapter.

14.10 The idea of cascading style sheets

In Word and FrameMaker, for example, the document is based on a single template which is stored on disk. When you create a new file, you are prompted as to which of the existing templates you would like to use, and you select one from the list. As you style the document you can then choose any of the styles in the template, and invent further styles of your own if you please. One way or another you always know that, if you choose xyz template, the document will start off with a certain predictable selection of styles.

With HTML style sheets, things are not quite so straightforward. Current discussion about style sheets is about layout *hints*. The word 'hints' is used because style sheets are meant to *suggest* to the browser how the document should be displayed rather than lay down hard and fast rules concerning this. So, when you display a document on the screen, the style sheet associated with it may suggest a selection of styles to adopt but this does not preclude the influence of other style sheets, user preferences or indeed the browser software itself superimposing their own stylistic opinions. The final document may well be the expression of a whole sequence of stylistic opinions which follow in a cascade. Håkon Lie, author of a recent style sheet proposal issued by the WWW consortium, explains that his style sheet proposal 'tries to soften the tension between the author and the reader' and much of his research into the area is centred on the tricky balancing act whereby he sees the author trying to give his or her document a distinct look and feel, with the reader imposing his or her preferences too. 'Designing a style sheet notation that fills both groups' needs is a challenge', writes Håkon. And indeed it must be!

14.10.1 The cascade

Håkon suggests that people will want to set up their browsers with their own style sheet specifying how they would like documents to look on their screen. Thus the reader with strong opinions on layout (and layout is certainly a subject on which many people do have strong opinions!) may supply an initial style sheet in anticipation of total control of the presentation. In practice, however, many users will hand over to the style sheets arriving with the incoming document.

Conflict resolution is based on each style declaration having a weight. By default the weight of the reader's declarations are less than the weights of declarations associated with the author's documents.

14.11 A selection of style sheet properties summarized

The CSS language is still in development and the precise properties with which it will allow you to control style and layout have not been fully finalized. The following diagrams show some of the properties likely to be offered by style sheets in these areas:

- Control of font/character style
- Style and layout for paragraphs, headings and other simple block-level elements
- Background colour and background images

14.12 Properties to control font, spacing of characters and line height

`font-size`

Value: `<length> | <percentage> | <number> | xx-small | x-small | small | medium | large | x-large | xx-large`
Initial value: `medium`
Example: `font-size: 12pt`

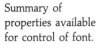

Summary of properties available for control of font.

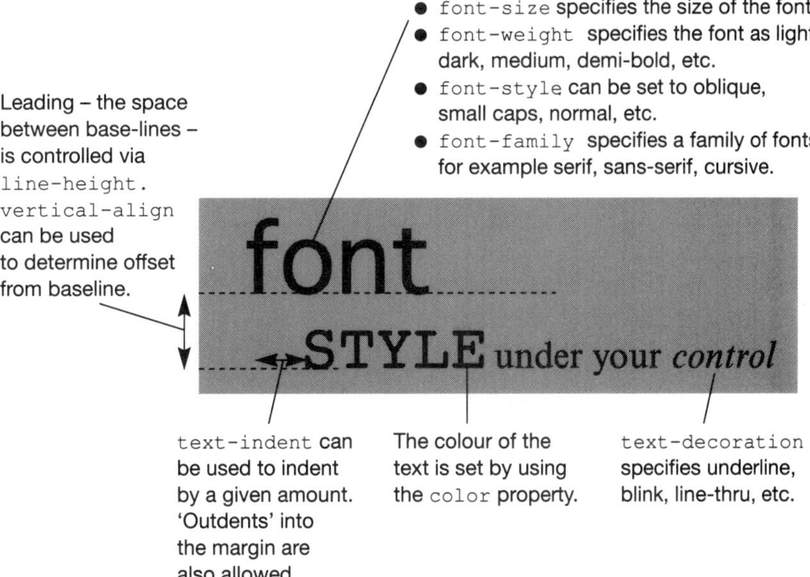

font-size specifies the size of the font.
font-weight specifies the font as light, dark, medium, demi-bold, etc.
font-style can be set to oblique, small caps, normal, etc.
font-family specifies a family of fonts, for example serif, sans-serif, cursive.
Leading – the space between base-lines – is controlled via line-height. vertical-align can be used to determine offset from baseline.
font
STYLE under your control
text-indent can be used to indent by a given amount. 'Outdents' into the margin are also allowed.
The colour of the text is set by using the color property.
text-decoration specifies underline, blink, line-thru, etc.

Font sizes can be set to an absolute height using `font-size`, or the font can be specified as 'small', 'medium', 'large' and so on. If defined, an absolute font size will take precedence. If the value is an integer number, this is then interpreted as relative to the parent element font size. A scaling factor of 1.5 is suggested between adjacent indexes, so, for example, if the 'medium' font is 10 pt, the 'large' font could be 15 pt. If the number is a floating point value, the browser should interpolate a font size if possible. Otherwise, it should round off to the closest integer index. Percentage is relative to the font-size of the parent element.

`font-family`

Value: `[ <family-name> | <generic-family> ] +`
Initial value: browser specific
Example: `font-family: "new century schoolbook" serif`

The value is a prioritized list of font family names and/or generic family names. List items are separated by white space. If the font family contains white space it must be quoted. In level 1 of CSS, the following generic families are defined:

- 'serif' (for example, Times)
- 'sans-serif' (for example, Helvetica)
- 'cursive' (for example, Zapf-Chancery)
- 'fantasy' (for example, Western)
- 'monospace' (for example, Courier)

Ideally, the style sheet writer should specify only one font, and the font manager should return the best alternative. However, since 'intelligent' font management of this kind is not yet available, as a second best a prioritized list of alternative families can be supplied by the author. The only problem is that then the browser must be able to judge whether or not a font has been successfully deployed, and how far it should proceed down the list. For example, if the style sheet asks for *Univers* and the window system is smart enough to suggest *Helvetica* (which looks almost identical) as a replacement, is this a success or a failure? The current style sheet specification has not yet dealt fully with this area.

`font`

Value: `font-size [ / line-height ] font-family [ font-weight ] [ font-style ]`
Initial value: not defined
Example: `font: 12pt/14pt Helvetica bold`

This is a conventional shorthand notation from the typography community to set `font-size`, `line-height`, `font-family`, `font-style` and `font-weight`. Setting the font property is equivalent to including separate statements on font at that point in the style sheet. Only one font family is allowed, to avoid ambiguity.

`font-weight`

Value: `extra-light | light | demi-light | medium | demi-bold | bold | extra-bold | <number>`
Initial value: `medium`
Example: `font-weight: demi-bold`
where `extra-light` = −3, `light` = −2, `demi-light` = −1, and so on

If the desired font weight is not available, the browser looks for substitutes. Non-integer font weights are allowed. This property allows you to set the text by either using keywords like 'light', 'demi-light' or a number.

`font-style`

Value: `normal | italic || small-caps | oblique || small-caps | small-caps`
Initial value: `normal`
Example: `font-style: italic`

If the preferred font style cannot be accomplished, the following (or similar) substitutions should be attempted by the browser:

```
italic  → oblique
oblique → italic
*       → normal
```

If small-caps are not available, capital letters of a smaller font size can be used to render small characters if the resolution of the output medium is appropriate for this.

text-decoration

Value: [none | underline | overline | line-through | box | blink] +
Initial value: none
Example: text-decoration: underline

Formatters should treat unknown values as 'box' (a simple rectangle). The colour of the decoration is the same as the colour of the text. If more than one colour is required, for example for 3-D boxes, the other colours should be based on the text colour. This property is not inherited but children elements should match their ancestor.

word-spacing **and** letter-spacing

Value: normal | <length>
Initial value: 0
Example: word-spacing: 0.1em letter-spacing: 0.2em

The browser is free to select the exact text spacing algorithm. Word and letter spacing may affect justification.

line-height

Value: <length> | <percentage>
Initial value: browser specific
Example: line-height: 120%

Line height refers to the distance between baselines. A percentage unit is relative to the font size of the element itself. For example:

```
P { line-height: 120%; font-size: 10pt }
```

Here, the line height would be 12pt. If there is more than one element on a formatted line, the maximum line height will apply. Authors should therefore be careful when setting line height on inline elements. Negative values are not allowed.

vertical-align

Value: baseline | sub | super | top | text-top | middle | bottom | text-bottom | <percentage>
Initial value: 0
Example: baseline-offset: sub

The property affects the vertical positioning of text: `sub` will make the text subscripted, while `super` will superscript the text.

`text-transform`

Value: `capitalize | uppercase | lowercase | none`
Initial value: `none`
Example: `text-transform: uppercase`

`capitalize` uppercases the first character of each word. `none` is used to neutralize an inherited value.

14.13 Layout at the paragraph level

`text-align`

Value: `left | right | center | justify`
Initial value: human language dependent
Example: `text-align: center`

This property applies to block-level elements only.

`text-indent`

Value: `<length> | <percentage>`
Initial value: `0`
Example: `text-indent: 3em`

This property only applies to the first formatted line of a block-level element. It may be negative, resulting in a line 'outdented' into the margin. An indent is not inserted in the middle of an element that was broken by another (such as `BR`). Percentage values are relative to the width of the parent element.

`padding`

Value: `<length> | <percentage> | auto{1,4}`
Initial value: `0`
Example: `padding: 20% 20%`

How much space to insert between the border of the frame and the content (for example, text or image). Consists of one to four values giving a length, percentage or 'auto'. The order is top, right, bottom, left. If there is only one value, it applies to all sides; if there are two or three, the missing values are taken from the opposite side. The colour of the padding area is controlled with the `background` property.

Summary of properties for control of layout and colour at the paragraph level.

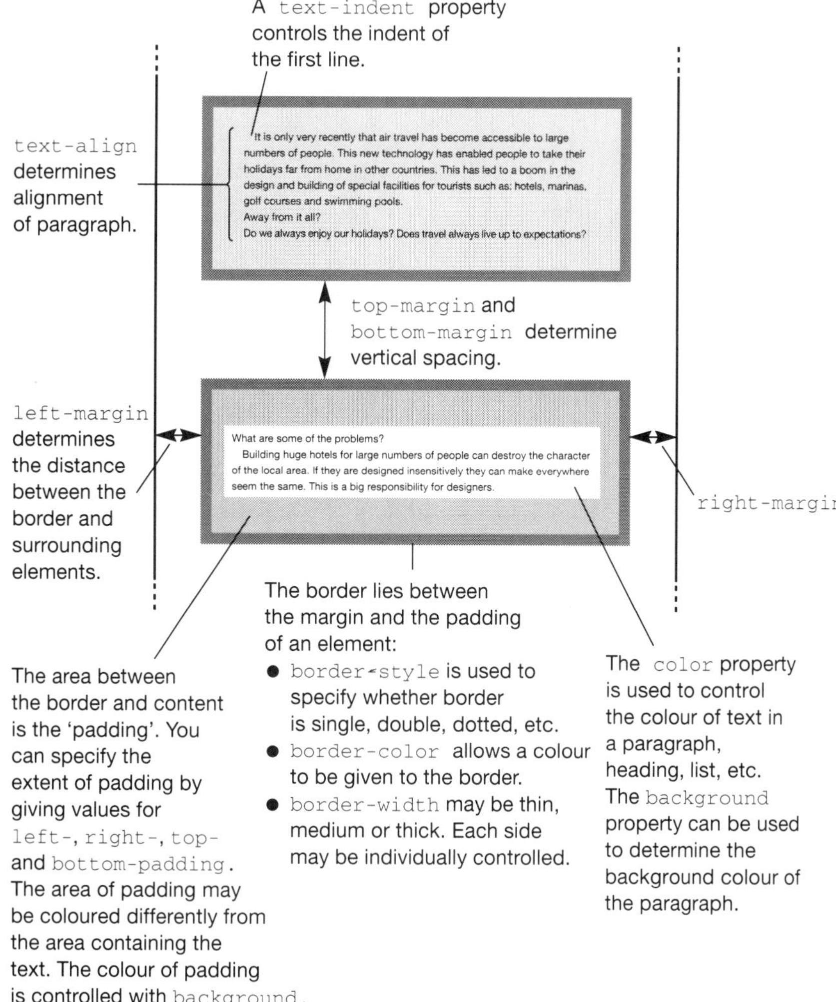

Style sheet properties to control the rendering of a paragraph of text
A text-indent property controls the indent of the first line.
text-align determines alignment of paragraph.
It is only very recently that air travel has become accessible to large numbers of people. This new technology has enabled people to take their holidays far from home in other countries. This has led to a boom in the design and building of special facilities for tourists such as: hotels, marinas, golf courses and swimming pools.
Away from it all?
Do we always enjoy our holidays? Does travel always live up to expectations?
top-margin and bottom-margin determine vertical spacing.
left-margin determines the distance between the border and surrounding elements.
What are some of the problems?
Building huge hotels for large numbers of people can destroy the character of the local area. If they are designed insensitively they can make everywhere seem the same. This is a big responsibility for designers.
right-margin
The border lies between the margin and the padding of an element:
● border-style is used to specify whether border is single, double, dotted, etc.
● border-color allows a colour to be given to the border.
● border-width may be thin, medium or thick. Each side may be individually controlled.
The area between the border and content is the 'padding'. You can specify the extent of padding by giving values for left-, right-, top- and bottom-padding. The area of padding may be coloured differently from the area containing the text. The colour of padding is controlled with background.
The color property is used to control the colour of text in a paragraph, heading, list, etc. The background property can be used to determine the background colour of the paragraph.

`margin-left, margin-right`

Value: `<length> | <percentage> | auto`
Initial value: `0`
Example: `margin-left: 2em`

The minimal horizontal distance between the element's box and surrounding elements. Horizontal margins may be negative. Percentage values are relative to the width of the parent element.

`margin-top, margin-bottom`

Value: `<length>`
Initial value: `0`
Example: `margin-top: 2em`

The vertical space between two blocks of text is the maximum of all bottom margin and top margin specifications between the two. Percentage values are relative to the width of the parent element. Vertical margins are $\geqslant 0$.

`margin`

Value: `<length> [ <length> [ <length> [ <length> ] ] ]`
Initial value: `0`
Example: `margin: 2em 1em`

The four lengths apply to top, right, bottom and left respectively. If there is only one value, it applies to all sides; if there are two or three, the missing values are taken from the opposite side. The property is shorthand for setting `margin-top`, `margin-right`, `margin-bottom` and `margin-left` separately. The individual browser declarations take precedence if the weights are otherwise equal.

`flow`

Value: `block | inline | canvas`
Initial value: undefined
Example: `flow: block`

This property decides if an element is block-level (for example, `H1` in HTML) or inline (for example, `EM` in HTML). For HTML documents, the initial value will be taken from the HTML specification. The `canvas` value is used to mark elements whose style properties will be applied to the canvas (for example, computer screen or sheet of paper) instead of the element itself. In HTML, it is suggested that the `BODY` element is given this role. This property is not inherited.

`width`

Value: `<length> | <percentage> | auto | from-canvas`
Initial value: `auto`
Example: `width: 100pt`

This property can be applied to text, but it is most useful with inline images and similar insertions. The width is to be enforced by scaling the image if necessary. When scaling, the aspect ratio of the image should be preserved unless the `height` property is set to anything but `auto`. Percentage values are relative to the width of the parent element. The `from-canvas` value means that the width of the element is such that the width and the margin add up to the width of the canvas. In HTML, `BODY` by default has this value.

`height`

Value: `<length> | auto | from-canvas`
Initial value: `auto`
Example: `height: 100pt`

This property can be applied to text, but it is most useful with inline images and similar insertions. The height is to be enforced by scaling the image if necessary. When scaling, the aspect ratio of the image should be preserved unless the `width` property is set to anything but `auto`. The `from-canvas` value means that the height of the element is such that the height and the margin add up to the height of the canvas. In HTML, `BODY` by default has this value.

`float`

Value: `left | right | none`
Initial value: `none`
Example: `float: left`

This property is most often used with inline images. With the value `none`, the image will be displayed where it appears in the text. With a value of `left` the margin properties will decide the horizontal positioning of the image and the text will float on the right side of the image. Vice versa with `right`.

`clear`

Value: `none | left | right | both`
Initial value: `none`
Example: `clear: left`

This property specifies if elements allow floating elements (normally images) to the left or right. With `clear` set to `left`, an element will be moved down to below any floating element on the left side.

`pack`

Value: `tight | loose`
Initial value: `tight`
Example: `H1 { pack: loose }`

If `pack` is set to `tight`, element boxes will move up vertically until they hit another element. With a value of `loose`, the element will not move up beyond any element with the same value in the `float` property.

`border-style`

Value: `<keyword> [ <keyword> [ <keyword> [ <keyword> ] ] ]`
Initial value: `none`
Example: `border-style: double`
Keyword values are: `none | dotted | single | double | thin-thick | thick-thin | beveled`

The four keywords apply to top, right, bottom and left respectively. If there is only one value, it applies to all sides; if there are two or three, the missing values are taken from the opposite side. The `thin-thick` (`thick-thin`) keyword requests a frame with the outer (inner) frame 'thin' and the inner (outer) frame 'thick'. The space between the two has the background colour of the cell. This property is not inherited. (If `UL` has a frame around it, you don't want each `LI` inside to inherit this frame.)

A border-style of `none` requests no visible frame around the element. However, the corresponding `border-width` must be non-zero for this to be achieved, otherwise the frame will be inherited from surrounding elements.

Additional suggested keyword values include: `dotted`, `wavy`, `baroque`, `filet`, `art-deco`, `raised`, `lowered`, `etched`, `shadow`.

`border-width`

Value: `<width> [ <width> [ <width> [ <width> ] ] ]`
Initial value: `medium`
Example: `border-width: thick thin`

A width is either a length or one of the keywords `thin`, `medium` or `thick`. The four widths apply to top, right, bottom and left respectively. If there is only one value, it applies to all sides; if there are two or three, the missing values are taken from the opposite side. A `border-width` of 0 requests the frame to be inherited from surrounding elements.

`border-color`

Value: `<color> | <url>`
Initial value: undefined
Example: `border-color: "http://www.pat.com/pats/concrete.gif"`

This attribute describes the colour of the frame surrounding an element.

14.13.1 Control of page breaks in printed versions of files

The page properties are used for paged media, for example paper and page-oriented screen browsers.

`page-break-after, page-break-before`

Value: <number> | never | discourage | neutral | encourage | always
Initial value: 0
Example: H1 { page-break-after: never }

Numbers can be from −2 to 2, corresponding, respectively, to the keywords. All `pagebreak-before` and `pagebreak-after` values that apply between two elements are combined according to the following table:

	−2	−1	0	1	2
−2	−2	−2	−2	−2	2
−1	−2	−1	−1	1	2
0	−2	−1	0	1	2
1	−2	1	1	1	2
2	2	2	2	2	2

In algorithmic terms: take the one with the largest absolute value; if they are the same, use the positive value.

`page-break-inside`

Value: <number> | never | discourage | neutral
Initial value: neutral
Example: PRE { page-break-inside: discourage }

Values can be −2, −1 or 0 meaning, respectively, never allow page-break inside element (`never`), discourage page-break inside element (`discourage`), or neutral about page-break inside element (`neutral`).

14.13.2 Properties of lists

`list-style`

Value: <url> | disc | circle | square | decimal | lower-roman | upper-roman | lower-alpha | upper-alpha | none
Initial value: none
Example: OL { list-style: lower-roman }

This property applies only to the children of the element where it is specified. In HTML, it is typically used on the `UL` and `OL` elements.

14.14 Control of the colour and background of elements

Style sheet control of backgrounds. Many elements can have a background colour or background image, including individual paragraphs, headings, list items, and so on.

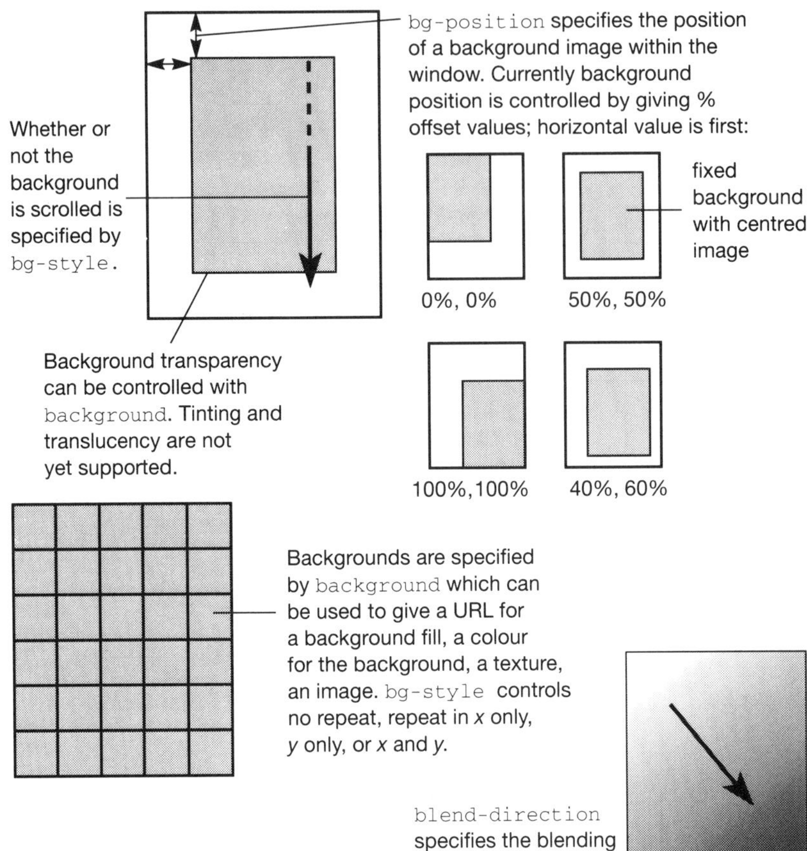

bg-position specifies the position of a background image within the window. Currently background position is controlled by giving % offset values; horizontal value is first:
Whether or not the background is scrolled is specified by bg-style.
fixed background with centred image
0%, 0%
50%, 50%
Background transparency can be controlled with background. Tinting and translucency are not yet supported.
100%,100%
40%, 60%
Backgrounds are specified by background which can be used to give a URL for a background fill, a colour for the background, a texture, an image. bg-style controls no repeat, repeat in x only, y only, or x and y.
blend-direction specifies the blending direction for two background colours.

These properties can be applied to a number of elements including all block-level elements and certain of those at character level. For example, the colour of an individual character cannot be set although of course the colour of an individual paragraph can. By associating a colour with the document `BODY` or even the HTML element (see Chapter 3) the whole document can be presented in the background colour of your choice.

You can specify a colour by using either its name, a hexdecimal code (see Chapter 14) or numerical values. The most basic list of colour names includes those common in the English language: black, white, red, green, blue, yellow, cyan, magenta, pink, brown, grey, orange, purple, turquoise, violet. Also, prefixing colour names with 'light-' or 'dark-' is allowed, for example 'red' and 'dark-red'.

Also, colour names in common use on the major GUI platforms should be supported.

The RGB colour model is being used in colour specifications. Other colour models should be kept in mind for later extensions.

Different ways to specify red:

- EM { color: #F00 }
- EM { color: #FF0000 }
- EM { color: 255 0 0 } /* integer range: 0–255 */
- EM { color: 1.0 0.0 0.0 } /* float range: 0.0–1.0 */
- EM { color: red }

`color`

Value: `<url>` || `<color>`
Initial value: browser specific
Example: `color: red`

This property describes the text colour of an element – its 'foreground' colour.

`background`

Value: [`<color>` | `<url>` | `transparent`] + [/ [`<color>` | `<url>` | `transparent`] +]
Initial value: `transparent`
Example: `background: "http://www.pat.com/pats/silk.gif" blue`

The background of a paragraph, a list item or indeed any other block-level element starts off 'transparent' in the sense that the colour of the background image of the parent element 'shows through'. In other words, if the general background colour of the document has been set to *blue* in the document body, then the background colour of all elements will be blue too, exactly as you would expect.

Of course, it is possible to change the backgound colour of any block-level element, and indeed it is possible to give such an element a background pattern too. Thus a paragraph might appear on a textured red background while the rest of the document is displayed on off-white. The extent of the colour and/or background image is controlled by the padding.

If there is an image referenced via a URL, this takes precedence over colour. The colour is used:

- to fill transparent regions of an image;
- while loading the image from the URL;
- if no URL is specified.

You can also specify a background that fades from one image/colour to another. This is done by using the delimiter '/' between *bg1* and *bg2* respectively. The resulting background is a fade between these. The `bg-blend-direction` property specifies the direction of the blending.

bg-style

Value: `[ repeat | repeat-x | repeat-y | no-repeat | scroll | fixed ] +`
Initial value: `repeat scroll`
Example: `bg-style: repeat-x scroll`

This property describes how the background image should be laid out. By default, the background image is repeated in both x and y directions, and the image is scrolled along with the other content. A 'fixed' background is fixed with regard to the screen.

bg-position

Value: `<percentage> [ <percentage> ]`
Initial value: `0% 0%`
Example: `bg-position: 50% 30%`

This property describes the initial position of a background image which has been specified with the `background` property. If only one value is given, it sets both the horizontal and vertical offset of the background image. If two values are given, the horizontal position comes first. With a value pair of `0% 0%`, the upper left corner of the image is placed in the upper left corner of the element. A value pair of `100% 100%` places the lower right corner of the image in the lower right corner of the element.

Instead of using percentage values, you can use keywords like 'left', 'centre' and so on.

bg-blend-direction

Value: `N | NW | W | SW | S | SE | E | NE`
Initial value: `S`
Example: `bg-blend-direction: NW`

This property is used to blend two different background colours. It specifies the direction of blending between *bg2* which is the background colour at the edge or corner of the screen and *bg1* which is the background colour at the opposite edge or corner. The values stand for North, North-west, West and so on, where `N` is the top of the window in which the document is displayed. The initial value is S, so if *bg1* is dark blue and *bg2* is light blue, the window will be dark blue at the top, smoothly blending through mid-blue to light blue at the bottom.

Specifying `bg-blend-direction: NW` would give light blue in the top left corner smoothly blending through mid-blue to dark blue in the bottom right corner. If only one background colour is specified, the blend direction is ignored. See the illustration earlier in this section.

14.15 Units

Length

- inches (in)
- pixels (px)
- centimetres (cm)
- millimetres (mm)
- ems (em) /* the width of the character 'M' */
- ens (en) /* half the width of an em */
- points (pt)
- picas (pc)

Percentage

In most cases, a percentage unit is relative to a length unit; `text-spacing` is an example of a property that is not relative to a length unit.

14.16 An example style sheet

```
BODY { width: from-canvas; height: from-canvas; margin: 0.5em 0 }
H1, H2, H3, H4 { margin-top: 1em; margin-bottom: 1em }
H5, H6 { margin-top: 1em }
H1, H2, H4, H6 { font-weight: bold }
H3, H5 { font-style: italic }

H1 { font-size: xx-large; align: center }
H2 { font-size: x-large }
H3 { font-size: large }

B, STRONG { font-weight: bold }
I, CITE, EM, VAR{ font-style: italic }
PRE, TT, CODE, KBD, SAMP { font-family: monospace }
```

```
ADDRESS { margin-left: 3em; font-style: italic}
BLOCKQUOTE { margin-left: 3em; margin-right: 3em; font-style: italic }
UL, DIR { list-style: disc }
OL { list-style: decimal }
MENU { margin: 0 0 }
LI { margin-left: 3em }

DT { margin-bottom: 0 }
DD { margin-top: 0; margin-left: 5em }

A.link { color: red }
A.visited { color: dark-red }
A.active { color: orange }
```

More information on style sheets

Cascading Style Sheets, level 1
W3C Working Draft
Available via `http://www.w3.org`
Authors: Håkon Lie and Bert Bos

15 EQUATIONS AND MATHEMATICS

Adrian finds maths mark-up as easy as telnetting an Archie site.

This chapter is a little more speculative than the rest of this book, because the standard for HTML's Math elements is neither finally agreed nor commercially implemented. But many of the features have been defined and prototyped, so the outcome will probably be much as described here. The chapter:

- introduces the way that HTML will handle maths (Section 15.1)
- describes the mathematical entities (Section 15.2)
- explains how to arrange and combine mathematical symbols (Section 15.3)
- and presents the special ARRAY tag last (Section 15.4), because it is a little more complicated.

The presentation of this chapter is similar to that in the rest of the book, but we have necessarily used some mathematical terms, such as sum, integral and limit. These are illustrated with HTML examples and formatted equations, which should make any unfamiliar words reasonably clear in their context. Readers afraid of maths can skip this chapter and come back to it later – the rest of HTML can be used without it.

15.1 A powerful new approach to maths ... coming soon

HTML 3 will be the first version of the language to handle maths. Not only mathematicians but chemists, physicists and engineers have clamoured for special easy-to-use tools to make equations and expressions easy to write. HTML's `MATH` is intended to cover most common user needs for mathematical discussion. With a little persistence and versatility, you will be able to express pretty much anything.

15.1.1 HTML's `MATH` and LaTeX

HTML is not designed as a maths representation language like ISO Standard 12083 Maths DTD, nor the mighty and venerable LaTeX. If you have a *very* complicated research paper to publish, you could if you wanted set it in LaTeX first, and run it through the latex2html filter to create its HTML representation. But after seeing `MATH` you will probably not want to use anything else.

`MATH` in fact complies quite closely with the LaTeX approach; since it has to use SGML entities and structure, it cannot exactly copy LaTeX, but readers used to typesetting with LaTeX will find HTML 3's `MATH` pleasantly intuitive.

15.1.2 Clean and compact

The notation is clean and compact. A superscript such as x^2 can be written in full as

```
x<SUP>2</SUP>
```

(These constructions are explained in full below.)

or in the handy shortref form as

```
x^2^
```

Subscripts are written similarly: x_i is just

```
x_i_
```

You can write superscripts and subscripts on the left or right of the variable, and you can even have both at once! (Similar but standalone `SUP` and `SUB` elements already exist outside `MATH`.)

15.1.3 Simple symbols

Another big simplification is in the choice of the most popular mathematical symbols. TeX fonts would swamp the font menu with subtle variations. HTML 3 tries to satisfy its technical users about 98% of the time; the remaining rare cases can be fixed slightly inelegantly – the mathematical equivalent of writing 'Goedel' instead of using an o-umlaut as in 'Gödel' – or in desperation put in as ready-made GIF or JPEG images. Work is under way on a scheme to download rare symbols as custom-made fonts to handle any special cases: this is more powerful than even a set of TeX fonts, as it can handle symbols that have not yet been invented!

15.1.4 Simple bracketing with `BOX` or `{...}`

Bracketing is handled using a single elegant construct, which can be written in full as

```
<BOX>...</BOX>
```

(These constructions are explained in full below.)

or in shortref form as

```
{...}
```

Several tags are available only within `BOX`, such as

```
<OVER>
```

for division,

```
<OF>
```

for function application, and

```
<LEFT> and <RIGHT>
```

for delimiters. So you can write 'A over B' very naturally as

```
<BOX> A<OVER>B </BOX>
```

or equivalently

```
{A <OVER> B}
```

and as you would expect, you can nest expressions. Similarly, you can write the function 'F of X' in HTML as the natural and readable phrase

```
{F <OF> X}
```

15.1.5 Simple parsing

This section is included for interest only, though we hope it will help you get the best from HTML. You can use MATH without needing to understand it.

The idea of using boxes greatly simplifies the work of the browser when handling mathematical formulae. The tokenizer identifies constants, variables, operators, functions and delimiters. The parser's first step is to make a tree (a hierarchy) of bounding boxes. Its second step is to size and position the necessary boxes. Its third and final step is to draw each item in the tree. There is no limit to the allowed depth of nesting of expressions.

How browsers handle mathematical expressions.

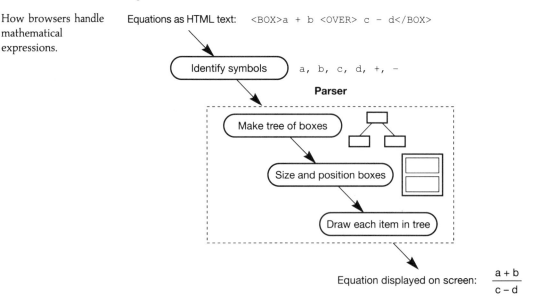

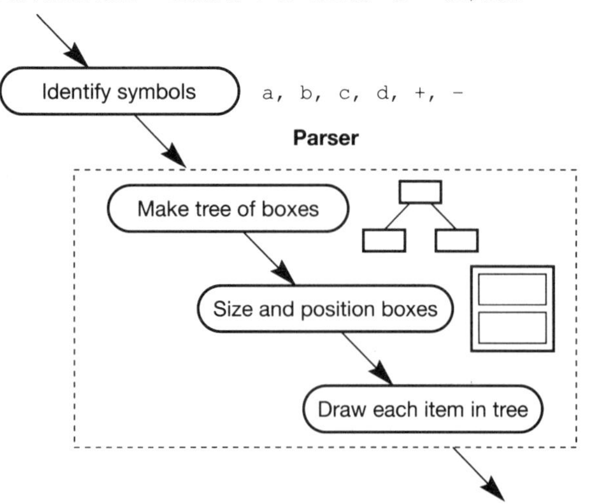

15.2 Math entities

Mathematicians use an enormously wide range of symbols, which they classify in many different ways. HTML 3 permits mathematicians to express themselves easily with a modest number of symbols chosen from the ISO math entities, combined with some very general rules for constructing formulae. In practice these should be enough for most purposes. This section looks at the symbols provided for maths; later sections introduce the rules which govern how symbols can be combined into equations and formulae.

15.2.1 Functions

A few function symbols are predefined in HTML 3. They include `sin`, `cos` and `tan`.

The HTML expression

```
<MATH>{&tan; <OF> &theta;}</MATH>      <!--tangent of an angle-->
```

which represents the trigonometric expression

$\tan\theta$

is understood to mean a single function, and not two unrelated symbols. This is nice, as it lets you forget the brackets round the expression to which the function is applied.

15.2.2 Operators

The usual arithmetic operators are recognized as infix function symbols (ones which come between the numbers or algebraic symbols that they are operating on), so that

$+ \; - \; * \; /$

have their normal meanings. One effect of this is that these symbols act as separators: $1 + 2$ is never confused with the number 12, for instance; and spaces are not required either side of the operators.

15.2.3 Continuation dots

Five kinds of ellipsis or continuation dots are provided to enable you to refer to terms in series which continue to infinity, or at least to some inconveniently large number N. They are

`&ldots;`	$\ldots$	(on the baseline)
`&cdots;`	$\cdots$	(on same level as the minus sign $-$)
`&vdots;`	$\vdots$	(3 vertical dots)
`&ddots;`	$\ddots$	(diagonal dots)
`&dotfill;`	....	(as wide as necessary)

15.2.4 Greek letters

All the lower-case letters of the Greek alphabet are provided as mathematical entities. They are written as `&name;` where *name* is the English spelling of the Greek letter, except that a few of the letters have (in addition to the normal forms) variants which are inconsistently named, such as `vepsilon`, `vsigma` and `vtheta` but (confusingly) `varpi`, `varrho` and `varphi`. For example:

`α`	α
`ω`	ω

15.2.5 Relations

The usual set of binary relations, yielding Boolean (truth-valued) results, is provided. For example:

`<`	$<$
`>`	$>$
`=`	$=$

15.2.6 Accents, arrows, pointers

Special tags are provided to put accents over or under mathematical symbols. They are

VEC, BAR, DOT, DDOT, HAT and TILDE

and their use is described later in this chapter. For example VEC $\vec{x}$ is written

```
<VEC>x</VEC>
```

15.2.7 Delimiters

When you want delimiters that match the size of the associated expression, you use the BOX element with the LEFT or RIGHT tags. For example:

```
<MATH><BOX>(<LEFT>x<OVER>1+x<RIGHT>)</BOX></MATH>
```

This is rendered as

$$\left(\frac{x}{1+x}\right)$$

This simple and general mechanism gives mathematicians using HTML 3 the power to represent all kinds of **new notations** that they may need to invent when describing novel concepts. BOX is discussed in full in Section 15.3.2.

Here are some common delimiters:

Symbol	*Entity*
( )	(not needed)
[ ]	(not needed)
| |	`∣ &/mid;`
{ }	`{ }`
< >	`< >`

For instance:

```
{&lcub; S - R &rcub;}
```

could be rendered

$$\{S - R\}$$

15.2.8 Other math symbols

Mathematicians love many strange, foreign and unpronounceable symbols. These include

`∞`	∞	(infinity)
`ℵ`	$\aleph$	(Hebrew Aleph)

which enable them to express concepts not known in daily speech. The symbols chosen for HTML 3 are those which mathematicians have most clamorously expressed a need for. Appendix D provides a rich set of proposed symbols.

15.2.9 Special spaces

Four special spatial entities are provided for fine control of white space in formulae. They are:

```
&sp;     &quadsp;
```

for normal, thin, m-width and extra-wide spaces respectively. You can't use them in normal text!

15.3 Arranging math symbols

15.3.1 MATH

By itself the $...$ tag does not do much: it just declares that something mathematical is going to happen. Text contained in the MATH element is normally formatted a bit specially. For instance, words are usually treated as variable names in italics, while functions (such as SIN), numbers and constants are rendered in an upright font. Spacing is also controlled automatically, so

```
<MATH>A+B</MATH>
```

(with no spaces) may well be typeset with preset spacing as

$$A + B$$

while your browser is perfectly within its rights to set **A B** (meaning A times B) as

$$AB$$

using the familiar mathematical convention of apposition to denote multiplication. If you want to insist on white space you can do so with the special spatial entities such as

```
A B
```

These spaces also act as token separators, just like normal spaces. Alternatively you can use the TEXT element (only within MATH) which works rather like PRE in normal text – any spaces you insert appear literally, which is convenient.

MATH can be included anywhere that you can write normal text in HTML 3. You are allowed to qualify MATH with just three attributes:

- ID to mark up a piece of mathematics as the target for a hypertext jump, for example:

  ```
  <MATH ID=quadratic>...</MATH>
  ```

- CLASS to identify which sort of expression is being drawn,
  - either for use with mathematical manipulation programs,
  - or to help browsers with style sheets or predefined renderings.

  For example:

  ```
  <MATH CLASS=chem>...</MATH>
  ```

  for chemistry. This is traditionally rendered with variables in an upright font, and browsers should comply with that convention.

- BOX (attribute) (not to be confused with the free-standing <BOX> element!) to draw a rectangular box around the formulae, for example:

  ```
  <MATH BOX> e=mc^2^ </MATH>
  ```

  might be rendered as

  $$\boxed{e = mc^2}$$

15.3.2 BOX (element)

A deep problem with mathematical expressions becomes clear as soon as you try to describe an equation to someone over the telephone: it is vital to explain which terms are bracketed together. What does 'A plus B over C' mean? In speech you may escape the ambiguity by saying either 'Ay-plus-Bee (pause) over Cee' or conversely 'Ay (pause) plus Bee-over-Cee' but in writing you have to be more definite.

Is it:

$$\frac{A+B}{C}$$

or $A + B/C$?

Mathematicians generally cheat and use a spatial analogy: the graphical layout indicates the bracketing. This is fine provided you can control the layout of the symbols. HTML 3 lets you do this in an easy-to-learn way.

BOX is the basic bracketing element for HTML 3 maths. You can choose to include delimiters if you need them. By itself, a BOX pair acts as logical but invisible brackets. Purely for convenience, you can write {...} in place of <BOX>...</BOX> – the meaning is the same.

For example,

```
<BOX>a + b<OVER>c - d</BOX>
```

and its equivalent

```
{a + b<OVER>c - d}
```

are both rendered as shown in the illustration.

$$\boxed{\frac{a+b}{c-d}}$$

The OVER element tells HTML that you want a visible division line. The similar ATOP element represents division by position (as does OVER), but leaves out the line between numerator and denominator.

If you want brackets round the expression, you tell BOX which delimiters to use: they are automatically stretched to fit. You can use round (...), square [...] and vertical line |...| brackets directly. You can also have curly brackets {...} which are represented in HTML 3 as { and } respectively: you obviously can't use {...} as these brackets are always interpreted by browsers to mean <BOX>...</BOX>.

For example, the curly-bracketed expression

```
{ &lcub; <LEFT> a + b<ATOP>c - d <RIGHT> &rcub; }
```

is rendered without a horizontal line as:

$$\left\{ {a+b \atop c-d} \right\}$$

You are quite free to format the source of your HTML how you like, as your browser will not mind. If you want to be able to read it, however, you should line up the opening and closing tags, and the left and right parts of your mathematical expressions, so you can see what goes with what. Of course, if you are really lucky you will get a syntax-directed HTML equation editor for Christmas, and it will count your tags and brackets, *and* format them symmetrically for you while you type.

The element BOX (or {...}) is a completely general organizer of mathematical expressions. You can combine it with a whole range of math symbols and symbol modifiers to create subtle mathematical effects.

You have already had an introduction to BOX, and should by now realize that it is a subtle but easy-to-use device which dramatically simplifies the writing of mathematical expressions in HTML 3. This is because the problem of bracketing things together – invisibly – recurs in a multitude of mathematical contexts.

The general syntax of a boxed expression is

```
<BOX> left-delim <LEFT> expression <RIGHT> right-delim </BOX>
```

where left-delim and right-delim are the symbols you want to use to mark off the left and right sides of the box, and expression is any mathematical expression at all. The whole thing can occur anywhere in a mathematical expression.

You will normally write {...} instead of actually using the BOX tag itself. Since both the left and right delimiters and their tags are optional, the most compact way to write an (invisible) boxed expression is simply

```
{ expression }
```

which could hardly be less fussy, could it?

Uses of `BOX`

There are at least four important purposes behind the use of `BOX` in your expressions:

(1) to **disambiguate** expressions by bracketing them (invisibly);

(2) to put **numerators over denominators**, with or without a dividing line;

(3) to insert **left and/or right delimiters** to symbolize the starts and ends of expressions;

(4) to create signs such as **integrals which stretch** to match the heights of expressions.

The `SIZE` attribute

There is only one attribute you can use to qualify `BOX`, which is `SIZE`. The possible sizes are:

`normal` (the default)

`medium`

`large`

`huge`

So, for example, you can write

```
<BOX SIZE=huge>
```

to create a deliberately oversized box. The effect is to stretch the left and right delimiters (if you supply any) vertically. If you want to use a size attribute, you have to use the `<BOX...>` syntax in full. You can't use `SIZE` with the short form `{...}`.

A box with `HUGE` vertical bars containing the variable **M**, for instance, looks like this in a typical browser:

and it is written in HTML as

```
<MATH>
     <BOX SIZE=huge> | <LEFT> M <RIGHT> | </BOX>
</MATH>
```

15.3.3 LEFT, RIGHT, OVER, ATOP, CHOOSE

<LEFT> and <RIGHT> may be replaced by <L> and <R> in the final HTML 3 specification.

These tags are specially designed to qualify the BOX element, and you should already have noticed them in use in the introduction to BOX at the start of this chapter. They have no attributes at all, so they appear only as basic tags, namely <LEFT>, <RIGHT>, <OVER>, <ATOP> and <CHOOSE>. Indeed, because they can only appear within BOX (or its short form {...}), they do not have closing tags (that is, there is no such thing as </ATOP>) either.

They have the following effects:

Tagged BOX *expression*	*Result in browser*
`{ [<LEFT> expr <RIGHT>] }`	[...] as left and right delimiters for expr
`{ expr1 <OVER> expr2 }`	expr1 with a dividing line over expr2
`{ expr1 <ATOP> expr2 }`	expr1 without a dividing line over expr2
`{ expr1 <CHOOSE> expr2 }`	like <ATOP> but bracketed

For example, to create the result:

$$\binom{n+1}{k}$$

you simply write the HTML expression:

```
<MATH>
     {n + 1<CHOOSE>k}
</MATH>
```

which can only be described as elegantly compact.

15.3.4 SUB **and** SUP

Superscripts and subscripts are the stuff of mathematical formatting, and it is common for mathematicians, physicists, chemists and engineers to use many of each. The approach chosen for HTML 3 allows subscripts to be subscripted, upper and lower limits to be draped around summation and integral signs, and individual elements to be both subscripted and superscripted on the left or on the right, simultaneously.

The basic syntax is simply

```
<SUB>...</SUB>
```

and

```
<SUP>...</SUP>
```

respectively.

You can use the attractively simple short forms

```
_item_
```

and

```
^item^
```

for items which are non-nested subscripts and superscripts respectively.

Inserting limits

A common requirement is to represent limits, as in

$$\sum_{n=0}^{\infty} v(n)$$

In the short form, you write simply

```
{&sum; _n = 0_^&inf;^ <of> v(n)}
```

where the symbols are interpreted as follows:

Symbol	*Interpretation*
`∑`	the summation (Greek letter Sigma) sign
`_n = 0_`	the subscripted lower limit, n = 0
`∞`	the infinity sign
`^∞^`	the superscripted upper limit, infinity
`v(n)`	the expression to be summated, a function of n

Notice that there must be no space between the subscript and the superscript if you are using the short form. You can write the same thing out in full if you insist. It looks like this:

```
<MATH>
      <BOX>
      &sum; <SUB>n = 0</SUB> <SUP>&infin;</SUP> <of> v(n)
      </BOX>
</MATH>
```

Nested subscripts or superscripts

If you need to draw nested subscripts, you have no choice but to use the long form. The syntax is a bit long, but could not be more straightforward. For instance:

```
X<SUB>a <SUB>i</SUB> </SUB>
```

gives, as you'd expect

$$X_{a_i}$$

If you have to handle a lot of these, for instance in matrices, we strongly suggest you get hold of a smart editor, or at least customize a word processor macro, to cut out the error-prone tedium of writing, and manually checking, all those repetitive </SUB> tags.

Subscripts and superscripts to the left of the term

In nuclear chemistry and in some mathematical formalisms, you need to put subscripts and superscripts on the left of math terms. The easiest way to do this is to use the short forms. For instance:

```
_4_^9^Be + _2_^4^He &rarr; _6_^12^C + _0_^1^n
```

gives

$$ {}_4^9\mathrm{Be} + {}_2^4\mathrm{He} \longrightarrow {}_6^{12}\mathrm{C} + {}_0^1\mathrm{n} $$

Tricks, dangers and ambiguities

There are some clear dangers with incautious mixing of left and right superscripts or subscripts – is the item supposed to apply to the term before or after it? The context will sometimes make things clear: there can only be one subscript on the left of a given term, so if there are apparently two, the first one must apply to the right of the preceding term – they can't both be printed in the same place. The same goes for two superscripts, and for both left and right placement.

In the absence of such disambiguating context, you should take care to bracket your expressions so there is no doubt as to their meaning – this may not affect the HTML parser, but it certainly makes your HTML easier for human readers. For instance,

```
{X_a_} {^b^Y}
```

can be seen at once to mean

$$ \mathrm{X_a}\ {}^{b}\mathrm{Y} $$

whereas the similar-looking expression

```
X_a_^b^Y
```

actually means

$$ \mathrm{X_a^b}\ \mathrm{Y} $$

because superscripts and subscripts immediately after a term are assumed to belong to it. You should never rely on these rules, both because of the risk of non-compliant parsers, and because you and other humans will be confused by your HTML. In case of doubt, always use brackets.

You can do exactly the same with the full forms <SUB> and <SUP>, but here there is a more direct way to disambiguate the direction (left or right) of association: you can insert an ALIGN attribute to insist on the direction.

For instance the verbose expression:

```
X <SUB ALIGN=right>a</SUB> Y <SUP ALIGN=left>b</SUP>
```

unambiguously gives

$X_a\ {}^{b}Y$

but at such length that you will surely prefer the short form.

15.3.5 ABOVE **and** BELOW

The ABOVE element draws a stretchy line, arrow, horizontal curly bracket (also known as a brace) or other mathematical accent ABOVE any mathematical expression you care to enclose in <ABOVE>...</ABOVE> tags. The default effect is a simple horizontal line above your expression:

```
<ABOVE>x + y</ABOVE>
```

gives

$\overline{x+y}$

Other horizontally stretchable symbols have to be named explicitly. For example, the curly bracket is &cub;. You tell ABOVE which symbol to use with the SYM attribute:

```
<ABOVE SYM="&cub;">
```

You can combine this behaviour with the use of SUP to put some text (or something else) above the centre of the curly bracket:

```
<ABOVE SYM="&cub;"> n(n - 1)(n - 2) &dots; (n - m + 1) </ABOVE>
<SUP> <TEXT>total of m factors</TEXT> </SUP>
```

which gives a beautiful horizontal curly-bracketed expression, with the curly bracket stretched to fit the text above which it lies. Notice that the SUP expression applies to the **whole** of the ABOVE expression:

$$\overbrace{n(n-1)(n-2)\ldots(n-m+1)}^{\text{total of m factors}}$$

The complete set of stretchy symbols you can use with the SYM attribute of ABOVE and BELOW is

`&line;`	a horizontal line (the default) (__)
`=`	a double horizontal line or equals sign (=)
`&cub;`	a horizontal curly bracket or brace (}) pointing up or down
`←`	a left arrow (←)
`→`	a right arrow (→)

`&hat;`	a circumflex accent or hat sign (ˆ)
`˜`	a Spanish tilde or 'not' sign ($\sim$)

The BELOW element works exactly like ABOVE, except of course that the stretchy symbol now appears underneath the enclosed expression. For example:

```
<MATH>
     { <BELOW SYM="&rarr;"> Z - Y </BELOW> }
</MATH>
```

gives

$$\underrightarrow{Z - Y}$$

You can use any of the symbols described for ABOVE with BELOW. The horizontal curly bracket necessarily has the point downwards in `<BELOW SYM="&cub;">`; if you want text centred below that, you use SUB.

Both ABOVE and BELOW can be used inside any math expression, and they can likewise contain any math expression. This makes a lot of work for your browser, but gives you a wide freedom to express mathematics naturally and directly.

15.3.6 VEC, BAR, DOT, DDOT, HAT and TILDE

These useful little elements are the mathematical equivalent of textual character mark-up with EM, STRONG and so on. They have no attributes. They draw the characters suggested (to the mathematician at least) by their names above their (presumably variable name) contents.

For example, you can put the variable x in between `<HAT>...</HAT>` tags:

```
<HAT>x</HAT>
```

gives

$$\hat{x}$$

The complete set of these math mark-up elements is as follows:

→	‾	·	··	^	~
VEC,	BAR,	DOT,	DDOT,	HAT,	TILDE

15.3.7 SQRT

The SQRT element wraps the familiar tick-with-a-tail symbol around its contents; like VEC and its fellows, it has no attributes. You just write

```
<SQRT>x + y</SQRT>
```

and you get

$$\sqrt{x+y}$$

15.3.8 ROOT...OF...

If you need higher roots (help!) you need of course to specify the radix as well as the radicand. You write

```
<ROOT>3 <OF> x + y </ROOT>
```

and you get

$$\sqrt[3]{x+y}$$

Like SQRT, ROOT has no attributes.

15.3.9 ...OF...

The OF element lets the mathematicians among you write functions in a most intuitive way. A mathematician explaining a function application on a chalkboard will say something like 'F of X minus Y' where F is the name of her function, and X minus Y is the function's argument, the thing that the function applies to. You can write this in HTML 3 as

```
<MATH>
      {F <OF> X - Y}
</MATH>
```

and the browser can render this as something like F(*X*-*Y*) depending on the style currently in force. The OF element makes it easy for rendering-to-speech browsers to speak HTML functions correctly out loud. You can combine the use of OF with any other MATH tags like OVER, and with subscripts and superscripts.

15.3.10 Writing integrals

Note: This section is advanced – non-technical readers can safely skip it.

Indefinite integrals

The tools already described are enough for you to write any integrals or differential equations that you need. You can represent the indefinite integral sign ∫ as a function in a box:

```
<MATH> { &int; <of>...
```

and the with-respect-to dx:

```
...<WRT> dx } </MATH>
```

The <WRT> element is not appropriate in some expressions, for example,

```
<MATH>{&int; <of> dx <OVER> 1+x}</MATH>
```

Definite integrals

The tags FROM and TO are being considered for use with limits, e.g. for integrals.

Definite integrals (those with limits above and below the integral sign) can be treated exactly like indefinite ones, with the addition of a subscript for the lower limit and a superscript for the upper limit. So, 'integral from 1 to 25 of x squared dx' can be written in HTML 3 as

```
<MATH>
      { &int;_1_^25^ <of> x^2^ <WRT> dx }
</MATH>
```

which can readily be translated into other formats.

A worked example

Suppose you want to write the integral

y = integral from 0 to infinity of sin x over 1 + x dx

to appear something like this:

$$y = \int_0^\infty \frac{\sin x}{1+x} dx$$

you use the special symbols and modifiers:

HTML	*Mathematics*
`∫`	integral symbol
`∞`	infinity symbol
`_symbol_`	subscripted symbol
`^symbol^`	superscripted symbol

You want the integral sign to have its limits below and above it, and you want the sign to span the same height as the expression that it governs. This is the same problem as with matrices, where the brackets must enclose the whole matrix. So, in the case of the integral, we can treat the symbol as the left half of a **box** enclosing the integrand. All that HTML requires is for you to indicate where the left-hand boxing symbol ends, using the tag <LEFT>.

The integral expression shown above is therefore written as

```
<MATH>
      y = {&int;_0_^&infin;^<of> {sin x<OVER>1 + x} <WRT> dx}
</MATH>
```

remembering that the curly brackets {...} are used to indicate box-grouping, and do not appear on the screen. The <WRT> element inserts white space between the expression and the '*dx*'.

All of this takes a long time to explain, but when you get used to it, you can write equations down in a few seconds.

Now that you have seen how to do the basics, as maths teachers love to say, you will want to write something *really* unpleasant, like a double integral containing a function with parameters, and some fractions. The beast looks like this:

$$\int_a^b \int_p^q \frac{f(x,y)}{1+1/x}\, dx\, dy$$

and you write it like this:

```
<MATH>
      {&int; _a_^b^ &sp;
       &int; _p_^q^ &sp; <LEFT>
            {f(x,y) <OVER> 1 + {1 <OVER> x}}
       <WRT> dx
       dy }
</MATH>
```

There are no special rules about how to lay out mathematical HTML, but as this example shows, you can make life easier for yourself and other human readers, if you indent the source text, and arrange repeating items in columns. Use white space, tabs and new lines wherever necessary between symbols (except for tricky uses of __ and ^^ where separators can change the meaning): Web browsers do not mind.

15.3.11 TEXT

The TEXT element lets you put in a few words of plain literal text (including accents if you need to write non-English characters) in the middle of any piece of maths mark-up, without having to write '&sp;' for any spaces you need to insert. There are no attributes allowed. For example:

```
<MATH>...<TEXT>G&ouml;del's Theorem</TEXT>...</MATH>
```

gives

...Gödel's Theorem...

15.3.12 B, T and BT

These elements (T and BT ONLY allowed in MATH!) let you override the normal convention beloved of mathematicians of writing variables and constants in plain italics. Numbers, operators, delimiters and other symbols are not affected.

- `<B>` puts variables and constants (which are already in *italics*) into ***boldface***.
- `<T>` puts them into an upright font instead of *italics*.
- `<BT>` puts them into a **boldface upright** font.

For instance

```
<BT>x = <SQRT> y^2^ - 3c </SQRT></BT>
```

gives something like

$$\mathbf{x} = \sqrt{\mathbf{y}^2 - \mathbf{3c}}$$

You can improve on the rather messy construction using <B> by exploiting the built-in arrangements for chemical formulae.

Chemists like to have chemical element symbols such as **As** (for Arsenic) and **Be** (for Beryllium, another poisonous metal) in **bold**, so to mark up your chemical formulae consistently, you should sub-class your MATH with CLASS=chem:

```
<MATH CLASS=chem>...</MATH>
```

Browsers are also likely to understand classes such as VECTOR, TENSOR and MATRIX as indicating special formatting. Other conventions may exist or be defined in style sheets. The default style is suitable for school-type mathematics.

15.4 ARRAY

HTML 3's mathematical array model looks quite complicated at first glance, but is actually highly regular and allows mathematicians to write many kinds of arrays on Web pages. Arrays can be written only within the MATH element.

The model is quite similar, too, to the TABLE model, with ROW for TR and ITEM for TD. Another point of similarity is that you can make array cells, like table cells, span rows or columns with ROWSPAN or COLSPAN. Unlike TABLE, you can explicitly give ARRAYs particular kinds of boundary with the LDELIM and RDELIM symbols.

An ARRAY consists of at least one ROW. A ROW consists of at least one ITEM. Inside arrays, items can be subscripted or superscripted, or in fact described using any MATH mark-up that you want.

You now know enough to write down a basic array:

```
<MATH>
     <ARRAY>
          <ROW><ITEM>a <ITEM>b <ITEM>c
          <ROW><ITEM>1 <ITEM>2 <ITEM>3
     </ARRAY>
</MATH>
```

which results as you'd expect in the array

$$\begin{array}{ccc} a & b & c \\ 1 & 2 & 3 \end{array}$$

15.4.1 ALIGN (top, middle, bottom)

The default positioning for ARRAYs is middle, that is, with the middle row or midpoint aligned with the baseline of the preceding or following expression.

<ARRAY align=middle> causes the middle row of the array to be aligned with the surrounding baseline, like this:

	array line 1
Baseline of text is here →	array line 2
	array line 3

The slight complication here is that if the array has an even number of lines (for example, 4) then the alignment is halfway between lines (for example, between lines 2 and 3).

Similarly ALIGN=top or ALIGN=bottom aligns the top or bottom of the array with the baseline.

15.4.2 COLDEF

COLDEF lets you specify the alignment of columns in an array even though columns are actually defined implicitly! You can understand how much work is going on behind the scenes to ensure your mathematical expressions appear properly. COLDEF takes a string expression in quotation marks.

You write:

C	for a centred column
L	for a left-aligned column
R	for a right-aligned column
+/-/=	for a plus, minus, or equals sign to appear **between** columns.

This beautifully simple mechanism gives you control of the column structure of your arrays. For instance,

```
<ARRAY COLDEF="lcr">
```

at the head of a 3-column array like the example above makes the columns left-, centre-, and right-aligned respectively.

The tag

```
<ARRAY COLDEF="c + c = c">
```

makes the same array appear like this:

$$\begin{array}{c@{\;+\;}c@{\;=\;}c} a & b & c \\ 1 & 2 & 3 \end{array}$$

Any spaces in the COLDEF expression are ignored.

15.4.3 LDELIM **and** RDELIM

You can put in any character or character-entity as the left or right delimiters of your arrays. For example

```
<ARRAY COLDEF="c + c = c" LDELIM="[" RDELIM="]">
```

gives

$$\begin{array}{l} [a \quad + \quad b \quad = \quad c] \\ [1 \quad + \quad 2 \quad = \quad 3] \end{array}$$

The default is for no delimiters to be used at all. These attributes save having to use an enclosing BOX element with LEFT and RIGHT.

15.4.4 LABELS

The single word tag <LABELS> causes the math parser to treat the first row and the first column of your array as text labels. The affected items are displayed spaced apart from the body of the table.

You can see, if you reflect on the problem, that the **top left** item in an array with LABELS is in a strange situation – it is neither a row label nor a column label, but it must be present to enable the position of the other label items to be identified. What you have to do is to supply a **dummy** item in this position – it is always ignored! Of course, if you forget, the LABELS command will eat up your first column label, leaving you one short and with all the labels in the wrong place.

Here is a complete example showing what happens:

```
<MATH>
  <ARRAY COLDEF="c + c = c" LDELIM="[" RDELIM="]">        <LABELS>
      <ROW><ITEM>DUMMY     <ITEM>1st     <ITEM>2nd     <ITEM>3rd
      <ROW><ITEM>letters   <ITEM>a       <ITEM>b       <ITEM>c
      <ROW><ITEM>digits    <ITEM>1       <ITEM>2       <ITEM>3
  </ARRAY>
</MATH>
```

which creates an array thus:

$$\begin{array}{rccccc} & \text{1st} & & \text{2nd} & & \text{3rd} \\ \text{letters} & [\,\mathrm{a} & + & \mathrm{b} & = & \mathrm{c}\,] \\ \text{digits} & [\,1 & + & 2 & = & 3\,] \end{array}$$

with, as you will notice, a blank space where the DUMMY ought to have been. Notice also that the labels are ***outside*** the delimiters, which is what mathematicians like. If you really want a border round the whole array, you can put the array inside a table cell.

15.4.5 ROW

There is really hardly anything left to say about the ROW element. You already know that you use it inside ARRAYs, and that it contains ITEMs. It has no attributes at all. You never need to put in </ROW> as it is always obvious from the context when a row has ended.

15.4.6 ITEM

There is almost nothing to explain about ITEMs either. They can only be used inside ROWs, and they can contain any maths mark-up. You can always omit the closing </ITEM> tag. The only permitted tags are ALIGN, COLSPAN and ROWSPAN to control the positioning and size of individual items.

ALIGN (left, center, right)

The default behaviour is <ITEM ALIGN=center>, that is, horizontal centring of items within rows. Within an array, you can change the default behaviour globally using COLDEF. This in turn can be overridden locally by

<ITEM ALIGN=left> (or =center or =right). Obviously for speed and simplicity you should use COLDEF on whole columns rather than setting lots of individual items if you can avoid it.

COLSPAN

Array items can be set to span several columns, exactly like table cells. You write

```
<ITEM COLSPAN=3>
```

to make an item span three column widths. The value given must be a positive integer. By default it is 1. COLSPANs which would go beyond the right of the array are ignored.

ROWSPAN

ROWSPAN works exactly like COLSPAN, allowing array items to span several rows. For example:

```
<ITEM ROWSPAN=2>
```

makes that item span two row heights. ROWSPANs which would go below the bottom of the array are ignored.

15.5 Summary of maths

HTML 3's MATH constructs steer a skilful path between being simplistic and the massive complexities of specialized mathematics packages. MATH enables technical users to benefit from clear and direct rendering of a wide range of equations, formulae and symbols.

Because the approach, such as with BOX, is generic, it can handle symbolisms not known to HTML. Convenient short cuts are provided for several common operations. Special provision is made for the subscripted and superscripted prefixes and suffixes used in various forms of chemistry and physics. Style sheets may be defined to assist with equations used in other fields.

Note: An excellent article on the issues of representing math in SGML is given in:

ftp://ftp.elsevier.nl/pub/sgml/epsig_news_article.ps

16 CREATING YOUR OWN ARTWORK FOR THE WEB

In this chapter:

- Image size
- When and where to use graphics
- Colouring Web pages
- Image file formats – GIF, JPEG, PNG
- Java and VRML
- Image manipulation tools

16.1 Introduction

There is no reason why you should not produce your own artwork, photographs or other images for insertion into Web documents even if you are new to publishing on the Web. You can scan in images, use a drawing/painting package, the choice is yours. The format in which images must be is important. The choices are JPEG, GIF and PNG and you will need a graphics manipulation package or program to convert images to the right format. Each graphics format has its own strengths and weaknesses as explained later in this chapter. Overall you are aiming for as small an image as possible in terms of bytes, consistent with the quality of reproduction which you think is acceptable. There is nearly always some trade-off between quality and image size simply because you will need to compress an image to put it on the Web and compression nearly always involves some loss of detail.

16.2 Image size

Size of images in terms of bytes

If you want people to access your graphics over low-bandwidth modem links *and* in congested conditions (unfortunately often the case these days) then you are best avoiding large inlined images, especially on your home page or on other commonly used pages. Over a 28.8 K line images may be transferred at 2 Kbytes a second, and perhaps much less. 100 bytes a second is not uncommon during peak times for Web pages accessed over a low-speed connection from home.

When and where to use graphics

First appearances count for a lot. If your page looks dull, or takes a long time to load, users will quickly get bored and move on to another site. To prevent this, use an effective image or graphic at the top of your page and consider using background textures or colours to add extra impact. It is difficult to give a hard and fast rule, but I would recommend that you aim to keep image sizes to no more than around 20 to 40 Kbytes for rapid loading, and that you use the `WIDTH` and `HEIGHT` attributes to ensure the text appears quickly. Add smaller graphics for further effects: for bullets, rules and borders.

If your document is several screenfulls long, then you can think about placing additional large images further down, just so long as they aren't visible when the document is initially displayed. This works because they will be loaded while the user is busy reading the first part of the document. If you do want to provide access to a large graphic, consider having a smaller version (a thumbnail) in your document which can be clicked on to download the large graphic if and when users want to do so. In this case, it is helpful to indicate the size of the full image in Kbytes after the thumbnail, for example '(118 K)', as this gives users a feel for how long it would take to download before they choose to download it.

Colouring Web pages

Careful use of background textures or colours with coloured text and links can be effective, especially if you adopt conventions that apply recognizable styles for groups of pages according to the role each page plays, for example making all reference pages in one colour, and product brochures in another. Try to avoid large files for background textures, as these will significantly slow down the initial appearance of the page contents.

Things you need to know about colour

Computers display images as a series of rows of pixels. Pixels are coloured dots made up from red, green and blue primary colour components. On most machines red, green and blue components can be individually set to one of up to 256 different values each. High-end machines generally support what is called 24-bit truecolor. Images on these machines are held as a series of red, green and blue values with eight bits each. This gives excellent colour rendition for most purposes. Many machines now support 16-bit truecolor which uses two bytes per pixel (that is, five bits per component). This is noticeably not as good as 24-bit truecolor.

At the bottom end are 256 colour display modes. These limit the display to a palette of 256 colours in total at any one time, as compared with thousands for 16-bit truecolor and millions for 24-bit truecolor. In compensation, these 256 colours can be altered to meet the needs of what is currently being displayed. Images are held as a series of numbers that index into the colour palette. For this reason, this display mode is known as *Indexed Colour*. Games programs invariably want to run with Indexed Colour as it is faster than truecolor, and also permits special effects through dynamic changes to the colour palette.

In Windows 95 and the Mac OS, things are complicated by the ability for each window to select its own palette of colours. Unfortunately, the hardware only permits a system palette of 256 colours in total at any one time. The operating system does some magic to merge the colour needs for the top window and other windows, to select a reasonable compromise for the system palette. Luckily, this has little impact on authoring Web pages!

On truecolor display modes Web browsers render pixel values in images to the nearest available colour. For 16-bit truecolor this sometimes results in visible banding effects for smoothly varying parts of the image. This can be avoided if the browser is able to approximate 24-bit truecolor by dithering between the nearest available colours. For indexed colour, the browser has two choices: to choose a fixed palette (called a colour cube) and use that to dither all images, or to try to find an optimal palette for all of the images on the page. If more than 256 colours in total are required for the set of images, then the browser has to go through a process that determines the best compromise palette. The images are then dithered to this combined palette.

Current browsers use a fixed strategy. Mosaic optimizes the palette for the images on the current page, while Netscape uses a predefined colour cube. Many graphics designers hate colour cubes! It prevents them from achieving a subtle touch. For instance, the designer would like to use a texture composed of slightly different colours. On browsers based on colour cubes such textures are messed up by the dither patterns needed to approximate the colours. The carefully understated pattern is lost in the noise! This can be avoided if browsers use a more sophisticated strategy: use a colour cube when loading the images, and then switch to an optimized palette if this would make a significant improvement.

16.3 Image file formats

The GIF image format

The Graphics Interchange Format was created by CompuServe to allow users to download graphics efficiently on CompuServe's proprietary network. It later became the workhorse graphics format for the Web. In 1994 CompuServe announced that the LZW compression routine used in GIF infringes a Unisys patent. As a result Unisys requires a royalty for software supporting the GIF format. This resulted in a group of graphics developers joining forces to develop a new public domain image file format. PNG or the Portable Network Graphics format will be described in a later section.

GIF uses a lossless image file format. This means that the original pixel values can always be recovered when decoding a GIF file, unlike JPEG which will be explained in the next section. GIF images are limited to a palette of up to 256 colours. One of these palette entries can be designated as 'transparent'. This allows you to cut holes in a GIF image on a pixel by pixel basis. Copyright and other information can be included in text comment fields. For faster perceived downloading, you can interlace GIF image data. This means that the image will start to appear at a low resolution and gradually get more detailed as further scan lines are received.

GIF is excellent for images with large areas of the same colour. This allows the image to be compressed to a small fraction of its original size. For photographic images consider using the JPEG format instead, as in most cases you get better results with smaller file sizes. Until PNG becomes widespread, GIF remains the obvious choice when you want images with transparent areas, or which are unsuitable for encoding as JPEG. One problem with GIF is that images may look significantly different from one platform to the next. This is because platforms vary in how they map red, green and blue values to the signals used to drive the display device. The mapping is dependent on a parameter known as the gamma value for the display. The Macintosh partially compensates for an assumed gamma value in the image data, while the PC doesn't bother. To correct for this, the browser would like to know the gamma value assumed by the image file. Unfortunately, this was left out of the GIF specification. *C'est la vie!*

JPEG

JPEG (pronounced 'jay-peg') stands for the Joint Photographic Experts Group (the name of the committee that wrote the standard). It is designed for compressing full colour or grey scale images of natural, real-world scenes, such as scanned photographs and paintings. It is not effective for images with lettering, simple cartoons or line drawing. JPEG has trouble with very sharp edges which tend to come out blurred. Such edges are rare in scanned photographs though. Plain black and white images should never be encoded using JPEG. GIF and PNG are complementary to JPEG and do much better for graphics art. JPEG can't squeeze data as much for flat images with abrupt edges without introducing visible defects.

In general, non-photographic images should be left as GIF. If you do want to convert GIF images to JPEG then there are several points to look out for. If the image has large single-colour borders then you should crop these before encoding to JPEG. GIF images have 256 or fewer colours. As a result, encoding scanned photographs as GIF images will often require significant colour compression. This resultant dithering makes it difficult to re-encode the image data efficiently in JPEG. Conversion tools typically have to smooth the image data to reduce the noise introduced by dithering before encoding to JPEG.

Tip: when taking a photo for a Web page, use a large aperture setting to soft focus the background. This will reduce the JPEG file size

The take-home lesson is that if you want to create high-quality JPEG files with high compression levels then you will need low-noise 24-bit truecolor images to start from. The level of compression you can attain without sacrificing quality will then depend on the sharpness of detail. Try using a smoothing filter before encoding to JPEG, and adjusting the degree of smoothing and the 'quality' setting of the encoder. You should be able to achieve about 10:1 to 100:1 compression depending on the level of quality you need. GIF and PNG can only achieve this for very simple images. The trick is that JPEG throws away information that the eye doesn't notice. For instance, we have trouble discerning small variations in colour, although we are quite sensitive to variations in brightness. This explains why JPEG compresses full colour images much better than grey scale images.

JPEG doesn't support transparency. This is because such data is a poor fit to how JPEG encodes data. If you need transparency, then use GIF or PNG. JPEG files are generally in one of two formats, Baseline JPEG and the newer Progressive JPEG format. At the time of writing, relatively few browsers support Progressive JPEG, but this is likely to change rapidly thanks to free decoding software from the Independent JPEG Group. The new format reorganizes the encoded image data, so that the decoder can generate a low-quality image very quickly. The image is sent as several scans, which progressively increase the quality until all of the data has been decoded. Progressive JPEG files are actually slightly smaller (about 5%) than the traditional format. Low-cost utilities are now available for converting to the progressive format, for instance the JPEG Transmogrifier for Macs from inTouch Technologies, which is available as a standalone tool or as a PhotoShop plug-in. Another shareware tool for this is the ProJPEG PhotoShop plug-in from Aris. Free source code for JPEG is available from the Independent JPEG Group.

Portable Network Graphics

PNG (pronounced *ping*) is a new public domain image format created in 1995 by a group of graphics developers cooperating over the Internet. PNG is a great improvement on GIF and requires no licence fees for software supporting it, unlike GIF. It is expected that GIF will fade away as more and more companies add support for PNG. By Summer '96, the vast majority of new browsers will support PNG for inlined images. Free source code for PNG is available from the PNG Developers Group.

PNG is a lossless compression format and faithfully preserves all pixel values, unlike JPEG. PNG has improved compression over GIF. It works much better than GIF for smoothly varying images. In addition to palette-based images, PNG supports truecolor images with up to 48 bits per pixel, and grey scale images with up to 16 bits per pixel. This makes PNG a great choice for computer generated artwork. Unlike GIF, you can ensure your images look just as good on Windows, Macs and other platforms by including gamma values that allow the browser to apply platform-dependent colour and brightness corrections. PNG has a much faster interlacing technique too, so users will be able to see PNG images earlier when browsing on slow connections.

Many Web page designers have been exploiting GIF's transparency feature to add impact to their graphics. The technique has its pitfalls though. To avoid jaggies around text art and other graphics, designers employ a technique called anti-aliasing. This smooths rough edges by setting boundary pixels to a mixture of the foreground and background colours. This works great just so long as someone doesn't change the background colour. However, if the image background is transparent, then that is just what will happen! Netscape defaults to a grey background, so this is what most designers assume when they anti-alias their images. If your browser has a different background, then you will see a grey halo around the image where the boundary pixels are mixed with Netscape grey.

One solution is to set the background colour using the `BGCOLOR` attribute of the `BODY` element. PNG offers a more effective answer which also works correctly with background textures. For palette-based images PNG offers the same transparency feature as GIF. You can designate one of the palette entries to make pixels with that value transparent. For truecolor images, though, PNG offers a variable translucency feature. It allows you to create effects like fades, where an image fades into the background as you move from one side of the image to the other. It works by allowing you to specify a blend factor for mixing the image with the background on a pixel by pixel basis. The technical guys call this an 'alpha channel'. This is highly recommended for reliable anti-aliasing as well as offering a host of new effects for soft fades and shadows.

Java

Java is a new computer programming language from Sun Microsystems. It is an object-oriented language inspired by C++. Most people think that Java is a much better language; for instance, it saves programmers from having to take care to free up resources they no longer need, a common source of bugs. By the time this book is in the shops, several companies will be marketing Java development toolkits for a wide variety of platforms. Sun already provides a basic Java software development kit which can be downloaded for free for Windows 95/NT and Sun workstations.

HTML authors can use small Java programs (called *applets*) to add dynamic effects to Web pages. The page uses the HTML `INSERT` element to name applets. The browser downloads the applet across the net and then runs it. Java applets are compiled to a platform-independent byte code format. This allows different kinds of machines to execute Java applets, for example PCs, Macs and various kinds of UNIX boxes. Java applets are executed in a special environment that ensures they can't screw up the host machine. After all, you may have no idea where the applet comes from, much less whether the programmer was trustworthy.

The execution environment also provides a standard way for applets to draw to the screen and so on. The AWT library supporting this is key to the portability of Java applets. For further information see `http://java.sun.com/`. Addison-Wesley is publishing a series of books on Java in Spring and Summer '96, written by members of the team that developed Java. Note that one of the authors of this book, Dave Raggett, is using Java to develop a portable public domain editor/browser for HTML 3 and style sheets.

VRML

In late 1993, Dave Raggett became fascinated with the possibilities offered by virtual reality. Already, you could run impressive VR programs on high-end PCs and UNIX workstations. The game Doom showed amazing performance for simple maze-like worlds using a variety of techniques like textured surfaces and sprite animation for the bad guys. A general-purpose VR package, Superscape, showed what could be done to simplify authoring and exploring 3-D worlds on PCs. Dave wrote a short paper setting out his vision for extending the Web to support distributed VR, naming the new format the

Virtual Reality Markup Language[1] (or VRML). He later presented this at a 'birds of a feather' session run jointly with Tim Berners-Lee at the first International World Wide Web Conference held at CERN in May '94, and the next month at the Internet Society Conference in Prague. Mark Pesce also presented his work at the CERN conference, demoing a crude VR browser with active hypertext links.

Mark Pesce, Tony Parisi, Brian Behlendorf, Gavin Bell and many others rapidly established the VRML mailing list and Web page with the support of *Wired Magazine*. There was an extraordinary interest in the idea, and work commenced on determining the scope and representation for the initial release. Within 12 months the VRML 1.0 spec was ready, along with early prototypes. The authors would like to especially thank Mark Pesce for his tireless work in getting companies to support VRML. Work now continues with extending VRML in the light of experience. VRML 1.1 fixes a number of problems encountered with the initial spec, while the forthcoming VRML 2.0 will add behaviours. This will allow objects to move and be heard. Microsoft's Active VRML provides one approach to handling time-based properties. Other proposals are based on scripting behaviour, and Sun's Java seems well suited for this.

VRML is still at an early stage. The vision, described so well in the fiction of writers like William Gibson (*Neuromancer*) who coined the term Cyberspace, and Neil Stephenson (*Snow Crash*), is still far off from being realized. The next challenge is to find ways to scale up to virtual worlds with millions of polygons from many different servers. At the same time, we are looking for ways for people to meet together in rooms and communal spaces defined in cyberspace. Within a few years, combined improvements in bandwidth and real-time protocols will allow you to meet and talk with other people in lifelike 3-D worlds. Much of the basic research has already been done, and now awaits improvements in technology. We are also hoping for greater expressivity for artists whose imagination will make cyberspace worth visiting.

VRML browsers and editing tools are now available for most platforms. Pointers to these can be found in various places, for example Yahoo, Webreference (`http://webreference.com/vrml/`), the VRML Repository at `http://www.sdsc.edu/vrml/`, and the VRML FAQ (`http://www.oki.com/vrml/VRML_FAQ.html`). The VRML standards are held at `http://www.vrml.org/`, and the original VRML forum at `http://vrml.wired.com/`. We like the WebFX VRML Netscape plug-in from Paper Software, although the WebSpace Navigator from TGS and SGI is easier to navigate with. The Home Space Builder from Paragraph is an easy to learn 3-D scene editing tool for creating VRML worlds. For the more adventurous, try Virtus' Walkthrough Pro.

[1] It was later changed to the Virtual Reality Modelling Language.

16.4 Image manipulation tools for the Web

The following is a brief summary of what is available. You are recommended to search for up-to-date information on the Web. We liked the Net Tools page at `http://humanitas.ucsb.edu/shuttle/tools.html` which covers a wide range of topics in addition to graphics. The TRANSPARENT/INTERLACED GIF page is at `http://dragon.jpl.nasa.gov/~adam/transparent.html`. The PORTABLE NETWORK GRAPHICS home page is at `http://quest.jp.nasa.gov/PNG/`. Web Reference has a wide collection of articles comparing different tools and lots of other useful information at `http://webreference.com`. Yahoo has a good set of menus to browse. Finally, we recommend you just try any of the popular Web search sites and enter keywords such as *graphics utilities tools* and so on and surf around.

Most of the tools mentioned below are either free or low cost. If you expect to be creating a lot of graphics, then you may want to take the plunge and invest your time and money in the high-end tools like Adobe. This can be supplemented with a range of plug-ins, such as Kai's Power Tools. You will also need lots of memory and a 24-bit truecolor display system. A colour scanner and a pressure-sensitive drawing pad will come in handy. To get going though, you can use cheap drawing and painting packages to create your artwork. For photographic images, Kodak's PhotoCD process allows you to get high quality images for a few dollars extra using your regular camera, without the need to purchase a colour scanner.

Image maps

MapEdit 2.1 by Thomas Boutell is available for Windows and UNIX/X11. It can handle progressive JPEG and PNG as well as GIF. Another free tool for Windows is *MapTHIS*. *WebMap* is a similar tool for the Mac, but is restricted in the image formats it can handle. You can get around this using conversion tools like *Clip2GIF* or *GraphicsConverter*.

Transparency

We like *Clip2GIF* and *Icon2Gif*, both of which are Mac freeware. Icon2Gif lets you drag and drop desktop icons to generate GIFs of them. You can then convert them to PNG with *GraphicsConverter* (2.1.4 or later). Clip2GIF also provides a drag and drop conversion to interlaced GIF, and also supports JPEG. On UNIX, use *giftrans* or the *pbm plus* suite (for example `giftopnm orig.gif | ppmtogif -trans #CFCFCF > new.gif`).

Image conversion, colour reduction and filtering, and so on

For the Mac: *Clip2GIF* is a simple freeware tool, but we like *GraphicsConverter* or *GifConverter*. *DeBabelizer Lite limited edition for the Web* is available free and can be used to adjust a group of images to share a common palette, giving the browser an opportunity to show the images as the designer intended. It also allows you generate thumbnail images from full-sized images. The pay for version handles conversion between a wide range of other formats including interlaced GIF, JPEG, progressive JPEG and PNG. The *JPEG Transmogrifier* is used to convert baseline JPEG images to the Progressive JPEG file format. On Windows, some useful tools are *Lview Pro, PaintShopPro* and *HiJaak'95*. UNIX users can try *xv, xpaint, ImageMagik* and the *pbm plus* suite.

Image width/height for `IMG/INSERT` elements

Including the width and height attributes with inline images allows the user to see your document more quickly. The browser doesn't have to keep stopping while it waits to find out how large each image is. On the Mac *Equilibrium Software* provide freeware *PixStik* and *HTML Image+* (BBEdit extension) which simplify the task of finding out and entering these attributes. On UNIX you can try *Gifsize* which is a Perl routine that automatically adds width/height attributes to `IMG` elements in HTML files.

Graphics services over the Web

Some Web sites offer free graphics services via HTTP and HTML forms, for example design your own custom bullets and rules via the Interactive Graphics Renderer by Patrick Hennesy at Kansas State University (`http://www.eece.ksu.edu/IGR/`); VRL's Imaging Machine (`http://www.vrl.com/Imaging`) offers an interactive graphics processing service (scale, flop, shear, add transparency and other effects). MapMaker is a Web service from MIT for creating an image map file (`http://tns-www.lcs.mit.edu/cgi-bin/mapmaker`). MIT also hosts the Transweb page, which provides a transparency service. WebScript is a server add-on for dynamically creating images of text strings in a variety of fonts, sizes, colours and styles; see `http://www.giftlink.com/` for details. The Great Bevelizer allows you to enter a URL for your GIF image, and returns it as a 3-D bevelled button ready to be included in your documents.

POSTSCRIPT

The story of the World Wide Web with apologies to Alan Watts

Appendix A
EXAMPLES OF TAGS

<IMG SRC="apple.gif">

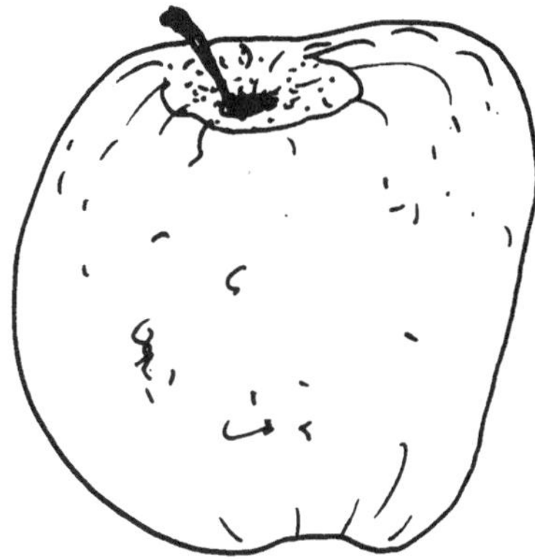

This appendix is a pure list of examples. Its function is to remind the reader of the syntax of particular tags where the general idea is remembered but some help with the details is needed. The examples do not do anything at all sensible, but we hope they are (individually) constructed correctly and will prove useful.

Extensions are shown where possible. These extensions are not guaranteed to work with browsers whether HTML 3 compliant or not. Their inclusion here is for practical purposes and does not constitute an endorsement of the extensions.

If you want to try the tags out in your browser, please insert a line or paragraph break (
 or <P>) after each example. Such separators have been omitted here for clarity. It has occurred to the authors that this appendix forms an interesting testbed for browsers which claim to be HTML 3 compliant. We are happy for it to be copied and used in this way provided that the authors' names and the publisher are acknowledged.

Finally, this list of examples is not comprehensive, but we have tried to include specimens of a wide range of HTML idioms.

Comments

```
<!--remarks like this are ignored by the HTML 3 parser-->
```

Head

```
<HEAD>                                                  <!--often omitted-->
<BASE HREF="http://my.dir/docs/thisdoc.html">           <!--URL of document itself-->
<ISINDEX>                                               <!--document already has a searchable index-->
<ISINDEX PROMPT="Enter keywords separated by commas">   <!--extension-->
<LINK REL=ToC HREF="thistoc.html">                      <!--table of contents-->
<LINK REL=banner HREF="ourlogo.html">                   <!--banner for top of page-->
<LINK REL=next HREF="nextdoc.html">                     <!--predefined next page-->
<LINK REL=stylesheet HREF="ourstyle.styl">              <!--associated style sheet-->
<NEXTID N=Z27>                                          <!--identifies next global identifier-->
<TITLE>Examples of HTML 3 tags</TITLE>                  <!--the only mandatory element in HTML 3-->
</HEAD>
```

Frameset

```
<!--divide up display area into rectangular containers--><!--must be directly after head-->
<FRAMESET ROWS="10%, 80%, 10%">                         <!--give first frame 10% of available height-->
   <FRAME SRC="ourlogo.html" SCROLLING="no">            <!--a non-scrolling frame for a logo panel-->
   <FRAME SRC="maintext.html" NAME="main">              <!--scrollable by default for the main text-->
   <FRAMESET COLS="100, *">                             <!--nested frameset-->
      <FRAME SRC="top.html" NORESIZE>                   <!--exactly 100 pixels wide, not resizeable-->
      <FRAME SRC="menubar.html">                        <!--relative-sized, occupies rest of the width-->
   </FRAMESET>
</FRAMESET>
```

Body

```
<!--main HTML text-->
<BODY ID="wasp">                                        <!--usually omitted in handwritten HTML-->
```

Banner

```
<!--at start of body only-->
<BANNER>Coffee, Tea, or Me?</BANNER>                    <!--displayed non-scrolling at top of page-->
```

Divisions

```
<DIV CLASS=chapter>1. Introduction                      <!--nested to show document structure-->
   <DIV CLASS=section>1.1 Purpose...</DIV>
   <DIV CLASS=section>1.2 Organization...</DIV>
   <DIV CLASS=section>1.3 Terminology Used...</DIV>
</DIV> <!--end of chapter 1-->
<DIV CLASS=abstract>...</DIV>
<DIV CLASS=appendix>...</DIV>
```

Headings

```
<H1>GENERAL HEADING</H1>                    <!--most browsers use large fonts-->
<H2>MAJOR HEADING</H2>                      <!--to distinguish the heading levels-->
<H3>Lieutenant heading</H3>                 <!--this should appear as 1.1.1 by default-->
<H4>Sergeant heading</H4>                   <!--this should appear as 1.1.1.1 by default-->
<H5>Corporal heading</H5>                   <!--some browsers may allow more levels...-->
<H6>Private heading</H6>                    <!--but 6 is the lowest defined in the standard-->
```

Paragraph

```
<P ALIGN=center>This is a formal paragraph.</P>    <!--usually omit the closing tag-->
<CENTER>NS centred text</CENTER>                   <!--extension--><BR>
```

Line break

```
line 1<BR>                        <!--unlike <P>, doesn't insert white space-->
line 2<BR CLEAR=left>             <!--extension, goes down until-->
                                  <!--left margin is free of floating images-->
                                  <!--also =right, =all (i.e. both margins)-->
<NOBR> </NOBR>                    <!--extension, forbids line breaks-->
<WBR>                             <!--extension, allow break even in <NOBR>-->
```

Horizontal tab

```
12345678<TAB ID="t8">                                 <!--set tabs in physical position-->
<TAB TO t8>
This line is indented to a predefined tab stop.<P>    <!--use tab-->
```

Hypertext link

- To an index of documents on the Web:

```
<A HREF="http://www.w3.org/"> Home of Short Acronyms </A>
```

- To a target section in same document, with inline graphic button:

```
<A HREF="#anchorage">
   <IMG SRC="alaska.gif">
   Jump to Anchorage Section
</A>
```

- Link target (somewhere in the document) in old and new styles:

```
<A NAME="anchorage">                              <!--deprecated-->
<DIV CLASS=section ID="anchorage">...</DIV>       <!--recommended-->
```

- To a target section in a related document:

```
<A HREF="hardware.html#req36">
   Requirement 36: Fail-Safe Data Storage
</A>
```

- Link target in "hardware.html" for the above:

```
<H3 ID="req36">Fail-Safe Data Storage</H3>
<P>The system <B>shall</B> preserve all data in the event of failure.</P>
```

- Link to bitmap image file:

```
<!--it is polite to warn users of large files-->

<A HREF="flowers.gif"> Basket of Flowers <I>(84 kilobytes)</I> </A>
```

- To bitmap image file with matching inline graphic icon used as button:

```
<A HREF="kk_image.gif">                      <!--main image-->
   <IMG SRC="kk_icon.gif">                   <!--icon is reduced from main image-->
   View of KaraKoram Range at Sunset
   <I>(171 kilobytes)</I>
</A>
```

- To footnote (generally pops up when anchor is clicked on):

```
<A HREF="#fn1"><I>explanans</I></A>                    <!--reference to footnote in link anchor-->
...
<FN ID="fn1"><P>thing which explains something</FN>    <!--the target footnote itself needs an id-->
```

Informational mark-up

```
<EM>emphasized words</EM>                           <!--usually italicized-->
<CITE>Hamlet, act 3, scene 1, line 12</CITE>        <!--typically italicized too-->
<CITE>Sophie, for exceptional bravery in venturing  <!--no formally required structure to CITE-->
    unarmed into a multi-user dungeon to rescue
    her son</CITE>
<STRONG>highlighted text</STRONG>                   <!--usually emboldened-->
<CODE>while not valid(input) do<BR>                 <!--usually fixed pitch-->
   getuser(input) </CODE>                           <!--but meaning is not same as PRE or TT-->
<CMD>format</CMD>                                   <!--computer program command-->
<ARG>c:</ARG>                                       <!--argument to a program command-->
<VAR>starship_velocity</VAR>                        <!--computer program variable-->
<ACRONYM>w3o</ACRONYM>                              <!--help to track down those acronyms-->
<PERSON>Rimsky-Korsakov</PERSON>                    <!--help to make index of people-->
<DEL>This sentence is obsolete.</DEL>               <!--legal, etc; can be struck through-->
<INS>This bit is new</INS>                          <!--legal, etc; newly inserted text-->
<KBD>MYFILE.GIF ENTER</KBD>                         <!--to be typed in by user-->
<AU>Ian Alexander</AU>                              <!--author's name-->
<DFN>grok</DFN>, to get a mental grip on a concept  <!--defining instance of a term-->
<LANG>en.uk</LANG>                                  <!--language context, see Appendix G-->
<Q>Then he said                                     <!--language-sensitive quotation marks-->
   <Q>I do, I do</Q>                                <!--alternating if nested,
and fainted.</Q>                                        e.g. "...'xxx'..." in UK-->
<ABBREV>fo</ABBREV> (short for the Foricas)         <!--abbreviation-->
<SAMP>###########</SAMP>                            <!--literal sequence of characters-->
```

Presentation mark-up

```
<B>Bold Face</B>
<I>Italics</I>
<TT>TeleType Font</TT>
<U>Underlined stuff</U>
<STRIKE>Strikethrough</STRIKE>
```

```
<BIG>BIG LETTERS</BIG>
<SMALL>The Fine Print</SMALL>
<SUB>subscripted</SUB>compared to normal
<SUP>superscripted</SUP>compared to normal
<FONT SIZE=2>Netscape's size 2 typeface</FONT>          <!--extension-->
<FONT SIZE=-1>NS size -1 relative to basefont (3)</FONT> <!--extension-->
<BASEFONT SIZE=6>NS basefont size set to 6...           <!--extension-->
<FONT SIZE=-1>NS size -1 relative to basefont (6)</FONT> <!--extension-->
```

Image

```
<!--see also OBJECT-->
<IMG SRC="whale.gif"                                     <!--bitmap image file-->
   UNITS="en"                                            <!--units: half width of letter M-->
   WIDTH=30                                              <!--(by default, units are pixels)-->
   ALT="Rorqual Whale, breaching"                        <!--text if image not shown-->
   ISMAP>                                                <!--server handles image clicks-->
<IMG SRC="banana.gif"                                    <!--lots of extensions allowing floating images-->
   ALIGN=right
   WIDTH=200
   BORDER=3
   VSPACE=10
   HSPACE=10>
```

Embedded object

```
                                                         <!--Netscape extension; will be dropped-->
<!--at its most basic, similar to IMG but capable of launching applications-->
<EMBED SRC="slides.ppt">                                 <!--application is PowerPoint-->
<EMBED SRC="pretty.bmp" WIDTH=200 HEIGHT=100>            <!--application is PaintBrush-->
```

Unordered list

```
<UL DINGBAT="caution"><LH>Things to Do</LH>              <!--list header optional-->
   <LI>Walk Dog
   <LI>Buy Milk
   <LI>Sew on Button
</UL>
<UL TYPE=square>                                         <!--extension; also =disc, =circle-->
   <LI>Conservative
   <LI>Traditionalist
   <LI TYPE=disc>Hippie                                  <!--further extension-->
</UL>
```

Ordered list

```
<OL><LH>Opening Decent Claret</LH>                       <!--list header optional-->
   <LI>Pull out the cork
   <LI>Let it breathe for an hour
   <LI>Pour gently.
</OL>
```

```
<OL TYPE=i START=5>                           <!--extension, roman numerals-->
   <LI>Centurion                              <!--type=A for capitals, =a for lower case-->
   <LI>Legate                                 <!--type=i for small roman, =I for large-->
   <LI>Gladiator
   <LI>Legionary
   <LI TYPE=I VALUE=10>Procurator             <!--further extensions-->
</OL>
```

Definition list

```
<DL><LH>Quite a Question</LH>
   <DT>The Goddess Parvati
      <DD>Initiate me into the knowledge of the Guru.
   <DT>The God Shiva
      <DD>The Guru is not different from the conscious Self.
</DL>
```

Figure (will be dropped; use `OBJECT` instead)

```
<!--more sophisticated than Image-->          <!--not yet implemented-->
<FIG SRC="nicodamus.jpeg">
   <OVERLAY SRC="nicolabel.gif">              <!--additional graphics to save duplication-->
   <CAPTION>Ground-dwelling spider
      <I>Nicodamus bicolor</I>                <!--mark-up allowed, unlike in IMG-->
   </CAPTION>
   <P>A small hairy spider, light fleshy red in color with a brown abdomen.
   <CREDIT>J.A.L. Cooke</CREDIT>
</FIG>
```

Table

```
<!--arrangement of HTML into rows and columns-->
<TABLE FRAME=box ID=scores>                   <!--lines separate THEAD, TBODY groups-->
   <CAPTION>a table for scores</CAPTION>      <!--as for FIG, caption applies to whole table-->
<COL ALIGN=left><COL ALIGN=right>             <!--column specifications-->
<THEAD VALIGN=top>                            <!--table head-->
   <TR><TH>name <TH>score
<TBODY VALIGN=middle>                         <!--(first) table body-->
   <TR><TD>Botham<TD>199                      <!--table data cells-->
   <TR><TD>Gower<TD>3
   <TR><TD>Gatting<TD>101
</TABLE>
<TABLE BORDER=5 CELLSPACING=5>                <!--thick frame, space between cells-->
   <TR><TD><IMG SRC="tony.gif">
      <TD><IMG SRC="paddy.gif">
      <TD><IMG SRC="john.gif">
   <TR><TD>Tony<TD>Paddy<TD>John              <!--table is used to organize images, texts,...-->
</TABLE>
```

Mathematics

```
<!--not yet implemented-->
```

- The definite integral from a to b of f(x) over $1 + x$:

```
<MATH>
   &int;_a_^b^ {f(x) <OVER> 1 + x} dx
</MATH>
```

Formulae

```
<!--achieved by sub-classes of MATH-->
```

- The compound $Fe_2{}^{2+}Cr_2O_4$:

```
<MATH CLASS=chem>                        <!--formatting rules for chemistry-->
   Fe_2_^2+^Cr_2_O_4_                    <!--variables are upright not italic-->
</MATH>
```

Horizontal rule

```
<HR>                                     <!--default is a solid bar across full page-->
<HR SRC="graticule.jpeg">                <!--use image as pattern for the rule-->
<HR CLASS=section>                       <!--style sheet defines handling of this rule-->
<HR SIZE=3>                              <!--extension, specifies thickness-->
<HR WIDTH=300>                           <!--extension, width across page-->
           <!--default Netscape measurement is pixels; % of document width also-->
<HR ALIGN=center>                        <!--extension; also =left, =right-->
<HR NOSHADE>                             <!--extension; force solid bar-->
```

Preformatted text

```
<PRE>"Sherman's dashing Yankee boys will never reach the coast"
       - So the saucy rebels said, and 'twas a handsome boast.
     But they had forgot, alas, to reckon with the host.
       (refrain) As we were Marching Through Georgia.
</PRE>
```

Admonishment (notes, cautions and warnings)

```
<NOTE CLASS=note SRC="warranty.gif">The Product is not implicitly or explicitly
   warranted fit for any purpose whatsoever, whether for use as software
   or for holding doors open.</NOTE>
<NOTE CLASS=caution>Using your notebook computer out of doors during
   thunderstorms could be dangerous.</NOTE>
<NOTE CLASS=warning>Do not test the smoke alarm with a naked flame.
   You might burn down your house.</NOTE>
```

Footnote

```
I am myself <A HREF="#fn3">indifferent honest</A>...
<FN ID="fn3"><I>indifferent honest</I> - moderately virtuous</FN>
```

Block quote

```
<BQ>
We were a self-centred army without parade or gesture, devoted to freedom,
the second of man's creeds, a purpose so ravenous that it devoured all
our strength, a hope so transcendent that our earlier ambitions faded in
its glare.
   <CREDIT>Introduction 'Foundations of Revolt',
      from: The Seven Pillars of Wisdom, T.E. Lawrence, 1926</CREDIT>
</BQ>
```

Address

```
<ADDRESS>
   Henry Tudor<BR>
   The White Tower<BR>
   London<BR>
   England<BR>
</ADDRESS>
```

Form

```
<!--obtain inputs from users-->
<FORM METHOD=post ACTION="http://www.hospital.gov/patients">
<P>Patient Number:                                   <!--text field-->
   <INPUT NAME="pid" SIZE=20>                        <!--visible size of field-->
<P>Criticality Category:                             <!--range field-->
   <INPUT NAME="crit" TYPE=range MIN=1 MAX=5>
<P>Site (please sketch in extent of injury or lesion):  <!--scribble on image-->
   <INPUT NAME="site" TYPE=scribble SRC="body.gif">
<P>Blood Group:                                      <!--radio buttons-->
   <INPUT NAME="bgp" TYPE=radio checked>A
   <INPUT NAME="bgp" TYPE=radio>B
   <INPUT NAME="bgp" TYPE=radio>AB
   <INPUT NAME="bgp" TYPE=radio>O
<P>Allergies:                                        <!--checkboxes-->
   <INPUT TYPE= checkbox NAME="alg">pollen
   <INPUT TYPE= checkbox NAME="alg">house dust
   <INPUT TYPE= checkbox NAME="alg">tartrazine
<P>Preferred Food:                                   <!--select menu-->
   <SELECT NAME="foo">
      <OPTION>omnivore
      <OPTION>vegetarian
      <OPTION>kosher
      <OPTION>vegan
      <OPTION>no salt
   </SELECT>
<P><TEXTAREA NAME="notes" ROWS=6 COLS=64>            <!--multi-line text area-->
   Please overtype this with any special notes.      <!--initial text in area-->
</TEXTAREA>                                          <!--end tag mandatory-->
```

```
<P>Existing Patient Record File (optional):          <!--file attachment-->
<INPUT NAME=rec TYPE=file ACCEPT="rec/*">            <!--accept only record files-->
<INPUT NAME=hhh TYPE=hidden>transaction prec 2       <!--hidden field for state info-->
<INPUT VALUE="Submit Patient Record" TYPE=submit>    <!--submit button-->
<INPUT TYPE=reset>                                   <!--reset button-->
</FORM>
               <!--end of examples of HTML 3 tags-->
</BODY>                                              <!--formal end of HTML 3 doc-->
```

Animation

The recommended way to animate Web documents is with Java applets (portable programs).

```
<MARQUEE BGCOLOR=navy BEHAVIOR=scroll SCROLLDELAY=20 HEIGHT=10% WIDTH=100% LOOP=99>Extension</MARQUEE>
```

Multimedia

```
<OBJECT=diagram.gif>
   <P>Diagram construction rules
</OBJECT>
```

Appendix B ALPHABETICAL LIST OF HTML ELEMENTS

Cross-references to other glossary entries are printed in **boldface** type. References in angle brackets <. . .> are HTML tags known to us. Tags are not case sensitive, so <a> is the same as <A>. Appendix A gives examples of the tags and their attributes in use.

The star rating for tags is necessarily approximate and conservative (the situation may well be better than is indicated here, and is certain to be different). It is to be interpreted as follows:

***	virtually guaranteed to be in the HTML 3 standard, already widely implemented
**	already implemented in some browsers, likely to be in the HTML 3 standard
*	proposed

The letter N is appended to ** ratings for tags implemented in Netscape Navigator 2.0.

<!-- --> ***

Comment, for example `<!--not case sensitive-->`. Comments can be seen in the HTML source (which users can view if they wish) but not when pages are displayed normally by browsers.

<A> ***

Link anchor, which can form either end of a hypertext jump; must always be qualified with 'HREF=...' (indicating the destination, so the anchor is the source: the usual situation) or 'NAME=...' (naming the source, so this is an HTML-2-type destination. In HTML 3 the preferred idiom is to put an ID attribute into a tag such as a heading or paragraph, for example `<H3 ID="price">`). It remains possible to put headings (for example, `<H3>...</H3>`) inside link anchors, but this is deprecated.

<ABBREV> *

Abbreviation.

<ACRONYM> *

Acronym, word made up of initial letters of other words.

<ADDRESS> ***

Address, postcode or zipcode, and other addressing information.

<APPLET>

Inserts a Java applet. The contents of the element are used as a fallback when the browser doesn't support Java. Java is a new programming language which can be used to add animations to HTML documents. Java applets are small programs that can be loaded across the Web. Note that APPLET is being superseded by the more general **OBJECT** tag which handles a wide variety of object types in addition to Java.

<ARG> *

Argument (parameter) within fragment of computer program (*see also* <**CMD**>).

<AU> *

Name of author.

<B> ***

Bold face.

<BANNER> *

Banner to appear, non-scrolling, at top of window, for things like corporate logos and navigation controls.

<BASE> ***

Base URL, the URL of the HTML document itself.

<BASEFONT> **N

Sets reference size of font for normal text. Offsets can be set with **FONT**.

<BIG> **N

Larger font than usual.

<BODY> ***

The whole body of an HTML document, that is, everything except the **HEAD**.

<BQ> *

Block quote, for sizeable chunks of quoted text. It is polite to include a <CREDIT> at the end of the quotation to acknowledge the author, source and date.

 ***

HTML forced line break.

<CAPTION> ***

Text caption to head a TABLE or a FIG figure. Can be aligned top, bottom, left, right of its object. The figure caption is available to users with text-only browsers, so you should design it to convey as much of the meaning of a figure as possible, while remaining brief.

<CITE> ***

Citation such as a reference to a scientific paper.

<CMD> *

Command name within computer program (*see also* <**ARG**>, <**VAR**>).

<CODE> ***

Specimen of computer program code (but *see also* <**CMD**>, <**ARG**>, <**VAR**>).

<COL> *

Column specification, for use within a TABLE element only.

<CREDIT> *

Accreditation of a quoted extract or figure to its author or source (*see also* <**BQ**>, <**FIG**>).

<DD> ***

Definition of a <DT> item within a <DL> list.

<DEL> *

Deleted characters, usually struck through with a horizontal line.

<DFN> *

Definition.

<DIR> **(obsolete)** **[*]**

Directory list. Use <UL plain> instead.

<DIV> *

HTML division to show document structure; needs to be qualified with 'CLASS=...' to indicate that your intentions are specified on a **style sheet**. You can use divisions for chapters, sections, parts, and so on. Notice that headings such as <H3> do not automatically create divisions.

<DL> ***

Definition list containing <DT> and <DD> items, normally paired.

<DT> ***

Term to be defined by a <DD> item within a <DL> list.

<EM> ***

Emphasized characters, usually italicized.

<EMBED> **(will be dropped)** **N

Embedded object, such as an image or application. Embedded objects are recorded as references to files in the same way as in images or hypertext links, but they also require helper applications, such as Microsoft Paintbrush for .bmp bitmaps on personal computers, so that they can be viewed. The arrival of **Java** means major changes for the Web in this area.

<FIG> **(will be dropped)**

The content of a FIG element defines a figure. The figure can be a mixture of text and images, and may be given a caption with the **CAPTION** element. Style sheets can be used to control whether the figure has a border and the interior colour and text styles.

<FONT> **N

Font size, either absolute or relative to **BASEFONT**. Preferred way of specifying fonts is with class attribute and a style sheet. Microsoft is trying to build styles into HTML, for example with <FONT FACE=Arial>, an approach plainly at odds with HTML's philosophy.

<FORM> ***

Form to be completed by the user. Various kinds of form input field are defined with the **INPUT** and **TEXTAREA** elements.

<FN> **

Footnote. Most browsers show footnotes in pop-up windows. Footnotes are referenced by hypertext links from elsewhere in an HTML page. For example, the footnote <FN ID=3>This...</FN> is referenced by <A HREF=#fn3>...</A>.

<FRAME> **N

Frame to occupy all or part of the browser's viewing area, resizing dynamically, and containing the document referenced in a URL. Since several frames can be included in an HTML page's <FRAMESET>, and any of them can be scrolling or static, frames provide a powerful way to set up two-dimensional displays.

<FRAMESET> **N

HTML structure appearing immediately after the document head in place of the document <BODY> and containing one or more <FRAME> elements, creating a display as a set of rectangular panels in place of a single viewing area. Framesets may be nested.

<HEAD> ***

HTML document header material such as title, author, document type. All of this, including the HEAD element itself, is optional except for <**TITLE**>.

<H1> ***

HTML heading level 1. Levels 1 through 6 are defined (for example, as <H6>); some popular browsers such as Netscape permit lower levels (7, 8, 9, ...) also.

<HR> ***

Horizontal rule. Can be qualified with 'SRC=...' to use an image, or 'CLASS=...' to use a style sheet to determine the style. Netscape allows various widths and patterns directly.

<I> ***

Italics.

<IMG> ***

Image (*see also* <**FIG**>); must be qualified by 'SRC=...' to indicate the file containing the (GIF or JPEG) image to display. Most suitable for small inline images.

<INPUT> ***

Field such as input text, radio button or checkbox for use within **FORM**.

<INS> *

Words recently inserted and possibly provisional (*see also* <**del**>).

<ISINDEX> ***

Indicates that a searchable index to the contents of the HTML page or related material already exists on the **server**, and provides an input field and button to start a search on the server. ISINDEX does not create such an index. Netscape allows a customized prompt for the field.

<KBD> ***

Keyboard input: denotes text to be typed in by the user. Often a typewriter font such as Courier.

<LANG> *

Language reference with which to render symbols; for example, in the context of Spanish (<LANG=es> where 'es' stands for España), quotation marks are typically «...» not "...".

<LH> ***

List header; optional text to introduce <**OL**> or <**UL**> or <**DL**> list.

<LI> ***

List item within an <**OL**> or <**UL**> list.

<LINK> *

Forward or reverse link to another page; used to predefine tours through HTML documents in which the user has only to press a NEXT or PREVIOUS button.

<MARQUEE> ?

Animated text, which scrolls left or right to attract attention. A Zippy Microsoft Extension.

<MATH> *

Mathematical and scientific equations and formulae. Will likely include ARRAY, BOX, ROOT, SQRT, TEXT and other elements.

<MENU> **(obsolete) [*]**

Menu list. Use <UL plain> instead.

<NEXTID> *

Identifier of the next item in a pre-planned path through a document.

<NOTE> **

Some kind of admonishment, distinguished by CLASS attribute (*see also* <**FN**>).

<OBJECT>

Inserts a multimedia object, for example a static image, a sound, a movie, an OLE control or a Java applet. OBJECT supersedes **IMG**, **EMBED** and **APPLET**. If the browser doesn't support the designated object, it tries the contents of the OBJECT element instead. In this way, you can provide a sequence of fallbacks to ensure that users can see something reasonable no matter what browser they are using.

<OL> ***

Ordered list; a list of <LI> items numbered in some way (*see also* <**UL**>).

<OPTION> ***

Menu item within a SELECT list (inside a **FORM**).

<OVERLAY> *

Image overlay, used to give <**FIG**> images a range of appearances without duplicating the basic graphical material (thus speeding transfer and display). Overlays are useful for presentations and explanations which build up images with successive layers of material.

<P> ***

Paragraph. Formally, P is a container for text, not a separator. In good HTML, all paragraphs begin with <P> although in practice no tag is required after block-level elements such as **H2**.

<PARAM>

The PARAM element specifies a named property which is used to initialize the class and is used in the context of **OBJECT**. PARAM elements can be combined with data streams for greater control.

<PERSON> *

Name of a person.

<PRE> ***

Preformatted text; instructs browser to accept any spaces and carriage returns literally so as to copy the layout as closely as possible. Normally the result is in a fixed-pitch font.

<Q> *

Inline quotation, in place of "...", `...' and so on. Symbols used are language-dependent.

<SAMP> ***

Symbols to be displayed literally instead of being interpreted.

<SELECT> ***

Menu for input from a predefined list of <OPTION> items, within a **FORM**.

<SMALL> **N

Smaller font than usual.

<STRIKE> *

Struck through.

<STRONG> ***

Strongly emphasized (often emboldened).

<SUB> ***

Subscripted.

<SUP> ***

Superscripted.

<TAB> *

Defines or applies tab stop for simple formatting of text into columns. Attributes include ID, INDENT, TO, ALIGN and DP.

<TABLE> ***

Table, structuring its contents into rectangular cells. Tables contain **<TR>** table rows which in turn contain **<TH>** table header cells (optionally) and **<TD>** table data cells.

<TBODY> **

Table body group specification, containing one or more **<TR>** for use within a **TABLE** element only. At least one TBODY element must exist in each table, but it can be implicit with no start or end tags.

<TD> ***

Ordinary table (data) cell.

<TEXTAREA> ***

Multi-line text field for use within **FORM**.

<TFOOT> **

Table footer group specification, containing one or more <TR> for use within a **TABLE** element only. At most one TFOOT is allowed in a table.

<THEAD> **

Table header group specification, containing one or more **<TR>** for use within a **TABLE** element only. At most one THEAD is allowed in a table.

<TH> ***

Table header cell.

<TR> * * *

Table row within a <**TABLE**>, containing <**TH**> or <**TD**> elements.

<TT> * * *

Teletype: a fixed-pitch font, usually Courier.

<U> *

Underlined (if the display device is capable of doing that).

<UL> * * *

Unordered list; a list of <**LI**> items bulleted in some way (*see also* <**OL**>).

<VAR> * *N

Program variable (placeholder) within fragment of computer program (*see also* <**CMD**>).

Appendix C
SPECIAL CHARACTERS

HTML allows you to refer to all Latin-1 characters by their numbers as listed here, bracketed by & ; symbols. For example, you can get the Cent sign ¢ by inserting the string &162; into your text.

The characters which are in the Added Latin-1 Entities (ISO 8879:1986) *also* have mnemonic HTML names, which you will probably find more convenient than their numeric references. For example

Á; for Á instead of **&192**; and

á; for á instead of **&224**;

Notice that (as this example illustrates) the HTML names are case sensitive. Most characters from 32 to 126 can simply be typed in directly, though spaces, tabs and line breaks may be ignored by browsers. Special care is needed with angle brackets < > (their codes are < >) since if inserted literally they are interpreted as tag boundaries.

Char	*English name*	*Latin-1*	*HTML*
		Characters 0–8 are unused.	
	Horizontal tab	9	(normally set and use tabs with <TAB>)
	Line feed	10	(normally use <P> or)
		Characters 11–31 are unused.	
	Space	32	
!	Exclamation mark	33	
"	Quotation mark	34	`"`
#	Number sign	35	
$	Dollar sign	36	
%	Per cent sign	37	
&	Ampersand	38	`&`
'	Apostrophe	39	
(	Left parenthesis	40	
)	Right parenthesis	41	
*	Asterisk	42	
+	Plus sign	43	
,	Comma	44	
-	Hyphen	45	
.	Period (full stop)	46	
/	Solidus (slash)	47	
0	*Digits*	48	
1		49	
2		50	
3		51	
4		52	
5		53	
6		54	
7		55	
8		56	
9		57	
:	Colon	58	
;	Semicolon	59	
<	Less than	60	`<` useful when *explaining* HTML
=	Equals sign	61	
>	Greater than	62	`>` useful when *explaining* HTML
?	Question mark	63	
@	Commercial at	64	
A	*Upper case letters*	65	
B		66	
C		67	
D		68	
E		69	
F		70	
G		71	
H		72	
I		73	
J		74	

Char	*English name*	*Latin-1*	*HTML*
K		75	
L		76	
M		77	
N		78	
O		79	
P		80	
Q		81	
R		82	
S		83	
T		84	
U		85	
V		86	
W		87	
X		88	
Y		89	
Z		90	
[	Left square bracket	91	
\	Reverse solidus	92	
]	Right square bracket	93	
^	Circumflex	94	
_	Horizontal bar	95	
`	Grave accent	96	
a	*Lower case letters*	97	
b		98	
c		99	
d		100	
e		101	
f		102	
g		103	
h		104	
i		105	
j		106	
k		107	
l		108	
m		109	
n		110	
o		111	
p		112	
q		113	
r		114	
s		115	
t		116	
u		117	
v		118	
w		119	
x		120	
y		121	
z		122	

Char	*English name*	*Latin-1*	*HTML*
{	Left curly brace	123	
|	Vertical bar	124	
}	Right curly brace	125	
˜	Tilde	126	
	Characters 127–160 are unused.		
¡	Inverted exclamation	161	
¢	Cent	162	
£	Pound	163	
¤	Currency	164	
¥	Yen	165	
¦	Broken vertical	166	
§	Section sign	167	
¨	Umlaut/diaeresis	168	
©	Copyright	169	`©`
ª	Feminine	170	
«	Left angle quote	171	
¬	Not sign	172	
-	Hyphen	173	(`` denotes a soft hyphen)
®	Reg. trade mark	174	`®`
¯	Macron	175	
°	Degrees	176	
±	Plus/Minus	177	
²	Superscript 2	178	
³	Superscript 3	179	
´	Acute accent	180	
µ	Micron	181	
¶	Paragraph sign	182	
·	Middle dot	183	
¸	Cedilla	184	
¹	Superscript 1	185	
º	Masculine	186	
»	Right angle quote	187	
¼	One quarter	188	
½	One half	189	
¾	Three quarters	190	
¿	Inverted question mark	191	
Á	A Acute	192	`Á`
À	A Grave	193	`À`
Â	A Circumflex	194	`Â`
Ã	A Tilde	195	`Ã`
Ä	A Diaeresis	196	`Ä`
Å	A Ring	197	`Å`
Æ	AE Diphthong	198	`Æ`
Ç	C Cedilla	199	`Ç`
É	E Acute	200	`É`
È	E Grave	201	`È`
Ê	E Circumflex	202	`Ê`

Char	*English name*	*Latin-1*	*HTML*
Ë	E Diaeresis	203	`Ë`
Í	I Acute	204	`Í`
Ì	I Grave	205	`Ì`
Î	I Circumflex	206	`Î`
Ï	I Diaeresis	207	`Ï`
Ð	Icelandic eth	208	`Ð`
Ñ	N Tilde	209	`Ñ`
Ó	O Acute	210	`Ó`
Ò	O Grave	211	`Ò`
Ô	O Circumflex	212	`Ô`
Õ	O Tilde	213	`Õ`
Ö	O Diaeresis	214	`Ö`
×	Multiplication	215	
Ø	O Slash	216	`Ø`
Ú	U Acute	217	`Ú`
Ù	U Grave	218	`Ù`
Û	U Circumflex	219	`Û`
Ü	U Diaeresis	220	`Ü`
Ý	Y Acute	221	`Ý`
Þ	Icelandic Thorn	222	`Þ`
ß	Small sharp S	223	`ß` (sz ligature)
á	a Acute	224	`á`
à	a Grave	225	`à`
â	a Circumflex	226	`â`
ã	a Tilde	227	`ã`
ä	a Diaeresis	228	`ä`
å	a Ring	229	`å`
æ	ae Diphthong	230	`æ`
ç	c Cedilla	231	`ç`
é	e Acute	232	`é`
è	e Grave	233	`è`
ê	e Circumflex	234	`ê`
ë	e Diaeresis	235	`ë`
í	i Acute	236	`í`
ì	i Grave	237	`ì`
î	i Circumflex	238	`î`
ï	i Diaeresis	239	`ï`
ð	Icelandic eth	240	`ð`
ñ	n Tilde	241	`ñ`
ò	o Grave	242	`ò`
ó	o Acute	243	`ó`
ô	o Circumflex	244	`ô`
õ	o Tilde	245	`õ`
ö	o Diaeresis	246	`ö`
÷	Division	247	
ø	o Slash	248	`ø`
ú	u Acute	249	`ú`
ù	u Grave	250	`ù`

Char	*English name*	*Latin-1*	*HTML*
û	u Circumflex	251	`û`
ü	u Diaeresis	252	`ü`
ý	y Acute	253	`ý`
þ	Icelandic thorn	254	`ð`
ÿ	y Diaeresis	255	`ÿ`

Entities for special symbols (added to Latin-1 for HTML/EN)

	English name	*HTML*
	Em space	` :`
	En space	` `
	Em dash	`—`
	En dash	`–`
	Non-breaking space	` `
	Soft hyphen	``
	Copyright sign	`©`
	Trade mark sign	`™`
	Registered sign	`®`

Appendix D
SPECIAL SYMBOLS

This appendix lists the currently proposed mathematical symbols (based on the Adobe Symbol font). The set is likely to change before the final HTML specification is agreed. Note that the HTML entities are case-sensitive.

	Name	*Symbol*	*Entity*
Characters			
Upper-case Greek	ALPHA	A	Α
	BETA	B	Β
	CHI	X	Χ
	DELTA	Δ	Δ
	EPSILON	E	Ε
	PHI	Φ	Φ
	GAMMA	Γ	Γ
	ETA	H	Η
	IOTA	I	Ι
	VARTHETA	ϑ	&varTheta;
	KAPPA	K	Κ
	LAMBDA	Λ	Λ
	MU	M	Μ
	NU	N	Ν
	OMICRON	O	Ο
	PI	Π	Π
	THETA	Θ	Θ
	RHO	P	Ρ
	SIGMA	Σ	Σ
	TAU	T	Τ
	UPSILON	Υ	Υ
	varsigma	ς	ς
	OMEGA	Ω	Ω
	XI	Ξ	Ξ
	PSI	Ψ	Ψ
	ZETA	Z	Ζ

	Name	*Symbol*	*Entity*
Characters			
Lower-case Greek	alpha	α	α
	beta	β	β
	chi	χ	χ
	delta	δ	δ
	epsilon	ϵ	ε
	phi	ϕ	φ
	gamma	γ	γ
	eta	η	η
	iota	ι	ι
	varphi	φ	ϕ
	kappa	κ	κ
	lambda	λ	λ
	mu	μ	μ
	nu	ν	ν
	omicron	o	ο
	pi	π	π
	theta	θ	θ
	rho	ρ	ρ
	sigma	σ	σ
	tau	τ	τ
	upsilon	υ	υ
	varomega	ϖ	&varomega;
	omega	ω	ω
	xi	ξ	ξ
	psi	ψ	ψ
	zeta	ζ	ζ

	Name	Symbol	Entity
Logical operators			
	logical NOT	¬	¬
	logical AND	∧	∧
	logical OR	∨	∨
	forall	∀	∀
	exists	∃	∃
	therefore	∴	∴
	implies	⊥	⊥
	if and only if	⟺	⇔
Set operators			
	set AND	∩	∩
	set OR	∪	∪
	superset	⊃	⊃
	equal superset	⊇	⊇
	subset	⊂	⊂
	equal subset	⊆	⊆
	set NOT	⊄	⊄
	member	∈	∈
	NOT member	∉	∉
	contains	∋	∋
Arrows			
Single	leftright	↔	↔
	left	←	←
	up	↑	↑
	right	→	→
	down	↓	↓
Double	double leftright	(*see* Logical operators)	
	double left	⇐	⇐
	double up	⇑	⇑
	double right	⇒	⇒
	double down	⇓	⇓
Infix comparison operators			
	equals	=	&equal;
	not equal	≠	≠
	approx equal	≈	≈
	identical	≡	≡
	congruent	≅	≅
	less or equal	⩽	≤
	greater or equal	⩾	≥
	proportional	∝	∝
Infix algebraic operators			
	plus	+	+
	minus	−	−
	plus or minus	±	±
	multiply	×	×
	divide	÷	÷
	circle plus	⊕	⊕
	circle multiply	⊗	⊗
	dot product	·	·
	sun or circle dot	⊙	⊙
Functions			
	function	*f*	&func;
	tilde	~	˜
	hat	^	&hat;
	left single quote	'	‘
	infinity	∞	∞
	club	♣	♣
	diamond	♦	♦
	heart	♥	♥
	spade	♠	♠
	degrees	°	°
	left double quote	"	“
	ellipsis	...	…
	mid	|	∣
	aleph	ℵ	ℵ
	null	∅	∅
	Product	∏	∏
	square root	√	□
	lozenge	◊	◊
	SUM	∑	∑
Geometric operators			
	angle	∠	∠
	triangle	∇	≜
	right angle	∟	&ang90;
	spherical angle	∢	∢
Calculus			
	partial differential	∂	∂
	integral	∫	∫
	contour integral	∮	∮
	surface integral	∯	&surfint;
	volume integral	∰	&volint;
	Cauchy integral	⨍	&cauchyint;
	edge integral	∲	&edgeint;
Delimiters	(Brackets for math can be chosen from the characters listed in Appendix C. With the exception of < > and { } which have special meanings in HTML 3, most common delimiters can be entered directly from the keyboard, so entity names are rarely used.)		

	Name	*Symbol*	*Entity*
	left curly brace	{	`{`
	right curly brace	}	`}`
	less than	<	`<`
	greater than	>	`>`
	lh single chevron	⟨	`⟨`
	rh single chevron	⟩	`⟩`
Reference marks			
	paragraph	¶	`¶`
	section	§	`§`
	dagger	†	`†`
	double dagger	‡	`‡`

	Name	*Symbol*	*Entity*
	hash or sharp	#	`♯`
	bullet	•	`•`
	check or tick	✓	`✓`
Ellipsis dots			
	baseline dots	. . .	`&ldots;`
	centre dots	⋯	`&cdots;`
	vertical dots	⋮	`&vdots;`
	diagonal dots	⋱	`&ddots;`
	dotfill*	....	`&dotfill;`

* as wide as necessary

Appendix E URL ORGANIZATION TYPES

Who's at that URL? This appendix lists the three-letter organization codes which are generally used. We can't help you with the rest of the URL, but luckily most companies and organizations are only too happy to announce themselves, so you shouldn't have too much trouble guessing whose pages are at www.microsoft.com, for instance. As you can see from the list, the codes mainly distinguish American institutions.

.com	American or international commercial venture (but many non-US firms use '.co.xx' where xx is their country code)
.edu	American educational institution (in contrast, non-US ones mostly use '.ac.xx')
.gov	American government agency
.int	International
.mil	American military (for example, US Navy)
.net	Network facilities company
.org	Non-profit organization (mostly American)

Appendix F
COUNTRY CODES

Addresses in URLs that do not use organization codes generally end with a two-letter country code. For example, the company `easynet.co.uk` is seen to be based in the United Kingdom. The country codes in common use are listed here. Country codes can also be used in Language Codes, such as `en.uk`, as described in Appendix G.

am	Armenia
ar	Argentina
at	Austria
au	Australia
be	Belgium
bm	Bermuda
br	Brazil
ca	Canada
ch	Switzerland
cl	Chile
cn	China
co	Colombia
cr	Costa Rica
cz	Czech Republic
de	Germany
dk	Denmark
ec	Ecuador
ee	Estonia
eg	Egypt
en	England
es	Spain
fi	Finland
fr	France
gb	Great Britain (most Brits use 'uk')
gr	Greece
hk	Hong Kong
hr	Croatia (Hrvatska)
hu	Hungary
id	Indonesia
ie	Ireland
il	Israel
in	India
is	Iceland
it	Italy
jm	Jamaica
jp	Japan
kr	Korea
kw	Kuwait
lt	Lithuania
lv	Latvia
mx	Mexico

my	Malaysia
nl	Netherlands
no	Norway
nz	New Zealand
pe	Peru
ph	Philippines
pl	Poland
pt	Portugal
ru	Russia
se	Sweden
sg	Singapore
si	Slovenia
sk	Slovakia
su	Soviet Union (yes, we know)
th	Thailand
tr	Turkey
tw	Taiwan
uk	United Kingdom
us	United States
uy	Uruguay
ve	Venezuela
za	South Africa

Appendix G
LANGUAGE CODES

The codes used to identify languages are described in the Internet RFC 1766 at `ftp://ds.internic.net/rfc/rfc1766.txt`. The list below is extracted from it. The language tag is composed of a primary language tag and zero or more subtags, as in '`en.uk`'. All tags are case insensitive.

In the first subtag:

- All 2-letter codes are interpreted as ISO 3166 2-letter Country Codes (see Appendix F) denoting the area in which the language is used.
- Codes of 3 to 8 letters may be registered with the IANA by anyone who feels a need for it.
- The information in the subtag may be:
  - Country identification, such as `en-us` (this usage is described in ISO 639);
  - Dialect or variant information, such as `no-nynorsk` or `en-cockney`;
  - Languages not listed in ISO 639 that are not variants of any listed language, which can be registered with the i- prefix, such as `i-cherokee`;
  - Script variations, such as `az-arabic` and `az-cyrillic`.

In the second subtag:

- Anything may be registered.

Additional language codes (1989 is the latest year with registrations):

ug	Uigur
iu	Inuktitut, *also called* Eskimo
za	Zhuang
he	Hebrew, *replacing* iw
yi	Yiddish, *replacing* ji
id	Indonesian, *replacing* in.

Unregistered examples for illustration purposes only:

Both official versions of Norwegian:	no-nynorsk, no-bokmaal
London slang:	en-cockney
North Sami ('Lappish'):	i-sami-no

Any useful subtags may be registered with IANA

2-letter code in first subtag is taken to be a country code

Appendix H DINGBAT ICONS

HTML provides a set of standardized dingbats for use in place of simple bullets or images. Their actual appearance may vary slightly on different browsers. Some typical icons and their intended purposes are given here.

Icon	*HTML*	*Purpose*
	`&archive;`	archive server
	`&audio;`	sound recording
	`&binary.document;`	data in binary format
	`&binhex.document;`	data in binhex format
	`&calculator;`	interactive calculating tool
	`&caution;`	warning of hazardous operation
	`&cd.i;`	an interactive CD-I session
	`&cd.rom;`	a read-only CD
	`&clock;`	clock or timing device
	`&compressed.document;`	document packed to store or send
	`&disk.drive;`	computer disk/diskette drive

Icon	*HTML*	*Purpose*
	`&diskette;`	computer diskette
	`&display;`	computer monitor or display
	`&document;`	unspecified document type
	`&fax;`	facsimile system or device
	`&filing.cabinet;`	group of folders or directories
	`&film;`	movie recording
	`&fixed.disk;`	computer hard disk
	`&folder;`	folder or directory
	`&form;`	fill-in form
FTP	`&ftp;`	FTP server
	`&glossary;`	glossary of (technical) terms
	`&gopher;`	Gopher server
	`&home;`	back to home/top page
	`ℑ`	still image or photograph
A Z	`&index;`	searchable index
	`&keyboard;`	keyboard as an input device
	`&mail;`	electronic mail tool
	`&mail.in;`	mail waiting to be opened
	`&mail.out;`	mail waiting to be sent
	`↦`	geographic map
	`&mouse;`	pointing device
	`&network;`	a computer network
NEW	`&new;`	draws attention to new item

Icon	*HTML*	*Purpose*
	`&next;`	to next item
	`¬ebook;`	notes or annotations
	`&parent;`	to parent item
	`&play.fast.forward;`	fast forward button
	`&play.fast.reverse;`	fast reverse button
	`&play.pause;`	pause button
	`&play.start;`	start button
	`&play.stop;`	stop button
	`&previous;`	to previous item
	`&printer;`	hardcopy device
	`&sadsmiley;`	'unfortunately', after an item
	`&smiley;`	'for fun', after an item
 STOP	`&stop;`	a serious error
Σ	`&summary;`	summary of document's message
	`&telephone;`	a telephone number
 TEL	`&telnet;`	telnet connection
	`&text.document;`	plain text
	`&tn3270;`	3270 terminal session (real or emulated)
	`&toc;`	table of contents
	`&trash;`	waste paper basket or dustbin
	`&unknown.document;`	data in unknown format
UU	`&uuencoded.document;`	uuencoded data

Appendix I
THE CYBERIA CAFÉ

Whitfield Street is a quiet backwater off Tottenham Court Road. It has Georgian brick terraces, a distant rumble of traffic, the sun glinting off the British Telecom Tower.

I sit on a gaily painted bench in a square by a playground to take a few notes and absorb the atmosphere. Connor from Dublin is sitting under a spread-out sleeping-bag with a banana and a couple of cans of Carlsberg lager. He leaves me about 10 seconds before engaging me in conversation.

'I used to play the computer machines constantly, before I came to London eight years ago', he says.

'Since I came to London, I stopped playing them ... and now when I go towards a computer, they are so advanced now, compared to when the first machines were, they're completely alien to me, I can't play them .... I dunno, some of the easier machines I can play, but the more up-to-date ones, I lose it completely. I used to live in snooker halls, arcades, things that were open 24 hours a day. It's changed now – most of the machines are that much more advanced now ....'

Connor trails off into repetition, is happy to speak into the tape-recorder.

'I got married, got a kid, got divorced, a lot of things. Also did a lot of drugs where we played. The drugs used to enhance your performance on the machines ... at times your fingers got tired pressing the buttons ... you'd miss a move, lose, take a break, have a bit of snooker to take you down a bit, then of course you'd be back on the machines. Some of me friends were constantly on the machines – it was like taking a drug.'

Connor used to spend up to £500 a day on his 'habit', a cocktail of pool, snooker, games and 'real' drugs. The games made up £250-worth per day. His favourite? '*Space Invaders*. As I say, this was 10 years ago.' What did he want?

'To beat them! Beat your mates at it! That was before you could buy home computers, tap in and get going. Once you're sucked in, you're in.' A police siren howls in the background.

I wonder if the Cyberia boys are doing the same thing.

'Yeah, it gets into your brain, it's an addiction thing, same as anything. It's the same as taking a drug. You get so spaced into the machine, as you do taking a drug. You can get so hyped out on that machine and wanting to beat it ... you can't let go, you have to stay, you have to beat it, you have to be best, and you know, you're not prepared for the machine to beat you.'

But the boys now are not playing a game, they can break into other people's machines, I suggest.

'I'm sure if they have home computers and good software, they can do what they want to do. What[ever] is possible through a machine, but they are just playing a game, they want to beat the system [like me]', Connor speculates.

I leave Connor on his bench and walk down the street to the Cyberia Café to see what they are really doing in there. Car parks and new concrete buildings have replaced some of the terraces, but they have evidently been controlled by the planners, as they are a similar height to the old houses of Fitzrovia, this area between Oxford Street, Fitzroy Street and Marylebone Road in London's downtown West End. There are little pubs like the Carpenter's Arms with flowers around their doors. The London Plane trees are fresh and green in the sunshine. There is a motorcycle park, showing how much money is about: a Honda Revere, a Polaris CX500, a Kawasaki Twin-Cam 16-valve, and more. Some prosperous-looking businessmen are having a smoke in their sleek Granadas and Sierras; it is an impromptu conference in the street. Down below the level of the road, there is a hobo's hostel, full of down-and-out men with coffee in paper cups. Next door is a fish bar and 'kebab with rice and yoghurt', dolmades and ratatouille. The Hope public house has an advertisement for Murphy's Stout: 'Buy 6, get one free, so like the Murphys there is no need to be bitter'.

Opposite is Pollock's Theatrical Print Warehouse, Pollock's Toy Museum, gaily painted like Victorian toys on the outside, inside play with puppets, coloured dominoes, magnetic kit moving toys, the tubes full of Spillikins pointed wooden sticks (remember those?). Masks and disguises. Then, across the road on the corner of Scala Street, W1, is the Cyberia.

The Cyberia Café, Internet Access, announces the window.

I sit down at the back. Half a dozen workstations along the front window, another inside. Windows workstations, all with big screens, comfortable and discreetly coloured. They have stereo loudspeakers.

Surprise, there are some women here. One of the machines has three women conversing (among them Ewa Pascoe, I discover), they are not punching buttons at all; two youngish men at machines by themselves, two older men dressed in check shirts, a sheepskin jacket over the chair, and all by himself a businessman in a dark suit punching away with his right index finger, bashing away very intently at something called Easynet.

At a table in the café, three men, two in white shirts, open-necked, one in a blue denim jacket, drinking coffee, portable phone, a bundle of papers, pen-computing tablets; they are gesticulating, I catch the word 'distributing', some form of computing is plainly being discussed.

The women are having something explained; they are doing very little on the machine but it is obviously the focus of attention. It looks like Mosaic on there....

The rest of the café is rather sparse. There is rather an attractively stripped floor, not varnished. A small bar, painted a dullish grey-green. A few cups of coffee, a few bottles of lemonade, tea, a few small buns, but food does not seem very important.

Cyberia's current artwork is by Alex Berka on a Mac, digitally reproduced by *The Colour Desk*, according to an art-gallery notice on the wall. 'The first quarrel' is a 36 × 38 inch colour inkjet print. A maiden in a flowery dress and the head of a gorilla in front of a French eighteenth-century four-poster bed with red, heavy gold velvet curtains, gold-and-plaster ceiling, tapestries, and on the maiden's head an enormous sunburst golden crown decorated with a Christ and saints' figures in niches among the rays. That seems to be a symbol of the Cyberia Café, the sunburst. The staff sport T-shirts with the word Cyberia in all four points of the compass, the four intermediate points marked with flashes.

Some rainforest plants, and to my surprise quite nice cut irises, tiger lilies and orange daisies brighten up the cerebral atmosphere. The first edition of the *Internet Magazine* is on sale at £1.50. The prices are low here for London: real espresso coffee is just 80p, cappuccino £1. The décor is sober with metallic greys, a little Cybernetic but not intensely so. Some soft piped music trickles out of the modestly sized speakers. Round glass tables, steel chairs with black plastic slats, silver paper in the office windows, white blinds, white bcbble lights, pale sand-coloured walls complete the décor. It is rather a quiet harmonious café.

Some people go up to the bar and ask about a machine; they make a booking for a time-slot about an hour ahead. I join them to try a coffee. It's long and strong from the espresso machine, which is a home-style portable 'until we get one plumbed in', says **Donna** behind the bar. She wears a black T-shirt with the Cyberia starburst, and explains that in a perfect world, coffee would be free to journalists, but that: 'We've had a lot of press attention and we'd be broke if...' – she trails off with a dizzy wave of the head, conveying the hordes of hyped-up hacks who have packed the bar in the past few weeks.

Phil comes behind the bar too, chats about the pricing, is astonished that Connor on the bench outside used to have a £250 habit on his space invaders.

'How did he get all that? At the most you'd spend £50 for a full day here, and if you were that interested, you would subscribe £57.34 including VAT for two months or (better) £168.97 for the year. Then you could download practically anything you wanted to play with!' Phil gives me the café's address, which is http:\\www.easynet.co.uk and their home page is home.htm – what could be simpler. I just have time to sip my coffee when

Ewa Pascoe, slim, pretty, self-possessed, comes briskly along to show me around. She was the woman doing the talking in the group at the workstation: 'I've been doing a lot of training this morning', she announces. It's easy to believe she has just done a couple of hours of weights and circuits, like the go-getting young women of Wall Street in sharp pinstripes worn over training shoes. But no:

'I was showing some customers around the Internet', she laughs. She is wearing a black miniskirt and a leopard-spotted shirt under a purple top.

'It's my normal work gear', she disclaims at once. She has a slight Central European accent, is blonde, and is, as I guess, Polish. She gestures calmly at the ruby-red lips in the bitmapped image:

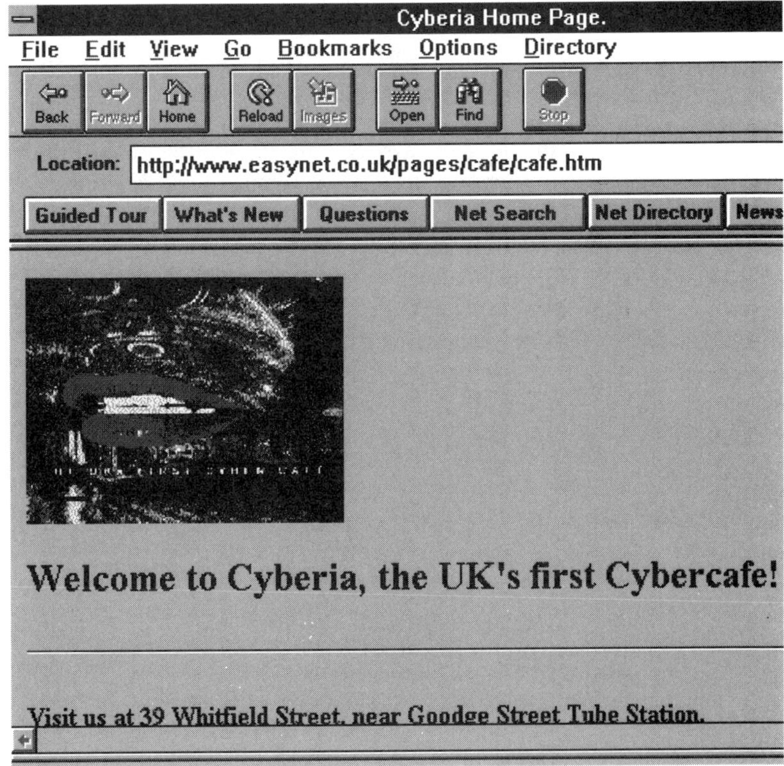

'Those are meant to be my lips', and indeed there is some resemblance. It seems she is rather the café's mascot: 'because my nickname is Europa'. She is still hoping to be carried away by Zeus in the guise of a bull, she says. She specializes in Human–Computer Interaction at the City University, where she is working on expert front-ends for psychologists with Imperial Cancer Research. She claims not to spend much time in the café, but all the press cuttings show her, the warm photogenic face of the chilly-sounding Cyberia.

She tells me about the band that played here on Friday; a 4-minute 'radio' program is available on the Internet, for those with the ability (or the patience) to download the 5-megabyte file for 3 minutes, 51 seconds worth of music and chatter.

'Ok, so we use the home pages for current event information, on Friday we had a live broadcast of a band, the *Charles Dexter Ward Experience*, and we wanted to have, at the same time, information about the band, so that people who were receiving the broadcast in Texas, Finland or Scandinavia, they could see the menu of what the band was playing with a little description of the music, and the people, so the broadcast is a little bit more than just pictures (via CUCM, the video conferencing system of the Internet), explaining the context of the event. The camera here, the band there....' Ewa rattles on, confident in her very human corner of cyberspace.

The café's network bandwidth is a business secret, Ewa says, with a smile. It is plainly ample, there is a huge file of the broadcast's music.

'We wanted to make sure that the full music from the whole album is there; commercial companies only provide a sample of 30 seconds of something-or-other, which is very annoying.' The Cyberia staff (and friends) know where they want to go, and they mean to get there. 'This is basically cutting the record label company out of the deal', she grins maliciously.

'We are trying to use the Internet to see how can we change other people's smart little businesses, and annoy them as much as possible, and use the technology to engineer what could be done. I don't think people mind paying; I mean, from what I've noticed, people are saying, well, we could contribute to the band, a fair amount, but that doesn't mean £11 per CD.'

They use the home page also for campaigns. 'All the current things going on like Green Screen Festival, which we are sponsoring, an environmental festival; so if anybody has anything interesting, non-profit-making, at the foot of the pages we will do that.'

There are titles like *No More Hiroshimas*, *The Internet Now* (the radio programme), 'On a lighter note, you wouldn't believe what you can find on the Web', *Guide to the UK* ('here is a sensitive map guide to the sights and sounds of Britain'). We take a look. Ewa explains: 'As a lot of visitors to the café are tourists, the French are used to Minitel for local information; and we have to tell them, uh-huh, there isn't any!'

So the café commissioned people all over Britain to make hypertexts of their local history, geography, pubs, restaurants, hotels: the Domesday Book as the BBC did not make it. Ewa has an opinion on that too.

'This is a role which the Tourist Board should be playing', says Ewa sourly. I chide her on her cynicism. 'Well, I'm an academic, so I'm cynical by definition!', she snorts.

I click on Winchester; a kilobyte of HTML later, we are in the city of King Arthur and King Alfred, with an attractive colour bitmap of the cathedral close (87 kbytes). There is a long list of pubs: I track down the Royal Oak Passage, a nice secret place I used to frequent as a boy – the narrow alley outside reduced the risk of being detected by the school authorities, or the police. The information is very detailed and accurate, but Ewa quickly chips in: 'Not everything is represented, some parts of the country are not so well covered.'

'It's a virtual trip, you don't really have to go to Winchester', she jokes: at least she still knows she is joking. We look up St Cross monastery, where you can still be offered a welcoming glass of free beer as a passing traveller. 'You get a virtual beer here', laughs Ewa. She steers me to the CyberCafé guide, the Home Page of which the café is plainly proud.

'There are still places for people to meet their friends, read the newspapers, discuss the important events of the day, and to read and answer their snail-mail correspondence', announces the Home Page. Those who still put inky pen to cellulose paper are evidently nostalgic oldies who like the bard to sing them stories by the fireside in the mead-hall before bedtime. For those more up-to-the minute, there is an email address: easynet.co.uk.

There are a couple of dozen Cybercafés around the world, listed online.

'Although none of them are as good as ours, because we have the best connection and full access to the Internet, including Mosaic', trumpets Ewa. 'The workstations get a 64-kilobit line, while the other cafés have one little terminal with text-based bulletin boards and charts.'

Keith Teare (a director) and David Roe (the MD) created the Easynet company, sister to the Cyberia, which works upstairs from the café, Ewa explains.

'We wanted to create something which would be very easy, even for children. The idea was to build a powerful and consistent system which was learnable and reliable, but which did not discourage people. Technophobes welcome!' The human-interface designer in Ewa shows through, the enthusiasm apparent.

'The email, the FTP, all the packages in our system are very similar, so once you learn on one, you can use another. Not too much transfer.... We selected purely Windows-based interfaces, and we are continuously trying to make it even more consistent in terms of what you see in the graphics, how you operate it.... One of the worst nightmares on the Internet is FTP-ing ... it never happens, basically. So we are using Archie for that.'

We go to archie.dot.ic.ac.uk, Imperial College, London. The file we want comes back into a single temporary directory on the Cyberia server, but Ewa is not impressed: 'So you see, it is still five more steps than it should be'. Ewa is striving for perfect simplicity on-screen. I notice only that it all seems much easier and faster than usual; a large bitmap arrives within a minute. Ewa immediately starts to paint it in bright colours. Then she rushes off to another appointment.

Andrew Blackburn works in the back office for Easynet. He could not be more different from Ewa Pascoe: slight, shy, inconspicuous, British, discreet. He quietly admits to having made the Internet Radio programme himself; he recorded some of the music onto tape from the mixing desk, some directly to disk, then edited it with the rather basic sound tool that comes with Windows. 'It was a bit difficult, but it's free and it works.' The end result: an HTML document full of music on the World Wide Web.

Under questioning, he says the clientele has changed from mainly journalists at first, to the general public now. There are plenty of regulars. 'At £168 per year, it is cheap, say some', he whispers. Andrew seems to find the antics of the press and public a little exaggerated. The phone rings and he excuses himself. He does have a proprietorial pride in the firm: 'We are just like any other Internet provider; but we pride ourselves on being easier than some of the others.'

Alexa Thomas is an actress over in England for six months from Florida State University. She's with the Study Abroad programme, which 'doesn't offer email to their students. It's a common problem, so a lot of foreign students come here to pick up their email and talk to their friends, that's what I do.' She works just down the street in London University.

'I'm not a techie at all, it's my first experience of computers beyond word-processing', she says in her nasal Florida drawl. 'This is really kind of a bit of an eye-opening experience as far as computers go. I'm afraid I've become addicted, I'm gonna have to have email when I get back home.' How long did it take to get addicted?

'God, a couple of weeks, then I realized, oh, it's great, even from the East Coast it takes a couple of weeks for a letter to get here; email is a lot quicker.' She has experimented with Mosaic, but email to friends in almost every university is why she comes into the café.

'I spend a lot of time here. A little less than half an hour every day, on Sundays a little longer.' She says that is probably how long she would spend writing to her friends if there wasn't a café here. She has a special rate for her email service, she comes in only at off-peak times.

'It's been wonderful to be able to talk to all my friends back home, I was worried ... phone calls are so ridiculously expensive and mail is so slow.' To Alexa, the short utterances and quick replies of email are more like talking than writing.

'You do get a lot of American students, a lot of businessmen in the lunch-breaks ... some do serious work, but often they just play around. There's definitely a variety of people here, not just computer junkies. Before

I came here I said, oh, that's so nerdy and so difficult, I don't know if I can do it; but when I came here and found out how easy it was, I got really into it. The Internet is a wonderful idea. We had a performance by a rock group the other week ... it's crazy to think they can perform here in Cyberia and be seen all over the world. Back in the States they had an Internet dance concert where they had one dancer in one city, another in another city, doing a dance together.' I inquire if she would like to act on the net.

'Maybe! I don't think the Internet or virtual reality will make the real thing obsolete. It's gonna be an addition to what we have already. A very interesting medium with a lot of possibilities. It's special function is that nothing else allows so many people from so far distant to talk together. The ability to see things and hear things at the same time. I joined the performance of the band, I was talking to and looking at a young man in California, it's a lot of fun, also educational. The Internet is a great way to casually experience whatever you choose to do, it kind of fits in with the whole relaxed atmosphere of the café, definitely a relaxing and enjoying experience.' Perhaps the Cyberia is for the Internet what the intellectual Viennese fin-de-siècle cafés were for Chess.

Alan Newton is a freelance Physics consultant, middle-aged, suited, solidly professional, with a Home Counties English accent. He works from home, needs to access data, and wonders if the Internet might help him. 'I've read about it in the literature, and I think that if I just log on, on my own without any help, it's a black hole into which I pour money. I saw an article about this place, and I thought, half an hour here will allow me to decide where to go and give me some pointers to go there. I've used CompuServe which is fine for fun stuff, but the impression I've got is that Internet has got much more real technical stuff, and hopefully somebody will confirm that for me in the next half hour or so.' We use Mosaic to find CERN, the European nuclear research centre, in a few keystrokes. Alan writes down CERN's URL (http://info.cern.ch) and browses The Particle Data Group at Lawrence Berkeley, Experiments at Helsinki, General Physics via Info.desy.de, and more. The Superconducting SuperCollider 'the greatest ruin of all time', laments one heading. Alan is confused that we have leapt from Germany to the USA in a couple of clicks.... I leave him looking through a dozen bookstore catalogues. 'Thank you for taking our exit off the international data highway', intones one of them.

Nico Macdonald commissions the graphics for Easynet, deals with the designers, works with the icons on the Web pages. He is reviewing a CD-ROM on one of the workstations as it won't run on his own Mac. An Apple Newton is on the desk for notes, addresses and appointments. He is one of the white-shirted young men I noticed earlier. He talks enthusiastically about the Net, graphics, business prospects. He is interrupted by Ivan Pope with an urgent question.

Ivan Pope publishes a magazine, *3W*, on the Internet. 'Since September 1993, first Internet magazine in the world. It's bi-monthly (every two months!), available internationally. Not a huge distribution, vaguely alternative.' Internet pages? 'www.3w.com/3w/ email to 3w@3w.com.' 'Shortest email address in the world!', I comment. 'Short and sweet!', he murmurs lovingly.

Geoff Turko from New Jersey is just calling up some things on a Skateboarding news net, surfing around the Net. He is short, young, fit, uses words economically, time is precious with the clock ticking away. 'I might find some things from my friends back home or something like that, finding out what's new, reading the messages.' Why?

'You can go down to the spots in London, but you're not gonna find out what's happening in the spots back home or in another part of the world.' Geoff is here for two years at the Architectural Association ... he breaks off to attend to a message. Today he has messages from Denmark. I thank him for his time. Another world.

Trystan Julliard is behind the bar, small, slight, blonde, but confident and energetic. She has been in the UK some years, comes from Silicon Valley of course, got married to an Englishman, has been with Cyberia since it started.

'I like computers, want to do something I enjoy, this is a really good place to grow in.' Her background? 'Silicon Valley, Dentistry, Travelling, Writing. Haven't gone to university.' Growth? 'The whole business will expand. I'm hoping to move up the ladder, into management.'

Trystan has taken on the soft-spoken air and idioms of the Englishwoman, but inside one quickly senses the excitement, the passion for technology, the boundless possibilities. She works behind the bar, helps to organize the Café.

'Neither of us, my husband or I, has any desire to go back to California. [England offers] a lot of growth, and a temperament I like. It's friendlier here; the cafés in the San Francisco area tend to be UNIX, text-only based. You have to be from the area, wearing an anorak to deal with that.' There are no anoraks in sight.

'No, that's just it, we're trying to get the normal people in, the everyday people, who have heard the hype, who want to try it out, find what all the hype has been about. Here's a place where they can do it without having a computer.' Soft, graceful piano music tinkles in the background as she reflects on the reality of a cyberspace café.

'The hype is starting to die down, it will go on for a little bit longer. If it doesn't there's going to be a big backlash, the Internet just can't deliver what the hype is promising. There are films where you just go tap-tap-tap and there is the information, and it just isn't like that.' What can the Net really deliver?

'A lot of fun, a lot of information if you really know how to look for it: that is the key thing, knowing how to look ... it's half pure logic and it's half pure intuition, knowing how to call something up, what somebody's going to call it. My own metaphor is trying to use somebody else's address book. Will it be under last name? first name? nickname? You've got to guess. The search engines are going to become even more sophisticated; they are already very clever. That is where the first AI is going to go.'

'I'm rarely behind the bar, usually I'm out as tech support, showing people around, most of the time.' How did she learn?

'You play. Ever since I was 16. Computers, the Internet, the whole culture, the mindset. I grew up with computers, in places where they were ubiquitous. The whole jargon around it ... it's not that different from growing up in surf country, it's just a part of knowledge and how things work.' A down side?

'I dunno. We'll find out as we go along. If you look at film as a metaphor: the Victorian Daguerrotypes ... and they had this technology starting, the film industry, they just didn't know where it was going to go. We just don't know. Can you imagine the Military [the DoD] imagining this when the ARPAnet got started? I'm not sufficiently prescient to imagine where all this is going to go.

'We get everything from little kids to grandmothers. We got one mom in who'd got no idea, but who wanted to email her son at university. The poor kid's gonna be shocked when he gets email from his mom!'

I.F.A.

GLOSSARY

Anchor A syntactic structure in HTML defining the start (or end – see description of the A tag) of a hypertext jump. Anchors generally use the A element with the HREF attribute, for example <A HREF="target.html"> <IMG SRC="target.gif"> Target</A>. Icons in the form of (small) IMG images can if desired be included with the anchor text. The LINK, REL and REV elements are also available to indicate various relationships between HTML pages. An alternative is to use an ISMAP mapped image containing hotzones, each of which forms a link anchor.

ANSI American National Standards Institute.

ASCII (American Standard Code for Information Interchange): the most common encoding of character data, using 7 bits (that is, 128 separate symbols) to represent the letters of the alphabet in upper and lower case, the digits, some control characters, and a very limited range of symbols such as $ and %. ASCII is used internally in most makes of computer (notably excluding IBM mainframes), and is essentially universally readable. It forms the lowest common denominator of data exchange, for instance by **email**. HTML provides a richer syntax but is itself written in ASCII, though it can also reference binary files such as **GIF** or **JPEG** images.

ATM Asynchronous Transfer Mode, a newer and faster way of sending data on a network. It may catch on, or it may be overtaken by even newer and faster modes.

Attribute Ancillary building-block used to qualify **elements** in **HTML** so as to alter their properties. For example, identifiers can be added to many elements such as <P> with the ID attribute, as in <P ID="example attribute definition">.

Author (vb) To write, as in 'to author some HTML'. A better word is 'design', since **hypertext** is a structure containing text and other items (such as graphics and tables).

BBC British Broadcasting Corporation.

Block A chunk of HTML formed by an **element** which automatically starts a new line for itself in most browsers. For example, <P> and <H3> and <UL>.

Block-level element An element which terminates the preceding paragraph. Block-level elements include H1-H6, HR, P, TABLE, FORM, ADDRESS, DIV, PRE, BQ, NOTE, BR, FN, UL, DL, OL, CAPTION, FIG, MATH.

BoF Birds-of-a-Feather meeting of the **IETF**.

Browser A **client** program for the Web. Browsers are supposed to comply with the **HTML** standard, or at least with some version of it. Most current browsers are based on HTML 1.0 or HTML+. Netscape, the market leader at the moment, is quickly taking up HTML 3 features, and with the exception of MATH is in fact already compliant with most of the standard. Browsers are available for personal computers, Macintoshes, UNIX boxes, and other kinds of computer. Most browsers can display graphics as well as text; a few such as Lynx are intentionally text-only, typically for an 80 × 24 character screen; others render text to speech or Braille.

CALS 'Continuous Acquisition and Life-cycle Support', formerly 'Computer-aided Acquisition and Logistics Support', formerly ... a US Navy/ Department of Defense approach to handling data, with much influence on HTML's **table** model.

CD-ROM Compact disc – read-only memory. Disk exactly like audio CD but containing about 600 megabytes of computer data. A cheap and portable form of storing information which is not constantly needed and which needs to be updated only occasionally (by making new CD-ROMs).

CERN Centre Européen de Recherche Nucléaire, the European laboratory for nuclear particle physics at Geneva and the mother of the World Wide Web. She has now thrown her children out into the dark Massachusetts forests. *See also* **MIT**.

Character-level element An element which allows the text to flow on without causing a paragraph break. Character-level elements include character tags such as `<I>`, `<SUB>` and `<STRONG>`, link anchors `<A>`, and inline images `<IMG>`, all of which can be thought of as 'part of the text'. Special characters such as the em-space ` ` and accented characters such as `ü` also work at this level.

Chunky (of a **hypertext**) Organized into small discrete units such as pages; *see also* **creamy**.

Clickable Piece of text or an image, active in the sense that when the screen cursor is placed over it and a mouse or other pointing device button is clicked, something, generally a **hypertext** jump, takes place.

Client A program which can run on some computer in a network, giving access to data stored on a **server** (computer or program). The client–server model effectively shares out the work (distributes it) across the network, minimizing the processing needed at any one place, so it is becoming the dominant style of network operation in most computing systems. **Browsers** are **Web** clients.

Compression Reduction of storage and transmission bandwidth needed for data, especially images (which can become very large: a holiday photograph 3 × 5 might need 2 megabytes of storage when uncompressed to give anything like photographic quality). Compression can be lossy, as with **JPEG**, or loss-free, as with **GIF**. Lossy compression allows very large reductions in data volume, at the price of some loss of quality. Loss-free compression offers more modest reduction. Compression techniques are rapidly improving; for example, fractal compression can render photographs with little loss in 1% or less (100:1 compression) of their original volume, but requires great computational power for the encoding step. Decoding fractals is much easier.

Content model The logical structure which defines which elements can be included within a given element in a document. For example, a form is allowed to include 'body.content', meaning that anything which can occur in the body of an HTML page is allowed inside a form – headings, text, blocks (*see* **block-level element**) and so on – without further explanation.

Context *see* **permitted context**.

Creamy (of a **hypertext**) Organized into large continuous sections to be read by scrolling or browsing through the text; *see also* **chunky**.

Delimiter Symbol with a specific meaning to HTML browsers; for example, the symbol sequence </ indicates the start of a closing tag, while the symbol > indicates the end of a tag.

DNS Internet Domain Name Server, a computer which returns to your machine the Internet Address corresponding to some Internet Domain name.

Download (vb) (1) To fetch files, such as **HTML** documents, over a network such as the **Internet**, from a **server**. It is quite easy to unwittingly import harmful computer **viruses** to your computer by this means – see that entry for details and safety precautions. (2) To run up an excessive phone bill waiting for someone else's idea of nice graphics and useful **shareware** to arrive through the mother of all electronic traffic jams.

DSSSL Document Style Semantics & Specification Language, a candidate source for HTML style sheets. It is pronounced to rhyme with Thistle. Unfortunately it is horribly complicated.

DTD Document Type Definition, such as the formal description of **HTML**, written in **SGML**.

DTP DeskTop Publishing, the business of creating finished and attractive documents at home or in a small office with a computer and a laser printer.

Dweeb Very insignificant and extremely young but over-enthusiastic Net-person (generally biologically male) whose social life and conversation is restricted to communication by electronic means.

Embedding Putting objects (such as images, texts, tables and data) belonging to application programs (such as image and text editors, spreadsheets and databases) into an HTML document as if they were just part of it. Embedding gives users a composite view of a system, with point-and-click access to any of the tools used to provide that view. The concept is already in wide use on personal computers and is likely to become very important on the Web.

Element Syntactic building-block in **HTML** able to stand by itself, unlike **attributes** which can qualify most elements. A typical element consists of a start tag, like `<H1>` or `<FORM>`, some text content, and a matching end tag, like `</H1>` or `</FORM>`. Some elements like `<HR>` have no content and hence do not require an end tag either. Many elements such as `<P>` do not require an end tag even though they have text content, as the start of the next similar element ends them implicitly.

Email Electronic mail. You can often send in replies or comments on **HTML** documents by writing email messages to their authors. Email is a much older service than HTTP and has its quirks, but is generally fast and reliable. No universally agreed way of encoding binary data or document mark-up exists for email messages, so it is wise to start transactions with plain **ASCII** text. The diverse encodings include BIN-HEX, UUENCODE, RTF and **MIME**; these depend for their success on your recipient's having the matching decoding software!

Emoticons Emetic little symbols such as `:-]` for 'glum' or `:-o` for 'astonished', you tilt your head to the left or (Einstein and all that) the page to the right, to see rather bad **ASCII** drawings of faces expressing emotions. These are supposed to lend depth of feeling to otherwise cold communications (what are words for?), or to draw the sting of otherwise stupidly aggressive messages. Their original and rightful place is in the Internet's Multi-User Dungeons (MUDs) where their terseness is part of the sport.

End tag The tag which closes an HTML **element**. The element name is preceded by an opening angle bracket and a slash, and is followed only by a closing angle bracket, for example `</TITLE>`. *See also* **start tag**.

En units Originally the width of a letter N in the current font; now defined as half the width of the widest character in the font, generally the letter M. If you allow 20 ens for a piece of text, you can be confident that there is room for at least 10 characters, and usually about 15 in mixed text.

Entity A symbol specially defined for use in HTML documents. For example, `&inf;` represents the mathematical infinity glyph ∞. The HTML entities are listed in Appendix B.

ETP Egg Transfer Protocol, used as example to explain **HTTP**, **FTP**, and so on. Each kind of data has an appropriate protocol for its safe transfer over the Internet.

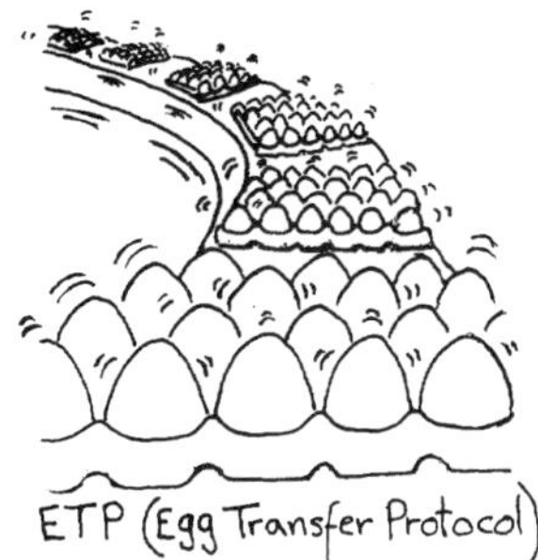
ETP (Egg Transfer Protocol)

FAQ (List of) Frequently Asked Questions; the rather repulsive term for a document which, like a scientific review, covers the field for newcomers to save everybody else from constant interruption by foolish questioning. Few FAQs are as well structured as reviews.

I've got all the FAQ's at my disposal

Flame **Internet** equivalent of driving one metre behind someone at 150 kilometres per hour in the fast lane, with your horn and headlights on, for half an hour, because they overtook you. Usually done with hastily written **email** messages.

Fixed-pitch Font in which all characters have the same width, as on a typewriter. Common examples are Courier and Elite.

Form An HTML document structure which creates, in a browser, the appearance of a fill-in form such as those ceaselessly produced by bureaucrats; more loosely, also such a visible structure in a browser. HTML forms consist mainly of named fields, each of which consists of a text label and a mechanism such as a text box or radio button for obtaining input from the user. There are also predefined form controls for submitting the contents of a completed form to the server, and for resetting a form to its initial (empty or default) state.

FTP (File Transfer Protocol) convenient, fast and reliable method of sending or receiving files of any sort over the **Internet**. FTP sites can be accessed directly from the Web, or with a specialized FTP client on any computer attached to the Internet. FTP works well on virtually every kind of computer, and FTP clients are normally supplied free with UNIX boxes, for example. Program files **downloaded** with FTP or any other protocol may contain **viruses** and should be checked before use. *See also* **MTP**.

FYI For Your Information, a relatively informal document describing an Internet standard.

Geek Older **dweeb**; unlike dweebs, a geek may be able to vocalize, but only Net-jargon comes out.

Generic attribute Property which can be applied to many different HTML elements. For example, the attributes `ID`, `LANG` and `CLASS` can all be used to qualify paragraphs `<P>`, headings `<H1>` to `<H6>`, `<TABLE>` and so on.

GIF (Graphics Interchange Format) A lossless **compression** algorithm and data format, originating from CompuServe and now very widely used on the Internet for transmitting and storing graphics. It is especially effective for compressing diagrams and images prepared on computers. *See also* **JPEG**.

Gopher (from 'go for it', but also a pun on the burrowing rodents of that name) A simple mechanism giving access to **ASCII** documents via an inordinate number of menus. Gopherspace was a precursor of the **Web**; its simplicity in use made it quite popular. As with the Web, Gopher menus could refer to each other in a simple way, so that the user could navigate rapidly around between Gopher sites with a few clicks of the mouse. The endless diet of similar-looking menus with similar titles ('search Gopher menus') and the rather small returns in terms of information (generally only short texts) make Gopher searches rather dull in comparison with **surfin'** the Web. As menu jumps are easily simulated by hypertext references, **HTTP:** now includes a Gopher mechanism, so if you have a Web **browser** you can try Gopherspace for yourself.

Home page(s) (1) HTML documents belonging to a person or an organization, and constituting his/her/its presence on the Web. (2) Top-level (index) HTML document of the set described in (1).

HTML Hypertext Mark-up Language (3.0), the subject of this book.

HTML Assistant A program made by H. Harawitz available as **shareware**, providing an easy and cheap way to write HTML for users of Microsoft Windows.

HoTMetaL A program made by SoftQuad, Inc., to edit **HTML** using paired symbolic tags. HoTMetaL is wise to the rules of HTML and can help you to avoid many types of error.

HTTP: HyperText Transfer Protocol, the email- and MIME-based mechanism for transferring chunks of **HTML** across the Internet. *See also* **Secure HTTP**, **ETP**.

HTTP -ng A coming-real-soon-now New Generation of HTTP: which will not be based on plain old email.

Hypertext Text (but also graphics, tables, diagrams, sound clips and other audio-visual media) represented in machine-readable form so that human users can move around from page to page by selecting predefined symbols with a pointing device. On the **World Wide Web**, the hypertext is written in **HTML** (the subject of this book), and jumps between pages are typically by means of underlined phrases, or by icons or buttons forming **anchors**. Broadly equivalent terms such as hypermedia and hypergraphics are sometimes used.

IAB Internet Architecture Board.

IESG Internet Engineering Steering Group.

IETF Internet Engineering Task Force.

Icon Small image, often arranged as a button which can be clicked (that is, in HTML it is within a hypertext **anchor**). Icons are supposed to be instantly recognizable, but their sheer variety and general incomprehensibility is becoming a stock joke.

IEEE Institute of Electronic and Electrical Engineering, a British body responsible for promoting many standards in engineering.

Infobahn No, we don't know what this is either. It seems to be one or more of the following: (1) what the **Internet** will become when everyone who is rich is using it; (2) what the telecommunications and cable TV companies would like us to use, namely, a lot of bandwidth in our sitting rooms which we pay for by the second as our kids order and watch yet another porno video; (3) the techno-saviour of western civilization as we know it, spreading electronic wisdom and knowledge from pole to pole and generally turning wicked savages into good Christians and white man's friends; (4) the death of family life, culture, the nuclear family and home-made apple pie, in which everyone will sit square-eyed in front of their monitors **surfing** the cyber-waves morning, noon, and night. We're sorry we can't help you further on this one.

Information Super-highway *See* **Infobahn**.

Internet (1) The global network of computers based on the Advanced Research Projects Agency Network (ARPAnet), founded in the 1960s, and now rapidly increasing. (2) The physical home of cyberspace and the **Infobahn**. (3) Useful word to put in newspaper headlines when introducing any dull piece of research, for example Internet Could Be Replaced By Brain-Implant Telepathy, Says Scientist.

IP Internet Protocol, familiar as part of **TCP/IP**.

ISDN Purely digital connection to the **Internet**, using a faster line (56 or 64 kbits per second; can be doubled-up to 128 kbits per second) than a normal telephone connection; offers very short setup times, unlike the slow dialling-in needed with phone lines; still generally too expensive for personal use, though this may change (if it does not, ISDN will probably disappear). *See also* **Modem**.

ISO International Standards Organization.

ISOC Internet Society and its board of trustees.

Java An interpreted programming language devised by Sun Microsystems, Inc. Programs are translated (compiled) into a completely portable intermediate code, which is a convenient short form for transmission on the Web. A Java client (probably free), a small program available for many different types of computer, interprets and obeys the code line by line. Since Java programs can be included with HTML documents, Java opens the door to a wide range of services that cannot be built into standard HTML. Its low cost, small size and interface to **Netscape Navigator** seem likely to obtain it wide acceptance.

JPEG An internationally agreed standard for lossy **compression** of images, especially photographs. Some quality is lost (images become more blurred and edges become indistinct) at high compression ratios. Typical photographs of people can safely be compressed to 15:1 or more with little noticeable degradation. JPEG is a relatively recent introduction on the Web but is likely to prove popular for photographs in particular. *See also* **GIF** and **MPEG**.

Jump Relaxed way of saying 'use a hypertext link'. A local jump is made entirely within one HTML page; other jumps are to pages on the same or remote servers. *See* **Link**.

A local jump

<A HREF = "#2">

LAN Local Area Network. If you are inside an organization which connects you to the Internet via a LAN, you get the **Web** for free, but at the price of even more delay than usual, if the LAN is at all busy (or if 1000 engineers are sharing a 64 kbyte Internet connection).

LaTeX A sophisticated but not especially friendly typesetting language widely used on UNIX machines and considered as one possible basis for HTML. HTML to LaTeX filters are available to format output for printing from Web pages. Incidentally the 'X' is meant to be a Greek letter Chi (χ) and should be pronounced 'kh'.

Latin-1 A widely used character set covering the letters, plain and accented, used in most European languages (except Greek and the Cyrillic alphabets), as well as a selection of common symbols. There is some variation in the arrangement of Latin-1 characters on different computers but this should be concealed by browsers (following the ordering shown in Appendix C).

Link Hypertext link, using <A> or <LINK> tags to connect a Web document to another document or image.

Mark-up By analogy with publishers' proofreading signs, the set of symbols used to indicate how a document is to be treated for display or printing on any device. **HTML** is a general-purpose mark-up language which can be interpreted or used to format text, organize data, create hypertext jumps or by specialized programs to transform the marked-up documents for use by other computer systems.

MIF A good and reliable document interchange format created by Frame Technologies, Inc. for use with FrameMaker.

MIME Multipurpose Internet Mail Extensions (Internet RFC 1590); a system to allow more interesting types of file to be sent by email, compared to the boring old text files supported by basic Internet Mail.

MIT Massachusetts Institute of Technology, the not-quite-all-male institution which is now the stepfather of the World Wide Web. *See also* **CERN**.

Modem MODulator/DEModulator; a signalling device which converts either way between digital signals, such as those coming from a computer's serial data port, and analog signals (modulated tones) which can be sent on a normal telephone line. In fact purely digital modems also exist, converting between local and long-distance signalling patterns. Most home users of the **Web** are connected to the **Internet** via a modem and telephone line. If you are buying a new modem for this purpose, the minimum useful speed is 14 400, and 28 800 is probably a better bet. Modem prices are falling rapidly. *See also* **ISDN**.

Mosaic *See* **NCSA**.

MPEG The video equivalent of **JPEG**. Most people's Internet connections (and most parts of the Internet itself) have too small a bandwidth to permit more than the smallest amount of video to be transmitted satisfactorily. This severe limitation will undoubtedly be attacked vigorously in the next decade, and the results will probably determine whether it is the Internet or some other network that achieves global dominance.

MTP Milk Transfer Protocol; *see* **ETP** for explanation.

NCSA National Center for Supercomputing Applications, the American home of the first successful graphical **browser**, Mosaic, the application which made the Internet and the World Wide Web household names.

Netscape Navigator The **browser** available on various types of computer made by Netscape Corp. Its concept derives closely from **NCSA** Mosaic, of which it is a more sophisticated re-implementation. It is currently available for free downloading and occupies about 70 or 75% of the browser market.

Nerd Male so into the Net that he forgets personal appearance. He is supposed to wear an anorak, but this hideous modern garment has nothing in common with the beautifully embroidered leather overshirt, *annoraaq*, worn by the Inuit of Greenland.

NSF American National Science Foundation.

Online (currently) Actively connected to the Web.

OSI Open Systems Interconnect[ion].

Page Loose term for an HTML document available on the Web. Documents can be much longer than the equivalent of a printed page, but the term is quite well established, as is the related **Home page**.

Parse To analyse a construct in some language to determine its structure, in order to translate or represent it appropriately. Each **HTML** document has to be parsed by a Web **browser** for display on a computer screen.

Patch An *ad hoc* attempted solution to a software fault.

PC Personal computer (once made by IBM) based on an Intel 80×86 microprocessor chip and traditionally running DOS/Windows operating systems, though nowadays multi-chip sets, networking, other manufacturers' chips, and even other operating systems make the distinction between PCs and computers in general increasingly indistinct.

Permitted context Places in a document where you can use an element; for example, the table header cell `TH` is only permitted in (the context of) a table row `TR`.

Publish To make available on the Web, generally in the form of HTML documents, though also as files of any other downloadable or executable type. The Web has already revolutionized the concept of publishing (paper and ink are no longer seen as essential ingredients, text does not have to be sequential, and so on). New arrivals like **embedding** and **Java** make the concept still more nebulous, as documents do not come into existence until viewed, and what comes into existence is probably different every time. The Web seems to be moving from broadcast publishing (everyone who visits a site sees some of the documents there) to narrowcast or even individual publishing (you see what you want to).

RFC Request for Comments, which sounds nice and vague, but is actually a virtually definitive document describing a proposed Internet standard.

Router A computer which directs data on the Internet.

RTF Rich Text Format, a word-processing document interchange format created by Microsoft. It is notoriously complex and difficult to parse reliably.

RTFM Read The Flaming Manual.

Secure HTTP: An updated version of **HTTP:** which includes encryption to protect sensitive data like credit-card details when transmitted over the Web; one of several competing protocols for the potentially lucrative market of payment on the Web.

Server A program (or computer running such a program) which provides a (data) service of some kind to its **clients**. A **Web** server uses **HTTP:** to provide its own set of **HTML** documents to Web users. For example, an organization may advertise its products or services on the Web by making available a set of Web pages on its own server; people can **download** this information from anywhere in the world connected to the **Internet**.

SGML Standard Generalized Mark-up Language, an international standard (ISO 8879:1986, Information Processing Text and Office Systems) for a method of describing the structure of a document of any type. The normal way to use SGML is to write a formal description (a **DTD**) in SGML syntax of how you want a particular type of document to be structured. SGML can also be used directly for unspecialized mark-up.

Shareware (1) Software which is available on free trial, and which can be freely distributed and copied provided the terms and conditions are also supplied; payment is usually required at the end of the trial period. Some shareware is issued commercially; other programs are written by individuals or places of learning. (2) Idiosyncratically configured software available free (if you ignore both your moral duty to pay for it, and your contribution to your telephone company's annual profits while you try to **download** it).

Smilies *see* **emoticons**.

Sneakernet (across building with floppy disk in hand, sneakers on feet) A fast reliable network transfer protocol, capable of 1.4 megabytes in a minute or two. Works much better than frayed Ethernet.

Sparc A kind of UNIX workstation manufactured by Sun Microsystems.

Standard width units *see* **width units**.

Start tag The tag which begins an HTML **element**. The element name is preceded only by an opening angle bracket, and may be followed by one or more **attributes**, each generally with an assigned value, for example `<H2 ID=introduction>`. *See also* **end tag**.

STD **Internet Standards Document.**

Style sheet A document, not itself written in HTML, associated explicitly (by a declaration) with an **HTML** page, defining the way in which various elements and classes (using the `CLASS` attribute in various elements) in the HTML are to be treated for display. For instance, a style sheet might specify 10 point Times Roman as the font for displaying `<P>` text on screen.

Surfing To spend (waste?) time browsing around the **Web** or the **Internet**, generally for pleasure. The practice is deprecated by companies that want their technical staff to be productive. Surfing, like reading dictionaries (when you were trying to look up a word), is an addictively serendipitous way of gathering facts but is less fruitful at finding out anything in particular. For serious information-gathering on the Internet, practical search methods include use of **WAIS** database indexes, **Gopher** menus, and beautifully prepared Web classifications and indexes such as Yahoo's (`http://www.yahoo.com`).

Table An arrangement of pieces of text or other data on a rectangular plan, possibly divided into a grid by horizontal and/or vertical lines and possibly surrounded by a ruled frame. Tables can have row and column headers, captions, a **table header**, and one or more **table bodies**.

Table header A single optional group of table rows at the top of a table, intended to be available to the user whenever table data is displayed, for instance by being fixed on screen while table data rows are scrolled.

Table body A group of table (data) rows treated as a unit, for example for bordering or alignment purposes. Tables can have any number of such groups.

Tag The mark-up structure in **HTML** which starts (**start tag**) or ends (**end tag**) an HTML element. A tag consists of a pair of angle brackets and whatever is inside them. Tags must contain at least the name of an element, for example `<P>`, `<MATH>` or `</MATH>`; start tags can also contain attributes and their values, for example `<P ALIGN=right>`. *See also* **element**, **attribute**.

Tao and the Art of Server Maintenance, etc. The Way of Effortless Being (The Track that can be Tracked is Not the True Track – literally 'Tao [which] Tao Not Tao'). *See* **Zen** for explanation.

TCP/IP Terminal Communications Protocol/ Internet Protocol. Actually no one knows or cares about the expansion of this acronym, which like radar has long since become a word in its own right. TCP/IP is the robust low-level means by which messages get sent on the Net.

Telnet A primitive mechanism for logging on to a remote computer (for example on the **Internet**) as if your computer was a terminal connected directly to it. Much early fun by hackers was conducted with nothing more sophisticated than cheap home computers, slow **modems** and Telnet.

URL Universal Resource Locator, the form of name used by **HTTP:** to identify servers and resources uniquely.

Veronica Supposedly 'Very Easy Rodent-Oriented Netwide Index to Computerized Archives'. This won *Byte* magazine's *The Really Stretching It Award* for worst acronym. A fairly useful companion in **Gopher**space, Veronica is now fading into peaceful oblivion as the Web takes over the world.

Virus A program designed to attach itself to other (innocent) files such as programs, and to replicate itself when those programs are executed. Some viruses display offensive messages on screen; others are designed to destroy data immediately or at particular times. Viruses can readily be transferred over the **Internet**, most frequently when games or other free programs are **downloaded** with **FTP** from unofficial sites. The safest approach is to fetch software only from reliable sources, such as major mirror sites, and to check all incoming files with an up-to-date virus checker before use.

VRML Virtual Reality Mark-up Language, a putative extension or supplement to HTML designed for low-bandwidth (that is, fast, even over the Internet) transmission and representation of moving images of seemingly solid objects on client displays. For example, you might one day be able to steer your browser 'through' a shop, literally browsing through the books, records or clothes on sale there. We doubt you'll be able to sniff the different kinds of coffee-beans, though.

WAIS (Wide Area Information Server, pronounced 'ways') Indexed databases on the Internet. WAIS databases can be searched very efficiently, and are beautifully indexed, for example by the University of Lund in Sweden. Thousands of databases containing trillions of bytes of scientific, technical and government data are freely available from many countries. There are a few public gateways to WAIS from the Web; more convenient and less crowded access is available if your organization provides WAIS clients and a WAIS server or gateway.

Web *See* **World Wide Web**. We have deliberately used a range of commonly used terms as synonyms for the Web: out there you will find all of them in use, so using only one is both artificial and monotonous.

Web page *See* **page**, **home pages**.

Width units Most **table** components can be sized either automatically or according to a specification supplied in a `WIDTH` attribute. This gives widths in a rich choice of units: pi – picas; pt – points; in – inches; em – em units; cm – centimetres; mm – millimetres; px – pixels (the awkward default). In some cases it is also possible to use percentages, for example the table's width as a percentage of the window or screen width. Finally, columns can be given relative widths by following their values with a star (*). No space is ever allowed between width values and width units; '3em' is right but '3 em' is not.

World, The The part of the world's human population rich enough to own or have access to a computer on the **Internet**. Nothing and nobody else deserves a mention.

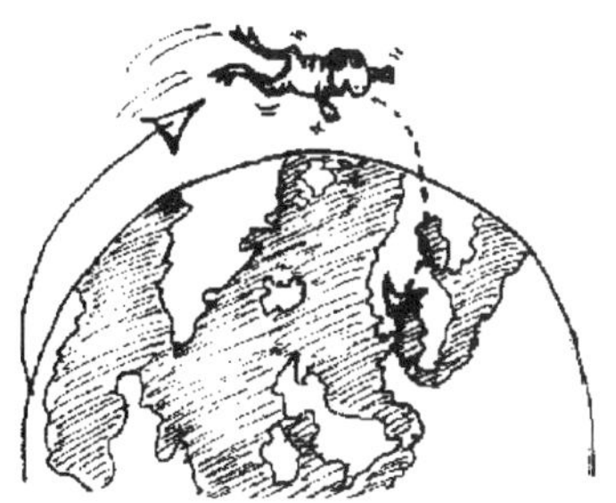

World Wide Web The set of all **hypertext** documents written in **HTML**, transmitted by **HTTP:** and residing on Internet computers; the abstract space in which readers can navigate around such documents in search of knowledge. The Web is criticized for lack of structure, but in fact there are good general and specific indexes which are widely known and used, and which enable even inexperienced users to find almost anything in a few minutes.

WYSIWYG (1) What You See Is What You Get. This is undoubtedly true when choosing a spouse, being sold secondhand cars, or unwisely buying squashy peaches in your street-market, but no computer screen ever accurately portrays what you will really get when you print a document out, as there are too many imponderables. (2) What You See Is What You Get: claimed performance of various word processors and other software tools in depicting printable output.

Xanadu Ted Nelson's long-running and pioneering project, reflecting his 1960s vision of a truly global hypertext with all the world's literature, and so on. The Web is a humble but practical successor to Nelson's vision. We are ashamed of the lack of recognition of this great man's achievement, and still more of the open abuse poured on him by *Wired*.

Yelnet Rapid and efficient information transfer protocol consisting of loudly enunciated data travelling from mouth to ear(s). Often much easier than **Telnet**. Quicker, too.

Zen and the art of . . . Zen is about being (part of) all that is. It is the opposite of separating reality into compartments, dealing electronically only with the most abstract of those. *See also* **Tao . . . .**

INDEX

D

E

F

G

W